2/19/03

29⁹⁵

CLYMER®

KAWASAKI

Z & KZ 900-1000 cc Chain & Shaft Drive • 1973-1981
(Includes C Series Police Models)

D1709678

The world's finest publisher of mechanical how-to manuals

PRIMEDIA
Business Magazines & Media

P.O. Box 12901, Overland Park, Kansas 66282-2901

FIRST EDITION
First Printing September, 1980

SECOND EDITION
Updated by Anton Vesley to include 1980 models
First Printing June, 1981
Second Printing August, 1982
Third Printing June, 1983
Fourth Printing March, 1984
Fifth Printing May, 1985
Sixth Printing July, 1986
Seventh Printing June, 1987
Eighth Printing July, 1988
Ninth Printing August, 1989
Tenth Printing August, 1990
Eleventh Printing August, 1991
Twelfth Printing August, 1992
Thirteenth Printing August, 1993
Fourteenth Printing January, 1995
Fifteenth Printing May, 1996
Sixteenth Printing August, 1997
Seventeenth Printing February, 1999
Eighteenth Printing January, 2001

THIRD EDITION
Updated by Ed Scott to include Police models
First Printing September, 2002

Printed in U.S.A.

CLYMER and colophon are registered trademarks of PRIMEDIA Business Magazines & Media Inc.

ISBN: 0-89287-837-1

Library of Congress: 2002111256

TOOLS AND EQUIPMENT: K & L Supply Co. at www.klsupply.com.

COVER: 1973 Z1 and photography courtesy of Richard Brett, Nottingham, England. Special thanks to www.classickawasaki.com for NOS parts.

2/19/03

CLYMER PUBLICATIONS
PRIMEDIA Business Magazines & Media
Chief Executive Officer Timothy M. Andrews
President Ron Wall

EDITORIAL

Editor
James Grooms

Technical Writers
Ron Wright
Ed Scott
George Parise
Mark Rolling
Michael Morlan
Jay Bogart

Production Supervisor
Dylan Goodwin

Lead Editorial Production Coordinator
Shirley Renicker

Editorial Production Coordinators
Greg Araujo
Shara Pierceall

Editorial Production Assistants
Susan Hartington
Holly Messinger
Darin Watson

Technical Illustrators
Steve Amos
Robert Caldwell
Mitzi McCarthy
Bob Meyer
Mike Rose

MARKETING/SALES AND ADMINISTRATION

Vice President,
PRIMEDIA Business Directories & Books
Rich Hathaway

Marketing Manager
Elda Starke

Advertising & Promotions Coordinator
Melissa Abbott

Associate Art Directors
Chris Paxton
Tony Barmann

Sales Manager/Marine
Dutch Sadler

Sales Manager/Motorcycles
Matt Tusken

Operations Manager
Patricia Kowalczewski

Sales Manager/Manuals
Ted Metzger

Customer Service Manager
Terri Cannon

Customer Service Supervisor
Ed McCarty

Customer Service Representatives
Susan Kohlmeyer
April LeBlond
Courtney Hollars
Jennifer Lassiter
Ernesto Suarez

Warehouse & Inventory Manager
Leah Hicks

The following books and guides are published by PRIMEDIA Business Directories & Books.

More information available at *primediabooks.com*

CONTENTS

CLYMER®

KAWASAKI

Z & KZ 900-1000 cc Chain & Shaft Drive • 1973-1981
(Includes C Series Police Models)

QUICK REFERENCE DATA

BREAKER PLATE

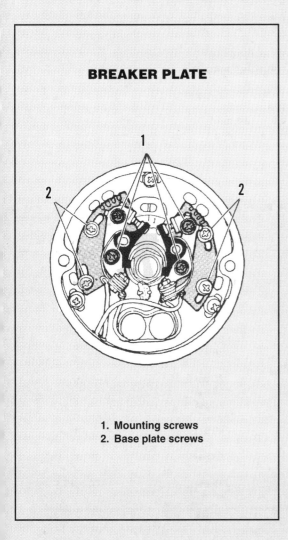

1. Mounting screws
2. Base plate screws

TIMING

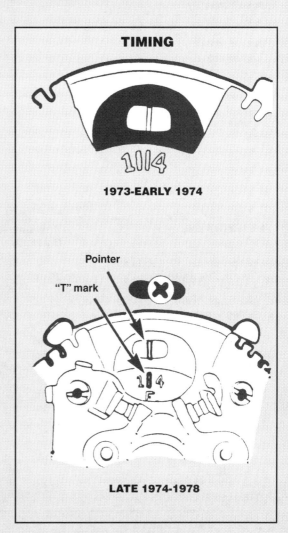

1973-EARLY 1974

Pointer

"T" mark

LATE 1974-1978

TUNE-UP SPECIFICATIONS

Spark plug gap	
1980 Z1R	0.039-0.043 in. (1.0-1.1 mm)
All others	0.028-0.032 in. (0.7-0.8 mm)
Spark plug type	
Normal riding conditions	Low speeds or cold weather
NGK:–B8ES	(below 50° F, 10° C)
ND:–W24ES-U	NGK:–B7ES
	ND:–W22ES-U
Valve clearance (cold)–intake and exhaust	
1979 & Later:	0.002-0.006 in. (0.05 – 0.15 mm)
1973–1978:	0.002-0.004 in. (0.05 – 0.10 mm)
Idle speed	
1000cc:	1,000 rpm
900cc:	900 rpm

KZ1000/900 CHASSIS ADJUSTMENTS

Clutch cable play	1/8 in (2-3 mm)
Brake lever play	
Z1R	1/8 in. (2-3 mm)
1973-1977	1/8-3/16 in. (3-5 mm)
Brake pedal play	
Disc brake	3/8 in. (8-10 mm)
Drum brake	1 in. (20-30 mm)
Drive chain play	
(on centerstand)	1 1/4 in. (30-35 mm)
(on sidestand)	1 in. (25 mm)
Throttle cable play	1/8 in. (2-3 mm)

TIRES AND TIRE PRESSURE

Model/Tire size	Pressure @ Load 0-215 lb.	Over 215 lb.	Over 365 lb.
Standard model (1979 and Later)			
Front 3.25V-19 4PR or MN90-19	28 psi	28 psi	—
Rear 4.00V-18 4PR or MP90-18	32 psi	40 psi	—
Standard model (1973-1978)			
Front 3.50H-19 4PR	28 psi	28 psi	—
Rear 4.00H-18 4PR	32 psi	36 psi	—
LTD, Classic			
Front ML90-10 LRB	26 psi	26 psi	—
Rear ML90-16T LRB	22 psi	24 psi	—
Front 3.2V-19 4PR	28 psi	28 psi	—
Z1R			
Rear 4.00V-18 4PR	32 psi	40 psi	
Shaft Drive			
Front 3.50V-19 4PR TUBELESS	28 psi	28 psi	28 psi
Rear 4.50V-17 4PR TUBELESS	32 psi	36 psi	40 psi

KZ1000/900 STANDARD FORK OIL

Model	Dry Capacity U.S. fl. oz. (cc)	Wet Capacity U.S. fl. oz. (cc)	Oil Level inches (mm)	SAE
Standard				
Police model	5.7 (170)	7.0 (208)	18.2 (463)	15W
1978—on	6.2 (184)	5.4 (160)	17.4 (441)	10W
1976–1977	5.9 (174)	4.7 (140)	16.8 (426)	10W
1974–1975	5.7 (170)	4.7 (140)	16.6 (422)	10W
1973	5.7 (170)	4.7 (140)	17.9 (455)	10W
Shaft drive	11.5 (340)	10.5 (310)	18.9 (480)	10W

NOTE: On 1978 and later models, check the fork oil level with the fork fully extended and the fork spring removed. On earlier models, leave the spring in place. Use non-detergent oil to retard foaming.

KZ1000/900 CARBURETOR SPECIFICATIONS (1980-1978 ½)

Item	1980 All	1979 Standard & Police Model	1979 LTD	1978 ½ All emission- controlled
Size/type	VM28SS	VM28SS	VM26SS	VM26SS
Main jet	No. 102.5 (No. 110 Shaft)	No. 102.5 (No. 110 Shaft)	No. 102.5	No. 102.5
Pilot jet	No. 15	No. 15	No. 15	No. 15
Jet needle	5CN29	5CN17-3	5CM18-3	5CN7-4
Needle jet	0-4	0-4	0-6	0-3
Cutaway	2.0	2.0	2.0	2.0
Idle mixture	–	1-1/8	(Full clockwise)	
Fuel level	4 mm	4 mm	4 mm	4 mm
Float height	26 mm	26 mm	26 mm	26 mm

KZ1000/900 CARBURETOR SPECIFICATIONS (1978-1977)

Item	1978 Standard Model	1978 Z1R	1977 Standard Model	1977 LTD
Size/type	VM26SS	VM28SS	VM26SS	VM26SS
Main jet	No. 105	No. 107.5	No 107.5	No. 105
Pilot jet	No. 15	No. 15	No. 17.5	No. 15
Jet needle	5DL31-3	5CN15-3	5CM8-3	5DL31-3
Needle jet	0-5	0-1	0-6	0-5
Cutaway	1.5	1.5	1.5	1.5
Idle mixture	1-1/4	1-3/8	1-1 1/4	1 1/4
Fuel level	4 mm	4 mm	3 mm	3 mm
Float height	26 mm	26 mm	25 mm	25 mm

KZ1000/900 CARBURETOR SPECIFICATIONS (1976-1973)

Item	1976	1975	1973-1974
Size/type	VM26SS	VM28SC	VM28SC
Main jet	No. 115	No. 112.5	No. 112.5
Pilot jet	No. 17.5	No. 17.5	No. 20
Jete needle	5DL31-3	5J9-2	5J9-3
Needle jet	0-6	0-8	P-8
Cutaway	1.5	1.5	2.5
Idle mixture	1-3/8	1-1/4	1 1/2
Fuel level	3 mm	3.5 mm	3.5 mm
Float height	22 mm	24 mm	24 mm

FASTENER TORQUES

Fastener	ft.-lb.	mkg
Engine		
Alternator rotor bolt		
1979 and later (12 mm)	95	13.0
1978 (10 mm)	50	7.25
1973-1977 (8 mm)	18	2.5
Camshaft cap bolts		
1979 and later	12	1.7
1973-1978 (chrome)	9	1.2
1973-1978 (dark)	7	1.0
Clutch hub nut	90	12.0
Crankcase bolts		
1000cc		
Small	90 in.-lb.	1.0
Large	18	2.5
900cc	70 in.-lb.	0.8
Crankshaft main bearing cap bolts	18	2.5
Cylinder head		
Bolts	8.5	1.2
Nuts	30	4.0
Engine mounting bolts	30	4.0
Engine mounting bracket bolts	17	2.4
Engine sprocket nut		
1000cc	60	8.0
900cc	100	13.5
Oil drain plug	22	3.0
Oil filter mounting bolt	15	2.0
Spark plugs	20	2.8
Shaft drive		
Front bevel mounting bolts	18	2.5
Front bevel drive gear nut	90	12.0
Front bevel driven gear bolt	90	12.0
Chassis		
Front axle clamp nuts	14	1.9
Front axle nut(s)	60	8.0
Fork triple clamp bolts		
Chain drive–upper bolt	14	1.9
Chain drive–lower bolt		
1000cc	30	4.0
900cc	40	5.7
Shaft drive–upper bolt	20	2.8
Shaft drive–lower bolt	15	2.0
Rear axle nut		
Chain drive	90	12.0
Shaft drive	100	14.0
Steering head top bolt		
Chain drive	35	4.5
Shaft drive	30	4.0
Swing arm pivot nut		
Chain drive	70	10.0
Shaft drive	11	1.5
Torque link nuts	22	3.0
Shaft drive		
Rear bevel mounting bolts	22	3.0
Rear bevel drain plug	15	2.0
Rear bevel pinion nut	90	12.0

INTRODUCTION

This detailed, comprehensive manual covers Kawasaki Z and KZ 900-1000 cc models. The expert text gives complete information on maintenance, tune-up, repair, and overhaul. Hundreds of photos and drawings guide you through every step. The book includes all you need to know to keep your Kawasaki running right.

The main body of this book (Chapters One through Twelve) contains service information for 1974 through 1979 motorcycles. The supplement at the end of the book covers the 1980 models including the 1979 through 1981 Police models.

If a procedure does not appear in the supplement, then it remains the same as for earlier models; follow the procedure described for the comparable 1979 model in the main body of this book.

Where repairs are practical for the owner/mechanic, complete procedures are given. Equally important, difficult jobs are pointed out. Such operations are usually more economically performed by a dealer or independent garage.

A shop manual is a reference. You want to be able to find information fast. As in all Clymer books, this one is designed with this in mind. All chapters are thumb tabbed. Important items are extensively indexed at the end of the book. Finally, all the most frequently used specifications and capacities are summarized in the *Quick Reference* pages at the front of the book.

Keep the book handy in your tool box. It will help you to better understand your Kawasaki, lower repair and maintenance costs, and generally improve your satisfaction with your bike.

CHAPTER ONE

GENERAL INFORMATION

The troubleshooting, maintenance, tune-up, and step-by-step repair procedures in this book are written specifically for the owner and home mechanic. The text is accompanied by helpful photos and diagrams to make the job as clear and correct as possible.

Troubleshooting, maintenance, tune-up, and repair are not difficult if you know what to do and what tools and equipment to use. Anyone of average intelligence, with some mechanical ability, and not afraid to get their hands dirty can perform most of the procedures in this book.

In some cases, a repair job may require tools or skills not reasonably expected of the home mechanic. These procedures are noted in each chapter and it is recommended that you take the job to your dealer, a competent mechanic, or a machine shop.

MANUAL ORGANIZATION

This chapter provides general information, safety and service hints. Also included are lists of recommended shop and emergency tools as well as a brief description of troubleshooting and tune-up equipment.

Chapter Two provides methods and suggestions for quick and accurate diagnosis and repair of problems. Troubleshooting procedures discuss typical symptoms and logical methods to pinpoint the trouble.

Chapter Three explains all periodic lubrication and routine maintenance necessary to keep your motorcycle running well. Chapter Three also includes recommended tune-up procedures, eliminating the need to constantly consult chapters on the various subassemblies.

Subsequent chapters cover specific systems such as the engine, transmission, and electrical system. Each of these chapters provides disassembly, inspection, repair, and assembly procedures in a simple step-by-step format. If a repair is impractical for the home mechanic it is indicated. In these cases it is usually faster and less expensive to have the repairs made by a dealer or competent repair shop. Essential specifications are included in the appropriate chapters.

When special tools are required to perform a task included in this manual, the tools are illustrated. It may be possible to borrow or rent these tools. The inventive mechanic may also be able to find a suitable substitute in his tool box, or to fabricate one.

The terms NOTE, CAUTION, and WARNING have specific meanings in this manual. A NOTE provides additional or explanatory information. A

CAUTION is used to emphasize areas where equipment damage could result if proper precautions are not taken. A WARNING is used to stress those areas where personal injury or death could result from negligence, in addition to possible mechanical damage.

SERVICE HINTS

Time, effort, and frustration will be saved and possible injury will be prevented if you observe the following practices.

Most of the service procedures covered are straightforward and can be performed by anyone reasonably handy with tools. It is suggested, however, that you consider your own capabilities carefully before attempting any operation involving major disassembly of the engine.

Some operations, for example, require the use of a press. It would be wiser to have these performed by a shop equipped for such work, rather than to try to do the job yourself with makeshift equipment. Other procedures require precision measurements. Unless you have the skills and equipment required, it would be better to have a qualified repair shop make the measurements for you.

Repairs go much faster and easier if the parts that will be worked on are clean before you begin. There are special cleaners for washing the engine and related parts. Brush or spray on the cleaning solution, let stand, then rinse it away with a garden hose. Clean all oily or greasy parts with cleaning solvent as you remove them.

WARNING
Never use gasoline as a cleaning agent. It presents an extreme fire hazard. Be sure to work in a well-ventilated area when using cleaning solvent. Keep a fire extinguisher, rated for gasoline fires, handy in any case.

Much of the labor charge for repairs made by dealers is for the removal and disassembly of other parts to reach the defective unit. It is frequently possible to perform the preliminary operations yourself and then take the defective unit in to the dealer for repair, at considerable savings.

Once you have decided to tackle the job yourself, make sure you locate the appropriate section in this manual, and read it entirely. Study the illustrations and text until you have a good idea of what is involved in completing the job satisfactorily. If special tools are required, make arrangements to get them before you start. Also, purchase any known defective parts prior to starting on the procedure. It is frustrating and time-consuming to get partially into a job and then be unable to complete it.

Simple wiring checks can be easily made at home, but knowledge of electronics is almost a necessity for performing tests with complicated electronic testing gear.

During disassembly of parts keep a few general cautions in mind. Force is rarely needed to get things apart. If parts are a tight fit, like a bearing in a case, there is usually a tool designed to separate them. Never use a screwdriver to pry apart parts with machined surfaces such as cylinder head or crankcase halves. You will mar the surfaces and end up with leaks.

Make diagrams wherever similar-appearing parts are found. You may think you can remember where everything came from — but mistakes are costly. There is also the possibility you may get sidetracked and not return to work for days or even weeks — in which interval, carefully laid out parts may have become disturbed.

Tag all similar internal parts for location, and mark all mating parts for position. Record number and thickness of any shims as they are removed. Small parts such as bolts can be identified by placing them in plastic sandwich bags that are sealed and labeled with masking tape.

Wiring should be tagged with masking tape and marked as each wire is removed. Again, do not rely on memory alone.

Disconnect battery ground cable before working near electrical connections and before disconnecting wires. Never run the engine with the battery disconnected; the alternator could be seriously damaged.

Protect finished surfaces from physical damage or corrosion. Keep gasoline and brake fluid off painted surfaces.

Frozen or very tight bolts and screws can often be loosened by soaking with penetrating oil like Liquid Wrench or WD-40, then sharply striking the bolt head a few times with a hammer and punch (or screwdriver for screws). Avoid heat unless absolutely necessary, since it may melt, warp, or remove the temper from many parts.

Avoid flames or sparks when working near a charging battery or flammable liquids, such as gasoline.

No parts, except those assembled with a press fit, require unusual force during assembly. If a part is hard to remove or install, find out why before proceeding.

Cover all openings after removing parts to keep dirt, small tools, etc., from falling in.

When assembling two parts, start all fasteners, then tighten evenly.

Wiring connections and brake shoes, drums, pads, and discs and contact surfaces in dry clutches should be kept clean and free of grease and oil.

When assembling parts, be sure all shims and washers are replaced exactly as they came out.

Whenever a rotating part butts against a stationary part, look for a shim or washer. Use new gaskets if there is any doubt about the condition of old ones. Generally, you should apply gasket cement to one mating surface only, so the parts may be easily disassembled in the future. A thin coat of oil on gaskets helps them seal effectively.

Heavy grease can be used to hold small parts in place if they tend to fall out during assembly. However, keep grease and oil away from electrical, clutch, and brake components.

High spots may be sanded off a piston with sandpaper, but emery cloth and oil do a much more professional job.

Carburetors are best cleaned by disassembling them and soaking the parts in a commercial carburetor cleaner. Never soak gaskets and rubber parts in these cleaners. Never use wire to clean out jets and air passages; they are easily damaged. Use compressed air to blow out the carburetor, but only if the float has been removed first.

Take your time and do the job right. Do not forget that a newly rebuilt engine must be broken in the same as a new one. Refer to your owner's manual for the proper break-in procedures.

SAFETY FIRST

Professional mechanics can work for years and never sustain a serious injury. If you observe a few rules of common sense and safety, you can enjoy many safe hours servicing your motorcycle. You could hurt yourself or damage the motorcycle if you ignore these rules.

1. Never use gasoline as a cleaning solvent.
2. Never smoke or use a torch in the vicinity of flammable liquids such as cleaning solvent in open containers.
3. Never smoke or use a torch in an area where batteries are being charged. Highly explosive hydrogen gas is formed during the charging process.
4. Use the proper sized wrenches to avoid damage to nuts and injury to yourself.
5. When loosening a tight or stuck nut, be guided by what would happen if the wrench should slip. Protect yourself accordingly.
6. Keep your work area clean and uncluttered.
7. Wear safety goggles during all operations involving drilling, grinding, or use of a cold chisel.
8. Never use worn tools.
9. Keep a fire extinguisher handy and be sure it is rated for gasoline (Class B) and electrical (Class C) fires.

EXPENDABLE SUPPLIES

Certain expendable supplies are necessary. These include grease, oil, gasket cement, wiping rags, cleaning solvent, and distilled water. Also, special locking compounds, silicone lubricants, and engine and carburetor cleaners may be useful. Cleaning solvent is available at most service stations and distilled water for the battery is available at supermarkets.

SHOP TOOLS

For complete servicing and repair you will need an assortment of ordinary hand tools **(Figure 1)**.

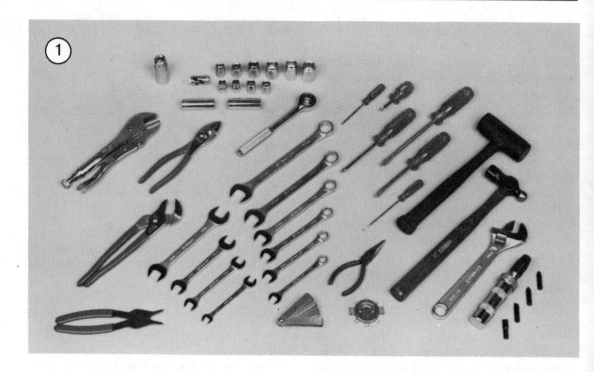

As a minimum, these include:

a. Combination wrenches
b. Sockets
c. Plastic mallet
d. Small hammer
e. Impact driver
f. Snap ring pliers
g. Gas pliers
h. Phillips screwdrivers
i. Slot (common) screwdrivers
j. Feeler gauges
k. Spark plug gauge
l. Spark plug wrench

Special tools required are shown in the chapter covering the particular repair in which they are used.

Engine tune-up and troubleshooting procedures require other special tools and equipment. These are described in detail in the following sections.

EMERGENCY TOOL KITS

Highway

A small emergency tool kit kept on the bike is handy for road emergencies which otherwise could leave you stranded. The tools and spares listed below and shown in **Figure 2** will let you handle most roadside repairs.

a. Motorcycle tool kit (original equipment)
b. Impact driver
c. Silver waterproof sealing tape (duct tape)
d. Hose clamps (3 sizes)
e. Silicone sealer
f. Thread lock
g. Flashlight
h. Tire patch kit
i. Tire irons
j. Plastic pint bottle (for oil)
k. Waterless hand cleaner
l. Rags for clean up

Off-Road

A few simple tools and aids carried on the motorcycle can mean the difference between walking or riding back to camp or to where repairs can be made. See **Figure 3**.

A few essential spare parts carried in your truck or van can prevent a day or weekend of trail riding from being spoiled. See **Figure 4**.

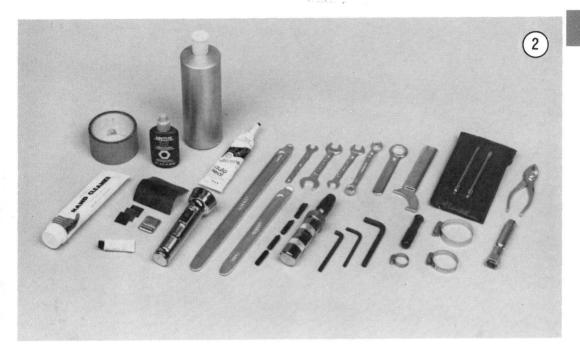

On the Motorcycle

a. Motorcycle tool kit (original equipment)
b. Drive chain master link
c. Tow line
d. Spark plug
e. Spark plug wrench
f. Shifter lever
g. Clutch/brake lever
h. Silver waterproof sealing tape (duct tape)
i. Thread lock

In the Truck

a. Control cables (throttle, clutch, brake)
b. Silicone sealer
c. Tire patch kit
d. Tire irons
e. Tire pump
f. Impact driver
g. Oil

WARNING
Tools and spares should be carried on the motorcycle – not in clothing where a simple fall could result in serious injury from a sharp tool.

TROUBLESHOOTING AND TUNE-UP EQUIPMENT

Voltmeter, Ohmmeter, and Ammeter

For testing the ignition or electrical system, a good voltmeter is required. For motorcycle use, an instrument covering 0-20 volts is satisfactory. One which also has a 0-2 volt scale is necessary for testing relays, points, or individual contacts where voltage drops are much smaller. Accuracy should be ± ½ volt.

An ohmmeter measures electrical resistance. This instrument is useful for checking continuity (open and short circuits), and testing fuses and lights.

The ammeter measures electrical current. Ammeters for motorcycle use should cover 0-50 amperes and 0-250 amperes. These are useful for checking battery charging and starting current.

Several inexpensive VOM's (volt-ohm-milli-ammeter) combine all three instruments into one which fits easily in any tool box. See **Figure 5**. However, the ammeter ranges are usually too small for motorcycle work.

Hydrometer

The hydrometer gives a useful indication of battery condition and charge by measuring the

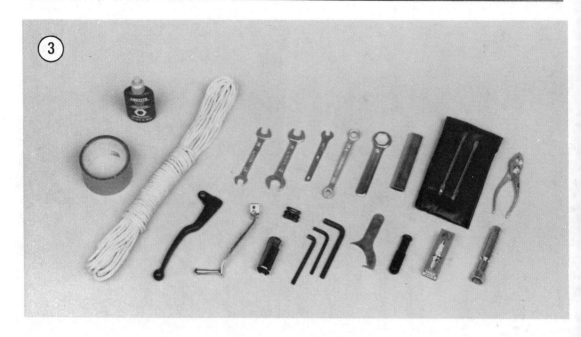

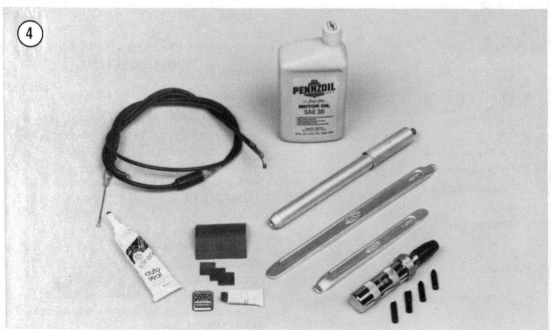

specific gravity of the electrolyte in each cell. See **Figure 6**. Complete details on use and interpretation of readings are provided in the electrical chapter.

Compression Tester

The compression tester measures the compression pressure built up in each cylinder. The results, when properly interpreted, can indicate general cylinder, ring, and valve condition. See **Figure 7**. Extension lines are available for hard-to-reach cylinders.

Dwell Meter (Contact Breaker Point Ignition Only)

A dwell meter measures the distance in degrees of cam rotation that the breaker points remain closed while the engine is running. Since

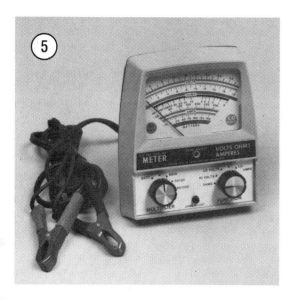

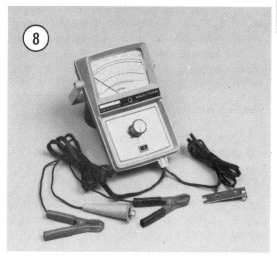

this angle is determined by breaker point gap, dwell angle is an accurate indication of breaker point gap.

Many tachometers intended for tuning and testing incorporate a dwell meter as well. See **Figure 8**. Follow the manufacturer's instructions to measure dwell.

Tachometer

A tachometer is necessary for tuning. See **Figure 8**. Ignition timing and carburetor adjustments must be performed at the specified idle speed. The best instrument for this purpose is one with a low range of 0-1,000 or 0-2,000 rpm for setting idle, and a high range of 0-4,000 or more for setting ignition timing at 3,000 rpm. Extended range (0-6,000 or 0-8,000 rpm) instruments lack accuracy at lower speeds. The instrument should be capable of detecting changes of 25 rpm on the low range.

> NOTE: *The motorcycle's tachometer is not accurate enough for correct idle adjustment.*

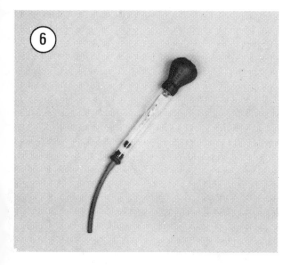

Strobe Timing Light

This instrument is necessary for tuning, as it permits very accurate ignition timing. The light flashes at precisely the same instant that No. 1 cylinder fires, at which time the timing marks on the engine should align. Refer to Chapter Three for exact location of the timing marks for your engine.

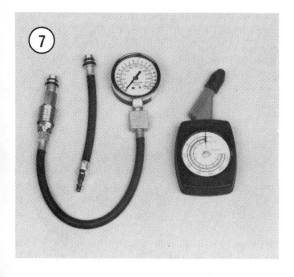

Suitable lights range from inexpensive neon bulb types to powerful xenon strobe lights. See **Figure 9**. Neon timing lights are difficult to see and must be used in dimly lit areas. Xenon strobe timing lights can be used outside in bright sunlight.

Tune-up Kits

Many manufacturers offer kits that combine several useful instruments. Some come in a convenient carry case and are usually less expensive than purchasing one instrument at a time.

Figure 10 shows one of the kits that is available. The prices vary with the number of instruments included in the kit.

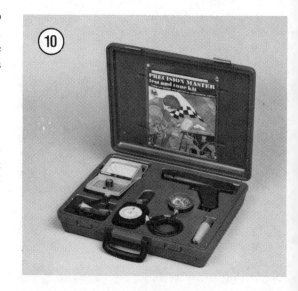

Manometer (Carburetor Synchronizer)

A manometer is essential for accurately synchronizing carburetors on multi-cylinder engines. The instrument detects intake pressure differences between carburetors and permits them to be adjusted equally. Quality manometers come with detailed instructions for use. See **Figure 11**.

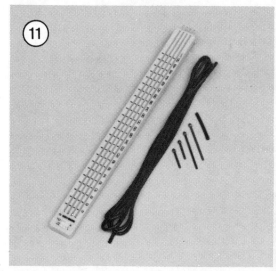

Fire Extinguisher

A fire extinguisher is a necessity when working on a vehicle. It should be rated for both Class B (flammable liquids – gasoline, oil, paint, etc.) and Class C (electrical – wiring, etc.) type fires. It should always be kept within reach. See **Figure 12**.

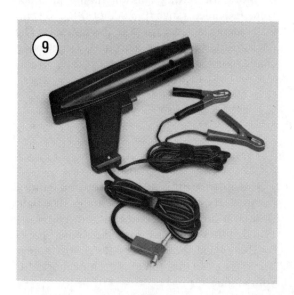

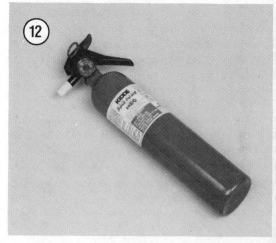

CHAPTER TWO

TROUBLESHOOTING

Troubleshooting motorcycle problems is relatively simple. To be effective and efficient, however, it must be done in a logical step-by=step manner. If it is not, a great deal of time may be wasted, good parts may be replaced unnecesarily, and the true problem may never be uncovered.

Always begin by defining the symptoms as closely as possible. Then analyze the symptoms carefully so thtat you can make an intelligent guess at the probably cause. Next, test the probably cause and attempt to verify it; if it's not at fault, analyze the symptoms once again, this time eliminating the first probably cause. Continue on in this manner, a step at a time, until the problem is solved.

At first, this approach may seem to be time consuming, but you will soon discover that it's not nearly so wasteful as a hit-or-miss method that may never solve the problem. And just a simportant, the methodical approach to troubleshoogint ensures that only those parts that are defective will be replaced.

The troubleshooting procedures in this chatper analyze typical symptoms and show logical methods for isolating and correcting trouble. They are not, however, the only methods; there may be saveral approaches to a given problem, but all good troubleshooting methods have one thing in common – a logical systematic approach.

ENGINE

The entire engine must be considered when trouble arises that is experienced as poor performance or failure to start. The engine is more than a combustion chamber, piston, and crankshaft; it also includes a fuel delivery system, an ignition system, and an exhaust system.

Befor ebeginning to troubleshoot any engine problems, it's important to understand an engine's operating requirements. First, it must have a correctly metered mixture of gasoline and air (**Figure 1**). Second, it must have an airtight combustion chamber in which the mixture can be compressed. And finally, it requires a precisely timed spark to ignite the compressed mixture. If one or more is missing, the engine won't run, and if just one is deficient, the engine will run poorly at best.

Of the three requirements, the precisely timed spark – provided by the ignition system – is most likely to be the cuplrit, with gas/air mixture (carburetion) second, and poor compression the lest likely.

STARTING DIFFICULTIES

Hard starting is probably the most common motorcycle ailment, with a wide range of problems likely. Before delving into a reluctant or non-starter, first determine what has changed

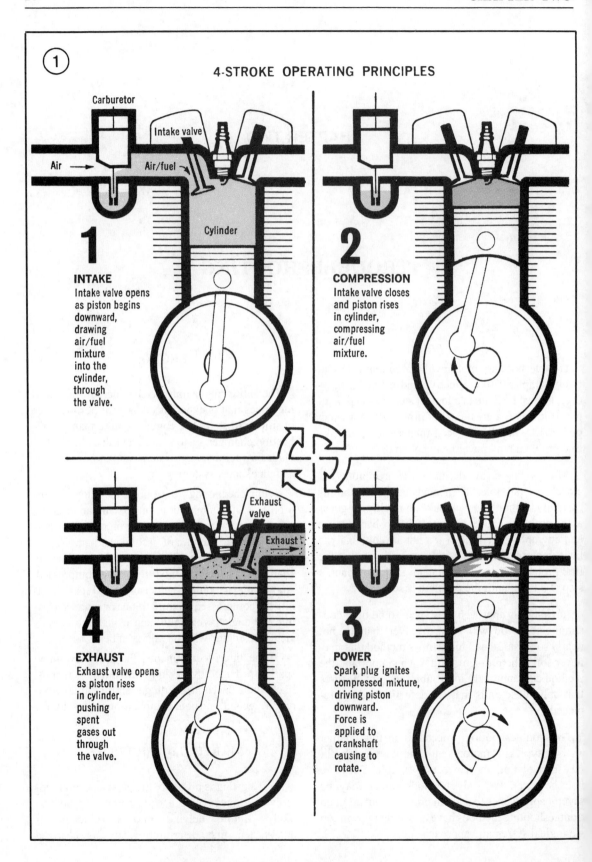

1

4-STROKE OPERATING PRINCIPLES

Carburetor

Intake valve

Air →   Air/fuel

Cylinder

1

INTAKE
Intake valve opens
as piston begins
downward,
drawing
air/fuel
mixture
into the
cylinder,
through
the valve.

2

COMPRESSION
Intake valve closes
and piston rises
in cylinder,
compressing
air/fuel
mixture.

4

EXHAUST
Exhaust valve opens
as piston rises
in cylinder,
pushing
spent
gases out
through
the valve.

Exhaust
valve

Exhaust →

3

POWER
Spark plug ignites
compressed mixture,
driving piston
downward.
Force is
applied to
crankshaft
causing to
rotate.

since the motorcycle last started easily. For instance, was the weather dry then and is it wet now? Has the motorcycle been sitting in the garage for a long time? Has it been ridden many miles since it was last fueled?

Has starting become increasingly more difficult? This alone could indicate a number of things that may be wrong but is usually associated with normal wear of ignition and engine components.

While it's not always possible to diagnose trouble simply from a change of conditions, this information can be helpful and at some future time may uncover a recurring problem.

Fuel Delivery

Although it is the second most likely cause of trouble, fuel delivery should be checked first simply because it is the easiest.

First, check the tank to make sure there is fuel in it. Then, disconnect the fuel hose at the carburetor, open the valve and check for flow (**Figure 2**). If fuel does not flow freely make sure the tank vent is clear. Next, check for blockage in the line or valve. Remove the valve and clean it as described in the fuel system chapter.

If fuel flows from the hose, reconnect it and remove the float bowl from the carburetor, open the valve and check for flow through the float needle valve. If it does not flow freely when the float is extended and then shut off when the flow is gently raised, clean the carburetor as described in the fuel system chapter.

When fuel delivery is satisfactory, go on to the ignition system.

Ignition

Remove the spark plug from the cylinder and check its condition. The appearance of the plug is a good indication of what's happening in the combustion chamber; for instance, if the plug is wet with gas, it's likely that engine is flooded. Compare the spark plug to **Figure 3**. Make certain the spark plug heat range is correct. A "cold" plug makes starting difficult.

After checking the spark plug, reconnect it to the high-tension lead and lay it on the cylinder head so it makes good contact (**Figure 4**). Then,

with the ignition switched on, crank the engine several times and watch for a spark across the plug electrodes. A fat, blue spark should be visible. If there is no spark, or if the spark is weak, substitute a good plug for the old one and check again. If the spark has improved, the old plug is faulty. If there was no change, keep looking.

Make sure the ignition switch is not shorted to ground. Remove the spark plug cap from the end of the high-tension lead and hold the exposed end of the lead about ⅛ inch from the cylinder head. Crank the engine and watch for a spark arcing from the lead to the head. If it's satisfactory, the connection between the lead and the cap was faulty. If the spark hasn't improved, check the coil wire connections.

If the spark is still weak, remove the ignition cover and remove any dirt or moisture from the points or sensor. Check the point or air gap against the specifications in the *Quick Reference Data* at the beginning of the book.

If spark is still not satisfactory, a more serious problem exists than can be corrected with simple adjustments. Refer to the electrical system chapter for detailed information for correcting major ignition problems.

Compression

Compression — or the lack of it — is the least likely cause of starting trouble. However, if compression is unsatisfactory, more than a simple adjustment is required to correct it (see the engine chapter).

An accurate compression check reveals a lot about the condition of the engine. To perform this test you need a compression gauge (see Chapter One). The engine should be at operating temperature for a fully accurate test, but even a cold test will reveal if the starting problem is compression.

Remove the spark plug and screw in a compression gauge (**Figure 5**). With assistance, hold the throttle wide open and crank the engine several times, until the gauge ceases to rise. Normal compression should be 130-160 psi, but a reading as low as 100 psi is usually sufficient for the engine to start. If the reading is much lower than normal, remove the gauge and pour about a tablespoon of oil into the cylinder.

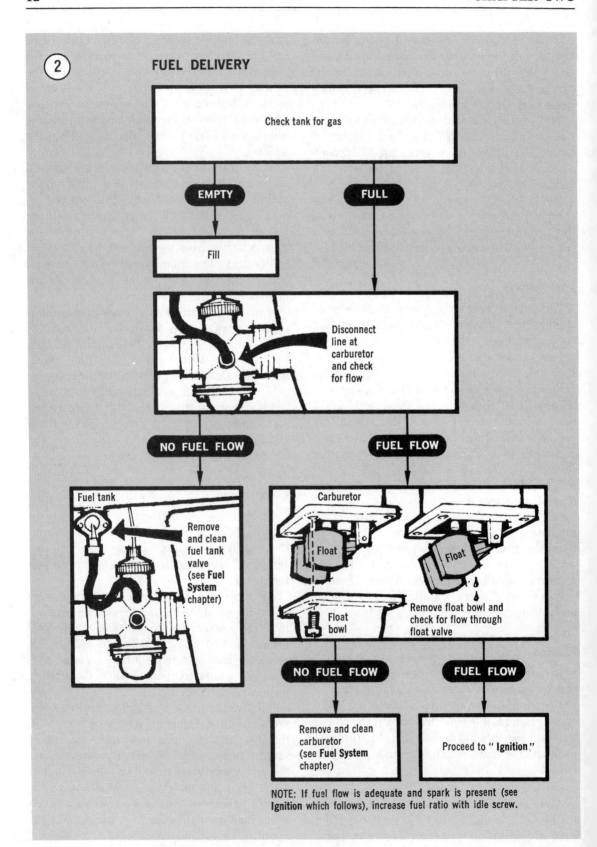

(2) FUEL DELIVERY

Check tank for gas

EMPTY

FULL

Fill

Disconnect line at carburetor and check for flow

NO FUEL FLOW

FUEL FLOW

Fuel tank

Remove and clean fuel tank valve (see **Fuel System** chapter)

Carburetor

Float

Float

Float bowl

Remove float bowl and check for flow through float valve

NO FUEL FLOW

FUEL FLOW

Remove and clean carburetor (see **Fuel System** chapter)

Proceed to " **Ignition** "

NOTE: If fuel flow is adequate and spark is present (see **Ignition** which follows), increase fuel ratio with idle screw.

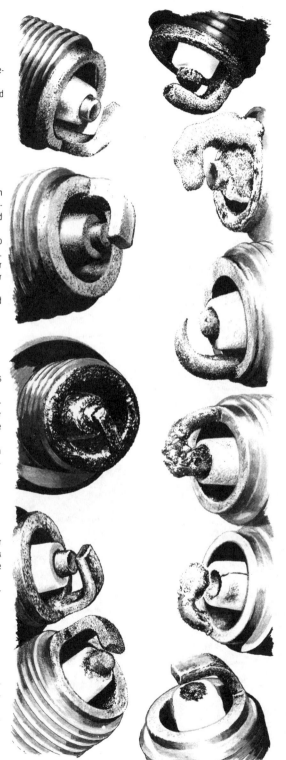

2

NORMAL
• Appearance—Firing tip has deposits of light gray to light tan.
• Can be cleaned, regapped and reused.

CARBON FOULED
• Appearance—Dull, dry black with fluffy carbon deposits on the insulator tip, electrode and exposed shell.
• Caused by—Fuel/air mixture too rich, plug heat range too cold, weak ignition system, dirty air cleaner, faulty automatic choke or excessive idling.
• Can be cleaned, regapped and reused.

OIL FOULED
• Appearance—Wet black deposits on insulator and exposed shell.
• Caused by—Excessive oil entering the combustion chamber through worn rings, pistons, valve guides or bearings.
• Replace with new plugs (use a hotter plug if engine is not repaired).

LEAD FOULED
• Appearance — Yellow insulator deposits (may sometimes be dark gray, black or tan in color) on the insulator tip.
• Caused by—Highly leaded gasoline.
• Replace with new plugs.

LEAD FOULED
• Appearance—Yellow glazed deposits indicating melted lead deposits due to hard acceleration.
• Caused by—Highly leaded gasoline.
• Replace with new plugs.

OIL AND LEAD FOULED
• Appearance—Glazed yellow deposits with a slight brownish tint on the insulator tip and ground electrode.
• Replace with new plugs.

FUEL ADDITIVE RESIDUE
• Appearance — Brown colored hardened ash deposits on the insulator tip and ground electrode.
• Caused by—Fuel and/or oil additives.
• Replace with new plugs.

WORN
• Appearance — Severely worn or eroded electrodes.
• Caused by—Normal wear or unusual oil and/or fuel additives.
• Replace with new plugs.

PREIGNITION
• Appearance — Melted ground electrode.
• Caused by—Overadvanced ignition timing, inoperative ignition advance mechanism, too low of a fuel octane rating, lean fuel/air mixture or carbon deposits in combustion chamber.

PREIGNITION
• Appearance—Melted center electrode.
• Caused by—Abnormal combustion due to overadvanced ignition timing or incorrect advance, too low of a fuel octane rating, lean fuel/air mixture, or carbon deposits in combustion chamber.
• Correct engine problem and replace with new plugs.

INCORRECT HEAT RANGE
• Appearance—Melted center electrode and white blistered insulator tip.
• Caused by—Incorrect plug heat range selection.
• Replace with new plugs.

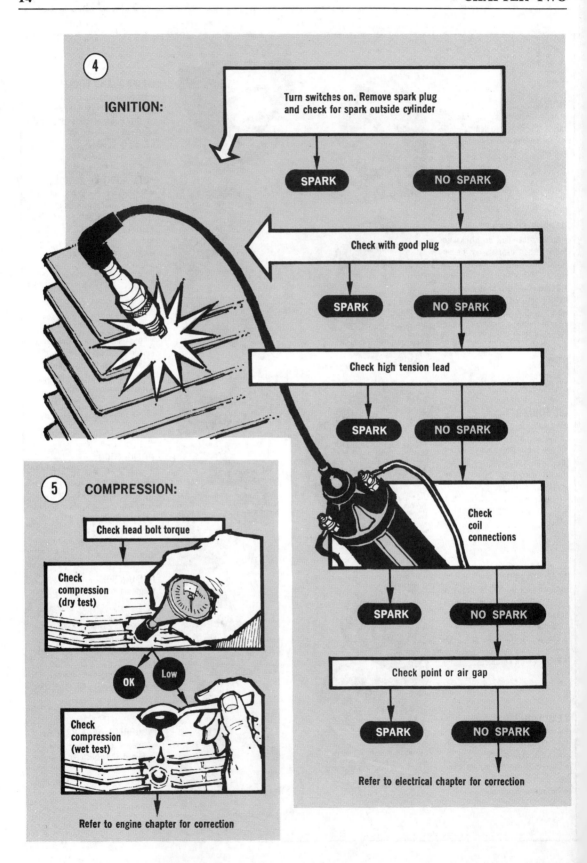

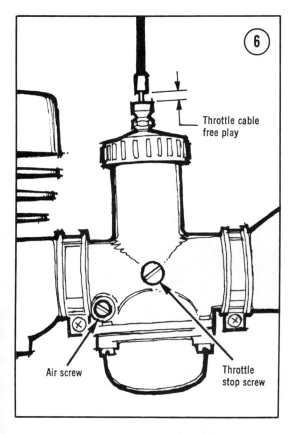

Throttle cable free play

Air screw

Throttle stop screw

Crank the engine several times to distribute the oil and test the compression once again. If it is now significantly higher, the rings and bore are worn. If the compression did not change, the valves are not seating correctly. Adjust the valves and check again. If the compression is still low, refer to the engine chapter.

> NOTE: *Low compression indicates a developing problem. The condition causing it should be corrected as soon as possible.*

POOR PERFORMANCE

Poor engine performance can be caused by any of a number of things related to carburetion, ignition, and the condition of the sliding and rotating components in the engine. In addition, components such as brakes, clutch, and transmission can cause problems that seem to be related to engine performance, even when the engine is in top running condition.

Poor Idling

Idling that is erratic, too high, or too low is most often caused by incorrect adjustment of the carburetor idle circuit. Also, a dirty air filter or an obstructed fuel tank vent can affect idle speed. Incorrect ignition timing or worn or faulty ignition components are also good possibilities.

First, make sure the air filter is clean and correctly installed. Then, adjust the throttle cable free play, the throttle stop screw, and the idle mixture air screw (**Figure 6**) as described in the routine maintenance chapter.

If idling is still poor, check the carburetor and manifold mounts for leaks; with the engine warmed up and running, spray WD-40 or a similar light lube around the flanges and joints of the carburetor and manifold (**Figure 7**). Listen for changes in engine speed. If a leak is present, the idle speed will drop as the lube "plugs" the leak and then pick up again as it is drawn into the engine. Tighten the nuts and clamps and test again. If a leak persists, check for a damaged gasket or a pinhole in the manifold. Minor leaks in manifold hoses can be repaired with silicone sealer, but if cracks or holes are extensive, the manifold should be replaced.

A worn throttle slide may cause erratic running and idling, but this is likely only after many thousands of miles of use. To check, remove the carburetor top and feel for back and forth movement of the slide in the bore; it should be barely perceptible. Inspect the slide for large worn areas and replace it if it is less than perfect (**Figure 8**).

If the fuel system is satisfactory, check ignition timing and breaker point gap (air gap in electronic ignition). Check the condition of the system components as well. Ignition-caused idling problems such as erratic running can be the fault of marginal components. See the electrical system chapter for appropriate tests.

Rough Running or Misfiring

Misfiring (see **Figure 9**) is usually caused by an ignition problem. First, check all ignition connections (**Figure 10**). They should be clean, dry, and tight. Don't forget the kill switch; a loose connection can create an intermittent short.

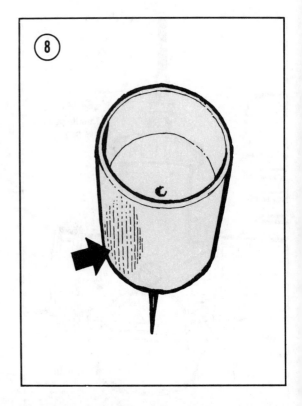

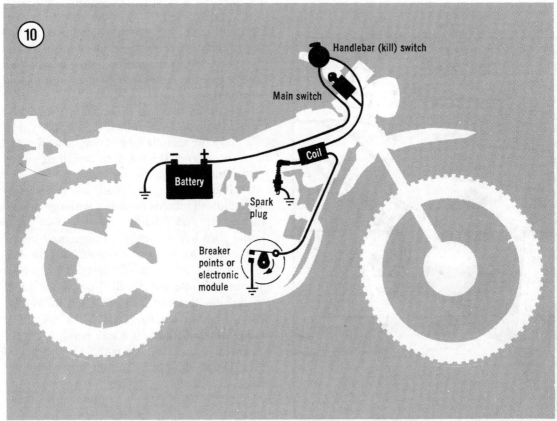

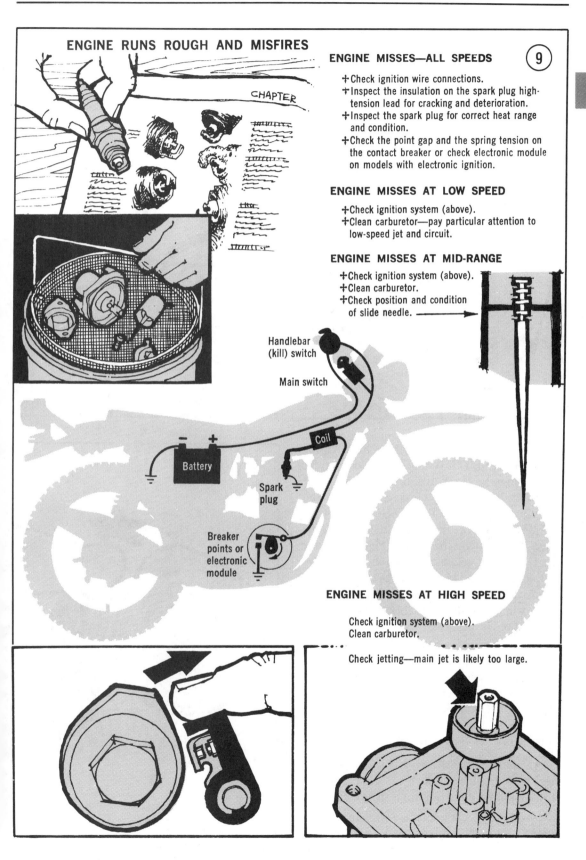

ENGINE RUNS ROUGH AND MISFIRES

CHAPTER

ENGINE MISSES—ALL SPEEDS ⑨

+Check ignition wire connections.
+Inspect the insulation on the spark plug high-tension lead for cracking and deterioration.
+Inspect the spark plug for correct heat range and condition.
+Check the point gap and the spring tension on the contact breaker or check electronic module on models with electronic ignition.

ENGINE MISSES AT LOW SPEED

+Check ignition system (above).
+Clean carburetor—pay particular attention to low-speed jet and circuit.

ENGINE MISSES AT MID-RANGE

+Check ignition system (above).
+Clean carburetor.
+Check position and condition of slide needle. ──────▶

Handlebar (kill) switch

Main switch

Coil

Battery

Spark plug

Breaker points or electronic module

ENGINE MISSES AT HIGH SPEED

Check ignition system (above).
Clean carburetor.

Check jetting—main jet is likely too large.

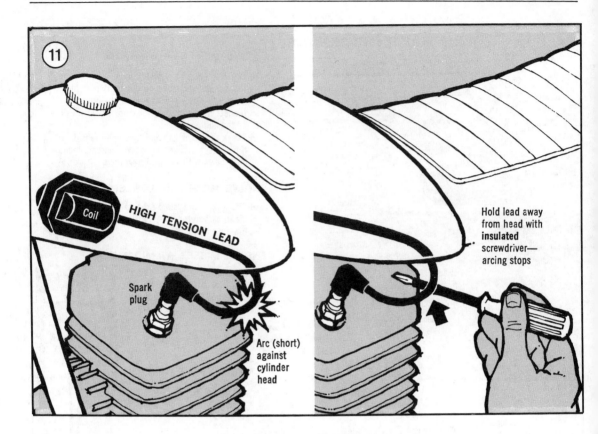

Coil

HIGH TENSION LEAD

Spark plug

Arc (short) against cylinder head

Hold lead away from head with **insulated** screwdriver— arcing stops

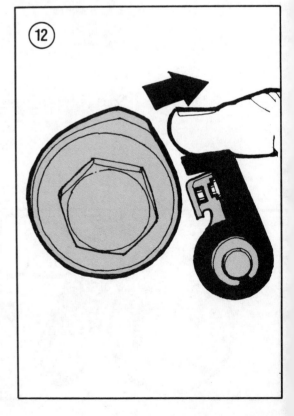

Check the insulation on the high-tension spark plug lead. If it is cracked or deteriorated it will allow the spark to short to ground when the engine is revved. This is easily seen at night. If arcing occurs, hold the affected area of the wire away from the metal to which it is arcing, using an insulated screwdriver (**Figure 11**), and see if the misfiring ceases. If it does, replace the high-tension lead. Also check the connection of the spark plug cap to the lead. If it is poor, the spark will break down at this point when the engine speed is increased.

The spark plug could also be poor. Test the system with a new plug.

Incorrect point gap or a weak contact breaker spring can cause misfiring. Check the gap and the alignment of the points. Push the moveable arm back and check for spring tension (**Figure 12**). It should feel stiff.

On models with electronic ignition, have the electronic module tested by a dealer or substitute a known good unit for a suspected one.

If misfiring occurs only at a certain point in engine speed, the problem may very likely be

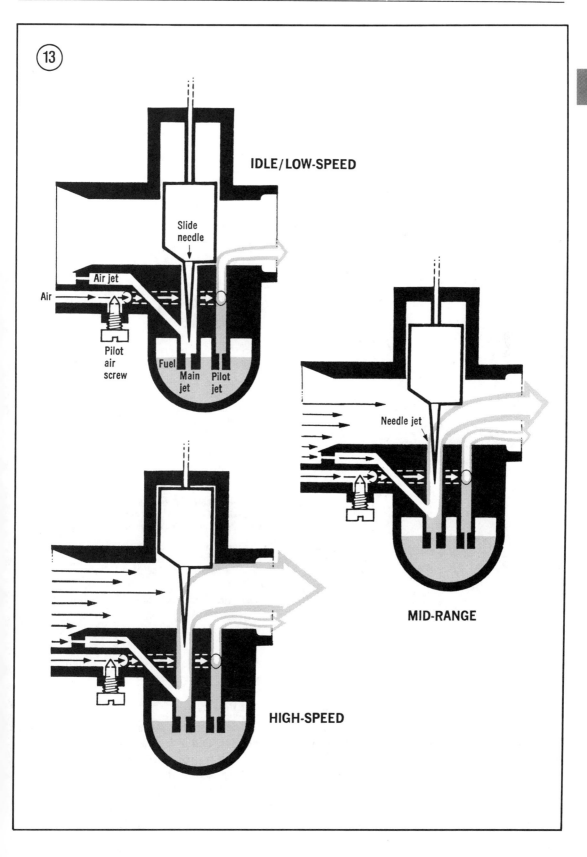

(13)

IDLE/LOW-SPEED

Slide needle

Air jet

Air

Pilot air screw

Fuel

Main jet

Pilot jet

Needle jet

MID-RANGE

HIGH-SPEED

2

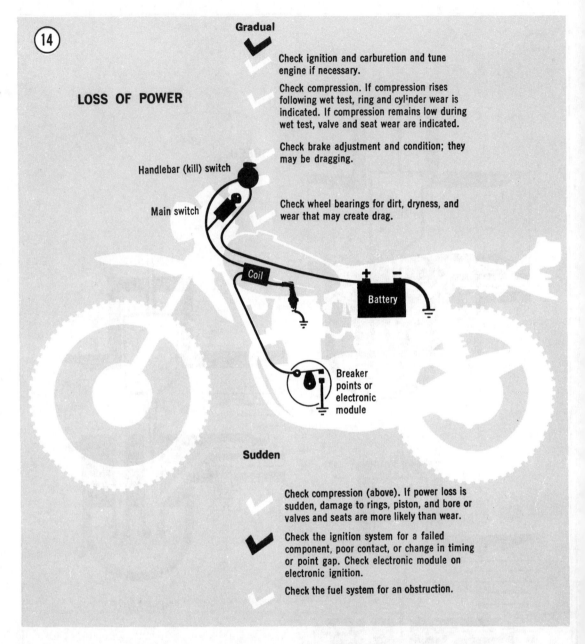

(14)

LOSS OF POWER

Gradual

Check ignition and carburetion and tune engine if necessary.

Check compression. If compression rises following wet test, ring and cylinder wear is indicated. If compression remains low during wet test, valve and seat wear are indicated.

Check brake adjustment and condition; they may be dragging.

Handlebar (kill) switch

Main switch

Check wheel bearings for dirt, dryness, and wear that may create drag.

Coil

Battery

Breaker points or electronic module

Sudden

Check compression (above). If power loss is sudden, damage to rings, piston, and bore or valves and seats are more likely than wear.

Check the ignition system for a failed component, poor contact, or change in timing or point gap. Check electronic module on electronic ignition.

Check the fuel system for an obstruction.

carburetion. Poor performance at idle is described earlier. Misfiring at low speed (just above idle) can be caused by a dirty low-speed circuit or jet (**Figure 13**). Poor midrange performance is attributable to a worn or incorrectly adjusted needle and needle jet. Misfiring at high speed (if not ignition related) is usually caused by a too-large main jet which causes the engine to run rich. Any of these carburetor-related conditions can be corrected by first cleaning the carburetor and then adjusting it as

described in the tune-up and maintenance chapter.

Loss of Power

First determine how the power loss developed (**Figure 14**). Did it decline over a long period of time or did it drop abruptly? A gradual loss is normal, caused by deterioration of the engine's state of tune and the normal wear of the cylinder and piston rings and the valves and seats. In such case, check the condition of the

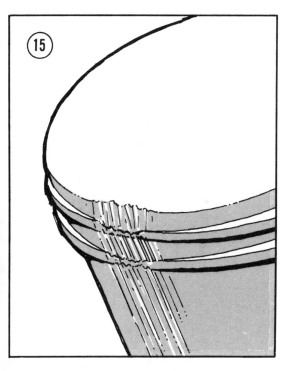

ignition and carburetion and measure the compression as described earlier.

A sudden power loss may be caused by a failed ignition component, obstruction in the fuel system, damaged valve or seat, or a broken piston ring or damaged piston (**Figure 15**).

If the engine is in good shape and tune, check the brake adjustment. If the brakes are dragging, they will consume considerable power. Also check the wheel bearings. If they are dry, extremely dirty, or badly worn they can create considerable drag.

Engine Runs Hot

A modern motorcycle engine, in good mechanical condition, correctly tuned, and operated as it was intended, will rarely experience overheating problems. However, out-of-spec conditions can create severe overheating that may result in serious engine damage. Refer to **Figure 16**.

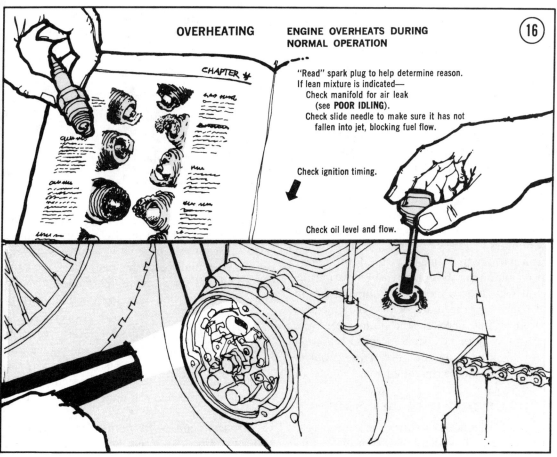

Overheating is difficult to detect unless it is extreme, in which case it will usually be apparent as excessive heat radiating from the engine, accompanied by the smell of hot oil and sharp, snapping noises when the engine is first shut off and begins to cool.

Unless the motorcycle is operated under sustained high load or is allowed to idle for long periods of time, overheating is usually the result of an internal problem. Most often it's caused by a too-lean fuel mixture.

Remove the spark plug and compare it to **Figure 3**. If a too-lean condition is indicated, check for leaks in the intake manifold (see *Poor Idling*). The carburetor jetting may be incorrect but this is unlikely if the overheating problem has just developed (unless, of course, the engine was jetted for high altitude and is now being run near sea level). Check the slide needle in the carburetor to make sure it hasn't come loose and is restricting the flow of gas through the main jet and needle jet (**Figure 17**).

Check the ignition timing; extremes of either advance or retard can cause overheating.

Piston Seizure and Damage

Piston seizure is a common result of overheating (see above) because an aluminum piston expands at a greater rate than a steel cylinder. Seizure can also be caused by piston-to-cylinder clearance that is too small; ring end gap that is too small; insufficient oil; spark plug heat range too hot; and broken piston ring or ring land.

A major piston seizure can cause severe engine damage. A minor seizure — which usually subsides after the engine has cooled a few minutes — rarely does more than scuff the piston skirt the first time it occurs. Fortunately, this condition can be corrected by dressing the piston with crocus cloth, refitting the piston and rings to the bore with recommended clearances, and checking the timing to ensure overheating does not occur. Regard that first seizure as a warning and correct the problem before continuing to run the engine.

CLUTCH AND TRANSMISSION

1. *Clutch slips*—Make sure lever free play is sufficient to allow the clutch to fully engage

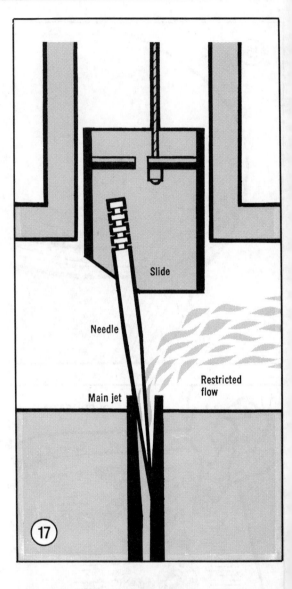

Slide

Needle

Restricted flow

Main jet

⑰

(**Figure 18**). Check the contact surfaces for wear and glazing. Transmission oil additives also can cause slippage in wet clutches. If slip occurs only under extreme load, check the condition of the springs or diaphragm and make sure the clutch bolts are snug and uniformly tightened.

2. *Clutch drags*—Make sure lever free play isn't so great that it fails to disengage the clutch. Check for warped plates or disc. If the transmission oil (in wet clutch systems) is extremely dirty or heavy, it may inhibit the clutch from releasing.

3. *Transmission shifts hard*—Extremely dirty oil can cause the transmission to shift hard.

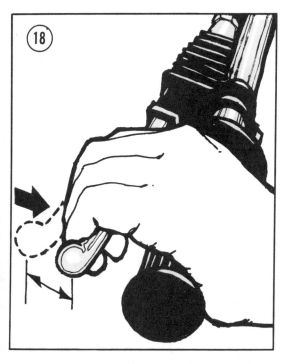

Check the selector shaft for bending (**Figure 19**). Inspect the shifter and gearsets for wear and damage.

4. *Transmission slips out of gear*—This can be caused by worn engagement dogs or a worn or damaged shifter (**Figure 20**). The overshift travel on the selector may be misadjusted.

5. *Transmission is noisy*—Noises usually indicate the absence of lubrication or wear and damage to gears, bearings, or shims. It's a good idea to disassemble the transmission and carefully inspect it when noise first occurs.

DRIVE TRAIN

Drive train problems (outlined in **Figure 21**) arise from normal wear and incorrect maintenance.

CHASSIS

Chassis problems are outlined in **Figure 22**.

1. *Motorcycle pulls to one side*—Check for loose suspension components, axles, steering

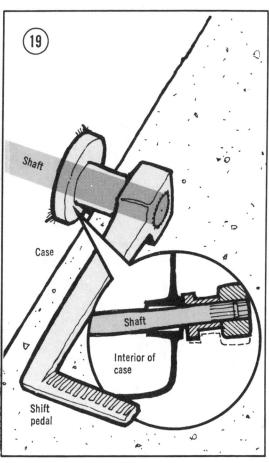

24

CHAPTER TWO

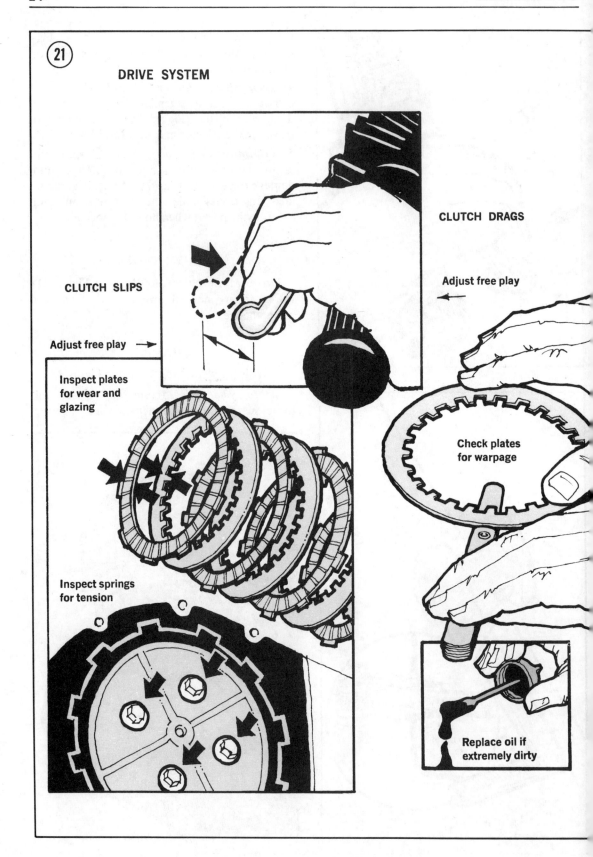

2

TRANSMISSION SLIPS OUT OF GEAR

TRANSMISSION SHIFTS HARD

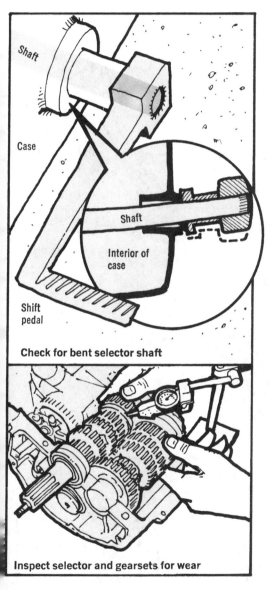

Check for bent selector shaft

Inspect selector and gearsets for wear

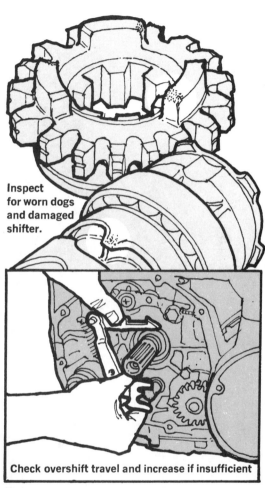

Inspect for worn dogs and damaged shifter.

Check overshift travel and increase if insufficient

TRANSMISSION IS NOISY

Check oil level

Disassemble and inspect (see Transmission chapter)

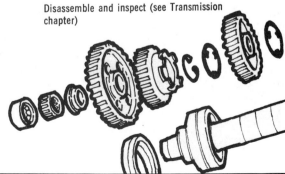

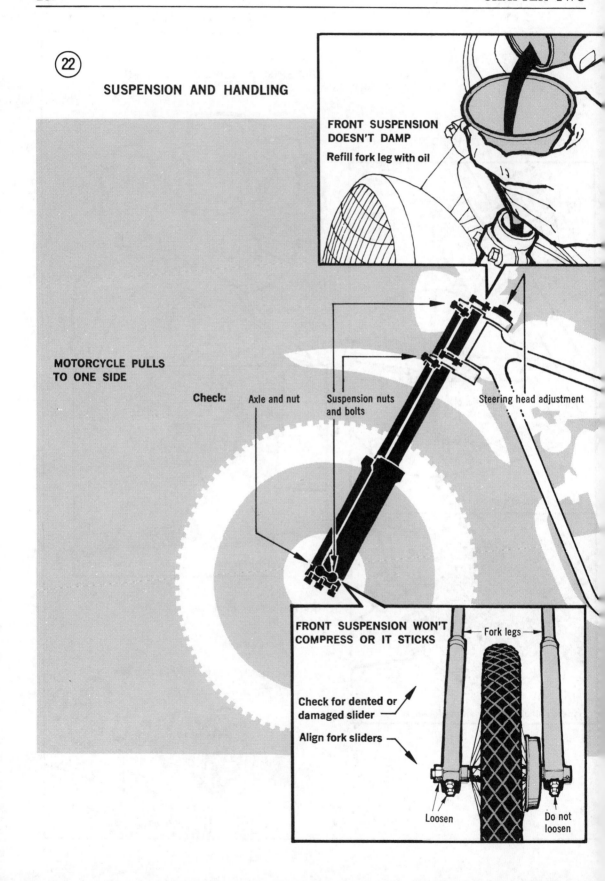

㉒

SUSPENSION AND HANDLING

FRONT SUSPENSION
DOESN'T DAMP

Refill fork leg with oil

MOTORCYCLE PULLS
TO ONE SIDE

Check: Axle and nut   Suspension nuts
and bolts   Steering head adjustment

FRONT SUSPENSION WON'T
COMPRESS OR IT STICKS   Fork legs

Check for dented or
damaged slider

Align fork sliders

Loosen   Do not
loosen

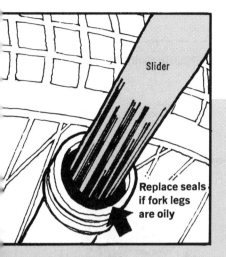

Slider

Replace seals if fork legs are oily

SUSPENSION AND HANDLING CONTINUED 2

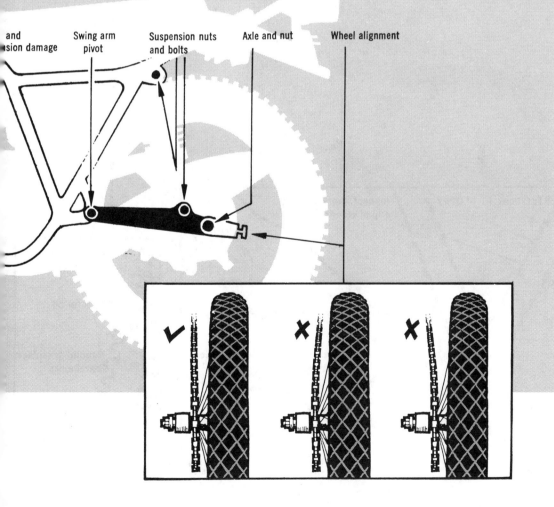

and
sion damage

Swing arm
pivot

Suspension nuts
and bolts

Axle and nut

Wheel alignment

SUSPENSION AND HANDLING CONTINUED

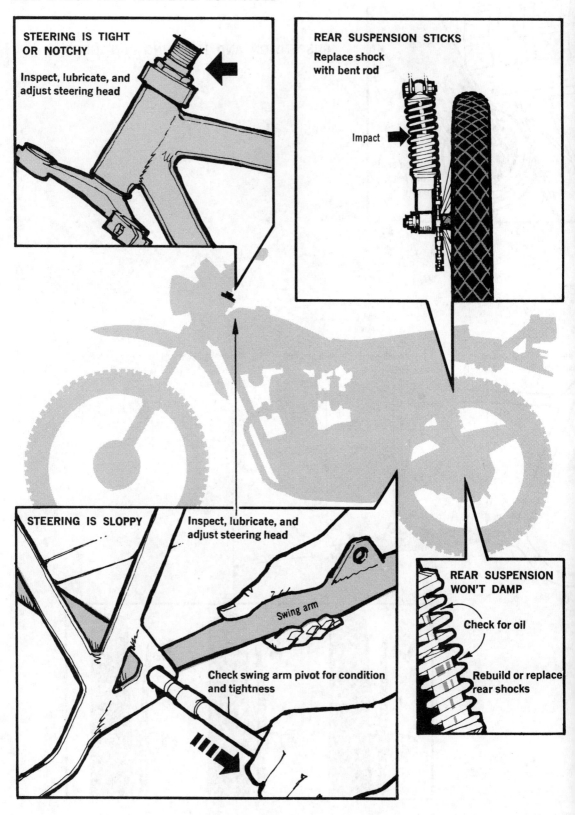

STEERING IS TIGHT OR NOTCHY

Inspect, lubricate, and adjust steering head

REAR SUSPENSION STICKS

Replace shock with bent rod

Impact

STEERING IS SLOPPY

Inspect, lubricate, and adjust steering head

Swing arm

Check swing arm pivot for condition and tightness

REAR SUSPENSION WON'T DAMP

Check for oil

Rebuild or replace rear shocks

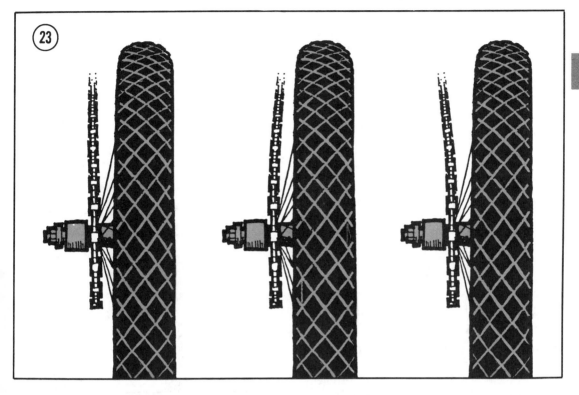

head, swing arm pivot. Check wheel alignment (**Figure 23**). Check for damage to the frame and suspension components.

2. *Front suspension doesn't damp*—This is most often caused by a lack of damping oil in the fork legs. If the upper fork tubes are exceptionally oily, it's likely that the seals are worn out and should be replaced.

3. *Front suspension sticks or won't fully compress*—Misalignment of the forks when the wheel is installed can cause this. Loosen the axle nut and the pinch bolt on the nut end of the axle (**Figure 24**). Lock the front wheel with the brake and compress the front suspension several times to align the fork legs. Then, tighten the pinch bolt and then the axle nut.

The trouble may also be caused by a bent or dented fork slider (**Figure 25**). The distortion required to lock up a fork tube is so slight that it is often impossible to visually detect. If this type of damage is suspected, remove the fork leg and remove the spring from it. Attempt to operate the fork leg. If it still binds, replace the slider; it's not practical to repair it.

4. *Rear suspension does not damp*—This is usually caused by damping oil leaking past

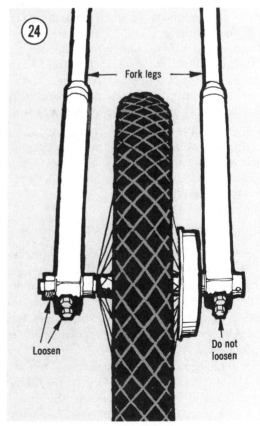

worn seals. Rebuildable shocks should be refitted with complete service kits and fresh oil. Non-rebuildable units should be replaced.

5. *Rear suspension sticks*—This is commonly caused by a bent shock absorber piston rod (**Figure 26**). Replace the shock; the rod can't be satisfactorily straightened.

6. *Steering is tight or "notchy"*—Steering head bearings may be dry, dirty, or worn. Adjustment of the steering head bearing pre-load may be too tight.

7. *Steering is sloppy*—Steering head adjustment may be too loose. Also check the swing arm pivot; looseness or extreme wear at this point translate to the steering.

BRAKES

Brake problems arise from wear, lack of maintenance, and from sustained or repeated exposure to dirt and water.

1. *Brakes are ineffective*—Ineffective brakes are most likely caused by incorrect adjustment. If adjustment will not correct the problem, remove the wheels and check for worn or glazed linings. If the linings are worn beyond the service limit, replace them. If they are simply glazed, rough them up with light sandpaper.

In hydraulic brake systems, low fluid levels can cause a loss of braking effectiveness, as can worn brake cylinder pistons and bores. Also check the pads to see if they are worn beyond the service limit.

2. *Brakes lock or drag*—This may be caused by incorrect adjustment. Check also for foreign matter embedded in the lining and for dirty and dry wheel bearings.

ELECTRICAL SYSTEM

Many electrical system problems can be easily solved by ensuring that the affected connections are clean, dry, and tight. In battery equipped motorcycles, a neglected battery is the source of a great number of difficulties that could be prevented by simple, regular service to the battery.

A multimeter, like the volt/ohm/milliammeter described in Chapter One, is invaluable for efficient electrical system troubleshooting.

See **Figures 27 and 28** for schematics showing

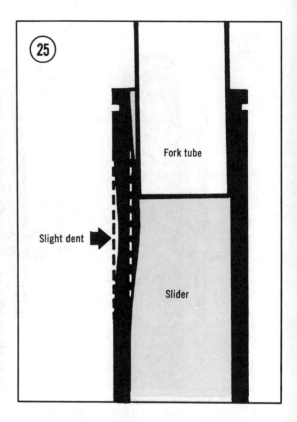

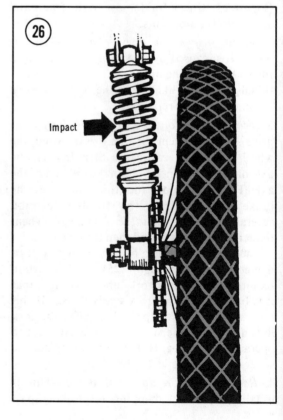

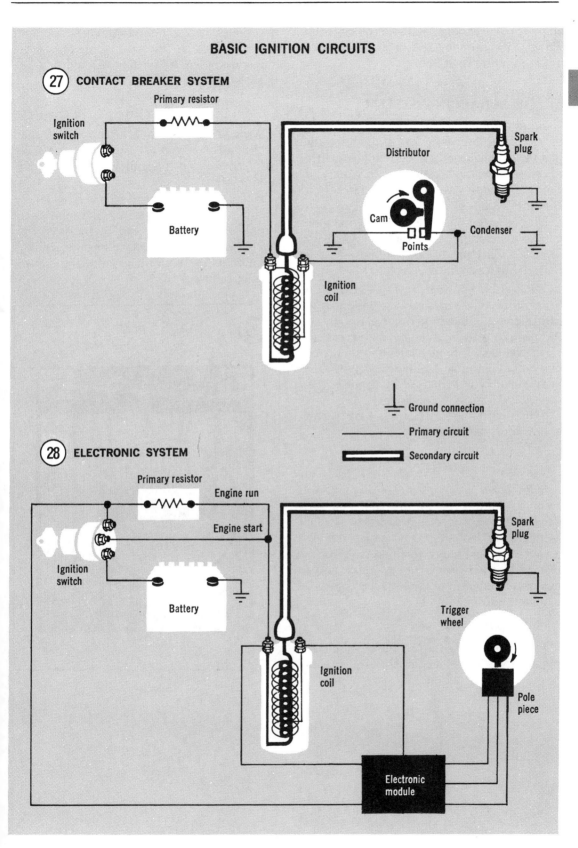

BASIC IGNITION CIRCUITS

(27) CONTACT BREAKER SYSTEM

Primary resistor

Ignition switch

Distributor

Spark plug

Cam

Condenser

Points

Battery

Ignition coil

Ground connection

Primary circuit

Secondary circuit

(28) ELECTRONIC SYSTEM

Primary resistor

Engine run

Engine start

Ignition switch

Spark plug

Battery

Trigger wheel

Ignition coil

Pole piece

Electronic module

simplified conventional and electronic ignition systems. Typical and most common electrical troubles are also described.

CHARGING SYSTEM

1. *Battery will not accept a charge*—Make sure the electrolyte level in the battery is correct and that the terminal connections are tight and free of corrosion. Check for fuses in the battery circuit. If the battery is satisfactory, refer to the electrical system chapter for alternator tests. Finally, keep in mind that even a good alternator is not capable of restoring the charge to a severely discharged battery; it must first be charged by an external source.

2. *Battery will not hold a charge*—Check the battery for sulfate deposits in the bottom of the case (**Figure 29**). Sulfation occurs naturally and the deposits will accumulate and eventually come in contact with the plates and short them out. Sulfation can be greatly retarded by keeping the battery well charged at all times. Test the battery to assess its condition.

If the battery is satisfactory, look for excessive draw, such as a short.

LIGHTING

Bulbs burn out frequently—All bulbs will eventually burn out, but if the bulb in one particular light burns out frequently check the light assembly for looseness that may permit excessive vibration; check for loose connections that could cause current surges; check also to make sure the bulb is of the correct rating.

FUSES

Fuse blows—When a fuse blows, don't just replace it; try to find the cause. Consider a fuse

a warning device as well as a safety device. And never replace a fuse with one of greater amperage rating. It probably won't melt before the insulation on the wiring does.

WIRING

Wiring problems should be corrected as soon as they arise — before a short can cause a fire that may seriously damage or destroy the motorcycle.

A circuit tester of some type is essential for locating shorts and opens. Use the appropriate wiring diagram at the end of the book for reference. If a wire must be replaced make a notation on the wiring diagram of any changes in color coding.

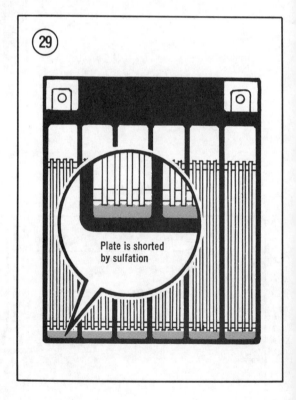

Plate is shorted by sulfation

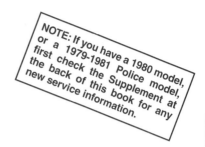

NOTE: If you have a 1980 model, or a 1979-1981 Police model, first check the Supplement at the back of this book for any new service information.

CHAPTER THREE

3

LUBRICATION, MAINTENANCE, AND TUNE-UP

SCHEDULED MAINTENANCE

This chapter covers all the regular maintenance you have to perform to keep your machine in top shape.

Regular maintenance is the best guarantee of a trouble-free, long lasting motorcycle. An afternoon spent now, cleaning and adjusting, can prevent costly mechanical problems in the future and unexpected breakdowns on the road.

> NOTE: *If you have a brand-new motorcycle, we recommend that you take the motorcycle to your dealer for the initial break-in maintenance at 500 miles.*

Emission-controlled Motorcycles

This manual covers U.S. emission-controlled motorcycles. We urge you to follow all procedures specifically designated for your bike. If you don't follow the maintenance schedule in this manual or if you alter engine parts or change their settings from the standard factory specifications (ignition timing, carburetor idle mixture, exhaust system, etc.), your bike may not comply with government emissions standards. In addition, since most emission-controlled bikes are carburetted on the lean side, any changes to emission-related parts (such as exhaust system modifications) could cause the engine to run so lean that engine damage would result.

All tables are found at the end of the chapter.

The procedures presented in this chapter can be easily carried out by anyone with average mechanical skills. The operations are presented step-by-step; if they are followed, it is difficult to go wrong.

When you need new parts, make sure you get the right ones. Note the frame serial number (VIN number) on the steering head (**Figure 1**), and the engine serial number on the engine case (**Figure 2**). Your dealer will often need these numbers to order the right parts for your bike.

There are 5 groups of maintenance items here. As the time and miles pass, start at the front of this chapter each time, and keep working deeper into it as more items become necessary:

a. Weekly or at every gas stop

b. Monthly or every 3,000 miles, whichever comes first

c. Every 6 months or 3,000 miles, whichever comes first

d. Every year or 6,000 miles, whichever comes first

e. Every 2 years or 12,000 miles, whichever comes first

Each group of items is summarized in the checklist (**Table 1**) at the end of this chapter. Detailed instructions on how to perform each item are given here.

WEEKLY MAINTENANCE

Tire Pressure

Tire pressure must be checked with the tires cold. Correct tire pressure depends a lot on the load you are carrying and how fast you are going. A simple, accurate gauge (**Figure 3**) can be purchased for a few dollars and should be carried in your motorcycle tool kit. See **Table 2** or your Tire and Load Data sticker (**Figure 4**).

Remove any embedded stones from the tires. Check each tire for bad cracks or cuts, and replace the tire if you find any.

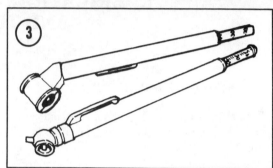

Brake Function

Check for a solid feel at the lever and at the pedal. If the hydraulic brakes feel spongy, perform *Brake Fluid Bleeding*, Chapter Eight.

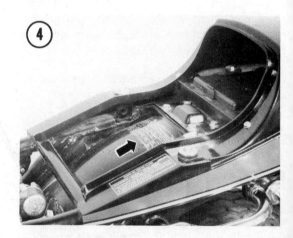

Brake Lever Play (1973–1978 only)

Check free play at the lever. It should be 1/8–3/16 in. (3–5 mm) at the ball end of the lever.

The clearance between the pads and disc(s) is automatically adjusted as the pads wear. The free play of the hand grip should be maintained to avoid brake drag.

Straighten the locking tab on the lockwasher and loosen the locknut. Turn the adjusting bolt in or out until the proper amount of free play is achieved.

After adjustment is completed, tighten the locknut and bend the locking tab up against the locknut.

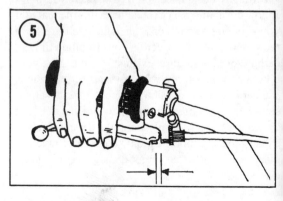

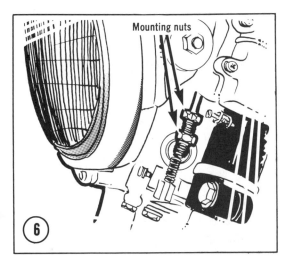

A. Free play   B. Pedal height

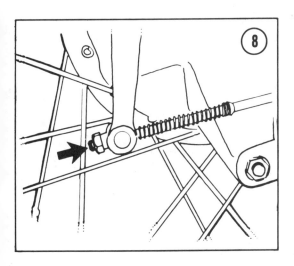

Brake Lever Play (Z1R)

There should be 1/8 in. (2-3mm) free play at the lever (**Figure 5**). The hydraulic brake pads adjust automatically, but the short cable link to the master cylinder will stretch with time and wear.

Loosen the locknut, turn the adjuster as required, and tighten the locknut.

If you can't get proper free play at the lever adjuster perform the following:

1. Remove the fairing.

2. Loosen the lever locknut and screw the adjuster in all the way.

3. Loosen the cable mounting nuts next to the headlight (**Figure 6**) and turn them as required to get proper free play.

4. If the mounting nut adjustment is insufficient, there is another adjuster on the cable guide behind the headlight.

Brake Pedal Height

Brake pedal *height adjustment* should not be required once you have set it right for you the first time, but it does affect pedal free play. Normal brake pedal height is about 1 in. (20–30mm) below the top of the footpeg. Adjust as follows:

1. Place the motorcycle on the centerstand.

2. Check to be sure that the brake pedal is in the at-rest position.

3. Loosen the locknut and turn the adjustment bolt to achieve the correct pedal height (**Figure 7**).

4. Tighten the locknut.

5. Adjust as described under *Brake Pedal Play*.

Brake Pedal Play (Drum Brake)

Adjust the brake pedal to the correct height as described earlier. Turn the adjustment nut on the end of the brake rod (**Figure 8**) until the brake pedal has ¾–1¼ in. (20–30 mm) free play. Free play is the distance the pedal travels from the at-rest position to the applied position when the pedal is depressed lightly by hand.

Rotate the rear wheel and check for brake drag. Also operate the pedal several times to make sure it returns to the at-rest position immediately after release.

Adjust the rear brake light switch as described under *Rear Brake Light Switch Adjustment*.

Brake Pedal Play (Hydraulic Disc Brake)

Adjust the brake pedal to the correct height as described earlier. Loosen the locknuts on the end of the brake pushrod. Rotate the pushrod until the brake pedal has ⅜ in. (8–10 mm) free play. Tighten the locknuts (**Figure 7**).

Free play is the distance the pedal travels until the pushrod contacts the master cylinder piston when the brake pedal is depressed lightly by hand.

Rotate the rear wheel by hand and check for brake drag. Also, operate the pedal several times to make sure it returns to the at-rest position immediately after release.

Adjust the rear brake light switch as described under *Rear Brake Light Switch Adjustment*.

Rear Brake Light Switch Adjustment

1. Turn the ignition switch ON.

2. Depress the brake pedal. The light should come on just as the brake begins to work.

3. To make the light come on earlier, hold the switch body and turn the adjusting locknuts to move the switch body *up*. Move the switch body *down* to delay the light (**Figure 9**). Tighten the locknuts.

> NOTE: *Some riders prefer the light to come on a little early. This way, they can tap the pedal without braking to warn drivers who follow too closely.*

Throttle Grip Inspection

Throttle cable free play should be 1/16–1/8 in. (2–3 mm) measured at the outer edge of the throttle grip flange (**Figure 10**). If adjustment is necessary, loosen the cable locknut and turn the adjuster (**Figure 10**) in or out to achieve the proper play. Tighten the locknut. If you can't get proper free play at the grip, see *Throttle Cable Adjustment*.

Make sure that the throttle grip rotates smoothly from fully closed to fully open. Check at center, full left, and full right positions of the steering.

Clutch Lever Play

The clutch cable should have about 1/16–1/8 in. (2–3 mm) play at the lever before the clutch

A. Later   B. Sooner

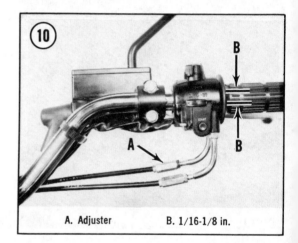

A. Adjuster   B. 1/16-1/8 in.

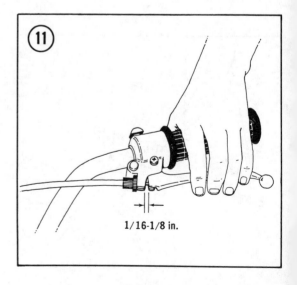

1/16-1/8 in.

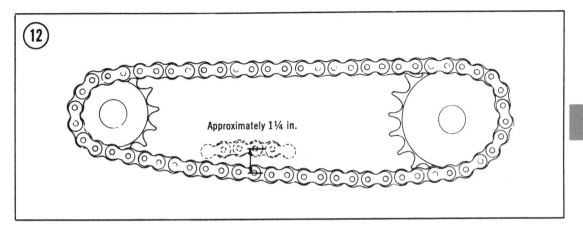

Approximately 1¼ in.

starts to disengage (**Figure 11**). Loosen the lock-nut, turn the adjuster as required, and tighten the locknut. If you can't get proper play at the lever, see *Clutch Adjustment*.

Steering

Check that the steering turns smoothly from side to side with no binding. Put the bike in NEUTRAL, lock the front brake, and rock the bike back and forth with your feet. If you can feel play or hear a "klunk," your steering has become too loose (see *Steering Play Inspection* in this chapter).

Drive Chain Play Inspection

1. Put the motorcycle on the centerstand.

2. Turn the rear wheel slowly until you locate the part of chain that stretches tightest between the 2 sprockets on the bottom chain run (the chain wears unevenly).

3. With thumb and forefinger, lift up and press down the chain at that point, measuring the distance the chain moves vertically.

4. The chain should have about 1¼ in. (30–35 mm) of vertical travel at midpoint (**Figure 12**). If it has less than 1⅛ in. (30 mm) or more than 1½ in. (40 mm) of travel, adjust the chain tension.

> *NOTE*
> *On models without a centerstand, measure chain play while on the side stand. The play should be about 1-1/8 in. (25-30mm).*

Drive Chain Play Adjustment

In adjusting the drive chain, you must also align the rear wheel. Rear wheel alignment is critical for safe handling. A misaligned rear wheel can sometimes cause speed wobbles and make cornering difficult, besides greatly increasing the wear of the tires, the rear chain, and the sprockets. All models have wheel alignment marks on the swing arm and notches in the chain adjusters. If each chain adjuster is moved the same number of alignment marks, the rear wheel should be aligned correctly.

If the drive chain is too loose or too tight, adjust it as follows:

1. Loosen the right side muffler mount, if required, to make it easier to get at the rear axle nut.

2. *Drum Brake:* Back off the brake adjuster nut (7) at the rear of the brake rod until it is flush with the end of the rod (**Figure 13**).

3. Remove the spring clip from the end of the bolt that mounts the torque link to the rear brake backing plate. Loosen the nut (8, **Figure 13**).

4. Remove the cotter pin (1) from the rear axle nut (2) and loosen the nut (**Figure 13**).

5. Loosen the locknuts on both chain adjusters (5, **Figure 13**).

6. Put the motorcycle on the centerstand.

7. If the chain was too tight, back out both chain adjuster bolts and kick the wheel forward until the chain tension is too loose.

8. Screw in both chain adjuster bolts until the chain tension is correct, so that the notch in each chain adjuster is positioned the same distance along the alignment marks cast into the swing arm (3, **Figure 13**).

9. When the adjustment is correct, sight along the chain from the rear sprocket to see that it is

correctly aligned. It should leave the top of the rear sprocket in a straight line. If it is cocked to one side or the other (**Figure 14**), the rear wheel is incorrectly aligned and must be corrected by turning the adjusters counter to one another until the chain and sprocket are correctly aligned. When the alignment is correct, recheck the free play.

> NOTE: *On **drum brake models,** before tightening the axle nut, spin the wheel and stop it forcefully with the brake pedal. Hold the pedal down while you tighten the axle nut. This centers the brake shoes in the drum, and will help prevent a "spongy" feel of the drum brake.*

10. Torque the rear axle nut to 85 ft.-lb. (12.0 mkg). Install a new cotter pin.

11. Tighten the chain adjuster locknuts.

12. Check the chain play again.

13. Torque the torque link nut to 22 ft.-lb. (3.0 mkg). Install the spring clip.

14. Tighten the right side muffler mounts, if loosened.

15. *Drum brake models:* Adjust brake pedal play.

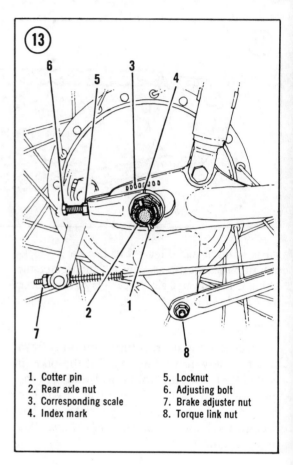

1. Cotter pin
2. Rear axle nut
3. Corresponding scale
4. Index mark
5. Locknut
6. Adjusting bolt
7. Brake adjuster nut
8. Torque link nut

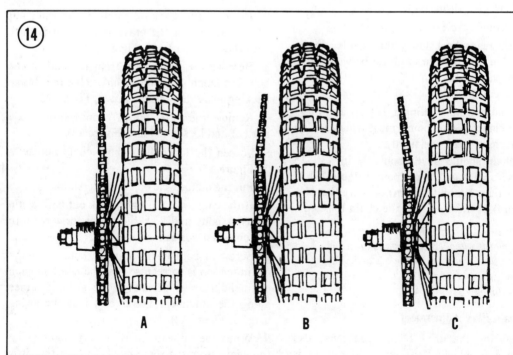

A   B   C

Drive Chain Lubrication

1. On 1973–1974 models, check that the rear chain is lightly oiled, but not dripping. If the chain is dry or dripping, adjust the chain oil pump (see *Chain Oil Pump Adjustment*). Hand lubricate the chain, in addition to the pump lubrication.

2. On 1975 and later models, place the motorcycle on its centerstand and oil as much of the bottom chain run as you can reach with SAE 30 motor oil or commercial chain lubricant.

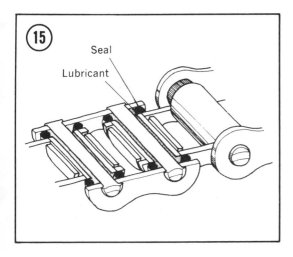

15

Seal

Lubricant

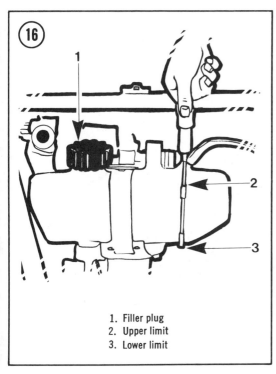

16

1

2

3

1. Filler plug
2. Upper limit
3. Lower limit

CAUTION
Drive chains on 1975 and later models have a permanent internal roller lubricant sealed in by 0-rings between the side plates (Figure 15). Do not use any solvent or chain lubricant not specifically approved for use on 0-rings. You could destroy the 0-rings and lose the permanent lubricant.

3. Rotate the wheel to bring the unoiled portion of the chain within reach. Continue until all the chain is lubricated.

Chain Oil Level (1973–1974)

1. Lift the seat. Take off the left side cover.

2. Use the dipstick to check the level in the chain oil tank (**Figure 16**).

3. When the tank is less than about ⅓ full, refill it with SAE 10W-30 or 10W-40 motor oil.

Chain Oil Pump Adjustment (1973–1974)

The chain oil pump should provide enough oil to keep the drive chain damp with oil. If the chain runs dry, or is dripping wet with oil while the motorcycle is moving, adjust the flow rate of the pump.

There is a slight difference between 1973 and 1974 model chain oil pumps. The 1973 pump has a flow rate cam plate marked from 0 to 5; 0 is the minimum flow rate, and 5 is the maximum. The 1974 flow rate cam plate is marked from 1 to 5; 1 is the minimum, and 5 is the maximum.

On both cam plates, the average flow rate is provided when the cam plate is set halfway between the minimum and maximum rates.

Adjust the flow rate as follows:

1. Remove the 2 screws on the left side of the engine that mount the chain oil pump cover to the chain cover. Remove the oil pump cover and its gasket.

2. *1973 only:* To increase the flow rate, rotate the cam plate counterclockwise so that the peg is closer to 5. To decrease the flow rate, rotate the cam plate toward 0 (**Figure 17**).

3. *1974 only:* Loosen the Phillips screw that clamps the cam plate. To increase the flow rate, rotate the cam plate counterclockwise so that the

Phillips screw is closer to 5. To decrease the flow rate, rotate the cam plate toward 1 (**Figure 18**). Tighten the screw.

4. Install the oil pump cover and its gasket.

Nuts, Bolts, Cotter Pins

Make a quick visual check of the axle suspension, control, and linkage fasteners.

    a. Axle nuts and clamp bolts.

    b. Top and bottom triple clamp bolts

    c. Shock absorber mounts

    d. Swing arm pivot

    e. Brake torque link

    f. Handlebar clamps

    g. Control lever and pedal pivots and links

Engine Oil Level

1. Wait several minutes after shutting off the engine before making the check, to give the oil enough time to run down into the crankcase.

2. Put the bike on its centerstand (or hold it level).

3. Look at the oil inspection window near the bottom of the clutch cover (lower right side of the engine) to see that the oil level visible through the window lies between the upper and lower lines on the clutch cover (**Figure 19**).

4. If the oil level lies beneath the lower line, add oil slowly, in small quantities, through the filler atop the clutch housing (**Figure 20**). Add enough to raise the oil level close to (but not above) the top line. Use SAE 10W-40, 10W-50, 20W-40, or 20W-50 motor oil designated "For Service SE".

> NOTE: *Too much oil in the engine will foul spark plugs, make smoke, cause a rapid buildup of carbon in the combustion chambers, and may cause oiling of the air cleaner through the crankcase breather.*

MONTHLY MAINTENANCE

These procedures should be performed every month or every 3,000 miles, whichever comes first. See **Table 1**.

Battery Electrolyte Level

Battery electrolyte level should be checked regularly, particularly during hot weather. Most batteries are marked with electrolyte level limit lines (**Figure 21**). Always maintain the fluid level between the 2 lines, using distilled water as required for replenishment. Distilled water is available at almost every supermarket. It is sold for use in steam irons and is quite inexpensive.

Overfilling leads to loss of electrolyte, resulting in poor battery performance, short life, and excessive corrosion. Never allow the electrolyte

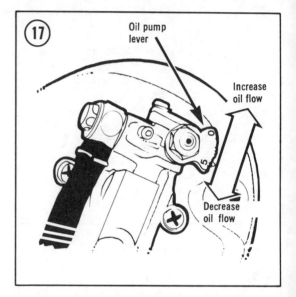

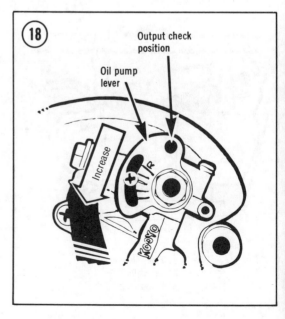

level to drop below the top of the plates. That portion of the plates exposed to air may be permanently damaged, resulting in loss of battery performance and shortened life.

1. Inspect the fluid level in all cells. On some models the battery must be removed to inspect it.

2. If the battery must be removed, disconnect the negative (−) ground cable first.

CAUTION
Be careful not to spill battery electrolyte on painted or polished surfaces. The acid is highly corrosive and will damage the finish. If it is spilled, wash it off immediately.

3. Remove the caps from the battery cells and add distilled water to correct the level. Never add electrolyte (acid) to correct the level.

4. When installing a battery, connect the positive (+) cable first. Make sure the wire terminals won't touch any metal parts when the battery is installed, and slide the rubber terminal boot (if equipped) over the terminal.

Brake Fluid Level Inspection

On models with translucent reservoirs or transparent windows, check that the fluid level is between the upper and lower level lines (**Figure 22**), or above the lower line (**Figure 23**).

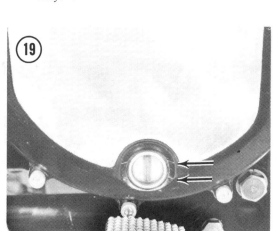

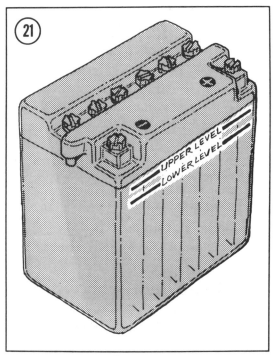

NOTE: *Hold the handlebar as close to horizontal as possible when checking fluid level.*

Brake Fluid Checking and Adding

1. Clean the outside of the reservoir cap thoroughly with a dry rag and remove it. Remove the washer and diaphragm.

2. The fluid level in the reservoir should be up to the upper level line (see **Figure 24**). Correct the level by adding fresh brake fluid.

> **WARNING**
> *Use brake fluid clearly marked DOT 3 only. Others may vaporize and cause brake failure. Never use old brake fluid or fluid from a container that has been left unsealed for a long time. Do not leave the reservoir cap off for any length of time (the fluid will absorb moisture from the air).*

> **WARNING**
> *Brake fluid is an irritant. Keep it away from your skin and eyes.*

> **CAUTION**
> *Be careful not to spill brake fluid on painted or plastic surfaces as it will destroy the finish. Wash immediately with soapy water and thoroughly rinse it off.*

3. Reinstall the washer, diaphragm, and cap. Make sure that the cap is tightly secured.

SIX MONTH MAINTENANCE

These procedures should be performed every 6 months or every 3,000 miles, whichever comes first.

This is the regular service interval that includes an engine *Tune-up, General Lubrication,* and *Chassis Maintenance* (see **Table 1**).

TUNE-UP

A complete tune-up should be performed every 3,000 miles (5,000 km) of normal riding. More frequent tune-ups may be required if the bike is ridden primarily in stop-and-go traffic. The purpose of the tune-up is to restore the performance lost due to normal wear and deterioration of parts.

Fluid level

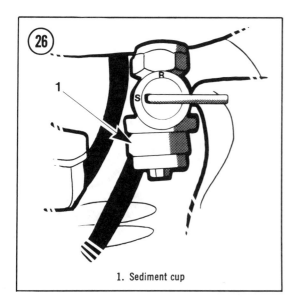

1. Sediment cup

These tune-up procedures are arranged so that you start with the jobs that require a "cold" engine and finish with the jobs that call for a fully warmed up engine. If you follow the sequence, you won't waste time waiting for your bike to cool down when required.

AIR CLEANER

A clogged air cleaner can decrease the efficiency and life of the engine. Never run the bike without the air cleaner installed; even minute particles of dust can cause severe internal wear.

Replace the element after 5 cleanings or every 6,000 miles (10,000 km), or any time the element

or gaskets are damaged. Inspect the air cleaner element more often if ridden in dusty areas.

Air Cleaner Maintenance

1. Lift the seat, take the cap off the air cleaner, and lift out the element (**Figure 25**).

> NOTE: *Some models require removing the tool tray and lifting the rear of the fuel tank.*

2. Tap the element lightly to remove most of the dirt and dust, then apply compressed air to the inside surface of the element.

3. Inspect the element, and make sure it is in good condition.

4. If the element is very dirty, replace it.

FUEL SYSTEM CLEANING

As water and dirt accumulate in the fuel tank and carburetor bowls, engine performance will deteriorate.

Manual Fuel Tap

1. Turn the fuel tap to S or OFF.

2. Remove the drain plug or sediment bowl from the bottom of the fuel tap (**Figure 26**).

3. Clean the screen above the sediment bowl, if applicable.

4. If there was water in the sediment cup, there may be water in the gas tank. Hold a clean glass container beneath the fuel tap, turn the lever to RESERVE, and notice whether the gasoline that comes out has any water mixed with it. After any water has been drained out, turn the fuel tap to OFF or S.

5. Install the drain plug, or sediment cup and gasket, being careful not to damage the petcock screen.

Vacuum Fuel Tap

1. Turn the fuel tap to ON.

2. Disconnect the fuel and vacuum lines from the tap (**Figure 27**).

3. Remove the fuel tank from the bike, or find a shallow drain pan or funnel to fit well under the fuel tap.

4. Turn the tap to prime (PRI) and check for water in the gas coming out. Keep draining water until there is only gasoline.

5. Turn the tap to ON and reconnect the fuel and vacuum lines. They're different sizes, so it's easy to connect them to the right fitting.

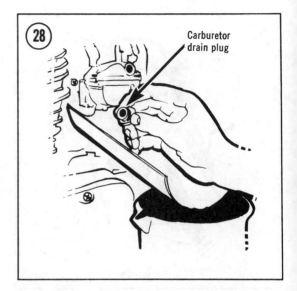

Carburetor Float Bowls

1. Hold a shallow pan or a funnel with tubing beneath a carburetor (**Figure 28**). Unscrew the drain plug from the bottom of the carburetor, and drain the float bowl.

2. Repeat for each of the 4 carburetors and install the drain plugs (**Figure 29**). Make sure the 0-rings on the drain plugs are in good condition.

3. If water came out of the float bowls, make sure you drain it out of the fuel tank too.

Fuel Line Inspection

Make sure none of the fuel lines are cracked or leaking. Replace any that have deteriorated.

SPARK PLUGS

Spark Plug Heat Range and Reach

It is important to use spark plugs of the correct heat range. If a spark plug has the correct heat range, it will create flame waves hot enough to prevent carbon from building up on its electrodes, but not hot enough to cause engine damage.

Too cold a spark plug will develop carbon deposits which can short circuit the plug, or glow and cause preignition, which can damage the engine. Too hot a spark plug can cause engine overheating and preignition.

The correct spark plug for normal operating conditions is the NGK B8-ES or ND W24ES-U, a 14 mm spark plug with ¾ in. reach. For high-speed operation in hot climates, the engine may prefer the B9-ES, a spark plug one heat range colder.

If you substitute another brand of spark plug, check the manufacturer's interchange chart to make sure the heat range and reach are correct. A plug with too long a reach may actually contact the valves and piston (**Figure 30**).

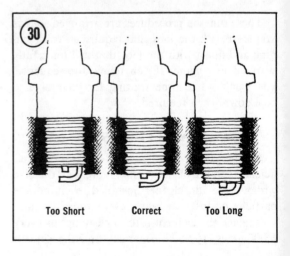

Too Short   Correct   Too Long

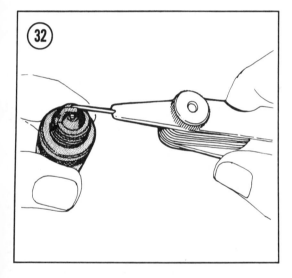

eroded electrodes, and excessive carbon or oil fouling (refer to Figure 3, Chapter Two, as a plug "reading" aid). Replace such plugs. If deposits are light, plugs may be cleaned in solvent with a wire brush or cleaned in a special spark plug sandblast cleaner.

CAUTION
Never sandblast an oily or wet plug. The grit will stick to the plug and later drop into the engine. After sandblasting dry plugs, clean them thoroughly, or you'll shorten your engine's life quite a bit.

5. Check the electrode gap of each spark plug with wire gauges (**Figure 32**). The gap should be 0.028–0.031 in. (0.7–0.8 mm). If any spark plug has a thinner or wider gap, correct it by bending the outer electrode with a gapping tool.

6. Check the spark plug gasket. If it is completely flattened, install a new one.

NOTE: *If you're going to adjust the cam chain and/or valve clearance, leave the spark plugs out until you're finished. It will be easier to turn the engine over precisely.*

7. Apply a small amount of anti-seize compound to the plug threads. Do not use oil or grease. Petroleum lubricants will turn to carbon and make the plugs stick when you next remove them.

8. Install the plugs, threading them in by hand until they seat. Then tighten them with a spark plug wrench:
   With *new* plug washers: ½ turn
   With *old* plug washers: ⅛ turn

Spark Plug Inspection

1. Grasp the spark plug leads (**Figure 31**) as near to the plug as possible and pull them off the plugs.

2. Blow away any dirt that has accumulated in the spark plug wells.

CAUTION
Dirt could fall into the cylinders when the plugs are removed, causing serious engine damage.

3. Remove the spark plugs with a spark plug wrench.

4. Inspect the spark plugs carefully. Look for plugs with broken center porcelain, excessively

CAM CHAIN ADJUSTMENT

In time, the camshaft chain and guides will wear and develop slack. The 1979 and later models have an automatic cam chain tensioner that is continually taking up slack. The 1973–1978 models require periodic cam chain tensioner adjustment to take up the slack and minimize engine noise. If neglected too long, the cam chain could break and cause severe engine damage.

When cam chain tension adjustment no longer quiets the cam chain, inspect the cam chain guide sprockets and tensioners (see *Cam Chain and Tensioner* in Chapter Four).

3

Adjustment (1973–1978)

1. Check that the ignition switch is OFF.

2. Remove the 2 timing cover screws and remove the cover and gasket (**Figure 33**).

3. Turn the crankshaft to the right (clockwise) a couple of full turns. Use the 17 mm bolt on the end of the crankshaft (**Figure 34**). This takes up the slack in the front run of the cam chain.

CAUTION
Do not rotate the crankshaft with the smaller inner bolt as it will damage the ignition advance mechanism.

NOTE: *Do not rotate the crankshaft counterclockwise as this will result in improper adjustment.*

4. Sight the hole in the contact point plate, and continue turning the crankshaft to the right until the T mark for a pair of cylinders (1 and 4, or 2 and 3) aligns with the pointer; see **Figure 35** and **Figure 36**.

5. Loosen the chain tensioner locknut and back out the tensioner bolt several turns (**Figure 37**). This allows a spring inside the tensioner to take up the cam chain slack.

6. Torque the tensioner bolt to 40 in.-lb. (0.5 mkg) on 900cc models and to 70 in.-lb. (0.8 mkg) on 1000cc models.

7. Tighten the locknut.

NOTE: *If you're going to check valve clearance or timing later, leave the timing cover off.*

8. Install the timing cover and gasket.

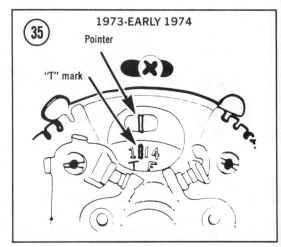

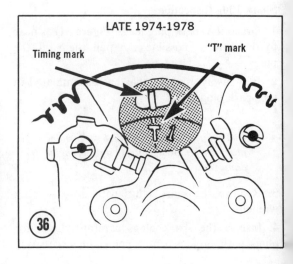

AIR SUCTION VALVES—1979 AND LATER

Suction Valve Operation

The air suction valves (reed valves) allow clean intake air to be sucked into the exhaust ports during negative exhaust pressure pulses. This helps complete combustion of unburned hydrocarbons in the exhaust system.

The air suction valves also prevent exhaust gas from backing up and flowing back into the air cleaner. If that happened, you would have an unplanned and unwanted EGR (exhaust gas recirculation) system. That would cut power a great deal and probably damage the engine.

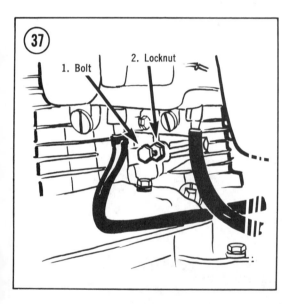

Suction Valve Inspection

1. Swing open the seat and remove the left side cover.

2. Turn the vacuum fuel tap ON.

3. Disconnect the fuel and vacuum lines from the fuel tap; raise the rear of the tank slightly, if required.

4. *Models with fuel gauge:* Disconnect the fuel tank sending unit wires.

5. Lift the rear of the fuel tank, and pull it back and off the bike.

> NOTE: *As a simple troubleshooting procedure, you can check the air suction valve function by disconnecting the long suction hose at the air cleaner housing (A, **Figure 38**). You should be able to blow through this hose into the exhaust system, and you should not be able to draw any air out of it because of the suction valve reeds. If you can draw air out of the hose, one or more of the suction valves is faulty.*

6. To inspect each valve individually, slide up the hose clamp and pull the hose off the air suction valve cover (B, **Figure 38**).

7. Remove the 4 bolts and flat washers and the suction valve cover (A, **Figure 39**).

8. Remove the reed valve assembly from the cylinder head cover (**Figure 40**).

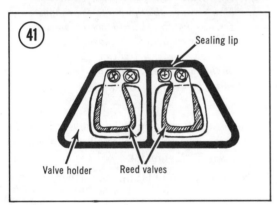

Sealing lip

Valve holder   Reed valves

9. Check the reed valves for cracks, folds, warpage or any other damage (**Figure 41**).

10. Check the sealing lip coating around the perimeter of the assembly. It must be free of grooves, scratches, or signs of separation from the metal holder (**Figure 41**).

> NOTE: *The valve assembly cannot be serviced, but must be replaced if defective.*

11. Wash off any carbon deposits between the reed and reed contact area with solvent.

CAUTION
Do not scrape off the deposits, or you will damage the assembly.

> NOTE: *If you're going to adjust valve clearance next, leave the air suction valve covers and fuel tank off.*

12. Install the air suction valves (see Chapter Seven, *Suction Valve Installation*).

13. Install the fuel tank (see Chapter Seven, *Fuel Tank Installation*).

VALVE CLEARANCE

Normal wear of the valves and valve seats decreases valve clearance and alters valve timing slightly. Insufficient valve clearance can lead to burnt valves and seats. Excessive valve clearance causes noisy operation and more rapid valve train wear.

> NOTE: *Check and adjust valve clearance with the engine cool, at room temperature.*

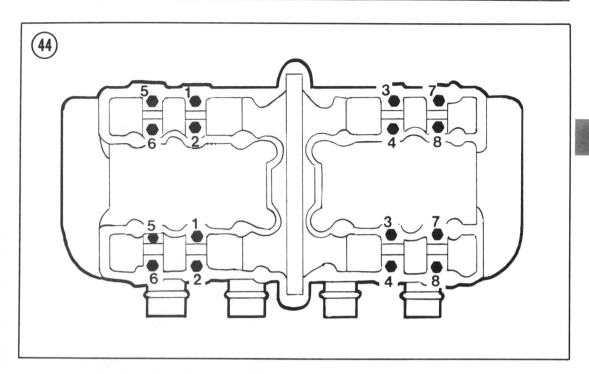

3

Valve Clearance Inspection

1. Disconnect the battery ground (−) cable (**Figure 42**).

2. Remove the fuel tank (see *Fuel Tank Removal,* Chapter Seven).

3. Pull the spark plug leads off the plugs.

4. Remove the screws securing the ignition cover and remove it and the gasket.

5. *Shaft drive*: Remove the ignition coils (**Figure 43**).

6. *1979 and later*: Remove the air suction valve covers (see *Suction Valve Inspection* in this chap-

ter). Tie the vacuum switch and air hoses up out of the way.

7. Remove the bolts (B, **Figure 39**) securing the valve cover. Tap around the perimeter with a plastic or rubber mallet to loosen the cover and remove it. Note which bolts have spark plug cable clamps attached.

8. Check that all 16 camshaft cap bolts are properly tightened (**Figure 44**). Following the sequence in **Figure 44**, torque all the cap bolts as follows:

   a. 1979 and later: 12 ft.-lb. (1.7 mkg)

   b. 1973-1978 chrome bolts: 9 ft.-lb. (1.2 mkg); Parkerized (dark) bolts: 7 ft.-lb. (1.0 mkg)

9. Remove the 2 timing cover screws, and remove the cover and gasket (**Figure 45**).

10. Rotate the crankshaft with a wrench on the outer 17 mm nut (**Figure 46**) until the line marks opposing each other on the intake camshaft sprocket line up with the valve cover surface (**Figure 47**).

CAUTION
Do not rotate the crankshaft with the smaller inner bolt as it will damage the ignition advance mechanism within the housing.

11. Insert a metric feeler gauge between the cam lobe and shim to check the clearance for the pair of intake valves that has some clearance (**Figure 48**, and **Table 3**). The clearance is measured correctly when there is a slight drag on the feeler gauge when it is inserted and withdrawn. Write down the clearance you measured.

> NOTE: *Some valves will be checked with the cam lobe pointing up, and some will be checked with the cam lobe pointing away from the opposite camshaft.*

> NOTE: *The cylinders are numbered 1 through 4, starting at the left side of the engine.*

12. Turn the crankshaft one full turn, so the camshaft you just checked turns ½ turn and the marks line up again.

13. Check the clearance for the pair of valves you didn't measure the first time.

14. Align the opposing marks on the exhaust camshaft with the valve cover surface (**Figure 49**), and measure the clearance for the 4 exhaust valves as you did in Steps 11-13.

15. If any valve's clearance is out of tolerance, skip ahead to *Valve Clearance Adjustment*. If all the valves' clearances are within specification (**Table 3**), continue this procedure to install the removed parts.

16. Place the valve cover gasket and the valve cover on the cylinder head. Install the valve cover bolts and washers, and the spark plug cable clamps as originally installed (**Figure 50**). Torque the valve cover bolts to 11 ft.-lb. (1.5 mkg) on 1978 and later models and to 9 ft.-lb. (1.2 mkg) on 1973-1977 models.

17. *1979 and later:* Install the 2 suction covers (**Figure 51**). Install a flat washer under each of the 8 bolts. Install the hoses on the suction covers and slide the hose clamps into place (**Figure 52**).

18. *Shaft drive:* Install the ignition coils (**Figure 53**).

19. Install the fuel tank; insert the front brackets carefully on the rubber grommets on the frame. Don't pinch any wires or control cables.

20. *Models with fuel level gauge:* Connect the fuel sending unit wires.

21. Connect the fuel line(s) to the fuel tap.

22. *Vacuum fuel tap models:* Connect the vacuum line to the fuel tap. The vacuum hose is the smaller of the two.

23. Connect the spark plug caps to the proper spark plug; the leads are numbered 1, 2, 3, 4 (left to right).

24. Connect the battery ground (−) cable.

> NOTE: *If you've had a problem with oil leakage at the valve cover gasket, remove the fuel tank and re-torque the valve cover bolts after the engine has run and cooled off.*

3

Valve Clearance Adjustment

To adjust the valve clearance, the shim located between the cam lobe and the valve lifter must be removed and replaced with one of a different dimension. The shims are available from Kawasaki dealers in increments of 0.05 mm and range in size from 2.0–3.2 mm. The dimension is marked on the shim surface.

This procedure pertains only to valves that need adjustment. Do not remove any shims whose clearance falls within the specified range.

1. Turn the crankshaft until the cam lobe points away from the lifter. Position the notch in the lifter so it points toward the opposite camshaft (**Figure 54**). This will allow easy shim removal.

2. Turn the crankshaft until the cam lobe is pushing down the lifter. Hold the lifter down (use a special Kawasaki Lifter Cup Holding Tool if available—**Figure 55**), and turn the crankshaft to rotate the cam lobe *away* from the tool (toward the opposite camshaft).

> **CAUTION**
> *When the valve lifter holder tool is fitted to a valve assembly and the crankshaft is turned to rotate the camshaft, it must be turned so the cam lobe turns away from the tool. If it is turned toward the tool, serious engine damage can result. (The camshaft rotates in the same direction as the crankshaft.)*

3. Remove the shim (**Figure 55**) and note the thickness marked on it, or measure the shim thickness with a micrometer.

4. Calculate the correct shim using this example. Refer to **Table 3**.

> NOTE: *The following numbers are for example only.*

EXAMPLE:

Actual measured clearance	0.52 mm
Subtract specified clearance	−0.15 mm
Equals excess clearance	0.37 mm
Existing shim number	220
Add excess clearance	+ 37
Equals new shim number	257
(round up to the nearest shim number)	260

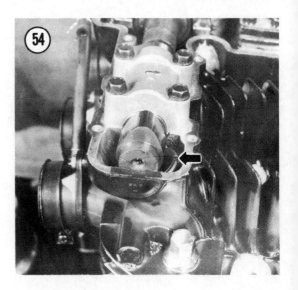

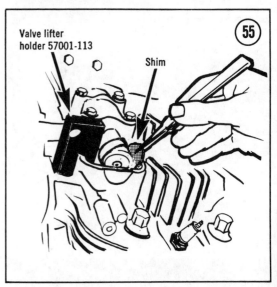

Valve lifter holder 57001-113   Shim

5. Insert the new shim on the valve lifter with the numbered side facing downward so the number will not be ground off by the action of the cam.

> **CAUTION**
> *Never put shim stock under a shim. The shim could come loose at high rpm and cause extensive engine damage. Never grind the shim; this can cause a fracture which can also cause extensive engine damage.*

> NOTE: *If the smallest available shim does not increase clearance to within acceptable limits, the valve seat is probably*

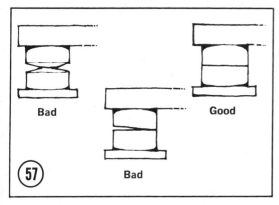

worn. *If this is the case, repair the valve seat, grind the valve stem slightly, and recheck the clearance.*

6. Turn the crankshaft until the cam lobe pushes down on the lifter and remove the special tool.

7. Rotate the crankshaft several times to fully seat the shim, and recheck the valve clearance.

8. Return to *Valve Clearance Inspection,* Step 16, and install the valve cover.

CONTACT POINTS—1973–1978

There are 2 sets of contact breaker points, each of which fires 2 of the cylinders (**Figure 56**).

The ignition will suffer if a set of points has a weak spring, dirty or eroded contacts, the wrong contact gap, or the wrong ignition timing. As point gap changes, so does ignition timing.

Contact Point Inspection and Cleaning

1. Remove the timing cover screws and remove the cover and gasket.

2. Through normal use, the surfaces of the breaker points gradually pit and burn. If the points are badly worn or pitted, replace them and the capacitors with new components. If they are not too badly pitted, they can be dressed with a few strokes of a clean point file or Flexstone (available at any auto parts store). Do not use emery cloth or sandpaper, as particles remain on the points and cause arcing and burning.

3. If points are still serviceable after filing, remove all residue with electrical contact point cleaner (in a spray can). Close the points on a piece of clean white paper such as a business card. Continue to pull the card through the closed points until no particles or discoloration are transferred to the card. Finally, rotate the engine and observe the points as they open and close. If they do not meet squarely (**Figure 57**) replace them as described under *Contact Point Removal/Installation.*

4. Rub a small amount of high-temperature grease into the felt that bears against the breaker point cam. If you use too much grease, the cam will sling it into the points, fouling them.

Contact Point Gap (With Feeler Gauge)

The gap for each set of points must be adjusted correctly before adjusting the ignition timing.

Adjust the gap as follows:

1. Rotate the crankshaft until one set of points is at its widest opening. Measure the gap between the contacts with feeler gauges. The correct gap is 0.012–0.016 in. (0.3–0.4 mm).

> NOTE: *There should be a **slight** drag on the feeler gauge as it is inserted and removed. Hold the feeler gauge loosely to make sure you're not prying the points open.*

2. If the gap measurement does not fall within the limits, slightly loosen the 2 screws that mount the fixed arm of that set of points (**Figure 58**).

3. Wedge a screwdriver into the pry point on the fixed arm base, and move the fixed arm away from the movable arm until the gap measures 0.014 in. (0.35 mm). Tighten the mounting

screws and recheck the gap. Check the ignition timing.

4. In the same manner, adjust the gap of the other set of breaker points.

Contact Point Gap (With Dwell Angle Meter)

The dwell angle is the number of degrees (or the percentage of 360 degrees) of breaker points camshaft rotation during which the points are closed and current can flow through them to the primary windings of the ignition coil. The breaker point gap can be adjusted with greater accuracy with a dwell angle meter than with feeler gauges.

Adjust the gap with a dwell angle meter as follows:

1. Connect the negative (−) dwell angle meter lead to the engine case, for ground. Connect the positive (+) lead to one set of the contact breaker points at the spring, or an exposed part of the wire.

2. If the dwell angle meter is calibrated in degrees, turn the selector knob to the single cam lobe position. If the switch does not have such a position, use the setting for the minimum number of cam lobes.

3. Start the engine and allow it to idle.

4. Read the meter. The reading for the correct gap on a meter calibrated in percentages is 53%; the correct reading on a meter calibrated in degrees is 190 degrees.

5. If the meter cannot be set for a single cam lobe, multiply the reading you get by the number of cam lobes the meter thinks it is checking, to get the desired reading.

6. If the dwell angle reading is not 190 degrees (or 53%), loosen slightly the 2 screws that mount the fixed arms of the breaker points (**Figure 58**).

7. Wedge a screwdriver against the pry point for the fixed arm, and move the fixed arm's contact point toward or away from the contact point on the movable arm until the correct reading on the meter is obtained. Tighten the screws.

8. In the same manner, adjust the gap for the other set of breaker points.

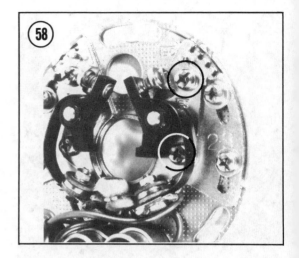

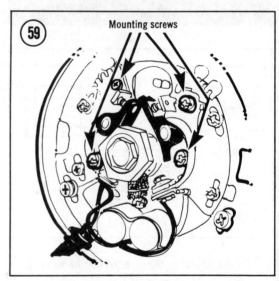

Mounting screws

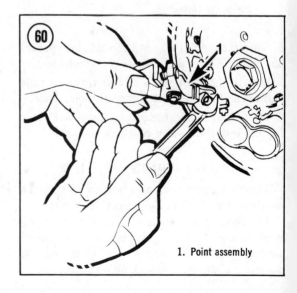

1. Point assembly

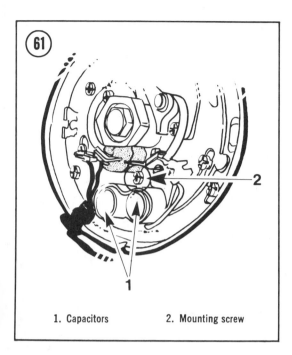

1. Capacitors   2. Mounting screw

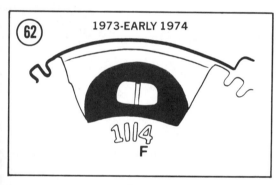

1973-EARLY 1974

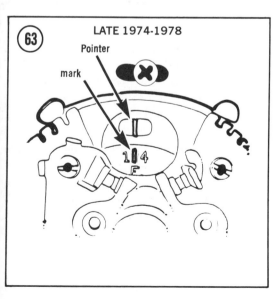

LATE 1974-1978

Contact Point and Condenser Removal

1. Remove the 2 screws that mount each breaker point assembly to its backing plate, and lift up the breaker points (**Figure 59**).

2. At the rear of the breaker point assembly, loosen the nut and remove the ignition coil wire and the condenser wire (**Figure 60**).

3. To take off the condensers, remove their mounting screw from the backing plate and lift them off as a pair (**Figure 61**).

IGNITION TIMING

See **Table 4** for ignition timing specifications.

Static Timing—1973–1978

There are two sets of contact breaker points and two ignition coils. The spark plugs in cylinders 1 and 4 are wired in series; so are the spark plugs in 2 and 3. When the left set of points opens, its ignition coil fires through the spark plugs in 1 and 4; the right set of points fires spark plugs 2 and 3.

Incorrect ignition timing can cause a drastic loss of engine performance and overheating. Clean the points and adjust their gap (as described earlier in this chapter) before adjusting timing.

Adjust static ignition timing as follows:

1. Remove the 2 ignition timing cover screws, and remove the cover and gasket.

2. Rotate the crankshaft until the right vertical line (the "F" mark) for cylinders 1 and 4 is aligned beneath the timing mark above and between the 2 sets of points (**Figures 62 and 63**).

> NOTE: *The left vertical line (the "T" mark) indicates TDC (top dead center). The right vertical line (the "F" mark) indicates ignition timing when the engine is running at idle.*

3. Connect one lead from an ohmmeter to the engine case, for ground. Connect the other lead to the left set of points (for 1 and 4). See **Figure 64**.

4. Loosen the 2 screws that mount the left-hand set of points to the backing plate, but don't loosen them too much. Pry point serrations in the edge of the contact breaker mounting plate are above

the top mounting screw. Insert a screwdriver in a pry point. See **Figure 65**.

5. Use the screwdriver to move the points plate to the right or left around the backing plate until the ohmmeter needle begins to fluctuate, showing that the points are beginning to open.

> *NOTE*
> *If you run out of travel while adjusting a set of points, loosen the 3 screws that mount the backing plate to gain more travel. This will alter the ignition timing for the other set of points, if it has already been adjusted.*

6. Tighten the breaker points mounting plate screws and check that the ohmmeter needle is still fluctuating. If not, repeat the adjustment.

7. Rotate the crankshaft until the "F" mark for 2 and 3 is aligned beneath the timing mark. Adjust the ignition timing for the right set of contact breaker points.

Dynamic Timing—All Models

Dynamic timing inspection is an alternate method of checking initial idle ignition timing, and it is the only way to check the advance mechanism function.

Ignition timing inspection is not required maintenance on 1979 and later models with transistorized ignition. Transistorized ignition timing is very stable, and once it is set properly, it should last the life of the motorcycle. However, the same mechanical advance mechanism is used on transistorized ignition models as on contact point ignition models, and it will affect timing if not maintained properly.

The procedures given here apply to both contact point and transistorized ignition systems.

1. Hook up a stroboscopic timing light according to manufacturer's instructions.

2. Start the engine and allow it to idle. Shine the timing light (**Figure 66**) on the timing mark.

At idle, the strobe light should flash and freeze the "F" line for 1 and 4 while aligned beneath the timing mark (**Figure 67**). If so, the ignition has been timed correctly and the ignition advance mechanism is functioning properly at idle.

3. Increase the rpm and continue aiming the timing light at the timing mark. The 1 and 4

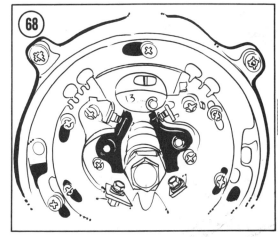

3

markings should appear to move to the left past the timing mark when the strobe light fires.

4. On 1973 and early 1974 models, the peg to the right of the 1 and 4 marks on the ignition advance mechanism should be aligned beneath the timing mark at 3,000 rpm; above that rpm the timing should not change again.

5. On late 1974 to 1976 models, the peg should be slightly to the right of the timing mark, and stabilized in that position at 2,350 rpm (**Figure 68**). The 1977–1978 models have an advance timing check mark slightly to the left of the peg.

6. On 1979 and later models, there is a double mark next to the peg that aligns at 3,400 rpm (**Figure 69**). If the advancer does not function correctly, see *Advancer Removal* in Chapter Eleven.

7. Shut off the engine. Move the spark plug connector to cylinder 3. Start the engine and let it idle. Use the timing light to check the initial timing of the right-hand set of points.

8. Install the ignition timing cover and its gasket.

THROTTLE CABLE ADJUSTMENT

Always check the throttle cables before you make any other carburetor adjustments. If free play isn't right it can throw all your adjustments off. Too much free play causes delayed throttle response (a jerky ride), and too little free play causes unstable idling.

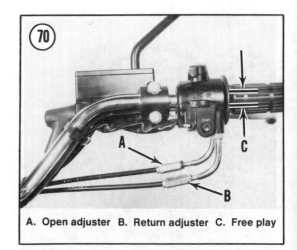

A. Open adjuster   B. Return adjuster   C. Free play

1. Check for about 1/16–1/8 in. (2–3 mm) of free play at the throttle grip flange (**Figure 70**).

2. *1976 and later:* Push the throttle grip completely closed (past the rest position) and check for *no* clearance between the throttle cable bracket and the pulley stop at the carburetor (**Figure 71**). This protects the carburetor linkage from excessive return cable stress.

3. *1973–1975:* To adjust, loosen both cable adjuster locknuts (**Figure 70**), take up all the slack with the open cable (front) adjuster, and turn the return cable (rear) adjuster to get your desired free play. Tighten the locknuts.

4. *1976 and later:*

   a. Loosen both throttle grip cable adjuster locknuts (**Figure 70**) and shorten both adjusters for maximum free play.

   b. Lengthen the return cable (rear) adjuster until there is *no* clearance between the throttle cable bracket and the pulley stopper when you push the throttle grip completely closed (**Figure 71**). Tighten the locknut.

   c. Lengthen the open cable (front) adjuster to get your desired free play. Tighten the locknut.

   > NOTE: *If all the adjustment range is used up at the throttle grip, use the adjusters at the carburetor end of the cables (Figure 72).*

5. Inspect the throttle cables from the grip down to the carburetors. Replace them if they're kinked or worn through.

WARNING
Riding with incorrectly adjusted or damaged throttle cables can cause loss of control.

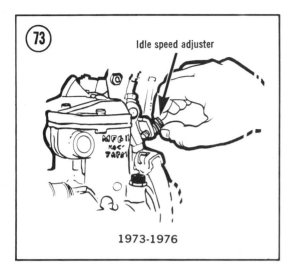

Idle speed adjuster

1973-1976

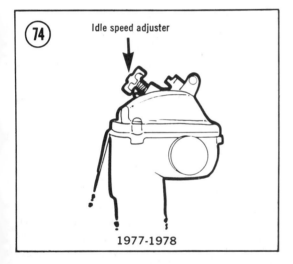

Idle speed adjuster

1977-1978

CARBURETORS

Idle Speed

Proper idle speed setting is necessary to prevent stalling and to provide adequate engine compression braking, but you can't set it perfectly with the bike's tachometer—it's just not accurate at the low end. You'll need a portable tachometer, or you're just as well off setting idle by ear and feel: if it stalls, set idle faster; if you want more engine braking, set idle slower.

1. Attach a portable tachometer, following the manufacturer's instructions.

2. Start the engine and let it warm up (about 5 minutes).

3. Turn the idle adjust knob (**Figures 73, 74, and 75**) to get 900 rpm on 900cc models or 1000 rpm on 1000cc models.

4. Rev the engine a couple of times to see if it settles down to the set idle speed. Readjust if necessary.

Idle Mixture

The idle fuel/air mixture affects low speed emissions, as well as idling stability and smooth transition to partial throttle openings. Adjustment is either by an air screw on the side of the carburetor (**Figure 76**) or a pilot screw (1977–1978 and LTD) on the bottom (**Figure 77**), depending on which year you have. Idle mixture should *not* be adjusted on emission-controlled bikes (made after January 1, 1978) unless the

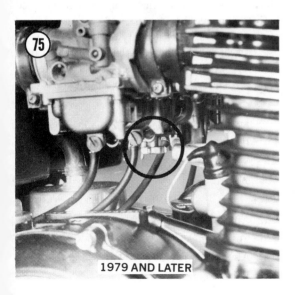

1979 AND LATER

factory settings have been altered. Earlier bikes should be adjusted at regular service intervals, and after carburetor synchronization.

CAUTION
Never turn the air screw or pilot screw in tight. You'll permanently damage the screw or the soft aluminum seat in the carburetor.

The standard idle mixture settings (**Table 5**) are ball-park figures, used to get the engine running after carburetor disassembly.

Idle Mixture Adjustment—1973-1976:

1. Start the engine and let it warm up (about 5 minutes).
2. Adjust the idle speed.
3. Turn each air screw (**Figure 76**) in or out slightly to the setting that gives the highest idle speed.

NOTE: *If any air screw can be turned to less than ½ turn from seating without affecting idle speed, there is probably something wrong with that carburetor.*

4. Reset idle speed, if necessary.
5. Repeat Steps 3 and 4 until idle speed cannot be further increased.
6. Back all 4 air screws out exactly ⅛ turn.

Idle Mixture Adjustment—1977-1978 (non-emission controlled):

1. Start the engine and let it warm up (about 5 minutes).
2. Adjust the idle speed.
3. Turn each pilot screw extender (**Figure 77**) in or out to the setting that gives the highest idle speed. Don't force the extender past its ½ turn range.
4. Reset idle speed, if necessary.
5. Repeat Steps 3 and 4 until idle speed cannot be further increased.

Idle Mixture Adjustment—1978 (emission controlled):

1. Turn each pilot screw extender (**Figure 77**) *counterclockwise* (viewed from the bottom) until it hits the stop.

2. Set idle speed to 1,000 rpm with an accurate tachometer.
3. Turn each pilot screw extender fully *clockwise* until it hits the opposite stop.
4. If idle speed has dropped *less* than 100 rpm, readjust idle with the idle adjuster knob (**Figure 74**).
5. If idle speed dropped *more* than 100 rpm, return each pilot screw an equal amount until the idle speed has dropped not quite 100 rpm (to just over 900 rpm). Wait a few minutes for the idle to stabilize. If the idle drop is less than 100 rpm, readjust idle with the idle adjuster knob. If more than 100 rpm, return the pilot screws some more until the drop is less than 100 rpm.

Idle Mixture Adjustment—1979

Air screw adjustment should *not* be necessary. The screws are secured with a dab of yellow paint at the factory. *Only if the factory setting has been altered,* turn each air screw (**Figure 76**) in until it seats lightly, then back it out 1⅛ turns. Readjust idle speed if necessary.

Carburetor Synchronization

Synchronizing the carburetors makes sure all the throttle slides are open the same amount at the same time. If they're not, an out-of-synch cylinder will fight the others, cutting power and gas mileage. If you have a bike with 4 separate exhaust pipes, you can check for a rough balance by listening to exhaust noise and feeling pressure at the mufflers. But the only accurate way is to use a set of vacuum gauges that measure all four cylinders at the same time. A typical set of gauges is shown in Chapter One.

NOTE: *Before you try to synchronize the carburetors, make sure all of the following are checked and adjusted first. If not, you're wasting your time—you won't get a good synch.*

a. Air cleaner
b. Spark plugs
c. Air suction valves (1979 and later)
d. Valve clearance

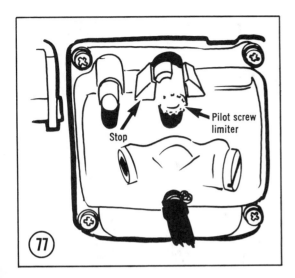

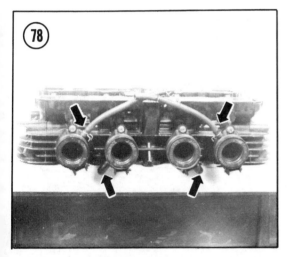

e. Contact points and ignition timing (1973–1978)

f. Throttle cable play

g. Carburetor holders and clamps tight

To synchronize the carburetors:

1. Start the engine, warm it up (about 5 minutes), check and adjust the idle speed, and stop the engine.

2. Remove the rubber caps from each carburetor holder vacuum tap. On 1979 and later models there is a vacuum line instead of a cap on carburetors 1 and 4 (**Figure 78**).

3. Connect the vacuum gauges to the carburetor holder vacuum taps, following the manufacturer's instructions.

4. Start the engine and check that each gauge is within the normal range (**Table 6**), and that the difference between any 2 cylinders is less than 0.8 in. (2 cm) Hg. If the difference is greater, shut off the engine and proceed as follows.

5. *1973–1975:* Loosen the synchronizing screw locknut next to the top of each carburetor (**Figure 79**). Your dealer can supply a handy special tool for doing this without removing the fuel tank. Otherwise, a wrench and screwdriver will do.

6. *1976 and later:* The synchronizing screws are inside the carburetors, so you'll have to remove the fuel tank to get at them. If you can synchronize the carburetors before the float bowls run dry, fine; if not, you'll have to supply fuel from a temporary hookup.

WARNING
When supplying fuel by temporary means, make sure the tank is secure and that all fuel lines are tight—no leaks.

a. Remove the fuel tank (see *Fuel Tank Removal*).

b. Remove the carburetor top covers (**Figure 80**).

WARNING
Make sure no dirt or parts fall into the carburetors, or you may wind up with a stuck throttle.

c. Loosen each synchronization screw lock. On *1976* models, flatten the lockwasher and loosen the lockbolt (**Figure 81**). On *1977 and later* models, loosen the locknut (**Figure 82**).

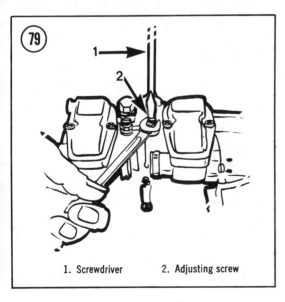

1. Screwdriver   2. Adjusting screw

7. Start the engine, let it idle, and turn each carburetor synchronization screw until each gauge reads within 0.8 in. (2 cm) Hg of the others. Adjust to keep idle speed low while doing this (go for the high vacuum reading).

8. Rev the engine and check that all carburetors return to within 0.8 in. (2 cm) Hg of each other. Readjust if necessary, and tighten the locknuts/bolts while holding the synchronization screws steady.

9. Reset idle speed and check that all carburetors have more than the minimum vacuum listed in **Table 6**. If any gauge reads less than the minimum, there may be an air leak—check all items (a through g) listed at the beginning of this procedure. If you still have a problem, there's probably trouble inside the carburetor. Disassemble the carburetor (see *Carburetor Disassembly,* Chapter Seven) and clean it, paying close attention to the starting fuel circuit.

10. *1973-1978:* Readjust idle mixture for any carburetor whose throttle slide was adjusted (see *Idle Mixture Adjustment*).

11. Stop the engine, remove the gauges, install the vacuum plugs/hoses, and install the carburetor tops and fuel tank if removed.

Rough Synchronization—Mechanical

Mechanical synchronization is not normally required, unless idle is so rough that a vacuum synchronization is impossible, or if a carburetor has been removed or the throttle linkage was disturbed. (See *Mechanical Synchronization* in Chapter Seven.)

CYLINDER COMPRESSION

A cylinder cranking compression check is not required *maintenance,* but it is the easiest way to check the internal condition of the engine: rings, valves and seats, etc. It's a good idea to check compression at each tune-up, write the values down, and compare it with the readings you get at the next tune-up. This will help you spot any developing problems before they cost too much gas and repair money.

1. Warm the engine to normal operating temperature. Make sure the choke is OFF.

2. Remove all the spark plugs.

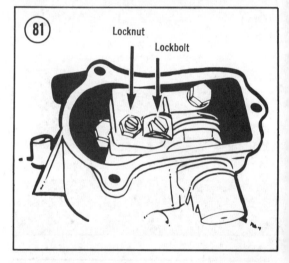

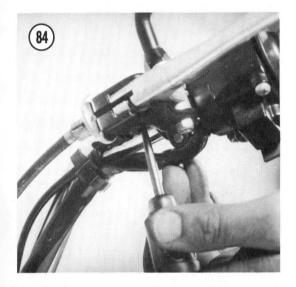

Readings should be from about 130-155 psi (9-11 kg/cm^2). A maximum difference of 10% between any 2 cylinders is acceptable.

Greater differences indicate worn or broken rings, leaky or sticky valves, blown head gasket or a combination of all.

If compression reading does not differ between cylinders by more than 10 psi, the rings and valves are in good condition.

If a low reading (10% or more) is obtained on one of the cylinders, it indicates valve or ring trouble. To determine which, pour about a teaspoon of engine oil through the spark plug hole onto the top of the piston. Turn the engine over once to distribute the excess oil, then take another compression test and record the reading. If the compression increases significantly, the valves are good but the rings are defective on that cylinder. If compression does not increase, the valves require servicing. A valve could be hanging open but not burned or a piece of carbon could be on a valve seat.

If any cylinder reads below 100 psi (7 kg/cm^2), check your readings with another gauge. It may be time to rebuild the top end (rings and valves).

LUBRICATION—6 MONTH/3,000 MILE

Engine Oil and Filter

The recommended oil change interval is 3,000 miles. The filter should be changed every other oil change.

If you ride hard, in dusty areas, or take a lot of short trips, change the oil more frequently.

Use SAE 10W-40, 10W-50, 20W-40 or 20W-50 motor oil with an API rating of SE or better. Try to use the same brand of oil. The use of oil additives is not recommended: anything you add to the engine also gets on the clutch plates and could cause clutch slippage or deterioration.

3. Connect the compression tester to one cylinder (**Figure 83**).
4. Turn the kill switch off, hold the throttle wide open, and crank the engine several revolutions until the gauge gives its highest reading. Record the figure and repeat for the other cylinders.

NOTE: *On models with a clutch activated starter lockout, have a friend hold the clutch lever in, or temporarily remove the lockout switch (**Figure 84**).*

When interpreting the results, actual readings are not as important as the difference between the readings. Individual gauge calibration varies widely.

NOTE
Never dispose of motor oil in the trash, on the ground, or down a storm drain. Many service stations accept used motor oil and waste haulers provide curbside used motor oil collection. Do not combine other fluids with motor oil to be recycled. To locate a recycler, contact the American Petroleum Institute (API) at www.recycleoil.org.

1. Put the motorcycle on the centerstand.
2. Start the engine and run until it is at normal operating temperature, about 5 minutes, then turn it off.

3. Put a drain pan under the crankcase and remove the drain plug (B, **Figure 85**). On models with a drain plug in the oil filter cover, remove that plug too.

4. The oil filter should be replaced every other engine oil change. If the oil filter is not to be changed, skip to Step 9.

> NOTE: *Before removing the filter cover, thoroughly clean off all road dirt and oil around it.*

5. To remove the oil filter, unscrew the bolt securing the filter cover (A, **Figure 85**) to the crankcase.

6. Remove the cover and the filter, discard the old filter and clean out the cover and the bolt.

7. Inspect the 0-rings on the cover and on the filter bolt (**Figure 86**); replace if necessary.

> NOTE: *Before installing the cover, clean off the mating surface of the crankcase—do not allow any road dirt to enter into the oil system.*

8. Insert the bolt into the cover and install the spring and washer. Insert the filter and reinstall into the crankcase. Torque the filter bolt to 14.5 ft.-lb. (2.0 mkg).

9. If you have a magnetic drain plug, clean any particles off of it. Install the engine oil drain plug and torque it to 22 ft.-lb. (3.0 mkg). Install the oil filter drain plug, if equipped.

10. Remove the oil filler cap from atop the clutch housing. Pour in the specified oil until it just reaches the upper line at the inspection window. The engine will hold about 3.9 qt. after changing the filter, or 3.2 qt. after only draining the oil. While adding the last pint, be sure to give the oil enough time to run down into the crankcase before checking the level in the inspection window.

> NOTE: *Too much oil in the engine may cause oiling of the air cleaner through the crankcase breather.*

11. Screw in the fill cap and start the engine, let it idle at moderate speed and check for leaks.

12. Turn off the engine and check for correct oil level within the oil level window.

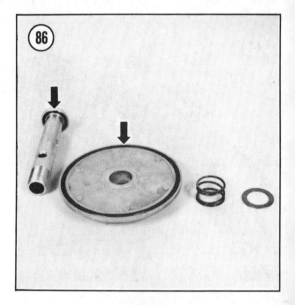

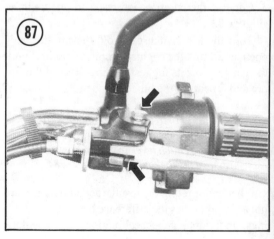

GENERAL LUBRICATION

Lever, Footpeg, and Stand Lubrication

Lubricate the clutch lever (**Figure 87**), front brake lever (**Figure 88**), rear brake pedal and linkage and footrest pivots (**Figure 89**), and side stand and centerstand pivots with motor oil.

Throttle Cable/Grip Lubrication

1. Remove the screws that assemble the twist grip housing. Remove the top half of the housing.

2. Remove the throttle cables from the twist grip.

3. Examine the exposed parts of the inner cables. Pull each inner cable up and down in its housing to determine by feel whether it is clean or gritty.

4. If the cables are clean, hold the top part of one cable vertical and spray it with Dri-Slide or one of the thin spray-on chain lubricants.

5. Hold the spray can close to the inner cable, near the top end of the cable housing, so that the lubricant will run down between the inner cable and its housing. Spray the cable until the lubricant runs out of the bottom of the cable housing at the carburetors. Lubricate the other cable in the same manner.

6. If the cables are dirty, spray them instead with a lubricant/solvent, such as LPS-25, or WD-40. Continue spraying the upper portion of the inner cable until the lubricant running out the bottom of the cable housing is clean.

7. Grease the twist grip assembly and the handlebar where the grip rotates.

8. Connect the throttle cables. The accelerator (opening) cable goes to the front of the housing. The decelerator (closing) cable goes to the rear.

9. Reassemble the twist grip housing. If the upper housing has a peg, it must fit into the handlebar hole (**Figure 90**).

10. Adjust throttle cable play at the grip (see *Throttle Grip Inspection*).

Clutch Cable Lubrication

1. In front of the engine, loosen the clutch mid-cable adjuster locknut and shorten the adjuster to give maximum free play (**Figure 91**).

2. At the clutch lever, loosen the adjuster locknut and shorten the adjuster, lining up the slots in the adjuster, nut, and lever (**Figure 92**).

3. Pull the cable housing (outer cable) free of the adjuster and swing the inner cable around to match the slot in the lever. Pull the cable and its fitting out of the lever.

4. At the top of the clutch cable, examine the exposed portion of the inner cable. If it is clean, hold the cable vertical and spray it with Dri-Slide or one of the thin spray-on chain lubricants.

5. Hold the spray can close to the inner cable, near the top end of the cable housing, so that the lubricant will run down between the inner cable and its housing. Spray the cable until it is lubricated along its entire length.

6. If the exposed portion of the inner cable is dirty, or the cable feels gritty while moving it up and down in its housing, spray it instead with a lubricant/solvent, such as LPS-25 or WD-40.

7. Re-connect the clutch cable and adjust free play at the lever.

Speedometer/Tachometer Cable Lubrication

Disconnect the cables at the lower end. Pull the inner cable out, apply a light coat of grease and reinstall the cables.

Swing Arm Lubrication (Chain Drive Only)

Chain drive models have a grease fitting on the swing arm (**Figure 93**).

1. Use a grease gun to force grease into the fitting on the swing arm, until the grease runs out both ends.

2. If grease will not run out of the ends of the swing arm, unscrew the grease fitting from the swing arm. Clean the fitting, and make certain that the ball check valve is free. Reinstall the fitting.

3. Apply the grease gun again. If grease does not run out both ends of the swing arm, remove the swing arm, clean out the old grease, install the swing arm, and lubricate it.

Carburetor Linkage Lubrication

Oil the carburetor choke linkage and accelerator pump pivots, if equipped (**Figure 94**).

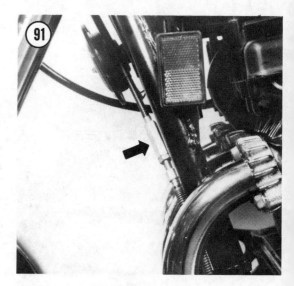

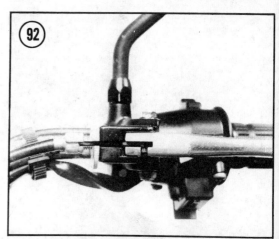

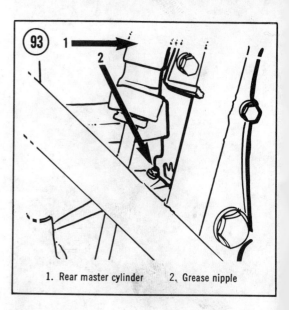

1. Rear master cylinder   2. Grease nipple

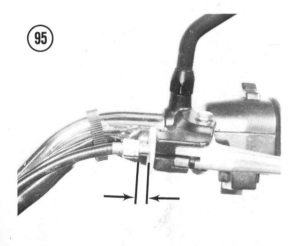

CHASSIS MAINTENANCE— 6 MONTH/3,000 MILE

Clutch Adjustment

As the clutch cable stretches, cable play will exceed the range of the handlebar adjuster. As the clutch plates and discs inside the engine wear, the clutch pushrod must be adjusted even when the cable play is within tolerance, or the clutch can slip and cause rapid wear.

Adjust the clutch as follows:

1. In front of the engine, loosen the clutch mid-cable adjuster locknut, and shorten the adjuster all the way (**Figure 91**).

2. At the clutch lever, loosen the locknut and turn the adjuster until 3/16–1/4 in. (5–6 mm) of threads are showing between the locknut and the adjuster body (**Figure 95**).

3. Remove the 2 clutch adjuster cover screws and the cover (**Figure 96**).

4. Loosen the locknut on the clutch adjusting screw inside the cover. Back out the screw 3 or 4 turns (**Figure 97**).

5. Screw in the clutch adjusting screw until the point is reached where it is hard to turn. Back out the screw ½ turn and tighten the locknut.

6. In front of the engine, lengthen the mid-cable adjuster until it has just taken all the slack out of the cable, and the clutch lever has no free play. Tighten the locknut.

7. Check that the lower end of the clutch cable (below the engine) is fully seated in its socket.

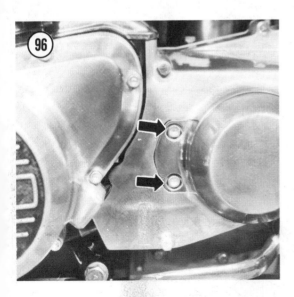

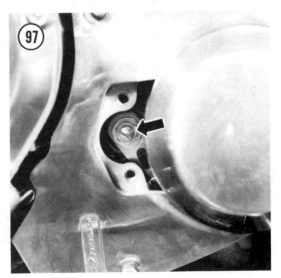

8. At the clutch lever, turn the adjuster as required to get 1/16–1/8in. (2–3 mm) of cable play at the clutch lever.

9. Install the clutch adjuster cover.

If the proper amount of adjustment cannot be achieved by using this procedure, the cable has stretched to the point that it needs replacing.

Tire Wear

Check the tread for excessive wear, deep cuts, and imbedded objects such as stones, nails, etc. On tires with inner tubes, if you find a nail in a tire, mark its location with a light crayon before pulling it out. This will help locate the hole in the inner tube. Refer to *Tire Changing* in Chapter Nine.

Check local traffic regulations concerning minimum tread depth. Measure with a small ruler. For speeds below 80 mph, Kawasaki recommends replacement when the front tread depth is 0.04 in. (1 mm) or less and rear tread depth is 0.08 in. (2 mm) or less. For higher speeds, the recommended limits are 0.06 in. (1.5 mm) for the front, and 0.12 in. (3 mm) for the rear. Tread wear indicators appear across the tire when tread reaches minimum safe depth. Replace the tire at this point.

Spokes and Rim Runout (1973–1978)

Cast aluminum wheels require no maintenance. For wire-spoked wheels, check as follows:

1. Tap each spoke with a wrench. The higher the pitch of sound it makes, the tighter the spoke. The lower the sound frequency, the looser the spoke. A "ping" is good; a "klunk" says the spoke is too loose.

2. If one or more spokes are loose, tighten them. If all the spokes are loose, tighten all spokes on one side, then all spokes on the other side. One-half to one turn of the spoke nipple should be sufficient.

3. Raise the front wheel off the ground and hold a ruler against the fork leg, close to the wheel rim. If the rim wobbles more than 1/8 in. (3 mm) side-to-side, or about 1/16 in. (2 mm) up and down, the wheels may need centering. Refer to Chapter Nine, *Wheels and Tires*.

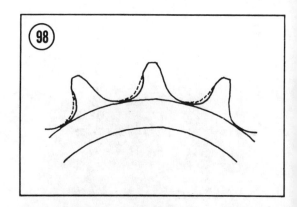

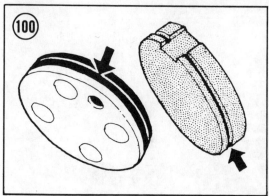

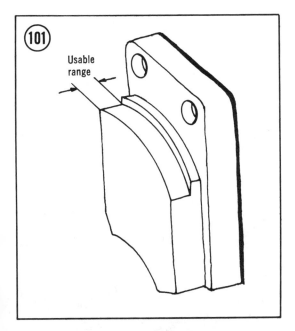

Usable range

3. Measure the length of any 20 links in the chain, from the center of the first pin you select to the 21st pin.

4. Twenty links in a new chain stretched tight are 15 in. (381 mm) long. If you measure more than 15-5/16 in. (389 mm) of length, install a new drive chain (see *Swing Arm Removal*, Chapter Ten).

5. If the drive chain is worn, inspect the rear wheel and engine drive sprockets for undercutting or sharp teeth (**Figure 98**). If wear is evident, replace the sprockets too, or you'll soon wear out a new drive chain (see *Rear Wheel Disassembly* in Chapter Nine and *Drive Sprocket Removal* in Chapter Six).

Brake Pads and Linings

The brake pads will wear more rapidly with severe use or riding in dusty areas.

Front Brake Pad Inspection:

1. Have a friend apply the front brake.

2. Shine a light between the caliper and the disc and inspect the brake pads (**Figure 99**).

3. *1973–1978:* If either pad has worn enough so that its red or green line is touching the disc, replace both pads as a set (**Figure 100**). See *Front Brake Pad Removal*, Chapter Eight.

4. *1979 and later:* If either pad has worn to the stepped 1 mm indicator (**Figure 101**), replace both pads as a set (see *Front Brake Pad Removal*, Chapter Eight).

Rear Brake Pad Inspection—Disc Brake:

1. Remove the pad cover from the caliper and inspect the brake pads (**Figure 102**).

2. If either pad has worn down to the stepped 1 mm indicator (**Figure 101**), replace both pads as a set. See *Rear Brake Pad Removal*, Chapter Eight.

3. Replace the pad covers.

Rear Brake Lining Inspection—Drum Brake:

1. Have a friend step on the brake pedal.

2. *1973–1974:* The brake cam lever should form an angle of 80–90 degrees with the brake rod

Drive Chain Wear

Kawasaki recommends replacing the drive chain when it has worn longer than 2% of its original length. If adjustment of a standard chain puts the chain adjuster notch behind the last index mark stamped on the swing arm, the chain should be replaced.

Inspect as follows:

1. With motorcycle on centerstand, screw in chain adjusters to move wheel rearward until the chain is taut (see *Drive Chain Play*).

2. Lay a scale along the top chain run.

(Figure 103). If the angle exceeds 100 degrees, disassemble the brake and inspect the linings. See *Rear Drum Brake Disassembly,* Chapter Eight.

3. *1974-1976:* Check the brake lining wear indicator on the backing plate (Figure 104). When the wear indicator pointer moves into the red range, or out of the USABLE RANGE, disassemble the brake and inspect the linings. See *Rear Drum Brake Disassembly,* Chapter Eight.

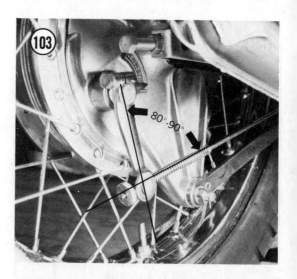

Steering Play Inspection

1. Prop up the motorcycle so that the front tire clears the ground.

2. Center the front wheel. Push lightly against the left handlebar grip to start the wheel turning to the right, then let go. The wheel should continue turning under its own momentum until the forks hit their stop.

> NOTE: *On some bikes, the wiring and control cables tend to stop the wheel movement. If the wheel stops too soon, make sure it's not because of wiring stiffness.*

3. Center the wheel, and push lightly against the right handlebar grip.

4. If, with a light push in either direction, the front wheel will turn all the way to the stop, the steering adjustment is not too tight.

5. Center the front wheel and kneel in front of it. Grasp the bottoms of the 2 front fork slider legs. Try to pull the forks toward you, and then try to push them toward the engine (Figure 105). If no play is felt, the steering adjustment is not too loose.

6. If the steering adjustment is too tight or too loose, readjust it as described under *Steering Adjustment* in Chapter Ten.

Front Fork Inspection

Lock the front brake and pump the forks up and down forcefully. You should hear the fork oil as it flows through its passages. There should be no binding. Inspect for fork oil leakage around the fork seals. If there is evidence of leakage, check the fork oil level (see *Fork Oil Change*). Check the upper and lower triple clamp mounting bolts for tightness (Figure 106).

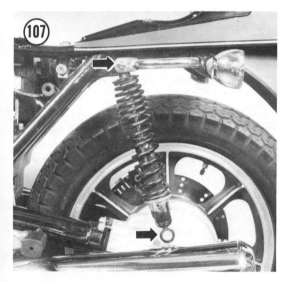

Rear Shock Inspection

Force the rear of the bike up and down. You should hear the fluid working. Check for fluid leakage. If there is fluid leakage replace the shocks; they are not rebuildable. Check the shock mounting bolts for tightness and their rubber bushings for wear (**Figure 107**). Make sure both shock absorbers are set at the same spring preload, left and right (**Figure 108**).

YEARLY MAINTENANCE

These procedures should be done every year or every 6,000 miles, whichever comes first. Maintenance items are listed in **Table 1**.

Fork Oil Change

1. Place a drain pan under the fork and remove the drain screw (**Figure 109**). Allow the oil to drain for at least 5 minutes.

> **WARNING**
> *Do not allow the fork oil to come in contact with any of the brake components. You could contaminate the disc and pads, reducing stopping power.*

2. With both of the bike's wheels on the ground and the front brake applied, push down on the handlebar grips to work the forks up and down. Continue until all oil is expelled.

3. Install the drain screw.

4. Repeat for the other fork.

5. Prop up the motorcycle so that the front tire just clears the ground.

6. Loosen a fork tube clamp bolt on one side of the top triple clamp (**Figure 110**).

7. Unscrew the fork tube plug (top fork bolt) from the fork tube (**Figure 110**).

> NOTE: *Some models require handlebar removal to loosen the fork tube plug.*

8. Fill the fork tube with about 4.7 oz. (140cc) 10W non-detergent fork oil on 1973–1977 models; 5.4 oz. (160cc) 15W non-detergent fork oil on 1978 and later chain drive models; or 10.5 oz. (310cc) 10W non-detergent fork oil on shaft drive models.

> NOTE: *The amount of oil poured in is not as reliable a measurement as the level of the top of the fork oil. You may have to add more oil later in this procedure.*

9. After filling both tubes, pump the forks several times to expel air from the upper and lower fork chambers.

10. Stick a long wire (at least 24 in.) down into the fork tube. Measure the distance from the top of the fork oil to the top of the fork tube. The distance should be—17-15/16 in. (455mm) on 1973 models; 18.7 in. (475mm) on 1974–1975 models; and 16.8 in. (426mm) on 1976–1977.

Remove the fork springs and check the distances for 1978 and later models. It should be 17.4 in. (441 mm) for chain drive and 18.9 in. (480 mm) for shaft drive.

11. If the oil level is low, fill to the specified level.

12. Install the fork springs (if removed) and the fork tube plug, and tighten the top triple clamp bolt.

13. Road test the bike and check for leaks.

Brake Fluid

To change the brake fluid, see *Brake Fluid Change* in Chapter Eight.

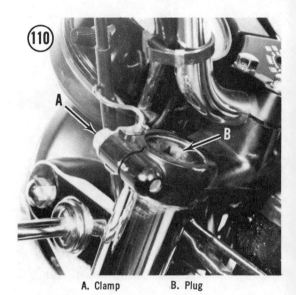

A. Clamp   B. Plug

Air Cleaner Replacement

Change the air cleaner element every year, or every 6,000 miles, whichever comes first. See *Air Cleaner Maintenance* earlier in this chapter.

Ignition Advance Lubrication

To lubricate the ignition advancer on both conventional and transistorized ignition systems, refer to *Advancer Removal/Installation* in Chapter Eleven.

Nuts, Bolts, Fasteners

Check all exposed nuts, bolts, cotter pins, safety clips and circlips. Pay particular attention to:

a. Control lever, pedal, and linkage pivots
b. Engine mount bolts
c. Handlebar clamp bolts
d. Top triple clamp bolts
e. Bottom triple clamp bolts
f. Front axle clamp nuts
g. Top shock absorber mounting nuts
h. Bottom shock absorber mounting bolts
j. Swing arm pivot
k. Rear brake torque link
l. Rear axle nut

This check is *especially* important on high mileage machines.

Rear Bevel Lube Level (Shaft Drive)

1. Put the bike on its centerstand.
2. Remove the rear bevel filler cap, and check that the lubricant level is just at the bottom of the filler threads (A, **Figure 111**).
3. If the level is low add hypoid gear oil API-rated "GL-5" or "GL-6" up to the filler opening. Check carefully for leakage.

Drive Shaft Joints (Shaft Drive)

At the *first* 6,000 mile service, and every 18,000 miles after that, grease the drive shaft sliding joints, front and rear.

Front:

Apply a thin coat of high temperature grease to the front drive shaft splines (see *Engine Removal,* Chapter Four, or *Drive Shaft Removal,* Chapter Ten).

Rear:

Coat the splines and pack the pocket forward of the splines with 25 cc (a little more than half a shot glass) of high temperature grease (see *Rear Bevel Removal,* Chapter Ten).

Swing Arm Lubrication (Shaft Drive)

At the *first* 6,000 mile service, and every 18,000 miles after that, lubricate the swing arm

tapered roller bearings. See *Swing Arm Removal,* Chapter Ten.

2 YEAR MAINTENANCE

These procedures should be done every 2 years or every 12,000 miles, whichever comes first. Maintenance procedures are listed in **Table 1**.

Speedometer Gear Housing Lubrication

1. Remove the speedometer gear housing (see *Front Wheel Disassembly*).
2. Pull the grease seal out of the speedometer gear housing and remove the speedometer drive gear.
3. Clean all old grease from the housing and gear, and apply high temperature grease.
4. Install a new grease seal and assemble the front wheel (see *Front Wheel Assembly,* Chapter Nine).

Wheel Bearing Lubrication

The 1979 and later models have sealed ball bearings in the wheel hubs. These require no lubrication for the life of the motorcycle.

The 1973–1978 models require periodic lubrication with high temperature grease. See *Front Wheel Disassembly* and *Rear Wheel Disassembly,* Chapter Nine.

Steering Stem Bearings

To lubricate the steering stem bearings, refer to *Steering Stem Disassembly* in Chapter Ten.

Rear Brake Cam Lubrication (Drum Brake)

1. Remove the rear wheel (see *Rear Wheel Removal,* Chapter Nine).
2. Take out the brake backing plate.
3. Wipe away the old grease, being careful not to get any of it on the brake shoes.
4. Sparingly apply high-temperature grease to the camming surfaces of the camshaft, the camshaft groove, and the brake shoe pivots (**Figure 112**). Do not get any grease on the brake shoes.
5. Reassemble the rear wheel and install it.

Rear Bevel Lube Change (Shaft Drive)

At the initial break-in maintenance, and every 18,000 miles after that (with no time limit), change the rear bevel drive lubricant.

1. Ride the motorcycle until the rear bevel drive is warm.

2. Put the bike on its centerstand.

3. Put a drain pan under the drive unit.

4. Remove the filler cap, remove the drain plug, and drain the lubricant (B, **Figure 111**).

> WARNING
> *Don't get any lubricant on the wheel or tire. Clean any off with a solvent.*

5. Install the drain plug and gasket.

6. Fill the drive unit to the bottom of the filler threads with hypoid gear oil API-rated "GL-5" or "GL-6." It will take *about* 7.8 oz. (230 cc).

7. Install the filler cap.

STORAGE

Several months of inactivity can cause serious problems and a general deterioration of bike condition. This is especially true in areas of weather extremes. During the winter months you should prepare your bike carefully for "hibernation."

Selecting a Storage Area

Most cyclists store their bikes in their home garages. If you do not have a garage, facilities suitable for long-term motorcycle storage are readily available for rent or lease in most areas. In selecting a building, consider the following points.

1. The storage area must be dry, free from dampness and excessive humidity. Heating is not necessary, but the building should be well insulated to minimize extreme temperature variations.

2. Buildings with large window areas should be avoided, or such windows should be masked (also a good security measure) if direct sunlight can fall on the bike.

3. Facilities near salt water (oceans) are not desirable.

4. Select an area with minimum risk of fire or theft. Check your insurance to see if your bike is covered while in storage.

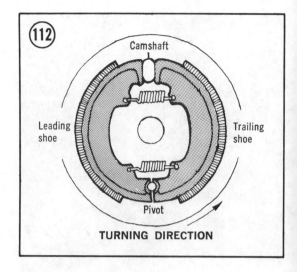

TURNING DIRECTION

Preparing the Bike for Storage

Careful preparation will minimize deterioration and make it easier to restore the bike to service later. Use the following procedure.

1. Wash the bike completely. Make certain to remove any road salt which may have accumulated during the first weeks of winter. Wax all painted and polished surfaces, including any chromed areas.

2. Run the engine for 20–30 minutes to stabilize oil temperature. Drain the oil, regardless of mileage since last oil change. Replace the oil filter and fill the engine with the normal quantity of fresh oil.

3. Remove the battery and coat the cable terminals with petroleum jelly. If there is evidence of acid spillage in the battery box, neutralize with baking soda, wash clean, and repaint the damaged area. Store the battery in a warm area and recharge it once a month.

4. Drain all gasoline from the fuel tank, interconnecting hoses, and carburetors. As an alternative, a fuel preservative may be added to the fuel. This preservative is available from many motorcycle shops and marine equipment suppliers.

5. Remove spark plugs and add a small quantity of oil to each cylinder. Turn the engine a few revolutions by hand to distribute the oil and install the spark plugs.

6. Check tire pressures. Move the machine to the storage area and store it on the centerstand.

7. Cover the bike with material that will allow air circulation. Don't use plastic.

After Storage

Before returning the motorcycle to service, thoroughly check all fasteners, suspension components and brake components. Make sure that the brake fluid level is correct and all brake hoses and connections are sound. Check all lubricant levels (engine oil, secondary and final drive gear oil) and top up if necessary. Make sure the battery is fully charged and the electrolyte level is correct before installing the battery. Fill the fuel tank with fresh gasoline.

Before starting the engine, remove the spark plugs and turn the engine over a few times to blow out the excess storage oil. Place a rag over the cylinder head to keep the oil from spraying over the motorcycle. Install new spark plugs and connect the spark plug leads. Make sure each plug lead snaps securely over each spark plug.

3

Table 1 MAINTENANCE CHECKLIST

Weekly/Gas Stop Maintenance	
Tire pressure	Check cold and adjust to suit load and speed
Brake function	Check for a solid feel
Brake lever play	1973–77: 1/8–3/16 in. (3–5 mm)
	Z1R: 3/16 in. (4–5 mm)
Brake pedal play	Drum Brake: About 1 in. (20–30 mm)
	Disc Brake: About 3/8 in. (8–10 mm)
Throttle grip	Check for smooth opening and return
	Free play: 1/16–1/8 in. (2–3 mm)
Clutch lever play	1/16–1/8 in. (2–3 mm)
Steering	Smooth but not loose
Drive chain play	About 1 1/4 in. (30–35 mm)
Drive chain	Lubricated—not dry
Chain oiler level	1973–74: Check
Nuts, bolts, cotter pins	Check axles, suspension, controls and linkage
Engine oil level	Check
Lights and horn	Check operation, especially brake light
Engine noise and leaks	Check
Kill switch	Check operation
Monthly/3,000 Mile Maintenance	
Battery electrolyte level	Check more frequently in hot weather
Disc brake fluid level	Check
6 Month/3,000 Mile Maintenance	
Air cleaner	Clean or replace
Fuel system	Clean carburetor bowls and fuel tank
Spark plugs	Check, clean, gap
Cam chain	1973–78: Adjust tension
Air suction valves	1979 and later: Check
Valve clearance	Check
Contact points	1973–78: Check gap, lube cam
Ignition timing	1973–78: Check, adjust
Throttle cables	Adjust
Carburetors	Adjust idle and synchronize
Engine oil and filter	Change (filter every other time)
General lube	Perform general lubrication
Clutch	Adjust
Tire wear	Check
Spokes and rim runout	1973–78: Check wire wheels
Drive chain wear	Check
Brake pads/linings	Check wear
Steering play	Check
Suspension	Check
(Continued)	

Table 1 MAINTENANCE CHECKLIST (continued)

Yearly/6,000 Mile Maintenance	
Fork oil	Change
Brake fluid	Change
Air cleaner	Replace
Ignition advance	Lube
Nuts, bolts, fasteners	Inspect/tighten
Rear bevel lube	Shaft Drive: Check level
Drive shaft joints	Shaft Drive: Grease at 6000 miles, then every 18,000 miles
Swing arm	Shaft Drive: Grease at 6000 miles, then every 18,000 miles
2 Year/12,000 Mile Maintenance	
Speedometer gear housing	Grease
Wheel bearings	1973–78: Grease
Steering stem bearings	Grease
Rear brake cam	900cc: Grease
Rear bevel lube	Shaft drive: Change (18,000 miles)

Table 2 TIRES AND TIRE PRESSURE

			Tire Pressure (psi) @ Load		
		Tire Size	0–215 lb.	215–365 lb.	Over 365 lb.
Shaft drive					
	Front	3.50V-19	28	28	28
	Rear	4.50V-17	32	36	40
Chain drive					
1979 and later	Front	3.25V-19	28	28	
	Rear	4.00V-18	32	40	
1973–78	Front	3.50H-19	28	28	
	Rear	4.00H-18	32	36	
Z1R	Front	3.25H-19	28	28	
	Rear	4.00H-18	32	36	
LTD	Front	ML90-19	26	26	
	Rear	MT90-16T	22	24	

Table 3 VALVE CLEARANCE INSPECTION

Model Year	Check Valve Pairs	Clearance
1973–78	1 and 3, or 2 and 4	0.002–0.004 in. (0.05–0.10 mm)
1979 and Later	1 and 2, or 3 and 4	0.002–0.006 in. (0.05–0.15 mm)

Table 4 IGNITION TIMING SPECIFICATIONS

Year	Initial	Advance
1979	10° @ 1000 rpm	40° @ 3400 rpm
1978½ (emission controlled)	10° @ 1000 rpm	40° @ 2350 rpm
1978 Z1R	10° @ 1450 rpm	40° @ 2350 rpm
Others	20° @ 1450 rpm	40° @ 2350 rpm
1977 LTD	20° @ 1450 rpm	40° @ 2350 rpm
Others	20° @ 1500 rpm	40° @ 2350 rpm
1975–76	20° @ 1500 rpm	40° @ 2350 rpm
1974 Late	20° @ 1500 rpm	40° @ 3000 rpm
Early	5° @ 1500 rpm	40° @ 3000 rpm
1973	5° @ 1500 rpm	40° @ 3000 rpm

Table 5 IDLE MIXTURE STANDARD SETTINGS

Year	1973–74	1975	1976	1977	1978	1979
Pilot/Air Screw (turns out)	1½	1¼	1⅜	1¼	1¼	1⅛

3

Table 6 CARBURETOR SYNCH VACUUM — INCHES Hg

Year	1973–75	1976	1977	1978–79
Normal range	7.9–9.8 in. (20–25 cm)	7.9–9.1 in. (20–23 cm)	9.4–11.0 in. (24–28 cm)	7.9–11.0 in. (20–28 cm)
Minimum	6 in. (15 cm)	6 in. (15 cm)	7.5 in. (15 cm)	6 in. (15 cm)

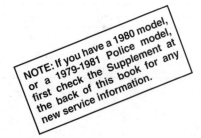

NOTE: If you have a 1980 model, or a 1979-1981 Police model, first check the Supplement at the back of this book for any new service information.

CHAPTER FOUR

ENGINE

This chapter provides complete service and overhaul procedures for the Kawasaki 900 and 1000cc engines. **Table 1** provides detailed specifications for the engine. **Table 2** provides tightening torques. All tables are at the end of the chapter.

This chapter is written in a general teardown sequence, so if you wish, you can work your way through several *Removal* and *Disassembly* sections skipping the *Installation* segments until you're ready to put it all back together. Otherwise, refer to the index and go to the section that describes the part you want to remove and tell you if any preparatory work is required.

Although the clutch and transmission are located within the engine, they are covered in separate chapters.

Service procedures for all models are virtually the same. Where differences occur, they are identified. Right now, before you start any work, go back and read the *Service Hints* in Chapter One. You will save yourself a lot of mistakes with those hints fresh in your mind.

ENGINE DESIGN

The unit construction combines the power plant, clutch, and transmission into one set of engine cases.

The crankcase is the front portion of the aluminum alloy engine cases, which are split horizontally. The built up (pressed together) crankshaft is mounted in 6 caged-roller main bearings.

The 4 pistons operate inside an alloy cylinder block with pressed-in cylinder sleeves. The alloy cylinder head houses the 2 overhead camshafts. Both camshafts are driven by a single chain from a sprocket on the crankshaft (between cylinders 2 and 3). The cam lobes depress lifter cups fitted to the tops of the valve stems, opening the valves.

The alternator and the starter motor clutch are mounted on the left end of the crankshaft. The ignition timing system (contact breaker points or electronic pickups) and advance mechanism are on the right end of the crankshaft.

The starter motor is mounted high in the left side of the engine to the rear of the cylinder block.

Engine lubrication is by wet sump, with the oil supply housed in the bottom of the crankcase. An oil pump, accessible from the bottom of the engine, feeds the main and big-end bearings, camshafts and valves, and some of the bearings on the transmission shafts.

The engine has been laid out so that most of the repairs can be done with the engine still in the frame. However, for repairs to the crankshaft, cam chain, transmission, or kickstarter ratchet, the engine must be removed from the frame.

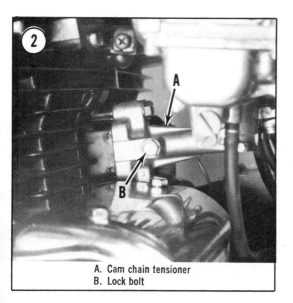

A. Cam chain tensioner
B. Lock bolt

BREAK-IN

Following cylinder servicing (boring, honing, new rings, etc.) and major lower end work, the engine should be broken in just as though it were new. The performance and service life of the engine depend greatly on a careful and sensible break-in.

For the first 500 miles, no more than ⅓ throttle should be used and speed should be varied as much as possible within the ⅓ throttle limit. Avoid prolonged, steady running at one speed, no matter how moderate, as well as hard acceleration.

Following the 500-mile service, increasingly more throttle can be used but full throttle should not be used until the motorcyle has covered at least 1,000 miles and then it should be limited to short bursts until 1,500 miles have been logged.

SERVICING ENGINE IN FRAME

Many components can be serviced while the engine is mounted in the frame:

a. Camshafts
b. Cylinder head and valves
c. Cylinder and pistons
d. Clutch
e. Alternator and ignition system
f. Carburetor assembly

We recommend that prior to engine removal and disassembly, the majority of parts be re-moved from the engine while it is still in the frame. By doing so you will reduce the weight of the engine considerably and make engine re-moval easier and safer.

CAM CHAIN AND TENSIONER

Proper cam chain tension is essential for safe operation, quiet running and maximum power. The cam chain itself (**Figure 1**) is endless and wraps around the crankshaft, so it can't be re-moved without splitting the crankcases (see *Crankshaft Removal*). The other guides and sprockets are removed as part of engine disassembly.

a. Top guide sprocket (see *Camshaft Installation*)
b. Front and rear guide sprockets (see *Cylinder Head Installation*)
c. Bottom guide roller (see *Cylinder Block Installation*)
d. Front guide rubber (see *Cylinder Block Installation*)

CHAIN TENSIONER (AUTOMATIC)

The 1979 and later models have an automatic tensioner that is continually self-adjusting (**Figure 2**). The bolt on the side is used only to lock the tensioner during engine disassembly/assembly. During normal operation, this short bolt doesn't touch the tensioner pushrod. The pushrod is free to move inward, but can't move out because of a one-way ball and retainer.

Locking the Tensioner (1979 and Later)

Remove the standard lock bolt (**Figure 2**) and install a longer bolt to lock the tensioner. Any 6 mm diameter bolt about 16 mm or longer will do. After your assembly work is done, remove the longer bolt and install the original bolt and washer.

Tensioner Removal (1979 and Later)

1. Lock the tensioner.
2. Remove the 2 tensioner mounting bolts (**Figure 3**) and the tensioner.

CAUTION
If the tensioner is not locked, do not loosen the tensioner mounting bolts with-out resetting the tensioner pushrod on reassembly.

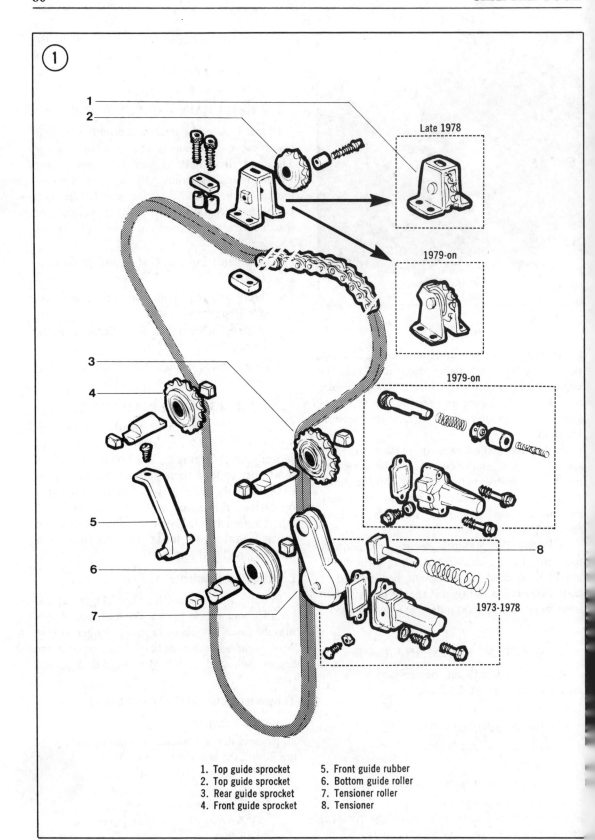

Late 1978

1979-on

1979-on

1973-1978

1. Top guide sprocket
2. Top guide sprocket
3. Rear guide sprocket
4. Front guide sprocket
5. Front guide rubber
6. Bottom guide roller
7. Tensioner roller
8. Tensioner

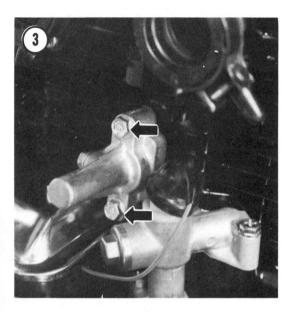

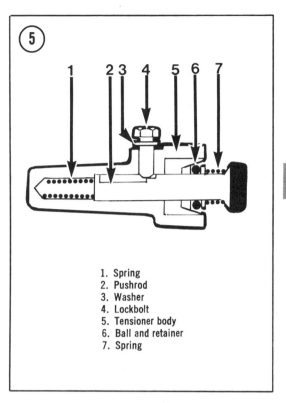

1. Spring
2. Pushrod
3. Washer
4. Lockbolt
5. Tensioner body
6. Ball and retainer
7. Spring

4

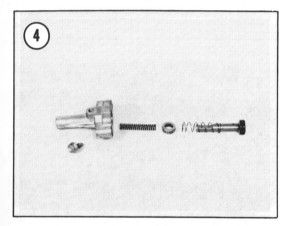

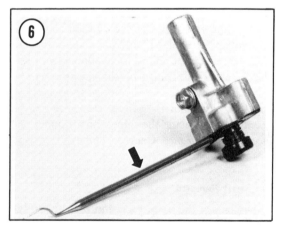

Tensioner Installation (1979 and Later)

1. Loosen the lock bolt and remove the pushrod and fine spring (**Figure 4**).

2. Compress the spring against the pushrod head and hold it in place temporarily with a wire or awl.

3. Make sure the heavy spring is in the tensioner (**Figure 4**), then insert the pushrod through the retainer and into the tensioner body with the pushrod flat facing the lock bolt (**Figure 5**).

4. Push the pushrod in as far as it will go and hold it while you tighten the lock bolt (**Figure 6**).

5. Remove the wire that kept the fine spring compressed.

6. Install the tensioner and gasket on the cylinder head.

7. When engine top-end assembly is complete, loosen the lock bolt, then tighten it again. This allows the tensioner to take up chain slack.

CAUTION
Do not loosen the lock bolt if the cams and top guide sprocket are not secure. The pushrod will overextend and lock, damaging the cam chain when the other parts are tightened.

CHAIN TENSIONER (MANUAL)

The 1978 and earlier models use a manually adjustable cam chain tensioner that does not take up chain slack until you loosen the locknut and bolt (**Figure 7**). No special procedures are necessary to assemble the manual tensioner.

CAMSHAFTS

The 2 overhead camshafts are mounted atop the cylinder head. The exhaust camshaft is at the front of the head, and the intake camshaft is at the rear. Each camshaft runs on 4 sets of split bushings, located beneath 2 bushing caps doweled to the cylinder head.

Camshaft sideplay is controlled by thrust faces on the camshaft riding against thrust faces on the insides of a camshaft bearing cap.

Each camshaft has 4 lobes and a drive sprocket in the center. Both camshafts are driven by an endless single row chain from the crankshaft.

In operation, the cam lobe strikes the top of the valve lifter cup fitted over the top of the valve stem. This lifts (pushes down) the valve off its seat in the top of the combustion chamber.

The shim in the top of the valve lifter cup is removable; it regulates the valve stem to cam lobe clearance. The shims are available from Kawasaki in a wide range of thicknesses. As the valve and valve seat wear, the cam/valve clearance decreases; but the proper clearance can be restored by replacing the shim with a thinner one (see *Valve Clearance*, Chapter Three).

Camshaft Removal

1. Disconnect the battery ground (–) cable (**Figure 8**).

2. Remove the fuel tank (see *Fuel Tank Removal*, Chapter Seven).

3. Pull the spark plug leads off the plugs.

4. Remove the screws (**Figure 9**) securing the ignition cover and remove it and the gasket.

5. Use a 17 mm wrench on the *outside* nut (**Figure 10**) and rotate the engine until the "T" mark for the No. 1 and 4 cylinders aligns with the fixed pointer (**Figures 11, 12, 13**). No. 1 and 4 cylinders are now at top dead center (TDC) on the compression stroke.

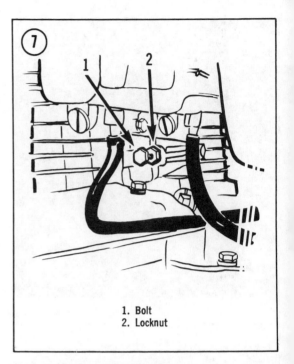

1. Bolt
2. Locknut

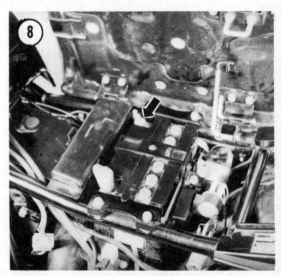

CAUTION
Do not rotate the crankshaft with the smaller inner bolt as it will damage the ignition advance mechanism unit located within the housing.

6. Disconnect the tachometer drive cable at the cylinder head.

7. Remove the bolt and pinion holder stop(s) (**Figure 14**) and remove the cable guide and tachometer drive gear from the cylinder head.

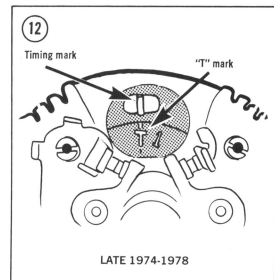

LATE 1974-1978

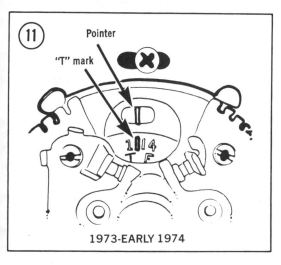

1973-EARLY 1974

4

8. *Shaft drive:* Remove ignition coils (**Figure 15**).

9. *1979 and later:* Slide up the lower hose clamps (**Figure 15**) and pull the hose off the air suction covers. Remove the 4 bolts and flat washers (A, **Figure 16**) securing the cover. Repeat these steps for the other cover. Tie the vacuum switch and air hoses up out of the way. Remove the air suction valve covers.

10. Remove the bolts (B, **Figure 16**) securing the valve cover. Note which bolts have spark plug cable clamps attached (only 1 side shown here).Tap around the perimeter with a plastic or rubber mallet to loosen the cover and remove it.

11. *1979 and later:* Lock the cam chain tensioner; remove the standard bolt (**Figure 17**) and install a 16 mm or longer bolt. Tighten it securely. Tensioner removal is not necessary.

12. *1973-1978:* Remove the 2 bolts securing the camshaft chain tensioner and remove it and the gasket.

13. Loosen the 4 Allen bolts (**Figure 18**) securing upper chain guide sprocket and carefully remove it.

NOTE: *Hold the 4 rubber dampers in place against the 4 bolts during removal to prevent accidently dropping them into the crankcase, through the cam chain cavity.*

CAUTION
If any of the rubber dampers fall into the crankcase, they must be removed prior to starting the engine. First, try retrieving them by removing the oil pan; if they cannot be located, the engine must be removed and disassembled. Do not run the engine with any of these loose parts in it.

14. Remove the 16 bolts (**Figure 19**) securing the camshaft bearing caps.

15. Gently tap the camshaft caps with a soft mallet to loosen them and lift them off (**Figure 20**). Mark the exposed bearing cap halves with a grease pencil so that you will be able to reassemble them in the same positions from which they were removed. Keep the bearing inserts in their original positions in the caps.

16. Remove the camshafts one at a time. Tie the cam chain up to the frame with wire or place a tool through the loop to prevent it from falling into the crankcase (**Figure 21**).

CAUTION
If the crankshaft must be rotated when the camshafts are removed, pull up on the cam drive chain and keep it taut while rotating the crankshaft. Make certain that the chain is positioned onto the crankshaft timing sprocket. If this is not done, the chain may become kinked and may damage both the chain and the timing sprocket on the crankshaft.

17. Remove the bearing inserts from the cylinder head and mark each as to location. Used inserts must be installed in their original position to prevent rapid wear.

Camshaft Inspection

Camshaft/bushing clearance inspection is described as part of the installation procedure (see *Camshaft Installation*).

1. Inspect the cam chain guide sprocket. If worn, install a new one.

2. Check the bearing journals for wear and scoring (**Figure 22**). If any bearing surface has a diameter less than 0.961 in. (24.42 mm), replace the camshaft with a new one.

3. Check the cam lobes for wear. The lobes should not be scored and the edges should be

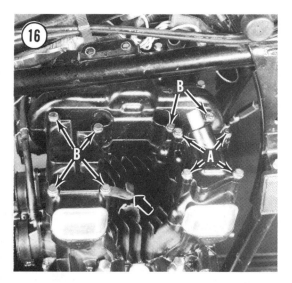

4

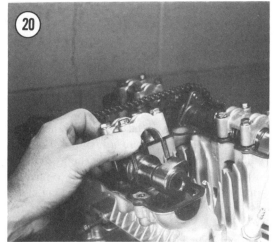

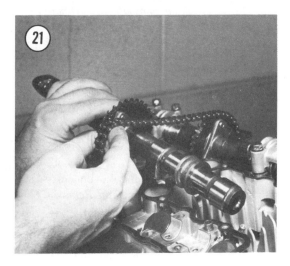

square. Slight damage may be removed with a silicon carbide oilstone. Use No. 100-120 grit initially, then polish with a No. 280-320 grit.

4. Even though the cam lobe surface appears to be satisfactory, with no visible signs of wear, it must be measured with a micrometer as shown in **Figure 23**.

5. On *900cc models,* replace the camshaft if the lobe height is less than 1.424 in. (36.16 mm) for intake or 1.404 in. (35.66 mm) for exhaust. On *1000cc models* replace the camshaft if lobe height is less than 1.422 in. (36.12 mm) for intake or 1.402 in. (35.62 mm) for exhaust.

6. Inspect the sprockets for wear. Check the condition of the chain damping rubber on each side of the sprocket (**Figure 24**). If it is starting to disintegrate it must be replaced, otherwise the bits of rubber will contaminate the engine oil and may cause excess engine noise.

7. When installing new cam sprockets, apply Loctite Lock 'N' Seal to the sprocket bolts and torque them to 11 ft.-lb. (1.5 mkg).

Camshaft/Bushing Clearance Inspection

To check camshaft/bushing clearance with Plastigage, follow the *Camshaft Installation* procedure, but leave the cam and bushings *dry* (use no lubricant). It is very important not to turn the cams while assembled dry. After checking clearance, remove and lubricate the cams and inserts.

Camshaft Installation

CAUTION
Do not install the camshafts in a cylinder head/valve assembly that has been removed from an engine; you will bend the valves, and the cams must be removed to install the head.

1. Make sure the tachometer drive gear is removed from the cylinder head.

2. Fit the bottom bushing halves for each camshaft into the cylinder head bosses from which they were removed.

3. Make sure that No. 1 and 4 cylinders are still at TDC. Refer to Step 5, *Camshaft Removal*.

CAUTION
Be sure to keep the camshaft drive chain taut if rotating the crankshaft.

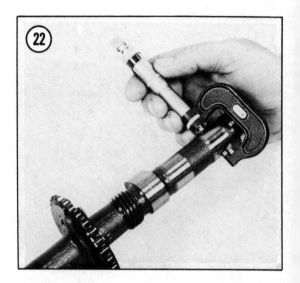

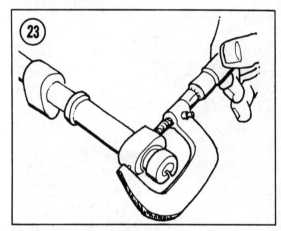

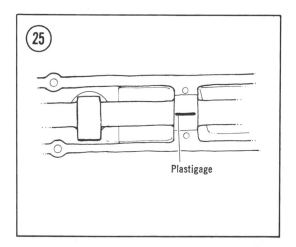

Plastigage

4. *If you are checking cam/bushing clearance with Plastigage*, cut strips of Plastigage and lay them lengthwise across each bottom bushing (**Figure 25**). Do not lubricate the journals or bushings.

5. Coat the camshaft journals and lobes with clean engine oil. Use molybdenum disulfide grease if new parts are being installed. Also coat the bushing halves in the cylinder head and the bearing caps.

6. Take care not to move the camshaft chain so that it will rotate the crankshaft; fit the exhaust camshaft to the chain. The exhaust camshaft has a tachometer worm gear on it (**Figure 22**). The notch on the end of the cam goes to the right side of the engine.

7. Position the exhaust camshaft on its bushing halves so that the small timing mark on the edge of the drive sprocket lies parallel to and just above the top surface of the cylinder head boss (**Figure 26**).

8. Pull the cam chain tight and fit it onto the exhaust cam sprocket.

9. Notice which pin in the camshaft chain lies parallel to or just above the timing mark on the exhaust camshaft sprocket. Beginning with the pin above that one as number 1, count off 28 pins along the chain in the direction of the intake camshaft, and mark the 28th pin.

10. Taking care not to rotate the crankshaft, fit the intake camshaft to the chain and the mounts so that the 28th pin in the chain lies directly above the arrow and the number "28" stamped on the rubber surface of the drive sprocket (**Figure 27**).

NOTE: *Install the cam with the notch on the end to the right-hand side of the engine.*

NOTE: *There will be considerable chain slack between 2 camshafts—this will be taken up by the chain tensioners.*

11. Check that the top halves of the split bushings are in place in the 4 bearing caps, in the same positions from which they were removed, and that the dowels are in place (**Figure 28**).

12. Put the bushing caps on the camshafts.

NOTE: *Each of the 4 bushing caps is numbered to match its location marked on the cylinder head, and cast with an arrow which should point toward the front of the engine (Figure 29).*

13. Insert the 16 cap bolts in the 4 bushing caps, and tighten the 4 left inside bolts just enough to seat the camshafts.

14. Following the sequence in **Figure 30**, torque all the cap bolts. On 1979 and later models, torque the bolts to 12 ft.-lb. (1.7 mkg). On 1973-1978 models, torque the chrome bolts to 9 ft.-lb. (1.2 mkg) and the Parkerized (dark) bolts to 7 ft.-lb. (1.0 mkg).

NOTE: *Do not rotate either camshaft with Plastigage material in place.*

15. *If you are checking cam/bushing clearance with Plastigage,* remove the bolts in the same sequence in which they were tightened. Remove the bearing caps carefully. Remove the camshafts and measure the width of the flattened Plastigage according to manufacturer's instructions (**Figure 31**). If any bushing has a clearance greater than 0.006 in. (0.16mm), replace all 4 sets of split bushings for that camshaft with new ones.

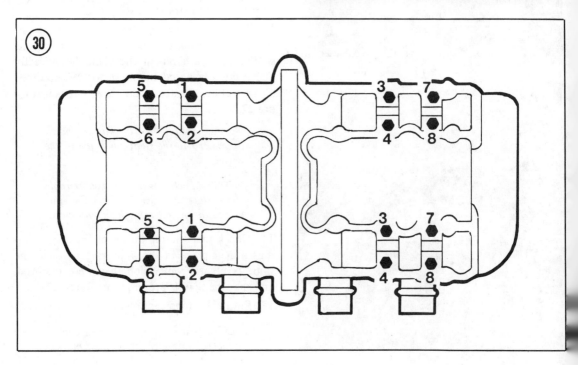

Clean all Plastigage from the cams and bushings and reinstall the camshafts (Steps 5 through 14).

16. Install the upper chain guide sprocket (**Figure 32**) and the 4 rubber dampers. If you have a KZ1000 with engine number between 22200 and 30000, check for a number "five" molded into the rubber dampers. If you don't have it, get new dampers from your dealer. The earlier parts wear out rapidly. Apply Loctite Lock 'N' Seal to the threads of the bolts before installing. Torque the bolts to 7 ft.-lb. (1.0 mkg).

NOTE: *Hold the 4 rubber dampers in place against the 4 bolts during assembly*

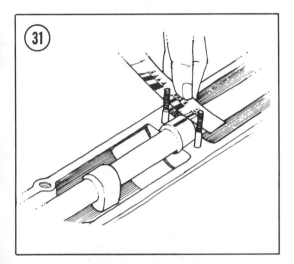

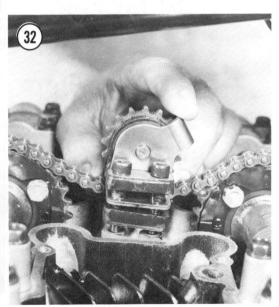

to prevent accidently dropping them into the crankcase, through the cam chain cavity.

CAUTION
If any of the rubber dampers fall into the crankcase, they must be removed prior to starting the engine. First, try retrieving them by removing the oil pan; if they cannot be located, the engine must be removed and disassembled. Do not run the engine with any of these loose parts in it.

17. *1973–1978:* Install the cam chain tensioner assembly on the cylinder block. Torque the mounting bolts to 14.5 ft.-lb. (1.0 mkg). Loosen the locknut and the bolt on the left side of the camshaft chain tensioner body, located on rear of cylinder block (**Figure 33**).

NOTE: *A spring inside the tensioner body will take up the slack in the camshaft chain.*

18. *1979 and later:* Unlock the automatic cam chain tensioner; remove the long bolt and install the original bolt and washer.

19. Before rotating the engine, make sure No. 1 and 4 cylinders are still at TDC and the timing marks on the camshafts are correctly aligned with the top of the cylinder head (**Figures 34-37**).

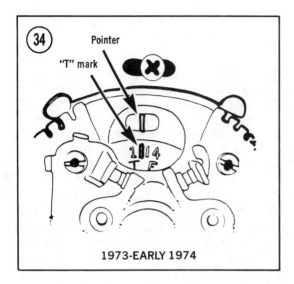

1973-EARLY 1974

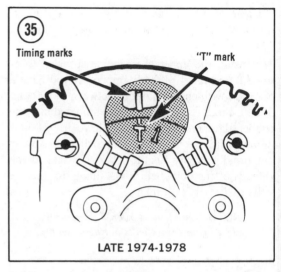

LATE 1974-1978

CAUTION
If any of these points are incorrect, rotating the crankshaft can cause severe internal damage to valves and pistons.

20. Rotate the crankshaft clockwise one complete revolution using a 17 mm wrench on the end of the crankshaft (**Figure 38**) until cylinders No. 1 and No. 4 are again at TDC.

CAUTION
If there is any binding while turning the crankshaft, stop. Determine the cause before proceeding.

Check to see that the timing marks on the camshaft sprockets are again aligned as they were when you installed the camshafts (**Figure 37**). If so, the cam timing is correct.

21. *1973–1978:* Tighten the cam chain tensioner lock bolt and locknut.

22. If you have replaced a camshaft or camshaft bushings with new ones, check the valve clearance now (see *Valve Clearance,* Chapter Three).

23. Install the tachometer drive. Coat the gearshaft with molybdenum disulfide grease and install the gear, O-ring (if equipped), guide/holder, stopper plate(s) and locking screw (**Figure 39**).

24. Coat the curved parts of the 4 rubber plugs at the ends of the cylinder head with liquid gasket sealer and install them (**Figure 40**).

25. Place the valve cover gasket and the valve cover on the cylinder head. Install the valve cover

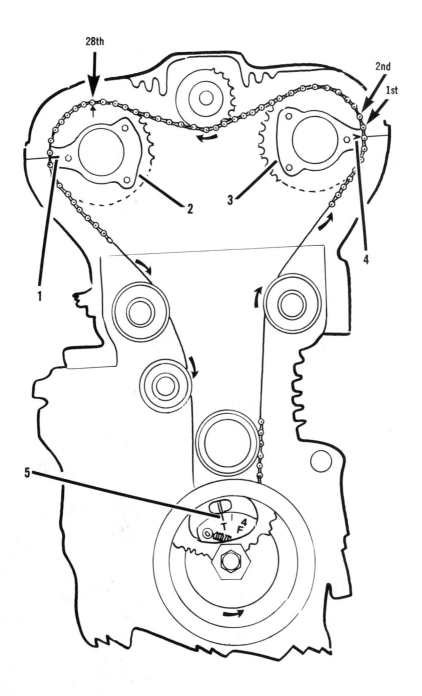

1. Timing mark
2. Inlet camshaft sprocket
3. Exhaust camshaft sprocket
4. Timing mark
5. #1, 4 TDC mark

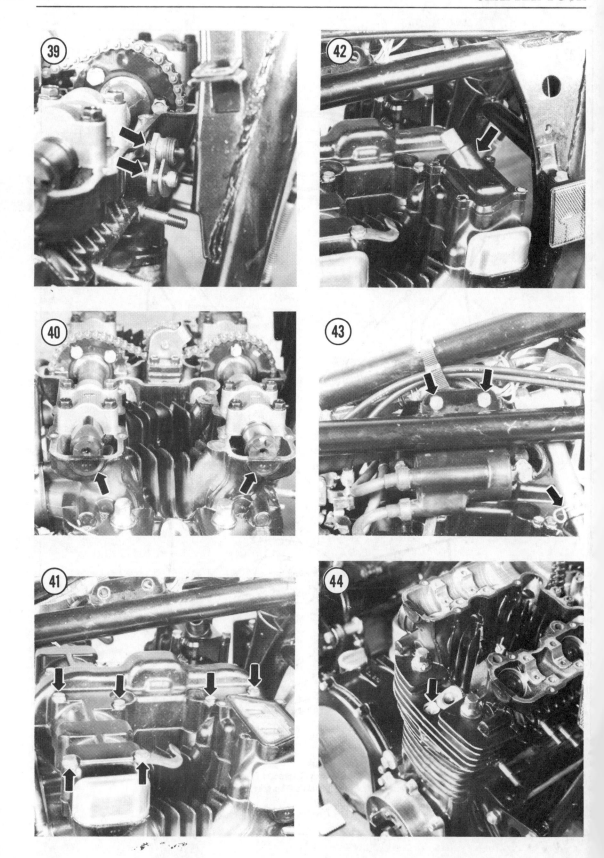

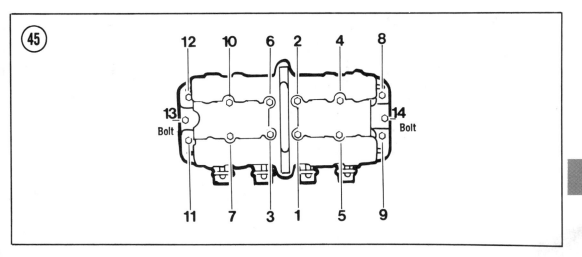

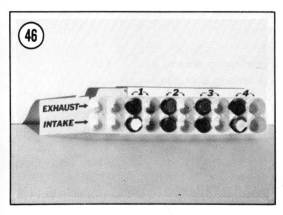

bolts and washers, and the spark plug cable clamps as originally installed (**Figure 41**). Torque the valve cover bolts to 11 ft.-lb. (1.5 mkg) on 1978 and later models, or to 9 ft.-lb. (1.2 mkg) on 1973–1977 models.

26. *1979 and later:* Install the 2 suction covers (**Figure 42**). Install a flat washer under each of the 8 bolts. Install the hoses on the suction covers and slide the hose clamps into place (**Figure 43**).

27. Install the ignition coils (**Figure 43** — shaft drive), fuel tank and battery ground lead. Install the ignition cover and gasket.

28. Check the idle and adjust if necessary.

29. After the engine has run and cooled off, re-torque the valve cover bolts.

CYLINDER HEAD

The alloy cylinder head has cast-in valve seats and pressed-in valve guides. Each valve operates against 2 coil springs, one inside the other.

As the valves and valve seats wear, the valves move closer to the camshaft, decreasing the clearance. When the clearance can no longer be restored by fitting thinner lifter cap shims, the end of the valve stem can be ground down once.

Engines manufactured prior to 1973 are equipped with a one-piece cylinder head gasket. The 1973 and later models are equipped with a 2-piece head gasket and an O-ring.

Cylinder Head Removal

1. Remove the camshafts (see *Camshaft Removal*).

2. Remove the exhaust system (see *Exhaust Removal*, Chapter Seven).

3. Remove the carburetor assembly (see *Carburetor Removal*, Chapter Seven).

4. Remove the 2 hex bolts located at the left and right ends of the cylinder head (shown removed in **Figure 44**).

5. Remove the 12 cylinder head nuts and washers (**Figure 45**).

6. Remove the valve lifters and shims at this time to avoid accidental mixup if they should come out while removing the head. Remove lifters and shims one cylinder at a time and place them into a container (like an egg carton — see **Figure 46**) marked with the specific cylinder and intake and exhaust. The No. 1 cylinder is on the left-hand side of the bike.

CAUTION
The lifters must be reinstalled into their original cylinder upon assembly.

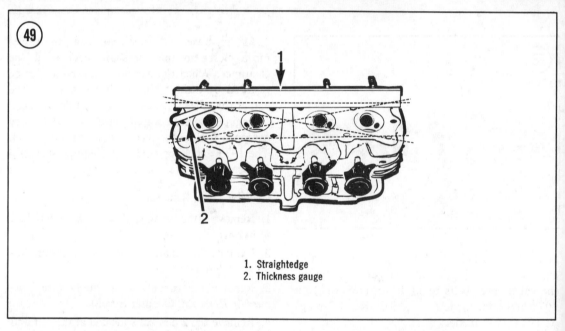

1. Straightedge
2. Thickness gauge

7. Loosen the head by tapping around the perimeter with a rubber or plastic mallet. If necessary, *gently* pry the head loose with a broad tipped screwdriver only in the ribbed areas of the fins (**Figure 47**).

> CAUTION
> *Remember the cooling fins are fragile and may be damaged if tapped or pried too hard. Never use a metal hammer.*

8. Lift the cylinder head straight up and off the studs and remove it.
9. Keep the cam chain tied up, and place a clean shop rag into the cam chain opening in the cylinder to prevent entry of foreign matter (**Figure 48**).

> NOTE: *If you are going to disassemble the valves yourself, go on to **Valve Removal**. Otherwise, take the cylinder head to a Kawasaki dealer for valve and valve seat work.*

Cylinder Head Inspection

1. Remove all traces of gasket from head and cylinder mating surface.

2. *Without removing the valves,* remove all deposits from the combustion chambers with a wire brush. A blunt scraper may be used if care is taken not to damage the head, valves, and spark plug threads.

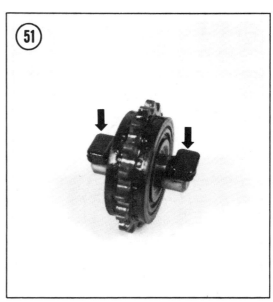

NOTE: *If one or more of the combustion chambers contained unusually large carbon deposits, check the valve guide and oil seals for those combustion chambers very carefully.*

3. After all carbon is removed from combustion chambers and valve intake and exhaust ports, clean the entire head in solvent.

4. Clean away all deposits on the piston crowns. Do not remove the carbon ridge at the top of the cylinder bore.

5. Check for cracks in the combustion chamber and exhaust ports. A cracked head must be replaced.

6. After the head has been thoroughly cleaned, place a straightedge across the gasket surface at several points. Measure warp by inserting a feeler gauge between the straightedge and cylinder head at each location (**Figure 49**). There should be less than 0.002 in. (0.05 mm) warp. If a small amount is present, the head can be resurfaced by a Kawasaki dealer or qualified machine shop.

Cylinder Head Installation

1. Check the condition of the front cam chain guide sprocket and the rear guide sprocket and

tensioner roller (**Figure 50**). Replace them if the sprocket teeth show signs of wear, or if the rubber is deteriorating.

2. Make sure the 4 rubber dampers on the guide sprocket and the cam chain tensioner shafts are bonded in place. The UP marks face up, away from the shafts (**Figure 51**).

NOTE: *The best adhesive to bond these dampers in place is one of the new "super glues" like Loctite Super Bonder, Permabond or equivalent. Read the manufacturer's instructions as this adhesive will stick your fingers together if you are not careful. Use it cautiously, and as instructed, and it will work wonders for you.*

NOTE: *If you have a very early Z1 prior to engine number 17089 that has a lot of cam chain noise, check to see that the guide roller shafts flats measure 0.30 in. (7.5 mm) high (Figure 52). If the shafts flats are only 0.18 in. (4.6 mm) high, you should get new shafts and dampers from your dealer to help quiet the cam chain. The cylinder block grooves must be widened by 0.020 in. (0.5 mm) on the inside (Figure 53) to accept the new roller shafts.*

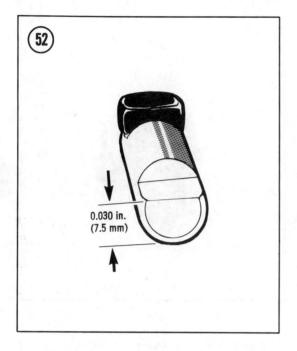

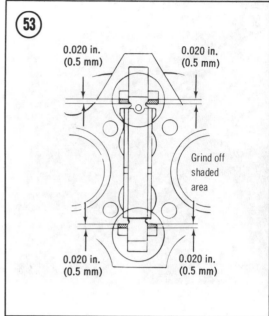

3. To install the cylinder head of a 1973 engine, lay a new cylinder head gasket on the cylinder block, with the wider crimped edges facing up (**Figure 54**).

4. To install the cylinder head on a 1974 or later engine, lay 2 new cylinder head gaskets (left and right are the same) on the cylinder block, with the wider crimped edges facing up. Place the O-ring in its groove between the 2 gaskets (**Figure 55**).

> NOTE: *Make sure the 2 locating dowels are in place.*

5. Place the cylinder head atop the cylinder block. Put the 12 washers and the 12 nuts on the studs.

> NOTE: *Copper washers are used at the outside corners of the cylinder head. These washers seal oil passages and must be in good condition to prevent oil leaks.*

6. Torque the cylinder head nuts first in the sequence shown in **Figure 56**. Tighten in 2 stages; first tighten to 18 ft.-lb (2.5 mkg) and second to 25 ft.-lb. (3.5 mkg) on 900cc models or to 29 ft.-lb. (4.0 mkg) on 1000cc models.

7. Install the 2 hex head bolts, at the left end and the right end of the cylinder head. Torque each one to 8.5 ft.-lb. (1.2 mkg).

8. Oil and install the valve lifters and shims in the same locations from which they were removed. Apply molybdenum disulfide grease if the parts are new.

9. Install the spark plugs.

10. Install the camshafts.

11. Install the carburetors, and adjust the throttle cables.

12. Install the exhaust system.

13. Install the gas tank.

14. Check idle and adjust the carburetors, if necessary.

VALVES

Removal

1. Refer to **Figure 57**. Remove the cylinder head (see *Cylinder Head Removal*).

2. Fit a valve spring compressor to the valve spring retainer and bottom of the valve head (**Figure 58**). Use the tool to press down the valve spring retainer and expose the split keepers on the valve stem. Remove the keepers.

3. Retract the compressor tool and remove it from the valve.

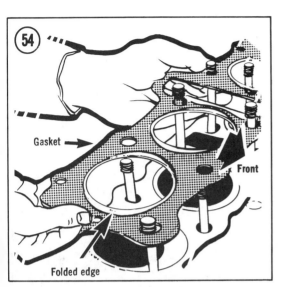

Gasket

Front

Folded edge

A. O-ring   B. Wide edge

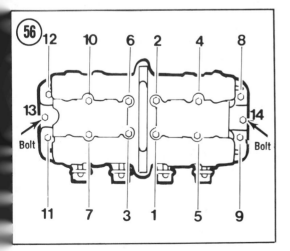

12 10 6 2 4 8

13   14

Bolt   Bolt

11 7 3 1 5 9

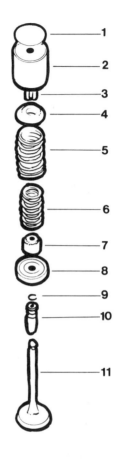

1
2
3
4
5
6
7
8
9
10
11

1. Shim
2. Valve lifter
3. Split keeper
4. Valve spring retainer
5. Outer valve spring
6. Inner valve spring
7. Oil seal
8. Valve spring seat
9. Circlip
10. Valve guide
11. Valve

CAUTION
Remove any burrs from the valve stem grooves before removing the valve. Otherwise the valve guides will be damaged.

4. Take out the valve spring retainer, the 2 springs, the spring seat, and the valve as shown in **Figure 59**.

Inspection

1. Clean valves with a wire brush and solvent.

2. Inspect the contact surface of each valve for burning (**Figure 60**). Minor roughness and pitting can be removed by lapping the valve as described under *Valve Lapping* in this chapter. Excessive unevenness of the contact surface is an indication that the valve is not serviceable. The contact surface of the valve may be ground on a valve grinding machine, but it is best to replace a burned or damaged valve with a new one.

Inspect the valve stems for wear and roughness and measure the vertical runout of the valve stem as shown in **Figure 61**. The runout should not exceed 0.002 in. (0.05 mm).

3. Measure valve stems for wear (**Figure 62**). Replace the valve if any stem diameter is less 0.270 in. (6.85 mm) on 900cc models or 0.272 in. (6.90 mm) on 1000cc models.

4. Remove all carbon and varnish from the valve guides with a stiff spiral wire brush.

5. Insert each valve in its guide. Hold the valve just slightly off its seat and rock it sideways. If it rocks more than slightly, the guide is probably worn and should be replaced. As a final check, take the head to a dealer and have the valve guides measured.

When guides are worn so that there is excessive stem to guide clearance or valve tipping, they must be replaced. Replace all, even if only one is worn. This job should only be done by a Kawasaki dealer, as special tools are required.

6. *On 900cc models:* Check valve spring free length with a vernier caliper. Replace any inner spring shorter than 1.38 in. (35 mm) and any outer spring shorter than 1.50 in. (38 mm). See **Figure 63**.

7. *On 1000cc models:* Valve springs must be checked for tension *while compressed*. See **Table 1** at the end of this chapter for compression specifications.

8. Measure each valve spring (inner and outer) for straightness by standing it on a flat surface and butting it against the vertical edge of a square (**Figure 64**). Install a new spring if the gap at the top is more than 0.075 in. (1.9 mm) on 900cc models or 0.060 in. (1.5 mm) on 1000cc models.

9. Check the valve spring retainer and valve keepers. If they are in good condition, they may be reused.

10. Inspect the valve seats. If worn or burned, they must be reconditioned. This should be performed by your dealer or local machine shop. If you are performing the work yourself, see **Table 1** at the end of this chapter for seat and width specifications (**Figure 65**).

Seats and valves in near-perfect condition can be reconditioned by lapping with fine carborundum paste. Lapping, however, is always inferior to precision grinding.

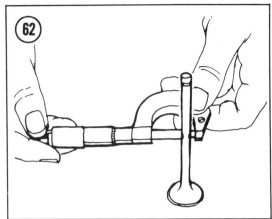

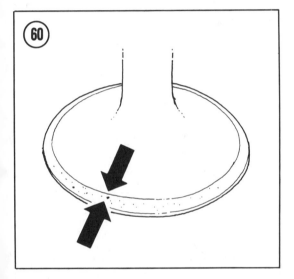

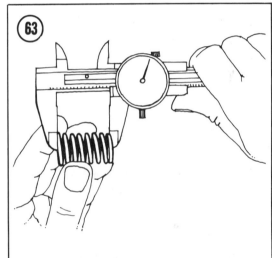

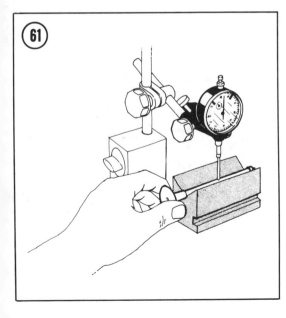

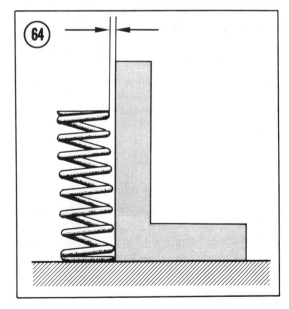

4

11. *1979 and later:* Check the air suction passages in cylinder head exhaust ports. Clean them if necessary (**Figure 66**).

Valve Lapping

Valve lapping is a simple operation which can restore the valve seal without machining if the amount of wear or distortion is not too great.

> NOTE: *Valve lapping is not a substitute for precision grinding or cutting of valves and their seats. Get a professional opinion on whether lapping will do the job before you settle for it.*

1. Coat the valve seating area in the head with a lapping compound such as Carborundum or Clover Brand.

2. Insert the valve into the head.

3. Wet the suction cup of the lapping stick (**Figure 67**) and stick it onto the head of the valve. Lap the valve to the seat by rotating the lapping stick in both directions. Every 5 to 10 seconds, rotate the valve 180° in the seat; continue lapping until the contact surfaces of the valve and the valve seat are a uniform grey (**Figure 68**). Stop as soon as they are, to avoid removing too much material.

4. Thoroughly clean the valves and cylinder head in solvent to remove all grinding compound. Any compound left on the valves of the cylinder head will end up in the engine and will cause damage.

After the lapping has been completed and the valve assemblies have been reinstalled into the head, the valve seal should be tested. Check the seal of each valve by pouring solvent into each of the intake and exhaust ports. There should be no leakage past the seat. If fluid leaks past any of the seats, disassemble that valve assembly and repeat the lapping procedure until there is no leakage.

Valve Stem Height

If the valve faces or seats were reground or recut, the valves will drop deeper into the cylinder head. Check valve stem installed height before you assemble the valves in the cylinder head. Otherwise you may not be able to get proper valve clearance with the available shims.

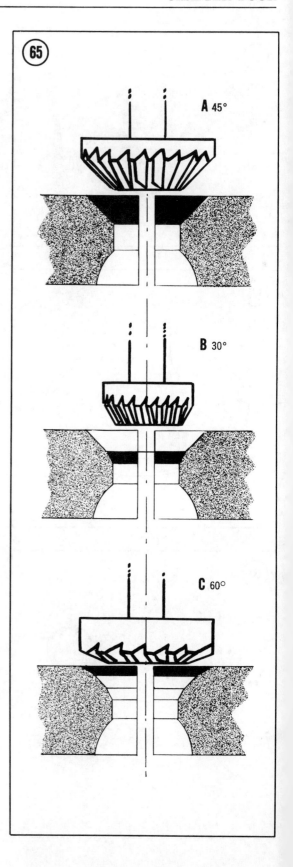

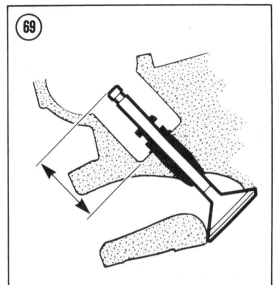

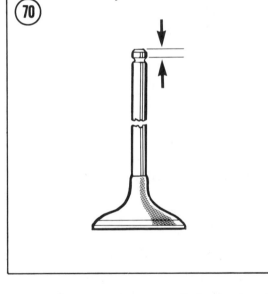

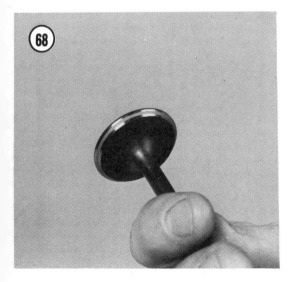

1. Insert the valve into the cylinder head and measure valve stem height (**Figure 69**).

2. If stem height is more than 1.499 in. (38.07 mm), the valve is too long for that cylinder. Swap valves, or grind a *maximum* of 0.012 in. (0.3 mm) off the valve stem end.

CAUTION
*If the valve stub (**Figure 70**) is ground to less than 0.165 in. (4.2 mm) the valve lifter may hit the spring retainer and drop the valve into the engine while running.*

Valve Installation

1. Refer to **Figure 71**. Remove the old oil seals and install new seals on the valve guides.

2. Coat the valve stems with molybdenum disulphide paste and insert them into the cylinder head.

3. On the valve stem, assemble the valve spring seat, the 2 valve springs, and the valve spring retainer.

> NOTE: *If variable pitch springs are used, install the springs with the closely-wound coils toward the cylinder head (Figure 72).*

4. Fit the valve spring compressor to the valve spring retainer and the bottom of the valve head. Use the tool to press down the retainer and expose the keeper groove on the valve stem. Fit the keepers and remove the spring compressor. Make sure the keepers are securely seated. Tap the stem end lightly with a hammer if necessary to jar the keepers into place.

> NOTE: *The 1000cc models use rounded grooves in the valve stems and keepers, along with iron valve guides instead of bronze (Figure 73). Do not use iron valve guides on earlier engines; rapid valve stem wear will result.*

5. Install the cylinder head (see *Cylinder Head Installation*).

6. Adjust valve clearance.

CYLINDER BLOCK AND PISTONS

The alloy cylinder block has pressed-in cylinder sleeves, which can be bored to 1 mm oversize.

Each piston is fitted with 3 rings. The top 2 rings are compression rings, to prevent compression blow-by into the crankcase. The bottom ring is an oil scraper ring, to keep excess oil out of the combustion chamber (**Figure 74**).

Cylinder and Piston Removal

1. Remove the camshafts (see *Camshaft Removal*).

2. Remove the exhaust system (see *Exhaust Removal*, Chapter Seven).

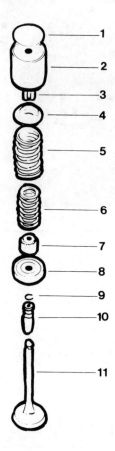

1. Shim
2. Valve lifter
3. Split keeper
4. Valve spring retainer
5. Outer valve spring
6. Inner valve spring
7. Oil seal
8. Valve spring seat
9. Circlip
10. Valve guide
11. Valve

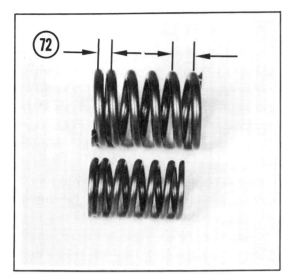

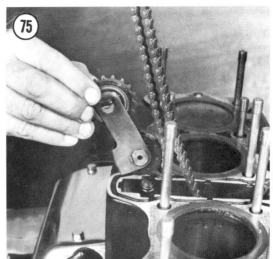

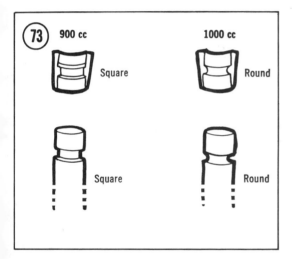

3. Remove the carburetor assembly (see *Carburetor Removal*, Chapter Seven).

4. Remove the cylinder head (see *Cylinder Head Removal*).

5. Remove the camshaft chain tensioner assembly and the guide sprocket from the top of the cylinder block (**Figure 75**).

> NOTE: *Be careful when removing these items as there are 2 small rubber dampers on top of each sprocket shaft. If they fall off, they will drop into the crankcase and will have to be removed.*

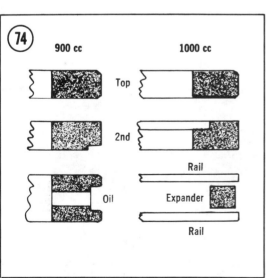

6. Loosen the cylinder by tapping around the perimeter with a rubber or plastic mallet (**Figure 76**). If necessary, *gently* pry the cylinder loose with a broad tipped screwdriver only in the ribbed areas of the fins.

CAUTION
Remember the cooling fins are fragile and may be damaged if tapped or pried too hard. Do not use a metal hammer.

NOTE: *Later models have a cast-in pry point at the cylinder base (Figure 77). Use the widest tool that will fit the slot. Do not hammer into the opening.*

7. Pull the cylinder straight up and off the pistons and cylinder studs.

NOTE: *Be sure to keep the cam chain wired up to keep it from falling into the crankcase.*

Keep track of the 2 dowel pins on the outermost front cylinder head studs.

8. To remove a piston, stuff rags into the top of the crankcase beneath the piston, to catch any small parts that might drop down.

9. Lightly mark the top of the piston with a 1, 2, 3 and 4 so that they will be installed into the correct cylinder. Remember No. 1 cylinder is on the left side.

10. Before removing the piston, hold the rod tightly and rock piston as shown in **Figure 78**. Any rocking motion (do not confuse with the normal side-to-side sliding motion) indicates wear on the wrist pin, rod small end, pin bore, or more likely, a combination of all three. If there is detectable rocking, install new pistons and wrist pins. Mark the piston and pin, so that they will be reassembled into the same set.

11. Remove the circlips from the wrist pin bores (**Figure 79**).

12. Heat the piston and pin gently with a small butane torch. The pin will probably slide right out. If not, heat the piston to about 140°F (60°C), or until it is too warm to touch, but not excessively hot. If the pin is still difficult to push out, use a homemade tool as shown in **Figure 80**.

CAUTION
When removing the wrist pin, take care not to put any side pressure on the piston to avoid bending the connecting rod; it was not designed to handle side loads.

13. After you remove the piston, remove the top ring by spreading the ends with your thumbs just enough to slide it up over the piston (**Figure 81**). Repeat for the remaining rings.

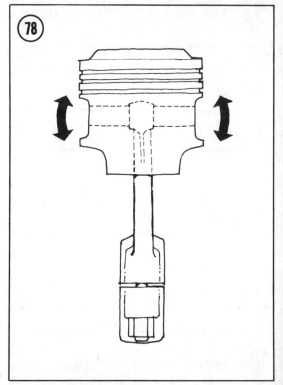

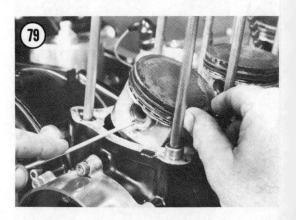

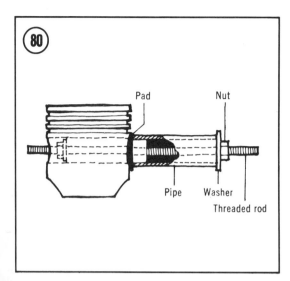

Pad · Nut · Pipe · Washer · Threaded rod

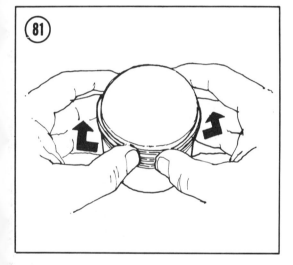

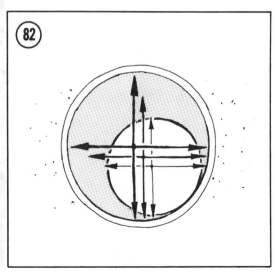

4

Cylinder Inspection

1. Measure the cylinder bores, with a cylinder gauge or inside micrometer at the points shown in **Figure 82**.

2. Measure in 2 axes—in line with the wrist pin and at 90° to the pin. If any measurement exceeds 2.60 in. (66.1 mm) on 900cc models or 2.76 in. (70.1 mm) on 1000cc models, or if the taper or out-of-round is greater than 0.002 in. (0.05 mm), the cylinders must be rebored to the next oversize and new pistons and rings installed. Rebore all cylinders even though only one may be faulty.

> NOTE: *The new pistons should be obtained first, before the cylinders are bored, so that pistons can be measured; slight manufacturing tolerances must be taken into account to determine the actual size and the working clearance.*

3. Check the cylinder walls for scratches; if evident, the cylinders should be rebored.

Piston Inspection

1. Carefully clean the carbon from the piston crown with a chemical remover or with a soft scraper. Do not remove or damage the carbon ridge around the circumference of the piston above the top ring. If the pistons, rings, and cylinders are dimensionally correct and can be reused, removal of the carbon ridges from the tops of cylinders will promote excessive oil consumption.

CAUTION
Do not wire brush piston skirts.

2. Examine each ring groove for burrs, dented edges, and wide wear. Pay particular attention to the top compression ring groove, as it usually wears more than the others.

3. Measure piston-to-cylinder clearance as described under *Piston Clearance* in this chapter.

4. Check piston wear; measure the outside diameter of the piston with a micrometer. Take the measurement 3/16 in. (5 mm) above the bottom

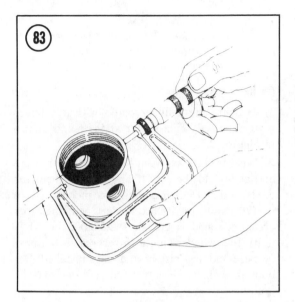

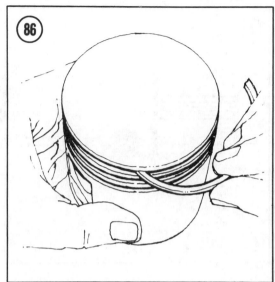

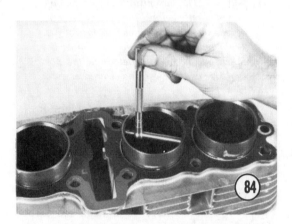

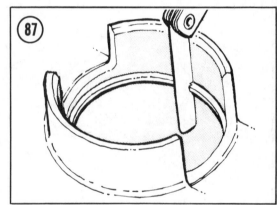

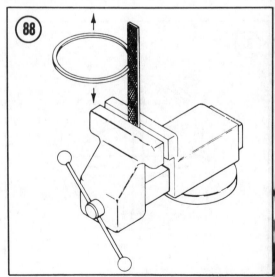

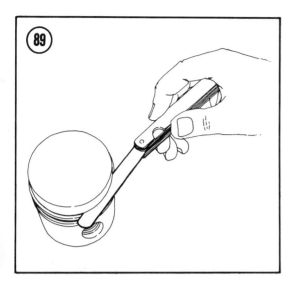

of the piston skirt, at a 90 degree angle to the wrist pin bores (**Figure 83**). If the diameter of the piston measures less than 2.50 in. (65.8 mm) on 900cc models or 2.75 in. (69.8 mm) on 1000cc models install new pistons.

Piston Clearance

1. With a cylinder gauge, measure the inside diameter of the cylinder just above its bottom edge where it will have undergone the least amount of wear (**Figure 84**).

2. To find the cylinder/piston clearance, subtract the outside diameter of the piston from the inside diameter of the cylinder.

3. The standard cylinder/piston clearance is 0.0025 – 0.003 in. (0.060 – 0.079 mm) on 900cc models or 0.0017 – 0.0026 in. (0.043 – 0.070 mm) on 1000cc models.

If a cylinder has not worn past the acceptable inside diameter limit, and installing a new piston will bring the clearance within tolerance, the cylinder block need not be bored. However, in no case should the cylinder/piston clearance be less than the minimum.

> NOTE: *You can also measure actual piston/cylinder clearance with a feeler gauge (Figure 85). The piston should be just free enough to slide with a light push. This method is **not** as accurate as micrometer measurement calculation.*

Piston Ring Inspection

1. Carefully remove all carbon from the ring grooves (an old ring piece makes a good scraper). See **Figure 86**. Inspect the grooves carefully for burrs, nicks, or broken and cracked lands. Recondition or replace the piston if necessary.

2. Check the end gap of each ring; insert the ring into the bottom of the cylinder bore and square it with the wall by tapping with the piston. Measure the gap with a feeler gauge (**Figure 87**). A new ring's gap should be 0.008 – 0.016 in. (0.2 – 0.4 mm) on 900cc models or 0.012 – 0.020 in. (0.3 – 0.5 mm) on 1000cc models.

If the gap is smaller than specified, hold a small file in a vise, grip the ends of the ring with your fingers, and enlarge the gap (**Figure 88**).

> NOTE: *An old ring can be re-used with an end gap up to 0.028 in. (0.7 mm) for 900cc models or 0.031 in. (0.8 mm) for 1000cc models.*

3. Install the rings on the piston.

> NOTE: *Install all rings with their markings facing up.*

4. Slide the rings around in their grooves to make sure there is no binding. Check the side clearance of each ring with a feeler gauge (**Figure 89**). Refer to **Table 1**.

If the clearance is incorrect, replace the pistons, or rings, or both.

Connecting Rod Inspection

1. Measure the inside diameter of the small ends of the connecting rods with an inside dial gauge. If the inside diameter measures more than 0.671 in. (17.05 mm) the whole crankshaft assembly should be replaced. Separate parts are not available.

2. Check each rod for obvious damage such as cracks and burns.

3. Check the connecting rod big-end bearing play; you can make a quick check by simply rocking the connecting rods back and forth (**Figure 90**). If there is more than a very slight rocking motion (some side-to-side *sliding* is normal), you should measure big-end bearing play. Get a professional opinion before you split the crankcases.

Refer to *Crankshaft Inspection*, in this chapter.

Cam Chain Inspection

Removal of the chain requires splitting the crankcases, but you can check cam chain wear on the 1000cc engines. Stretch a length of the cam chain with about a 10 lb. (5 kg) pull, and measure a 20-link length. If 20 links exceed 6.21 in. (157.8 mm), the cam chain must be replaced (see *Crankshaft Removal*).

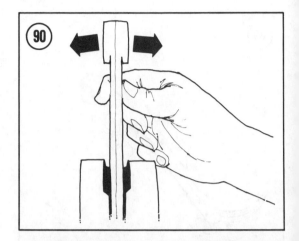

Piston and Cylinder Installation

1. Check the condition of the lower cam chain guide roller (**Figure 91**) and the front guide rubber (**Figure 92**). Replace them if the rubber has worn or deteriorated.

2. Make sure the 2 rubber dampers on the roller shaft are bonded in place.

3. Install the guide roller assembly in the crankcase, and check that the 2 hollow dowel pins are around the front outer cylinder studs (**Figure 93**).

4. Install the bottom oil ring on the piston with a ring expander tool, or by spreading the ends with your thumbs (**Figure 94**). On a 3 piece oil ring, install the expander first.

5. Install the second and top rings.

> NOTE: *Install all rings with their markings (Figure 95) facing up.*

6. Coat the connecting rod holes, piston pin, and piston holes with clean engine oil.

> CAUTION
> *Be sure to install the correct piston onto the same rod from which it was removed, No. 1, 2, 3, or 4.*

7. To install a piston, position it atop the rod so that the arrow on the piston crown faces forward (**Figure 96**).

> NOTE: *Up to 1979, new pistons were marked on top for selective fit with new wrist pins and cylinders. If many new parts are available, match a marked wrist pin (Figure 97) with an "A" piston, and an unmarked wrist pin with a "B" piston. Also it is preferable to match a numbered piston with a correspondingly numbered cylinder bore (Figure 98).*

8. Insert the piston pin and tap it with a plastic mallet until it starts into the connecting rod bush-

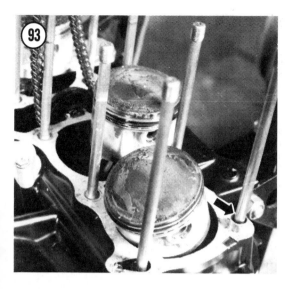

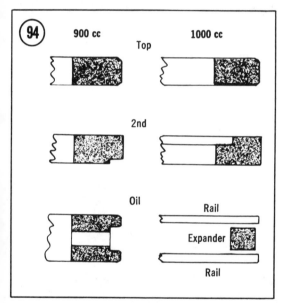

900 cc	1000 cc
Top	

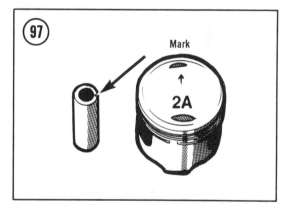

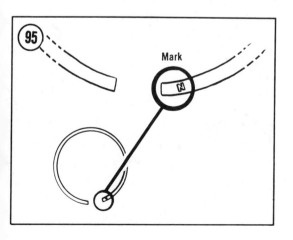

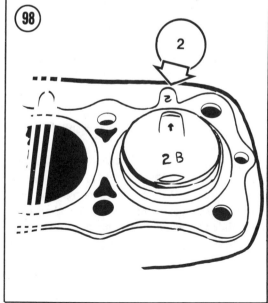

4

ing. If it does not slide in easily, heat the piston until it is too warm to touch but not excessively hot (140°F or 60°C). Hold the piston so that the rod does not take any shock. Otherwise, it may be bent. If the pin is still difficult to install, use the homemade tool shown in **Figure 99**, but eliminate the piece of pipe.

9. Install a new circlip on each side of the piston pin on all pistons. After installing each circlip, rotate it so that the gap lies at the bottom or top.

10. To minimize blow-by, rotate the top and bottom ring on each piston so that the ring ends face forward. Rotate the second ring so that its ends face the rear of the engine (**Figure 100**). With 3-piece oil rings, the 2 rails should each be offset about 30° to either side of the expander opening.

11. Check that the top surface of the crankcase and the bottom surface of the cylinder are clean prior to installing new gaskets. Blow out the oil passages with compressed air to remove any particles or dirt that may slow down oil flow.

12. Lay a new cylinder base gasket atop the crankcase. Make sure all holes align.

13. *1000cc:* Install a new O-ring around each of the 4 cylinder base spigots.

14. Apply a little sealant, such as GE Silicone Sealant, around the 4 inner rear cylinder studs (**Figure 101**). Wipe off any excess.

15. Install a piston holding fixture under the 2 inner pistons protruding out of the crankcase opening (**Figure 101**).

> NOTE: *These fixtures may be purchased or may be homemade units of wood. See **Figure 102** for dimensions.*

16. Apply assembly oil to the piston rings and cylinder walls. Use molybdenum disulfide grease on *new* pistons.

17. Carefully install the cylinder onto the cylinder studs (**Figure 103**) and slide it down over the inner 2 pistons. Compress each piston ring with your fingers as the cylinder starts to slide over it. Then slide the cylinder over the outer pistons.

18. Remove the piston holding fixture and push the cylinder down all the way.

19. Install the cylinder head as described under *Cylinder Head Installation* in this chapter.

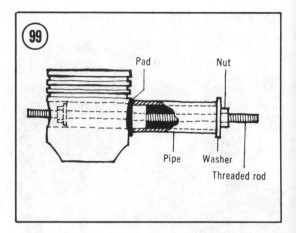

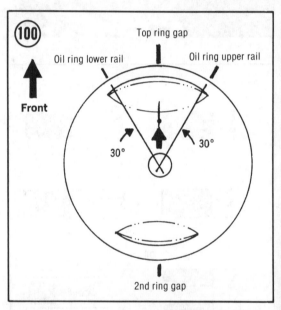

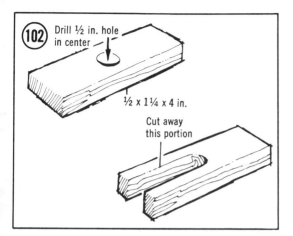

(102) Drill ½ in. hole in center

½ x 1¼ x 4 in.

Cut away this portion

(103)

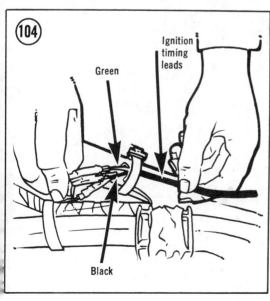

(104)

Green

Ignition timing leads

Black

ENGINE REMOVAL/INSTALLATION

Engine removal is required to split the crankcases for crankshaft, cam chain, clutch outer housing, transmission, and kickstarter ratchet service. Although the following parts can be left attached for engine removal, we recommend that you remove them first.

    a. Camshafts

    b. Cylinder head

    c. Cylinder block and pistons

    d. Clutch hub and plates (Chapter Five)

    e. Alternator rotor (Chapter Twelve)

It makes for handling a much lighter engine; and while the engine is in the frame, you can use the rear brake to lock the drive train, instead of resorting to makeshift or expensive tools. Once the engine is removed from the frame, some parts (like the alternator, drive sprocket, and clutch) can not be removed from the engine without special tools.

Engine Removal (Chain Drive)

1. Disconnect the battery ground (–) cable.

2. Drain the engine oil; remove the engine oil drain plug and the oil filter drain plug, if equipped.

3. Remove the fuel tank (see *Fuel Tank Removal*, Chapter Seven).

4. Remove the exhaust system (see *Exhaust Removal*, Chapter Seven).

5. Pull the spark plug caps off the spark plugs.

6. Under the top frame tube, unplug the connectors joining the black wires and the green wires (**Figure 104**).

7. At the front of the cylinder head, unscrew the tachometer drive cable and remove it from the head.

8. Remove the carburetor block as an assembly (see *Carburetor Removal*, Chapter Seven).

9. Take the screen off the top of the air cleaner.

10. Atop the engine cases, work the oil breather hose clamp up the hose. Pull the hose off the oil breather.

11. Remove the air cleaner housing.

12. *1979 and later:* If you didn't remove the cylinder head, loosen the vacuum switch hose clamps and remove the vacuum switch and hose

assembly (**Figure 105**); then remove the left air suction valve cover.

13. The starter relay is behind the side cover. Pull down the rubber cap and unbolt the starter cable from the solenoid (**Figure 106**). Remove the cable from the cable clamp.

14. Unplug the blue alternator cable connector behind the side cover (**Figure 106**).

15. Unbolt the negative (black) battery wire from its ground on the engine. If other wires are grounded by the same bolt, release them also (**Figure 107**).

16. Unscrew the 2 cap nuts that mount the right front footpeg assembly to the motorcycle frame. Remove the footpeg assembly from its mounting studs.

17. Remove the chain cover (see *Sprocket Cover Removal,* Chapter Six).

18. Remove output sprocket (see *Drive Sprocket Removal,* Chapter Six).

19. To the rear of the kickstarter lever, remove the brake light switch from its mount. Unhook the spring.

20a. *Drum brake:* On the right side of the rear wheel, unscrew the brake rod nut until it is flush with the rear of the brake rod.

20b. *Disc brakes:* Remove the 2 rear master cylinder mounting bolts and the side cover bracket, if equipped.

21. Loosen the locknut on the brake pedal positioning bolt. Back out the bolt far enough to depress the pedal below the frame rail tube (**Figure 108**).

22. Place the motorcycle on its centerstand and a jack beneath the engine. Jack up the engine just enough to take the weight off the engine mount bolts.

23. Remove the short engine mount bolt from the lower center bracket on each side of the frame (**Figure 109**).

24. On the right side of the frame, remove the 2 upper rear bracket mounting bolts. Remove the bracket.

25. Remove the 2 lower center bracket mounting bolts on the right side of the frame. Remove the bracket.

26. Remove the 2 front bracket mounting bolts on the right side of the frame. Remove the bracket.

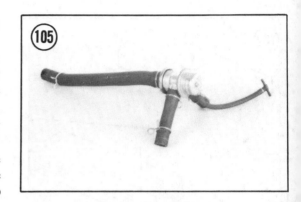

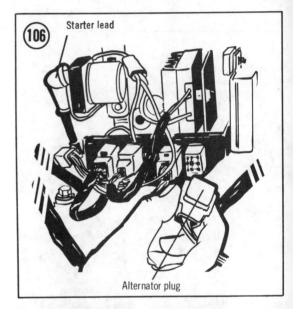

Starter lead

Alternator plug

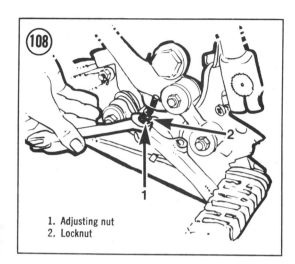

1. Adjusting nut
2. Locknut

27. Remove the (long) front, lower rear, and upper rear engine mount bolts.

28. Pull the engine up slightly and to the right side so that it clears the lower front and rear right mounting support brackets.

WARNING
*If the recommended parts have **not** been removed, this final step requires 2 people to safely remove the engine from the frame.*

Pull the engine out through the right side of the frame. Take it to your workbench for further disassembly.

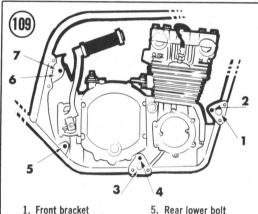

1. Front bracket	5. Rear lower bolt
2. Front bolt	6. Rear upper bracket
3. Lower center bracket	7. Rear upper bolt
4. Lower center bolt	

Engine Removal (Shaft Drive)

1. Disconnect the battery ground (–) cable.

2. Drain the engine oil; remove the engine oil drain plug and the oil filter drain plug, if equipped.

3. Remove the fuel tank (see *Fuel Tank Removal*, Chapter Seven).

4. Remove the exhaust system (see *Exhaust System Removal*, Chapter Seven).

5. Disconnect the spark plug wires and remove the 2 ignition coils (**Figure 110**).

6. Slide the hose clamps up (**Figure 110**), and remove the vacuum switch and hose assembly (**Figure 111**).

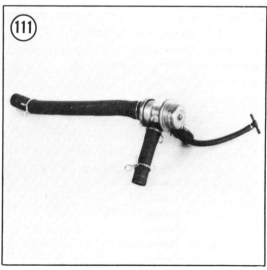

7. Remove the left air suction valve cover.

8. Under the left side cover, disconnect the 6-pole alternator connector (**Figure 112**).

9. Remove the 2 brackets from the air cleaner housing (**Figure 112**).

10. Loosen the clamp (**Figure 112**) connecting the silencer to the air cleaner housing, and remove the housing.

11. Under the right side cover, remove the 3 bolts and open the electrical panel (**Figure 113**).

12. Disconnect the starter lead from the starter solenoid (**Figure 114**).

13. Disconnect the 4-pole pickup coil connector (**Figure 115**), then close the electrical cover.

14. Remove the rear brake light switch (**Figure 116**).

15. Disconnect the battery ground lead at the rear of the engine (**Figure 117**).

16. Remove the 2 rear master cylinder mounting bolts (**Figure 116**), then push the brake pedal down below the frame tube.

17. Remove the right footpeg assembly.

18. Remove the side marker reflectors from the downtubes.

19. Disconnect the tachometer cable at the cylinder head.

20. Remove the front bevel gearcase (see *Front Bevel Removal,* Chapter Six).

21. Remove the shift linkage and shift shaft; spread the arms from the shift drum, turn the shift shaft counterclockwise (to the left), and pull the shaft and linkage out (**Figure 118**).

22. Take a final look all over the engine to make sure everything has been disconnected.

23. Loosen, then remove, all engine mounting bolts and nuts (**Figures 119 and 120**).

> NOTE: *The upper rear mounting bolt has 2 spacers.*

> NOTE: *Bolt removal will be easier if you jack or lever the engine up slightly to take the weight off the bolts.*

WARNING
Keep your hands clear as you remove the bolts. The engine can easily smash your fingers.

A. Housing brackets   B. Alternator plug   C. Clamp

26. See **Figure 121**. Pull the engine up slightly and to the right side so that it clears the lower front and rear right mounting support brackets.

> WARNING
> *If the recommended parts have **not** been removed, this final step requires 2 people to safely remove the engine from the frame.*

Pull the engine out through the right side of the frame. Take it to the workbench for further disassembly.

Engine Installation

If you have removed the recommended parts (camshafts, cylinder head, block and pistons, alternator, and clutch) leave them off until you have installed the bare engine in the frame. Otherwise 2 people will be required for installation.

> NOTE: *Bolt removal will be easier if you jack or lever the engine up slightly to take the weight off the bolts.*

> WARNING
> *Keep your hands clear as you install the bolts. The engine can easily smash your fingers.*

1. Install the engine through the right side of the frame.

2. Install the 3 engine mounting brackets loosely with 2 front nuts and lockwashers and 4 bolts with lockwashers (**Figures 119, 120**).

3. Lift the engine and insert the 3 long bolts. The upper rear bolt has 2 spacers.

4. Insert the 3 short bolts with lockwashers. The 2 bolts under the middle of the engine get nut plates (**Figure 122**).

5. Tighten the engine mounting bracket bolts to 17.5 ft.-lb. (2.4 mkg).

6. Tighten the engine mounting bolts to 29 ft.-lb. (4.0 mkg).

7. To assemble the rest of the motorcycle, reverse the removal procedures, noting the following.

All models: After connecting multiple-pin plastic connectors, make sure none of the male pins have popped out of place. Tug on the wires to find a loose pin, and push loose pins back into place until you feel the locking tang seat fully.

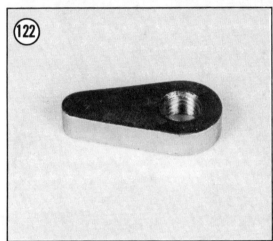

After installing the engine, secure the ignition timing leads in the clamps attached to the bottom crankcase (**Figure 123**).

Route the alternator and starter leads behind the shift mechanism cover tabs or bevel drive case tabs (**Figure 124**).

1977 and later: When installing the footpeg assemblies, lubricate the damper rubbers with soapy water to prevent damper damage.

Make sure the air cleaner ducts are installed with the "UP" marks up and the "L" marked

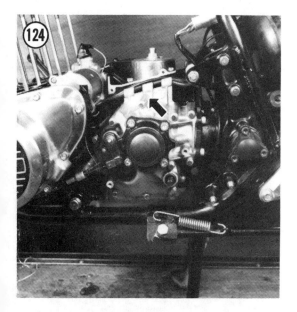

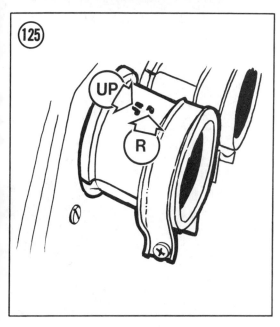

duct on the left and the "R" duct on the right (**Figure 125**).

1979 and later: The air suction valve cover bolts have a flat washer. Torque the bolts to 11 ft.-lb. (1.5 mkg).

1979 and later chain drive: The ignition coil resistor attaches to the coil front mounting bolts with the leads facing forward.

8. Adjust the throttle cables, clutch, rear brake, and rear brake light switch (see Chapter Three).

9. Check that the drain plugs are installed and add engine oil (see Chapter Three).

10. Start the engine and check for leaks.

OIL PUMP

The oil pump, which is geared to the crankshaft, is in the bottom of the crankcase toward the left side of the engine. The low pressure double gear pump pulls oil through a coarse mesh screen and pushes it through the filter to trap the finer particles. (If the filter becomes clogged, a bypass valve routes the oil—still dirty—around the filter.)

From the filter, the oil goes through the oil pressure switch, which turns off the warning light on the instrument panel whenever: (a) the engine rpm exceeds 1,300; and (b) there is oil coming through the lines. Beyond that point the oil flow is split among 3 passageways. The first passageway goes to the crankshaft main bearings and big-end bearings, the spray from which lubricates the cylinder walls and the wrist pins. The second passageway leads to the camshaft bushings; after the oil leaves the bushings it lubricates the cams and the valves. The third passage directs oil to the transmission main shaft and output shaft bearings. After lubricating the engine components, the oil eventually drips back down into the crankcase sump.

Oil Pressure Check

To check the functioning of the oil pump, remove the plug from the oil pressure check point on the right side of the crankcase, and screw in the fitting of an oil pressure gauge (Kawasaki special tool available). See **Figure 126**. Start the engine and run it long enough to warm the oil to 140° F (60° C). Hold rpm steady at 3,000, and

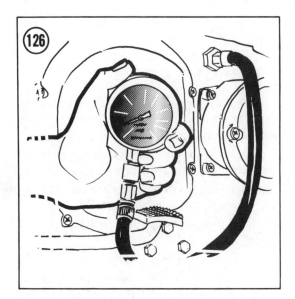

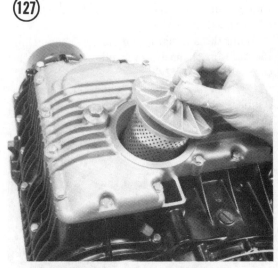

check the gauge. The gauge should read 2.8 psi. If the pressure is less than 2.0 psi, check the lubrication system.

Oil Pump Removal

The oil pump can be removed without removing the engine from the frame. For clarity, the engine is shown removed.

1. Drain the engine oil (see Chapter Three).

2. Remove the oil filter (**Figure 127**).

3. Remove the exhaust system (see *Exhaust Removal,* Chapter Seven).

4. Remove the 17 bolts and washers that mount the oil pan to the crankcase (**Figure 128**). Remove the oil pan, gasket, and O-ring.

5. Remove the 3 bolts and washers that mount the oil pump to the crankshaft (**Figure 129**). Pull out the oil pump and its driving gear.

Oil Pump Disassembly

1. See **Figure 130**. Inspect the outer housing for cracks (**Figure 131**).

2. Pop off the circlip that mounts the driving gear to its shaft (**Figure 132**). Take off the driving gear, the alignment pin, and the shim.

3. Remove the pump body screws.

4. Alternately tap the ends of the 2 gearshafts gently with a plastic mallet, to loosen the pump body cover.

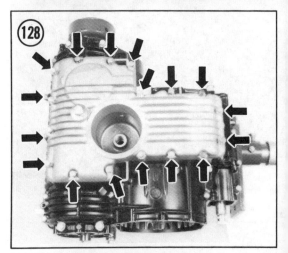

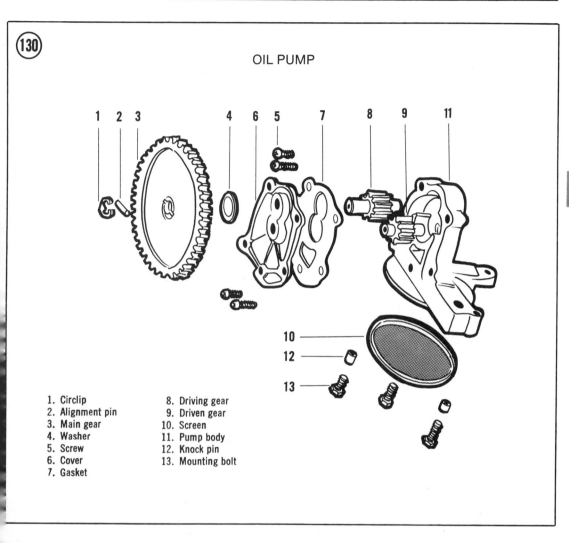

OIL PUMP

1. Circlip
2. Alignment pin
3. Main gear
4. Washer
5. Screw
6. Cover
7. Gasket
8. Driving gear
9. Driven gear
10. Screen
11. Pump body
12. Knock pin
13. Mounting bolt

4

5. Remove the pump body cover and its gasket.

6. Remove the 2 pump gears from the body and inspect their teeth for damage. If either gear has damaged teeth, replace the pump assembly with a new one.

7. Assemble the 2 pump gears into the body. With feeler gauges, measure the clearance between the teeth of each gear and the sides of the pump body, at the points where the teeth run closest to the body (**Figure 133**).

8. Install a new oil pump if either clearance is greater than 0.004 in. (0.1 mm) on 900cc models or 0.0055 in. (0.14 mm) on 1000cc models.

9. Gear end clearance can be checked by laying Plastigage across the gears (**Figure 134**) and assembling the cover and gasket. Follow the Plastigage instructions to check the clearance. Clearance should be 0.0004 – 0.002 in. (0.01 - 0.05 mm). If clearance is greater, a thinner gasket is available, or the pump body can be lapped on plate glass covered with No. 320 sandpaper.

Oil Pump Assembly

1. See **Figure 130**. Clean the mating surfaces of the pump body and the cover with a blunt edge scraper.

2. Fit a new gasket to the pump body, and put on the cover.

3. Apply Loctite to the pump body screws and install them.

4. Mount the shim, alignment pin, driving gear, and the circlip on the pump shaft.

5. After assembly, rotate the gear to make sure it turns freely.

Oil Pump Installation

1. Check the oil passage O-ring (A, **Figure 135**) and the oil pan O-ring. Install new ones if damaged.

2. Fill the pump with engine oil to prime it.

3. Check that the 2 dowel pins are in place (B, **Figure 135**).

4. Install the pump in the engine. If it will not seat, rotate the driving gear enough to mesh it with the crankshaft gear.

5. Apply Loctite to the 3 pump mounting bolts. Install them and torque each one to 70 in-lb. (0.8 mkg).

6. Install the oil pan and a new gasket.

7. Install the exhaust system.

8. Install the oil filter (see Chapter Three).

9. Add engine oil (see Chapter Three).

CRANKCASE SEPARATION

1. Remove the ignition advance mechanism (see *Advancer Removal,* Chapter Eleven).

2. Remove the 6 screws that mount the right engine cover. Remove the cover and its gasket (**Figure 136**).

3. Remove the clutch cover and gasket (**Figure 137**). Disassemble the clutch *if* you plan to remove the outer clutch housing from the transmission input shaft after splitting the engine cases (see *Clutch Removal,* Chapter Five).

4. Remove the mounting bolt at the bottom of the kickstarter lever if equipped. Pull kickstarter lever off the kickstarter shaft.

5. Remove the 4 bolts that mount the kickstarter mechanism cover to the engine (**Figure 138**). Pull off the cover and its gasket (**Figure 139**).

6. Pull the slotted spring guide off the kickstarter shaft. Unhook the nearest end of the kickstarter return spring from the shaft. Unhook the other end and take out the spring.

7. Remove the alternator cover with stator (see *Alternator Removal,* Chapter Eleven). If you plan to perform the crankshaft inspections that

require removal of the outer main bearings, remove the alternator rotor and starter clutch.

8. Remove the starter motor cover (**Figure 140**).

9. Remove the 2 starter motor bolts (**Figure 141**).

10. Pry the starter loose and disconnect the starter cable (**Figure 142**).

> CAUTION
> *Do not tap on the starter motor shaft.*
> *You will damage the motor.*

11. Remove the starter idler shaft and gear (**Figure 143**).

12. *Chain drive models*:

   a. Remove the gearshift linkage cover (**Figure 144**).

   b. Remove the output shaft collar and O-ring (**Figure 145**). Use a bearing puller if necessary.

   c. Move the shift arms away from the shift drum and pull out shift shaft and linkage.

13. Remove the engine from the frame (see *Engine Removal*).

14. Remove the 5 engine case bolts from the top of the engine, noting the location of the 2 cable clamps (A, **Figure 146**).

15. Turn the engine over and remove the oil pump (see *Oil Pump Removal*).

> CAUTION
> *Set the engine on wood blocks to protect*
> *the cylinder studs.*

16. With the oil pump out of the way, remove the 8 large bolts on either side of the crankshaft (**Figure 147**). Do *not* remove the main bearing cap bolts at the middle of the crank.

17. Remove the 17 smaller bolts shown in **Figure 148**. Note the 2 lead clamp positions (A, **Figure 148**).

18. Use 2 engine bolts as jacking screws in the locations shown in **Figure 149**. It should not be necessary to pry or use a mallet. If you encounter resistance, check for bolts you may have missed. Don't overlook the upper bolt under the starter motor (**Figure 146**).

19. Lift the bottom half off.

4

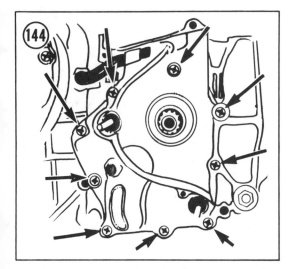

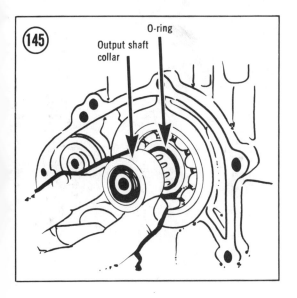

O-ring

Output shaft
collar

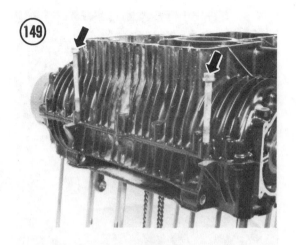

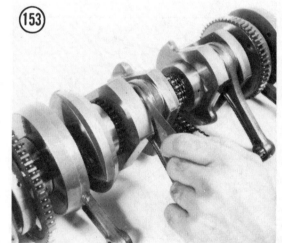

CRANKSHAFT AND CAM CHAIN

Once the crankshaft is removed, the cam chain can be replaced. The crankshaft and connecting rod assembly is pressed together and separate parts are not available from Kawasaki. There are very few specialty shops able to repair this kind of crankshaft, so in most cases you can inspect the crank and rods but only replace the whole assembly if some part is faulty. See your Kawasaki dealer if you suspect crankshaft trouble.

Crankshaft Removal

1. Split the engine cases (see *Crankcase Separation*).

2. With the engine upside down, remove the 4 bolts from the bearing cap mounted on the center of the crankshaft. Remove the bearing cap (**Figure 150**).

> NOTE: *The bearing cap is machined in combination with the engine case. If the bearing cap is damaged, both it and the engine cases must be replaced as a set.*

3. Lift the crankshaft out of the engine case. Take off the cam chain (**Figure 151**).

Crankshaft Inspection

1. Carefully examine the condition of the crankshaft bearings (**Figure 152**). They must spin freely without excessive play or roughness.

2. Check connecting rod big-end side clearance with feeler gauges (**Figure 153**). If clearance exceeds 0.024 in. (0.6 mm), replace the crankshaft assembly.

3. Check No. 5 bearing outer race side clearance with feeler gauges (**Figure 152**). This bearing determines crankshaft side play. If play exceeds 0.020 in. (0.5 mm) on 900cc engines, or 0.024 in. (0.6mm) on 1000cc engines, replace the crankshaft assembly.

4. If these checks are satisfactory, take the crankshaft to your dealer or local machine shop. They can check crankshaft alignment and inspect for cracks. Check against measurements given in **Table 1** at the end of this chapter.

5. Inspect the cam chain for wear (see *Cam Chain Inspection*).

Crankshaft and Cam Chain Installation

1. Turn the upper engine case upside down.

2. Check that the oil passages are clean and that the bearing dowel pins are in place (C, **Figure 154**).

3. Position the cam chain on the crankshaft and lay the crankshaft in place (**Figure 155**). Rotate each bearing outer race until its alignment hole mates with its dowel pin.

4. Oil the crank bearings.

5. Insert the main bearing cap with its arrow pointing to the front of the engine.

6. Insert the bearing cap bolts loosely, and tighten them in 2 stages to 18 ft.-lb. (2.5 mkg) in a cross pattern (**Figure 156**).

CRANKCASE ASSEMBLY

Assemble the crankcases with the engine upside down.

> CAUTION
> *Set the engine on wood blocks to protect the cylinder studs.*

1. When assembling new crankcase halves, seat the bypass valve steel ball evenly in the upper crankcase half. Insert a soft rod against the ball and lightly hammer it. Install a new lockwasher, tighten the bolt, and bend up an ear of the lockwasher (**Figure 157**).

2. In the upper crankcase half, 2 crankcase dowel pins, 2 transmission bearing alignment

rings (B, **Figure 154**), and 3 transmission and
kickstarter dowel pins must be in place (A,
Figure 154).

3. Check that all oil passages are clear and that
the oil passage O-ring is in place and in good condition (A, **Figure 156**). If the O-ring has a flat
side, face it toward the top of the engine.

4. Install the transmission shafts and the kickstarter ratchet assembly in the upper engine half
(**Figure 158**). Rotate the bearings until the dowel
pins seat and make sure the alignment rings are
fully seated in the bearing and case grooves.

> NOTE: *If you are using new engine
> cases and the old alignment rings won't
> fit, thinner rings are available.*

5. Rotate the shift drum to the NEUTRAL position
(**Figure 159**).

6. Align the transmission gears in the NEUTRAL
position (**Figure 160**).

7. Make sure the crankcase mating surfaces are
completely clean and dry.

8. Apply a light coat of gasket sealer to the sealing surfaces of the bottom half. Cover only flat
surfaces, not curved bearing surfaces. Make the
coating as thin as possible.

CAUTION
Do not block the oil breather return passage with sealant.

9. Assemble the engine cases, fitting the arm of
the middle shifter fork into the groove in 3rd gear
on the input shaft, and the arms of the other 2
shifter forks into the grooves of their gears on the
output shaft.

10. Seat the upper case half onto the lower and
tap lightly with a plastic or rubber mallet—do
not use a metal hammer as it will damage the
cases.

11. Loosely install the 8 large (8 mm) bolts on
either side of the crankshaft. Use Loctite Lock
'N' Seal or equivalent on the 2 bolts indicated (A,
Figure 161), and use liquid gasket sealant under
their bolt heads.

12. Torque the 8 large bolts in 2 stages to 18 ft.-
lb. (2.5 mkg), following the sequence numbers on
the bottom of the engine.

13. Loosely install the 17 smaller (6 mm) engine
case bolts in the bottom case. Apply Loctite to
the threads of the bolt indicated (B, **Figure 162**)

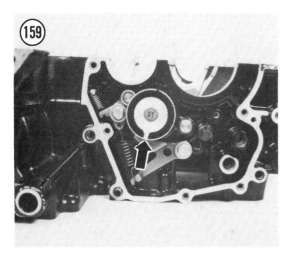

and liquid gasket under its head. Remember to reinstall the cable clamps where shown (A, **Figure 162**).

14. Torque the 17 smaller bolts to 70 in.-lb. (0.8 mkg) on 900cc models or to 90 in.-lb. (1.0 mkg) on 1000cc models.

15. Turn the transmission input and output shafts to see that they are free, and while spinning the output shaft, shift the transmission (turn the shift drum) through all gears to make sure the transmission is working right.

NOTE
These motorcycles have neutral locating balls inside output 4th gear. When operating correctly, the neutral locator will not allow the transmission to shift up from NEUTRAL as long as the output shaft is **not** *turning.*

16. Install the oil pump (see *Oil Pump Installation*).

17. Turn the engine over and insert the 5 upper crankcase bolts. Use Loctite on the bolt indicated (B, **Figure 163**) and liquid sealant under its head. Don't forget the 2 lead clamps (A, **Figure 163**).

18. Torque the 5 upper crankcase bolts to 70 in.-lb. (0.8 mkg) on 900cc models or to 90 in.-lb. (1.0 mkg) on 1000cc models.

19. Install the clutch cover. If you disassembled the clutch, assembly may be easier after the engine is in the frame.

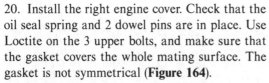

20. Install the right engine cover. Check that the oil seal spring and 2 dowel pins are in place. Use Loctite on the 3 upper bolts, and make sure that the gasket covers the whole mating surface. The gasket is not symmetrical (**Figure 164**).

21. Install the ignition advance mechanism (see *Advancer Installation,* Chapter Eleven).

22. See **Figure 165**. Put the kickstarter spring on the kickstarter shaft, and hook the end of the spring closer to the engine case. Rotate the kickstarter shaft clockwise as far as it will go. Work the near end of the spring into its hole in the kickstarter shaft.

23. Put the slotted spring guide on the kickstarter shaft.

24. Install the kickstarter cover and gasket.

25. Install the starter motor, idler gear and shaft.

26. Install the alternator stator. If you removed the rotor, assembly may be easier after the engine is in the frame.

27. *Chain drive models:*

    a. Install the output shaft O-ring and collar.

    b. Install the shift linkage and cover (see *Shift Linkage Installation,* Chapter Six).

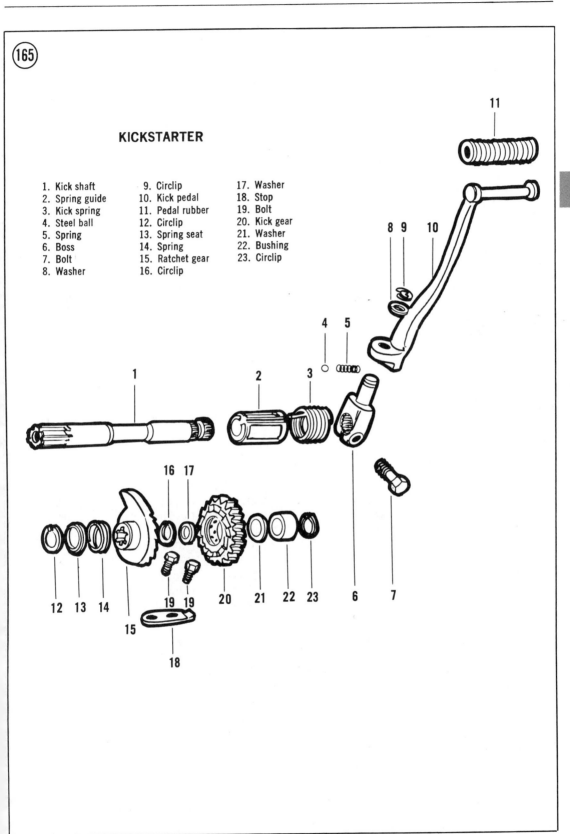

(165)

KICKSTARTER

1. Kick shaft
2. Spring guide
3. Kick spring
4. Steel ball
5. Spring
6. Boss
7. Bolt
8. Washer

9. Circlip
10. Kick pedal
11. Pedal rubber
12. Circlip
13. Spring seat
14. Spring
15. Ratchet gear
16. Circlip

17. Washer
18. Stop
19. Bolt
20. Kick gear
21. Washer
22. Bushing
23. Circlip

4

Table 1 ENGINE SPECIFICATIONS

Component	1000 cc		900 cc	
	Standard	Wear Limit	Standard	Wear Limit
Camshaft height				
Intake	1.429 in. (36.30 mm)	1.422 in. (36.12 mm)	1.429 in. (36.30 mm)	1.422 in. (36.12 mm)
Exhaust	1.409 in. (35.80 mm)	1.402 in. (35.62 mm)	1.409 in. (35.80 mm)	1.402 in. (35.62 mm)
Camshaft journal/ bearing clearance	0.001–0.003 in. (0.020–0.070 mm)	0.006 in. (0.16 mm)	0.001–0.003 in. (0.020–0.070 mm)	0.006 in (0.16 mm)
Camshaft journal diameter	0.963 in. (24.47 mm)	0.961 in. (24.42 mm)	0.963 in. (24.47 mm)	0.961 in. (24.42 mm)
Camshaft runout	0.001 in. (0.02 mm)	0.004 in. (0.10 mm)	0.001 in. (0.02 mm)	0.004 in. (0.10 mm)
Camshaft end play	0.010–0.016 in. (0.25–0.40 mm)	N/A	0.010–0.016 in. (0.25–0.40 mm)	N/A
Camshaft chain (length-20 links)	6.13 in. (155.6 mm)	6.21 in. (157.8 mm)	6.13 in. (155.6 mm)	6.21 in. (157.8 mm)
Cylinder head warp	N/A	0.002 in. (0.05 mm)	N/A	0.002 in. (0.05 mm)
Combustion chamber volume				
Chain drive	2.20 cu. in. (36 cc)	N/A	2.20 cu. in. (36 cc)	N/A
Shaft drive	2.12 cu. in. (34.7 cc)	N/A	2.12 cu. in. (34.7 cc)	N/A
Valve head thickness	0.037 in. (0.95 mm)	0.020 in. (0.50 mm)	0.037 in. (0.95 mm)	0.020 in. (0.50 mm)
Valve stem bend	0.001 in. (0.01 mm)	0.002 in. (0.05 mm)	0.001 in. (0.01 mm)	0.002 in. (0.05 mm)
Valve stem diameter				
Intake	0.275 in. (6.97 mm)	0.272 in. (6.90 mm)	0.275 in. (6.97 mm)	0.270 in. (6.86 mm)
Exhaust	0.274 in. (6.96 mm)	0.272 in. (6.90 mm)	0.274 in. (6.96 mm)	0.270 in. (6.86 mm)
Valve guide ID	0.276 in. (7.008 mm)	0.279 in. (7.08 mm)	0.276 in. (7.008 mm)	0.280 in. (7.10 mm)
Valve/guide clearance				
Intake	0.004 in. (0.092 mm)	0.010 in. (0.25 mm)	0.001 in. (0.035 mm)	0.004 in. (0.10 mm)
Exhaust	0.004 in. (0.107 mm)	0.009 in. (0.24 mm)	0.002 in. (0.045 mm)	0.004 in. (0.10 mm)
Valve seat width	0.04 in. (1.0 mm)	N/A	0.05 in. (1.25 mm)	N/A
Valve spring tension				
Inner	61 lb. @ 0.93 in. (27.6 kg @ 23.6 mm)	54 lb. (24.7 kg)	N/A	N/A
Outer	114 lb. @ 1.01 in. (51.6 kg @ 25.6 mm)	102 lb. (42.6 kg)	N/A	N/A
Cylinder ID	2.756 in. (70.010 mm)	2.760 in. (70.10 mm)	2.599 in. (66.01 mm)	2.602 in. (66.10 mm)
Piston diameter	2.754 in. (69.95 mm)	2.748 in. (69.80 mm)	2.596 in. (65.94 mm)	2.590 in. (65.80 mm)
Piston/clyinder clearance	0.002–0.003 in. (0.05–0.07 mm)	N/A	0.0025–0.003 in. (0.06–0.08 mm)	N/A

Table 1 ENGINE SPECIFICATIONS (continued)

Component	1000 cc		900 cc	
	Standard	Wear Limit	Standard	Wear Limit
Piston ring/groove clearance				
Top	0.002 in. (0.06 mm)	0.006 in. (0.15 mm)	0.0025 in. (0.06 mm)	0.007 in. (0.18 mm)
2nd (and 900cc oil ring)	0.002 in. (0.05 mm)	0.006 in. (0.15 mm)	0.001 in. (0.03 mm)	0.006 in. (0.15 mm)
Piston ring thickness				
Top	0.046 in. (1.18 mm)	0.043 in. (1.10 mm)	0.057 in. (1.45 mm)	0.054 in. (1.36 mm)
2nd	0.046 in. (1.18 mm)	0.004 in. (1.10 mm)	0.058 in. (1.48 mm)	0.055 in (1.40 mm)
Oil (900 cc)	N/A	N/A	0.098 in. (2.48 mm)	0.094 in. (2.40 mm)
Piston ring groove width				
Top	0.049 in. (1.24 mm)	0.052 in. (1.33 mm)	0.059 in. (1.51 mm)	0.063 in. (1.60 mm)
2nd	0.048 in. (1.23 mm)	0.052 in. (1.32 mm)	0.059 in. (1.51 mm)	0.063 in. (1.60 mm)
Oil	0.099 in. (2.52 mm)	0.102 in. (2.60 mm)	0.099 in. (2.51 mm)	0.102 in. (2.60 mm)
Piston ring gap (installed)				
Top & 2nd	0.016 in. (0.4 mm)	0.032 in. (0.8 mm)	0.012 in. (0.3 mm)	0.028 in. (0.7 mm)
Piston ring free gap				
Top	0.28 in. (7 mm)	0.25 in. (6.3 mm)	0.35 in. (9 mm)	0.24 in. (6 mm)
2nd	0.32 in. (8 mm)	0.28 in. (7.2 mm)	0.35 in. (9 mm)	0.24 in. (6 mm)
Oil (900 cc)	N/A	N/A	0.31 in. (8 mm)	0.20 in. (5 mm)
Piston pin diameter	0.669 in. (16.997 mm)	0.668 in. (16.96 mm)	0.669 in. (16.997 mm)	0.668 in. (16.96 mm)
Piston pin hole	0.670 in. (17.008 mm)	0.672 in. (17.08 mm)	0.670 in. (17.008 mm)	0.672 in. (17.08 mm)
Connecting rod small end ID	0.669 in. (17.009 mm)	0.671 in. (17.05 mm)	0.669 in. (17.009 mm)	0.671 in. (17.05 mm)
Connecting rod bend & twist	0.002 in./4 in. (0.05 mm/100 mm)	0.008 in. (0.20 mm)	0.002 in./4 in. (0.05 mm/100 mm)	0.008 in. (0.20 mm)
Connecting rod big end clearance				
Radial	0.001 in. (0.023 mm)	0.003 in. (0.08 mm)	0.001 in. (0.023 mm)	0.003 in. (0.08 mm)
Side	0.014 in. (0.35 mm)	0.02 in. (0.6 mm)	0.014 in. (0.35 mm)	0.02 in. (0.6 mm)
Crankshaft				
Runout	0.002 in. (0.04 mm)	0.004 in. (0.10 mm)	0.002 in. (0.04 mm)	0.004 in. (0.10 mm)
#5 bearing side clearance	0.001 in. (0.25 mm)	0.020 in. (0.5 mm)	0.001 in. (0.25 mm)	0.024 in. (0.6 mm)

NOTE: "N/A" means "Not Applicable"

4

Table 2 ENGINE TORQUE AND LOCKING AGENT

Fastener	Chain Drive		Shaft Drive	
	Foot-pounds	Kilogram-meter	Foot-pounds	Kilogram-meter
Breather cover bolt	14.5	2.0	11	1.5
Camshaft cap bolts	9 (1973-78 chrome)	1.2		
	7 (1973-78 dark)	1.0		
	12 (1979-later)	1.7	12	1.7
Camshaft chain tensioner bolt	70 in.-lb.	0.8	N/A	N/A
Camshaft chain guide screw (front)	Use locking agent		Use locking agent	
Camshaft chain guide sprocket shaft bolt	80 in.-lb.	0.9	N/A	N/A
Camshaft chain guide sprocket Allen bolts	70 in.-lb.	0.8	90 in.-lb.	1.0
Camshaft sprocket bolts	11	1.5	11	1.5
Carburetor holder screws	Use locking agent		Use locking agent	
Carburetor mounting screws	Use locking agent		Use locking agent	
Clutch hub nut	100	13.5	90	12
Clutch release screws	Use locking agent		Use locking agent	
Clutch spring bolts	90 in.-lb.	1.0	95 in.-lb.	1.1
Crankcase bolts				
1000 cc: 6 mm	90 in.-lb.	1.0	90 in.-lb.	1.0
8 mm	18	2.5	18	2.5
900 cc: 6 mm	70 in.-lb.	0.8	N/A	N/A
Crankshaft main bearing cap bolts	18	2.5	18	2.5
Cylinder head				
Bolts	104 in.-lb.	1.2	104 in.-lb.	1.2
Nuts	30	4.0	30	4.0
Cover bolts	104 in.-lb.	1.2	11	1.5
Alternator				
Stator Allen bolts	90 in.-lb.	1.0	90 in.-lb.	1.0
Cover screws	Use locking agent		Use locking agent	
Rotor bolt	18	2.5	95	13
Engine drain plug	22	3.0	22	3.0
Engine mounting bolts	30	4.0	30	4.0
Engine mounting brackets	17	2.4	17	2.4
Engine sprocket nut				
1000 cc:	60	8.0	N/A	N/A
900 cc:	100	13.5	N/A	N/A
Shift linkage cover	Use locking agent		Use locking agent	
Neutral indicator switch	11	1.5	11	1.5
Oil breather cover bolt	15	2.0	11	1.5
Oil filter drain plug	15	2.0	N/A	N/A
Oil filter mounting bolt	15	2.0	15	2.0
Oil pan bolts	90 in.-lb.	1.0	90 in.-lb.	1.0
Oil passage plug	Use locking agent		Use locking agent	
Oil pressure indicator switch	50 in.-lb.	0.6	50 in.-lb.	0.6
Oil pump cover screws	Use locking agent		Use locking agent	
Oil pump mounting bolts	70 in.-lb.	0.8	70 in.-lb.	0.8
Return spring pin	Use locking agent		14.5	2.0
Right engine cover screws	Use locking agent		Use locking agent	
Spark plugs	20	2.8	20	2.8
Starter				
Clutch Allen bolts	25	3.5	30	4.0
Motor lead terminal nuts	40 in.-lb.	0.5	40 in.-lb.	0.5
Motor retaining bolts	90 in.-lb.	1.0	90 in.-lb.	1.0
Stud bolts				
Cylinder	Less than 90 in.-lb.	1.0	Less than 90 in.-lb.	1.0
Exhaust	Less than 40 in.-lb.	0.5	Less than 40 in.-lb.	0.5
Timing advancer bolt	18	2.5	18	2.5
Front bevel mounting bolts	N/A	N/A	18	2.5
Front bevel drive gear nut	N/A	N/A	90	12.0
Front bevel driven gear bolt	N/A	N/A	90	12.0

CHAPTER FIVE

CLUTCH

CLUTCH OPERATION

The clutch is a wet multi-plate type which operates immersed in the engine oil. It is mounted on the right end of the transmission input shaft. The inner clutch hub is splined to the input shaft and the outer housing can rotate freely on the input shaft. The outer housing is geared to the crankshaft.

Between the 2 clutch hubs is a sandwich of clutch plates. Every other plate (including the inner one and the outer one) is a friction plate which is locked to the outer housing and must turn whenever it turns. The remaining metal plates are locked to the inner hub; when they turn, it turns.

Atop this sandwich of clutch plates is the pressure plate. There are coil springs that press the pressure plate in against the rest of the plates. This pressure, or friction, jams the plates together, which locks together the clutch hubs. Then the crankshaft can turn the transmission input shaft.

To disengage the clutch, a pushrod extending through the hollow output shaft pushes a steel ball, which pushes a shorter pushrod with a plate which pushes the pressure plate outward from the clutch. With the pressure gone, the outer housing and the alternate plates locked to it continue to turn, but the other plates (thus the inner hub) stop turning.

CAUTION
The clutch friction discs are bathed in the same oil you put in the engine. Do not add STP or use any of the new "super-slippery" oils. You will cause clutch slippage.

Clutch Release (Chain Drive)

The clutch release mechanism is mounted to the rear of the chain cover. The 2-piece mechanism consists of a spiral gear with an arm riding in a base with a spiral gearing. The clutch cable is attached to the arm; when pulled, it rotates the spiral gear which is cammed outward from the base. The adjusting screw in the spiral gear then pushes against the clutch pushrod, which extends through the hollow transmission input shaft and–through additional linkage–operates the clutch.

The 1978 and later chain drive clutch releases have a ball bearing spiral ramp for smoother action.

All of the clutch components except the outer housing can be removed without splitting the engine cases.

Clutch Release (Shaft Drive)

The shaft drive model clutch release is mounted inside the front bevel drive case. It uses a slightly different ball and ramp system but it works the same as the chain drive clutch release.

The shaft drive clutch inner hub is connected to the transmission input shaft through a damper cam and spring plate for additional shock absorption. Otherwise, it works the same as a chain drive clutch.

CLUTCH CABLE REPLACEMENT

1. Shorten the mid-cable adjuster (in front of the frame down tube) to give maximum cable free play.

2. Line up the slots on the adjuster and clutch lever, and disconnect the cable from the lever (**Figure 1**).

3. *Chain drive:* Remove the engine sprocket cover (see *Sprocket Cover Removal,* Chapter Six).

4. *Shaft drive:* Loosen the 2 starter cover bolts and remove the 4 front bevel cover bolts (**Figure 2**) and the cover.

5. Remove the cotter pin and disconnect the clutch cable from the clutch release lever (**Figures 3 and 4**).

6. Remove the old cable, routing the new cable through all the same locations, clips, and guides that the old cable used.

7. Install the cable ends, with a new cotter pin at the bottom.

8. Replace the covers and adjust the clutch (see Chapter Three).

CLUTCH RELEASE (CHAIN DRIVE)

Refer to **Figure 5**.

Clutch Release Removal

1. Place the bike on the centerstand.

2. Shift the transmission into NEUTRAL.

3. Remove the left front footpeg and gearshift lever.

4. Remove the 2 bolts securing the starter motor cover and remove it (**Figure 6**).

5. Remove the 4 bolts securing the engine sprocket cover and remove it (**Figure 6**).

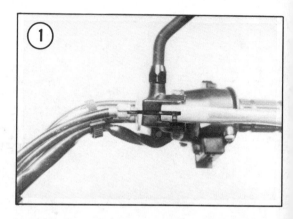

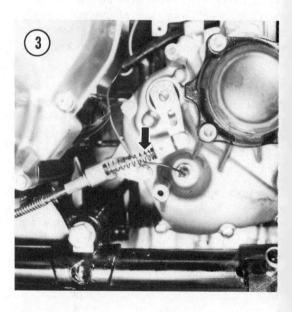

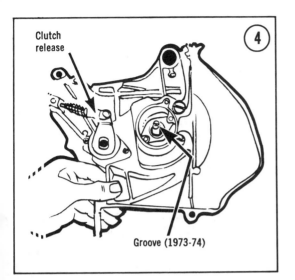

④

Clutch release

Groove (1973-74)

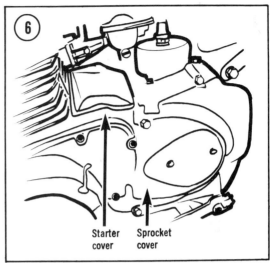

⑥

Starter cover   Sprocket cover

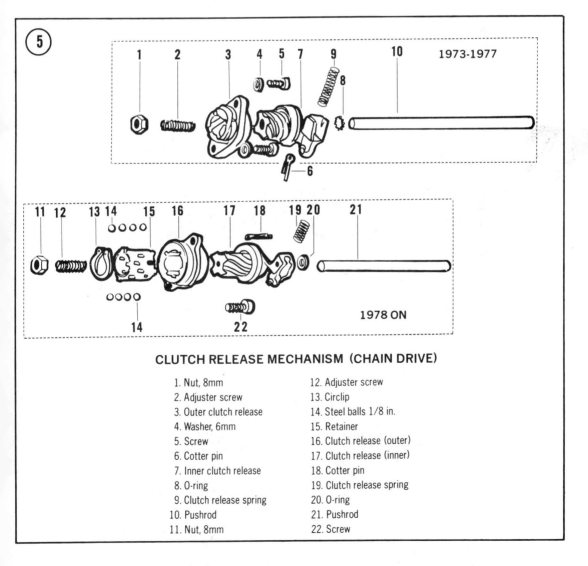

⑤

1973-1977

1   2   3   4   5   7   9   10   8

6

11 12 13 14 15 16 17 18 19 20 21

14   22

1978 ON

CLUTCH RELEASE MECHANISM (CHAIN DRIVE)

1. Nut, 8mm	12. Adjuster screw
2. Adjuster screw	13. Circlip
3. Outer clutch release	14. Steel balls 1/8 in.
4. Washer, 6mm	15. Retainer
5. Screw	16. Clutch release (outer)
6. Cotter pin	17. Clutch release (inner)
7. Inner clutch release	18. Cotter pin
8. O-ring	19. Clutch release spring
9. Clutch release spring	20. O-ring
10. Pushrod	21. Pushrod
11. Nut, 8mm	22. Screw

5

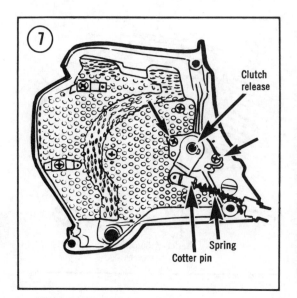

Clutch
release

Spring

Cotter pin

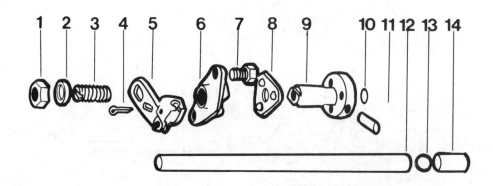

CLUTCH RELEASE MECHANISM
(SHAFT DRIVE)

1 2 3 4 5 6 7 8 9 10 11 12 13 14

1. Locknut
2. Flat washer
3. Adjusting screw
4. Cotter pin
5. Clutch release lever
6. Ball ramp
7. Allen bolt
8. Ball assembly
9. Release shaft
10. O-ring
11. Knock pin
12. Pushrod
13. Steel ball
14. Pushrod

6. Remove the clutch release lever cotter pin (**Figure 7**). Remove the cable tip from the lever.

7. Remove the 2 screws that mount the base to the chain cover (**Figure 7**).

8. Remove the circlip and separate the outer and inner release gears.

Clutch Release Inspection (Chain Drive)

Refer to **Figure 5**.

Clean all parts in solvent and thoroughly dry with compressed air. Check the balls for wear or pitting; replace if necessary.

NOTE: *Replace all balls even though only a few may be worn.*

Inspect the grooves in the inner and outer release gears. If they show signs of wear, replace the entire assembly. Upon reassembly, push the inner gear back and forth in the direction of the shaft without turning it. If there is excessive play, replace the entire assembly.

Clutch Release Installation (Chain Drive)

1. Apply grease to all parts prior to assembly.

2. Insert the inner gear into the outer gear. They must be installed so that when the 2 gears are fully meshed, the clutch release lever will be positioned in relation to the outer release gear as shown in **Figure 7**.

NOTE: *The machined side of the outer release gear must face **up**.*

3. Install the circlip.

4. Install the mechanism into the cover and apply Loctite Lock N' Seal to the screws prior to installation.

NOTE: *The clutch release lever must be installed as shown in **Figure 7**.*

5. Install the cable into the lever and install a new cotter pin.

6. Install the engine sprocket cover, starter motor cover, footpeg, and gearshift lever.

7. Adjust the clutch as described under *Clutch Adjustment* in Chapter Three.

CLUTCH RELEASE (SHAFT DRIVE)

Refer to **Figure 8**.

Clutch Release Removal

1. Place the bike on the centerstand.

2. Shift the transmission into NEUTRAL.

3. Remove the front bevel gear case (see *Front Bevel Removal,* Chapter Six).

4. Remove the clutch adjusting screw locknut, flat washer, and release lever (**Figure 9**).

5. On the inside of the gear case, remove the release shaft and ball assembly (**Figure 10**).

Clutch Release Installation (Shaft Drive)

Refer to **Figure 8**.

1. If there is any damage, replace the release lever balls and ramp as a set.

2. Apply grease to all parts before assembly.

3. Install the release shaft with the stop pin pointing as shown in **Figure 11**.

4. Install the release lever, shaft, and locknut.

5. Connect the clutch cable to the lever and install a new cotter pin.

6. Install the front bevel gear case (see *Front Bevel Installation,* Chapter Six).

7. Adjust the clutch (see Chapter Three).

CLUTCH PLATES AND HUB

Clutch Removal (Chain Drive)

Refer to **Figure 12**.

1. Put the bike on its centerstand, and put a drain pan under the clutch cover.

2. Remove the screws holding the clutch cover in place (**Figure 13**).

3. Gently free the cover by tapping it with a soft mallet. Remove the cover.

4. Remove the 5 bolts holding the clutch spring assembly to the hub (**Figure 14**). Remove the

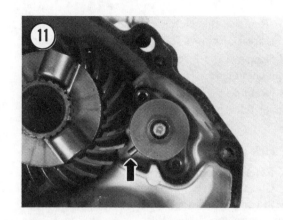

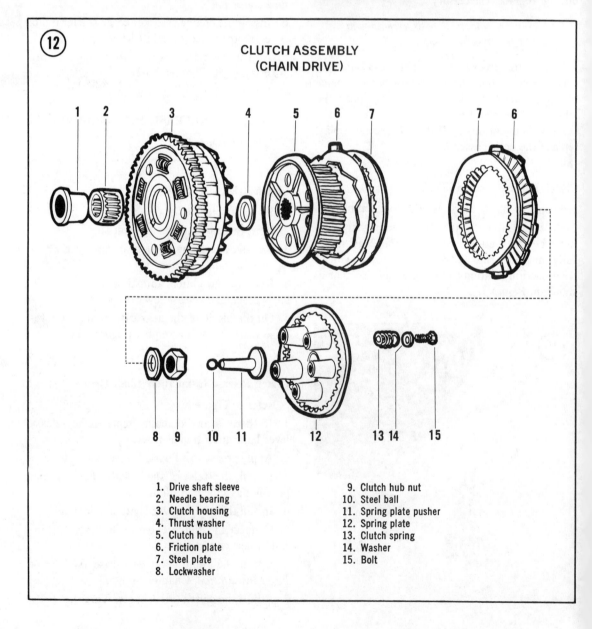

**CLUTCH ASSEMBLY
(CHAIN DRIVE)**

1. Drive shaft sleeve
2. Needle bearing
3. Clutch housing
4. Thrust washer
5. Clutch hub
6. Friction plate
7. Steel plate
8. Lockwasher
9. Clutch hub nut
10. Steel ball
11. Spring plate pusher
12. Spring plate
13. Clutch spring
14. Washer
15. Bolt

washers and clutch springs (**Figure 15**) and then the pressure plate (**Figure 16**).

5. Remove the friction plates and discs (**Figure 17**).

6. Remove the pressure plate pusher (**Figure 18**) and the steel ball behind it.

7. With a socket on a breaker bar, remove the clutch nut from the input shaft (**Figure 19**).

NOTE: *A special tool is required to keep the outer housing from turning—see*

your Kawasaki dealer; or, a screwdriver can be held between one of the clutch housing gear teeth and the inside of the engine cases. Be careful not to slip or damage the gear or cases. The clutch nut is **tight**.

8. Remove the washer, inner clutch hub, and thrust washer from the input shaft.

NOTE: *The clutch outer housing can not be removed without splitting the engine cases.*

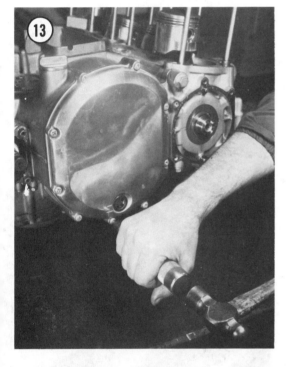

Clutch Removal (Shaft Drive)

Refer to **Figure 20**.

1. Put the bike on its centerstand, and put a drain pan under the clutch cover.

2. Remove the bolts holding the clutch cover in place (**Figure 21**).

3. Gently free the cover by tapping it with a soft mallet. Remove the cover.

> NOTE: *If you have a special clutch holding tool, remove the clutch bolts, pressure plate, and friction plates and discs. If not, use the rear brake to hold the clutch outer housing as follows.*

4. Remove the circlip and pressure plate pusher from the pressure plate (**Figure 22**).

5. Remove the short pushrod and the steel ball behind it (**Figure 23**).

6. Pry out the staked area of the clutch hub nut with a punch (**Figure 24**).

CAUTION
Do not damage the input shaft.

7. Shift the transmission into fifth gear, and step on the brake pedal.

8. With a socket on a breaker bar, loosen the clutch nut from the input shaft (**Figure 25**).

9. Remove the 6 pressure plate bolts, washers and springs (**Figure 26**).

10. Remove the pressure plate, friction plates and discs (**Figure 27**).

11. Remove the clutch hub nut and spined washer.

12. Remove the clutch inner hub, splined collar, and washer (**Figure 28**).

> NOTE: *The outer clutch housing can not be removed without splitting the engine cases.*

Clutch Inspection

1. Clean all clutch parts in petroleum-based solvent such as kerosene and thoroughly dry them.

2. Measure the thickness of each friction disc at several places around the disc as shown in **Figure 29**. Replace any plate that measures less than 0.140 in. (3.5 mm) on chain drive models or 0.110 in. (2.7 mm) on shaft drive models.

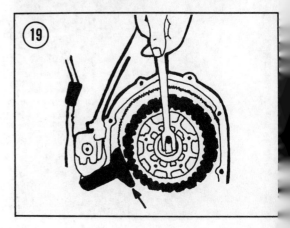

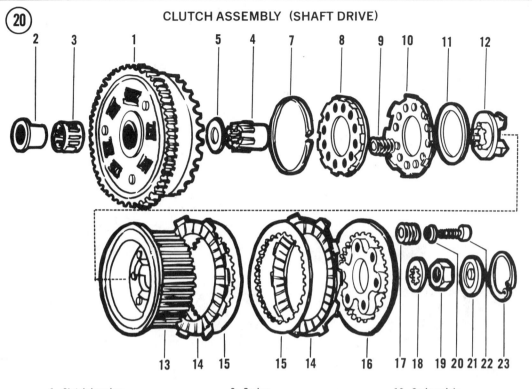

CLUTCH ASSEMBLY (SHAFT DRIVE)

20

1. Clutch housing
2. Sleeve
3. Needle bearing
4. Splined collar
5. Thrust washer
7. Circlip
8. Damper spring plate
9. Spring
10. Damper spring seat
11. Seat stop
12. Damper cam follower
13. Clutch hub
14. Friction plate
15. Steel plate
16. Spring plate
17. Spring
18. Splined washer
19. Nut
20. Washer
21. Spring plate pusher
22. Allen bolt
23. Circlip

5

21

22

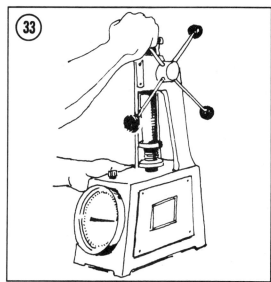

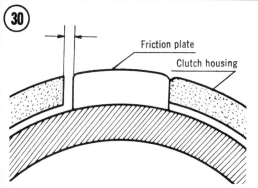

Friction plate

Clutch housing

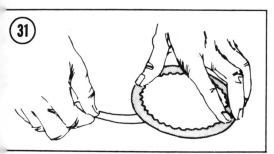

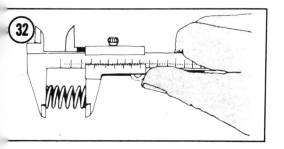

3. Insert a friction plate into the outer clutch hub, and rotate the plate until one side of each tab on it is butted up against a side wall of the hub. With feeler gauges, measure the clearance between the other side of each tab and the other side wall of the hub (**Figure 30**).

4. Replace any plate with clearance greater than 0.020 in. (0.5 mm). If the side walls of the outer hub are chewed up or badly worn, replace the outer hub.

5. Lay each plate on a flat surface. If there is a gap between any part of the clutch plate and the flat surface, measure the gap with feeler gauges (**Figure 31**).

6. Replace any plate with a warp greater than specified in **Table 1**.

7. Inspect the clutch springs.

    a. *900cc:* With calipers, measure the free length of each clutch spring (**Figure 32**). Replace *all* springs if *one* has a free length less than 1.27 in. (32.3 mm).

    b. *1000cc:* The clutch springs must be checked *while compressed* (**Figure 33**)—47 lb. (21.5 kg) @ 0.93 in. (23.5 mm) on chain drive models and 39 lb. (17.5 kg) @ 0.87 in. (22.1 mm) on shaft drive models.

8. Visually inspect the outer splines that mount the steel clutch plates to the inner hub. If the splines are unevenly worn or notched, replace the inner hub with a new one.

Clutch Installation

Reverse the removal procedure. Refer to **Figures 12 and 20**. Note the following:

a. If new friction plates are installed, oil them to prevent seizure.

b. *Chain drive:* Install the washer under the clutch hub nut with the OUT SIDE mark facing out.

c. Torque the hub nut to 100 ft.-lb. (13.5 mkg) on chain drive models or to 90 ft.-lb. (12.0 mkg) on shaft drive models.

d. Apply molybdenum disulfide grease to the steel ball and short pushrod.

e. Cross-tighten the pressure plate spring bolts gradually and evenly.

f. Add engine oil and adjust the clutch (see Chapter Three).

Table 1 CLUTCH PLATE WARP SPECIFICATIONS

	Friction Plate	Steel Plate
900 cc	0.012 in. (0.30 mm)	0.016 in. (0.40 mm)
1000 cc		
Chain drive	0.012 in. (0.30 mm)	0.014 in. (0.35 mm)
Shaft Drive	0.014 in. (0.35 mm)	0.014 in. (0.35 mm)

NOTE: If you have a 1980 model, or a 1979-1981 Police model, first check the Supplement at the back of this book for any new service information.

CHAPTER SIX

TRANSMISSION

6

This chapter covers all parts that transmit power from the clutch to the drive chain: the basic transmission itself, the kickstarter ratchet gears, the shift drum that moves the gears in the transmission, the shift linkage that turns the shift drum, the drive sprocket and chain oil pump (early models), and the front bevel drive gearcase on the shaft drive models.

See **Table 1** at the end of this chapter for specifications not given in the text.

TRANSMISSION OUTER PARTS (CHAIN DRIVE)

Several transmission parts can be repaired without splitting the engine cases. These outer parts are the:

  a. Drive sprocket cover
  b. Chain oil pump
  c. Drive sprocket
  d. Shift linkage

Each of these outer parts is described in the following section.

DRIVE SPROCKET COVER

The chain cover mounts the chain oil pump (1973-1974 only) and the clutch release mechanism. Remove the cover to gain access to the clutch release mechanism; it need not be removed for repairs to the chain oil pump.

Sprocket Cover Removal

1. *1973-1974:* On the left side of the engine, remove the 2 screws that mount the oil pump cover to the chain cover. Remove the oil pump cover and its gasket.

2. *1973-1974:* Push the hose clamp on the oil intake tube far enough down to the tube to free it from the chain oil pump nipple. Pull the tube off the pump. Plug the end of the tube with a screw to prevent oil from leaking out (**Figure 1**).

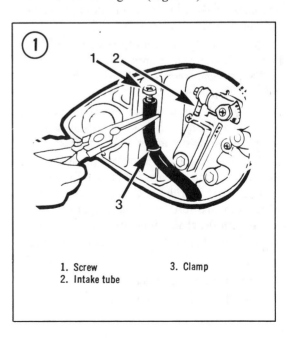

1. Screw   3. Clamp
2. Intake tube

3. Unscrew the 2 cap nuts that mount the left front footpeg assembly to the motorcycle frame. Remove the footpeg assembly from its mounting studs.

4. Remove the clamp bolt from the rear of the gearshift lever. Pull the lever off the selector shaft.

5. On the left side of the engine behind the cylinder block, remove the 2 screws and flat washers that mount the starter motor cover (**Figure 2**). Remove the cover and its gasket.

6. Remove the 4 bolts that mount the sprocket cover to the engine (**Figure 2**). Remove the sprocket cover, being careful not to damage the selector shaft oil seals or the chain oil pump shaft in the rear.

7. *If you are installing a new cover:* at the rear of the chain cover, remove the cotter pin securing the clutch cable to the clutch release mechanism. Unhook the clutch cable (**Figure 3**).

Sprocket Cover Installation

1. Butt the bottom end of the outer clutch cable against its stop in the front of the chain cover.

2. Fit the clutch release spring to the exposed inner clutch cable.

3. Hook the bottom clutch cable fitting into the cable mount on the arm of the clutch release mechanism. Insert the cotter pin through the cable mount, and spread its legs.

4. *1973–1974:* At the rear of the chain cover, rotate the oil pump shaft until the slot in the shaft will be positioned horizontally when the cover is mounted (**Figure 4**).

5. *1973–1974:* Rotate the rear wheel until the pin in the end of the transmission output shaft is aligned to fit the slot in the oil pump shaft.

6. Press the chain cover into place on the engine. Be careful not to damage the oil seal around the shift shaft. If it will not bottom, rock the rear wheel back and forth until the output shaft will couple with the chain oil pump shaft.

7. Install the 4 bolts that mount the chain cover.

8. Install the starter motor cover and gasket.

9. Install the gearshift lever.

10. Install the left front footpeg.

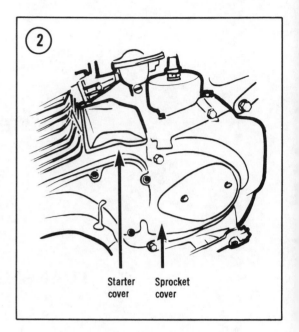

Starter cover   Sprocket cover

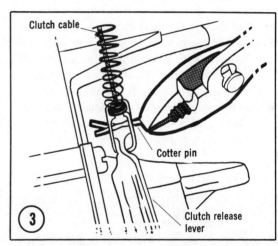

Clutch cable

Cotter pin

Clutch release lever

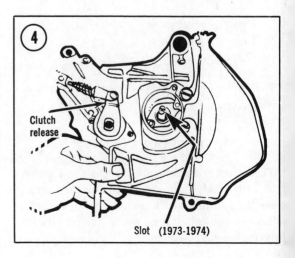

Clutch release

Slot (1973-1974)

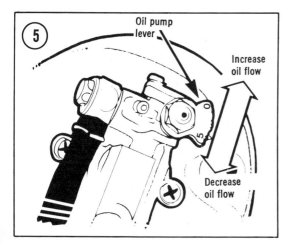

5

Oil pump lever

Increase oil flow

Decrease oil flow

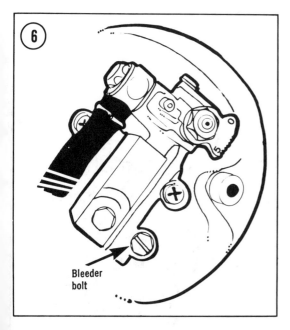

6

Bleeder bolt

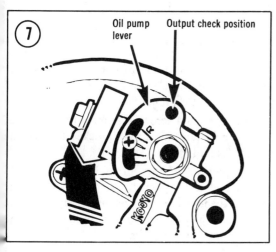

7

Oil pump lever   Output check position

11. *1973–1974:* Install the chain oil pump intake tube.

12. *1973–1974:* Install the oil pump cover.

CHAIN OIL PUMP (1973–1974 MODELS ONLY)

The chain oil pump was discontinued with the 1975 model, when the sealed O-ring drive chain was added.

Operation

The chain oil pump is connected to the transmission output shaft, which is hollow. Oil flows from the reservoir (behind the left side cover), through the pump, through the output shaft, and out around the output sprocket to the rear chain.

The flow rate is varied in 2 ways. An adjustable cam varies the amount of oil delivered by each rotation of the pump shaft (**Figure 5**). Since the pump is driven by the transmission output shaft, the rpm of the pump shaft varies with that of the output shaft.

Bleeding the Pump

If the chain oil tank runs dry, the pump will get an air lock which must be bled. Unscrew the bleeder bolt on the pump body (**Figure 6**). Run the engine with the bike on the centerstand, in gear, until oil flows out of the bleeder hole. Screw in the bleeder bolt.

Testing the Pump

All 1974 models have a redesigned pump with a built-in device, as indicated by a hole drilled in the upper right corner of the flow rate plate (**Figure 7**). To use the test device, remove the oil pump cover, remove the Phillips screw that locks the flow rate plate, rotate the plate counterclockwise until the additional hole in the plate is aligned with the screwhole, and install and tighten the Phillips screw.

Put the motorcycle on the centerstand. Start the engine, shift into first gear, and hold the rpm at 2,000 for 2 minutes. Shut off the engine and observe the rear chain. If it has been well oiled, the pump is working properly; reset the flow rate plate. If the chain has not been oiled properly, remove the pump and replace it with a new one (**Figure 8**).

Chain Oil Pump Removal

1. Remove the 2 screws that mount the oil pump cover to the chain cover. Remove the oil pump cover.

2. Push the hose clamp on the oil intake tube far enough down the tube to free it from the chain oil pump nipple. Pull the tube off the pump. Plug the end of the tube with a screw to prevent oil from leaking out.

3. Remove the 2 Phillips, pump-mounting screws. Remove the pump from the chain cover.

> NOTE: *Repair parts are not available. If the pump is faulty, install a new unit.*

Chain Oil Pump Installation

1. To install the pump on the chain cover, note the positioning of the pin on the end of the transmission output shaft. Rotate the pump shaft so that its slot will be aligned with the pin when the pump is installed.

2. Fit the pump to the chain cover. If the pump shaft will not engage the output shaft, put the motorcycle in gear and work the rear wheel back and forth until the 2 shafts will engage.

3. Apply Loctite to the 2 pump mounting screws. Install the screws.

4. Fit the oil intake tube and its clamp to the pump nipple.

5. Remove the bleeder screw. Bleed the air out of the pump. Install the bleeder screw.

6. Fit the oil pump cover and its gasket to the chain cover. Install the 2 mounting screws.

DRIVE SPROCKET

The drive sprocket is on the left end of the transmission output shaft, behind the sprocket cover. The drive chain is endless—it has no master link. To remove the drive chain, remove the drive sprocket from the output shaft, and remove the swing arm (see *Swing Arm Removal,* Chapter Ten).

Drive Sprocket Removal

1. Remove the drive sprocket cover (see *Sprocket Cover Removal*).

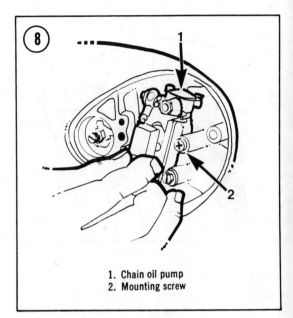

1. Chain oil pump
2. Mounting screw

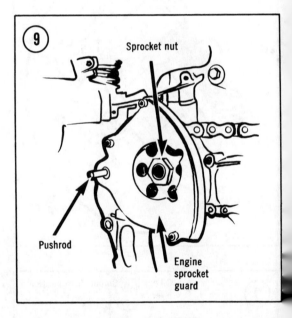

Sprocket nut

Pushrod

Engine sprocket guard

2. Pull the clutch pushrod out of the transmission input shaft, to the left of the drive sprocket (**Figure 9**).

3. Remove the 4 screws that mount the sprocket guard in front of the output sprocket. Remove the guard (**Figure 9**).

4. At the end of the output shaft, use a cold chisel and a hammer to bend the tab of the washer behind the sprocket nut away from the nut. Use a hammer and a drift to flatten the tab against the output sprocket.

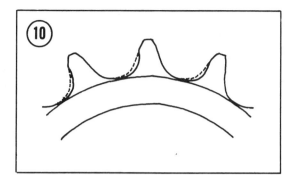

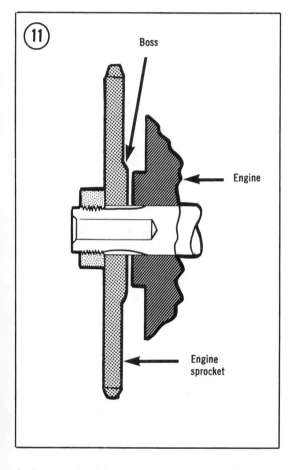

Boss

Engine

Engine
sprocket

5. Loosen the drive sprocket nut (**Figure 9**).

> NOTE: *To keep the sprocket from turning, have an assistant hold the rear brake on to hold the chain taut.*

6. Remove the sprocket nut, the tab washer, and the sprocket from the output shaft.

> NOTE: *If necessary to provide slack, adjust the drive chain as described in Chapter Three.*

Drive Sprocket Installation

1. Inspect the teeth on the sprocket. If the teeth are visibly worn, replace the sprocket (**Figure 10**).

2. Position rear chain on the sprocket. On 1975 and later models the raised boss must face the transmission to provide adequate clearance for the drive chain (**Figure 11**).

> WARNING
> *If the 1975 and later drive sprocket is installed with the raised boss facing out, chain failure and wheel lockup may result.*

3. Fit the sprocket to its splines on the output shaft. If the sprocket won't go on the shaft because the rear chain is too tight, move the rear wheel forward in the swing arm to loosen the chain.

4. Butt the tab washer against the output sprocket, so that the tang on the washer fits into one of the sprocket holes.

5. Loosely install the drive sprocket nut.

6. Torque the sprocket nut to 100 ft.-lb. (13.5 mkg) on 900cc models or to 60 ft.-lb. (8.0 mkg) on 1000cc models.

> NOTE: *To keep the sprocket from turning, have an assistant hold the rear brake on to hold the chain taut.*

7. Bend up one side of the tab washer against the side of the nut.

8. Position the sprocket guard in front of the drive sprocket. Install the 4 mounting screws.

9. Insert the clutch pushrod into the transmission input shaft.

10. Install the sprocket cover.

11. If necessary, reposition the rear wheel in the swing arm, to adjust the tension of the rear chain.

SHIFT LINKAGE (CHAIN DRIVE)

Inside the transmission, gears are shifted by shifter forks, which are moved from side to side by the camming slots cut into the cylindrical shifter drum. The linkage (outside the engine cases) that converts up-and-down motions of the gearshift lever into rotation of the shifter drum is the gear selector mechanism (**Figure 12**).

The shift lever is mounted to one end of the selector shaft. At the other end of the shaft is an

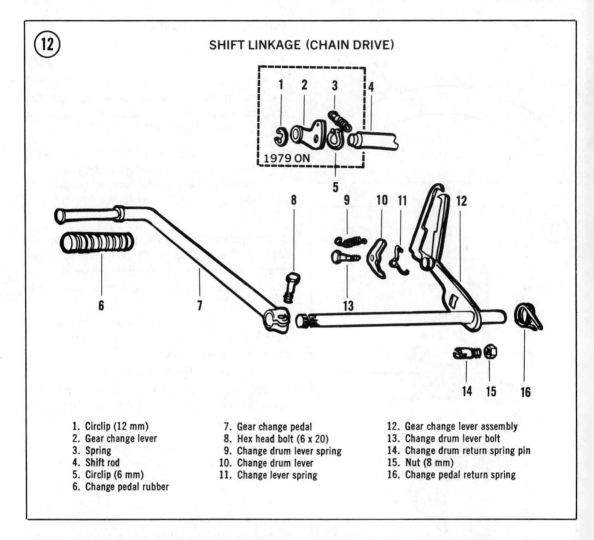

SHIFT LINKAGE (CHAIN DRIVE)

1979 ON

1. Circlip (12 mm)
2. Gear change lever
3. Spring
4. Shift rod
5. Circlip (6 mm)
6. Change pedal rubber
7. Gear change pedal
8. Hex head bolt (6 x 20)
9. Change drum lever spring
10. Change drum lever
11. Change lever spring
12. Gear change lever assembly
13. Change drum lever bolt
14. Change drum return spring pin
15. Nut (8 mm)
16. Change pedal return spring

arm with 2 hinged pawls. The pawls rest against pegs protruding from the left end of the shifter drum. When the selector shaft is rotated, the pawls grasp the pegs and rotate the shifter drum.

The 2 legs of the strong hairpin return spring on the selector shaft arm rest against a stationary centering peg. When the shift lever is released, the return spring brings the selector shaft back to its center position.

A spring loaded detent is mounted to the left end of the shifter drum. It locks the pegs of the shifter drum into their new position after the shift has been made, to prevent the transmission from jumping out of gear.

1979 and later: An external neutral detent lever arm is added to assist neutral holding (**Figure 13**). This external neutral detent replaces the earlier models' internal shift drum neutral detent.

Shift Linkage Removal (Chain Drive)

1. Remove the drive sprocket cover (see *Sprocket Cover Removal*).

2. Remove the drive sprocket (see *Drive Sprocket Removal*).

3. Put an oil pan under the shift linkage cover, and remove the neutral indicator lead.

4. Remove the 9 screws and the shift linkage cover (**Figure 14**). Tap the cover loose with a soft mallet, if necessary. Use care; the cover is positioned with a dowel.

5. Remove the output shaft collar (**Figure 15**). Use a bearing puller, if necessary.

6. Refer to **Figure 16**. Note carefully how the shifter shaft assembly pawls engage on the shifting drum. To remove the shift shaft, pull the

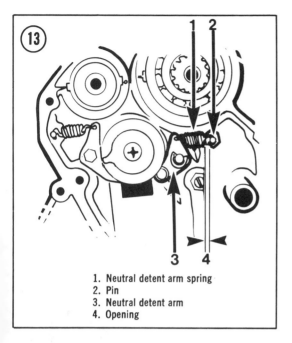

1. Neutral detent arm spring
2. Pin
3. Neutral detent arm
4. Opening

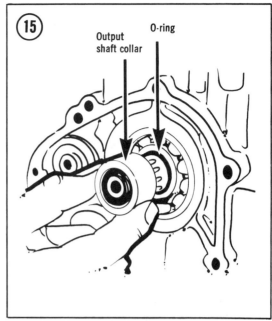

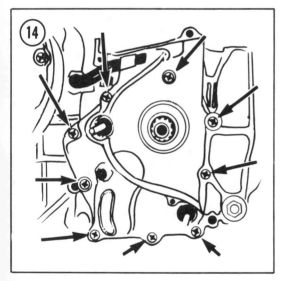

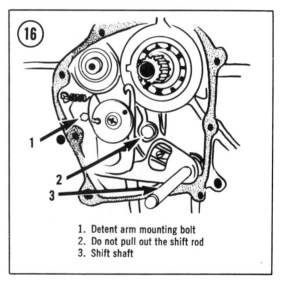

1. Detent arm mounting bolt
2. Do not pull out the shift rod
3. Shift shaft

pawls away from the shifting drum and slide out the shaft assembly.

> NOTE: *Do not pull the shift rod (Figure 16) out. If it is pulled out by 1½ in. (40 mm), the internal shift forks within the crankcase will fall to the bottom of the oil pan. This would require removal and disassembly of the engine to reposition them.*

7. Remove the gear position detent arm and spring (**Figure 16**).

8. *1979 and later:* Remove the neutral detent arm and spring (**Figure 13**).

9. To expose the pegs on the shifter drum, remove the screw from the cover plate, and remove the plate.

Shift Linkage Inspection (Chain Drive)

1. If the transmission fails to shift gears, check for: a weak pawl spring; bent, worn, or binding pawls; worn shifter drum pegs; a broken return spring; or a broken return spring stop.

2. If the transmission undershifts or overshifts, check for: a binding, bent, or worn detent; a weak detent spring; bent or worn pawls; worn pegs; a loose return spring stop; or a bent or weak return spring.

3. If the transmission jumps out of gear, check for: a binding, bent, or worn detent; or a weak detent spring.

4. To check the tension of the detent spring, measure its free length with calipers (**Figure 17**). Replace the spring if it measures more than:

   a. 0.98 in. (25 mm) on 1973–1976 models

   b. 0.96 in. (24.5 mm) on 1977 models

   c. 0.94 in. (23.9 mm) on 1978 models

   d. 0.94 in. (23.9 mm) — 1979 and later models with detent spring

   e. 1.26 in. (32.0 mm) — 1979 and later models with neutral spring

5. Replace any other broken, bent, binding, or worn parts, including shifter drum pegs.

Shift Linkage Installation (Chain Drive)

Refer to **Figure 12**.

1. If any of the shifter drum pegs were replaced, make certain that the long peg (which turns on the "neutral" light) is installed as shown in **Figure 18**.

2. Install the gear position detent on its mount to the left of the shifter drum. Install the mounting screw, being careful not to jam the detent. Attach the detent spring with the opening facing down.

3. *1979 and later:* Install the neutral detent arm on the shift rod end. Install the circlip and attach the detent spring with its opening facing down (**Figure 13**).

4. Install the cover plate on the shifter drum, if removed. Use Loctite if there is no lockwasher.

5. Make sure the return spring pin (**Figure 19**) is not loose. It must protrude out from the crankcase by 0.8 in. (20 mm) for it to work effectively. Readjust if necessary.

6. Be sure the return spring and pawl spring are properly in place on the shaft. **Figure 20** shows the proper position for the pawl spring (a) and the return spring (b).

7. Install the shift mechanism and shaft; place the shift arm and overshift limiter onto the pins on the shift drum.

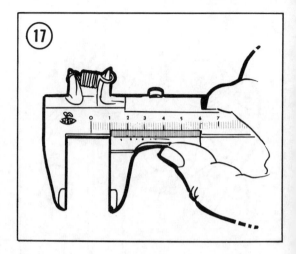

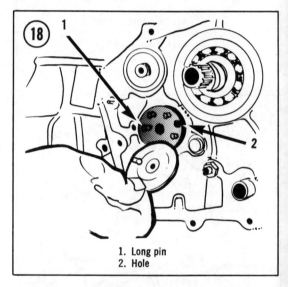

1. Long pin
2. Hole

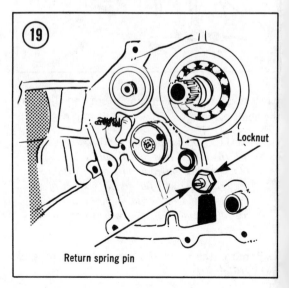

Locknut

Return spring pin

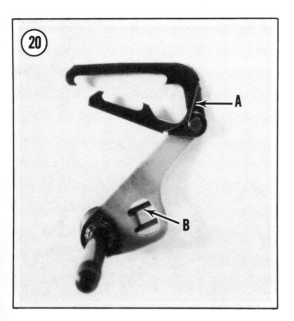

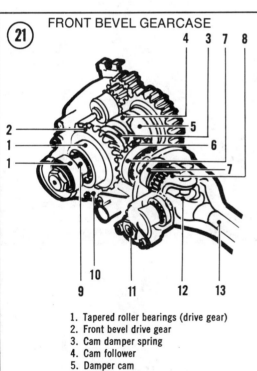

FRONT BEVEL GEARCASE

1. Tapered roller bearings (drive gear)
2. Front bevel drive gear
3. Cam damper spring
4. Cam follower
5. Damper cam
6. Front bevel driven gear
7. Tapered roller bearings (driven gear)
8. Drive shaft sliding joint
9. Front bevel drive gear shaft
10. Front bevel gear case
11. Swing arm pivot shaft
12. Universal joint
13. Drive shaft

8. Install the shift linkage cover with dowel and 9 screws.

9. Put the sprocket spacer on the output shaft.

> NOTE: *The spacer is installed after the transmission cover so as to avoid damaging the output shaft oil seal.*

10. Mount the neutral light wire.

11. Install the drive sprocket (see *Drive Sprocket Installation*).

12. Install the drive sprocket cover (see *Sprocket Cover Installation*).

TRANSMISSION OUTER PARTS (SHAFT DRIVE)

Some transmission parts can be repaired without splitting the engine cases. These outer parts are the:

a. Front bevel drive

b. Shift linkage

The outer parts are described in the following sections.

FRONT BEVEL DRIVE

Shaft Drive

The front bevel drive gearcase is mounted on the left side of the engine cases, connecting to the transmission output shaft through a damper cam (**Figure 21**). Trouble should be very infrequent, as long as the recommended lubrication is adhered to (see Chapter Three). The front bevel drive shares oil with the engine for lubrication.

Bevel gear backlash, tooth contact patterns, and tapered roller bearing preload are all critical to bevel drive strength, quietness and longevity. Assembly to the proper tolerances requires several special tools and a high degree of skill. In the event of bevel drive trouble, we recommend you remove the unit from the motorcycle and take it to your Kawasaki dealer for repair.

The shaft drive clutch release is mounted on the inside of the front bevel gearcase, requiring bevel case removal for replacement. The front bevel gearcase must also be removed before removing the engine from the frame, and to service the shift linkage.

Front Bevel Removal

1. Put the bike on its centerstand.

2. Put an oil pan under the front bevel case.

3. Loosen the 2 starter cover bolts.

4. Remove the left footpeg assembly.

5. Put the transmission in NEUTRAL and remove the shift pedal bolt and the pedal.

6. Remove the 4 front bevel cover bolts and the cover (**Figure 22**).

7. Remove the clutch release lever cotter pin and disconnect the clutch cable from the lever (B, **Figure 23**). Pull the cable free of the gear case.

8. Disconnect the neutral wire at the switch (A, **Figure 23**).

9. Pull the coupling dust cover forward off the swing arm flange.

10. Turn the rear wheel until you can see a hole in the smooth rim of the coupling (**Figure 24**). In the hole is a pin that locks the coupling in the forward position.

11. Push the coupling lock pin in about 3/16 in. and push or pry the coupling back off the bevel drive output gear.

> NOTE: *The drive shaft and coupling are spring loaded to the front. Use only enough force to free the coupling on the side by the lock pin. If necessary, remove the rear wheel and loosen the 4 rear bevel drive nuts at the swing arm to take some load off the coupling (see **Rear Bevel Removal**, Chapter Ten).*

12. Remove the 11 front bevel case bolts (**Figure 25**).

13. Tap the case with a soft mallet to free it, and remove the bevel case and gasket. The damper cam follower and spring should come off with the bevel case (**Figure 26**).

Front Bevel Inspection

See **Figure 27**. Although it may be practical for you to disassemble the bevel drive for inspection, you cannot replace the bearings or seals (which require bearing removal) without special tools. If there is trouble in the drive unit, it may be best to remove the unit, take it to your Kawasaki dealer, and let him overhaul it.

Check the wear pattern on the bevel teeth (**Figure 28**). Check for the following characteristics:

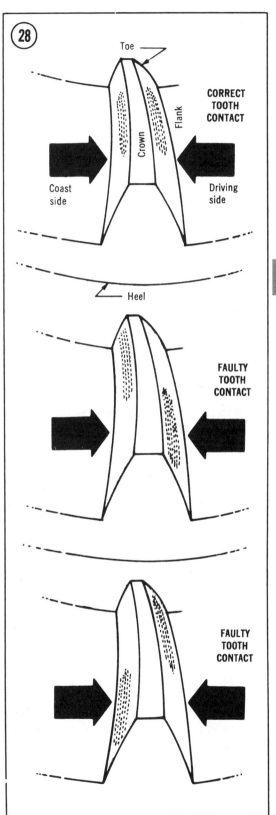

6

a. Some clearance between top of teeth and top of pattern.

b. No distinct lines indicating high pressure areas.

c. Marks on adjoining teeth should be directly opposite each other.

d. Both drive and coast patterns should be fairly well centered on teeth. Check bevel gear backlash at the driven gear bevel teeth. Standard backlash is 0.005–0.007 in. (0.13–0.18 mm).

Front Bevel Installation

1. Install the 2 dowel pins (A, **Figure 29**) and a new gasket.

2. Turn the bevel output gear until the lockpin faces up (**Figure 30**). Make sure the lock pin spring is inside the gear.

3. Check that the clutch release screw end is not protruding above the shaft (**Figure 31**).

4. Coat the clutch pushrod end and the bevel output gear with molybdenum disulfide grease.

5. Align the damper cam and cam follower, and install the front bevel case over the shifter shaft and onto the engine. Take care not to damage the shift shaft oil seal.

> NOTE: *If the spring-loaded coupling is too tight, remove the rear wheel and loosen the 4 rear bevel drive nuts at the swing arm to provide adequate play (see **Rear Bevel Removal**, Chapter Ten).*

6. Tighten the 11 bevel case bolts.

7. Align the lock pin hole on the bevel output gear with the hole in the drive shaft coupling (**Figure 32**).

8. Insert the lock pin and push it in just enough to let the coupling slide forward over the gear.

> NOTE: *Don't push the lock pin in too far. It can fall inside the bevel drive gear.*

9. Maneuver the coupling as required to allow the lock pin to spring out and seat in the coupling.

10. If the rear bevel mounting nuts were loosened, torque them to 22 ft.-lb. (3.0 mkg).

11. Slip the coupling dust cover back over the swing arm flange.

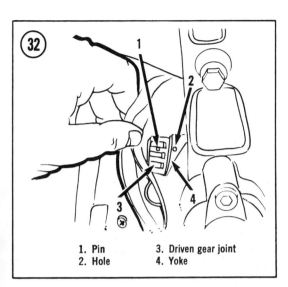

1. Pin
2. Hole
3. Driven gear joint
4. Yoke

12. Connect the neutral indicator wire to the switch.

13. Connect the clutch cable and install a new cotter pin.

14. Install the front bevel cover, 4 bolts and washers.

15. Tighten the starter cover bolts.

16. Install the shift pedal.

17. Install the footpeg.

18. Add engine oil and check the level.

SHIFT LINKAGE (SHAFT DRIVE)

The shaft drive shift linkage functions the same as the chain drive model's, but the parts are newly designed (**Figure 33**).

6

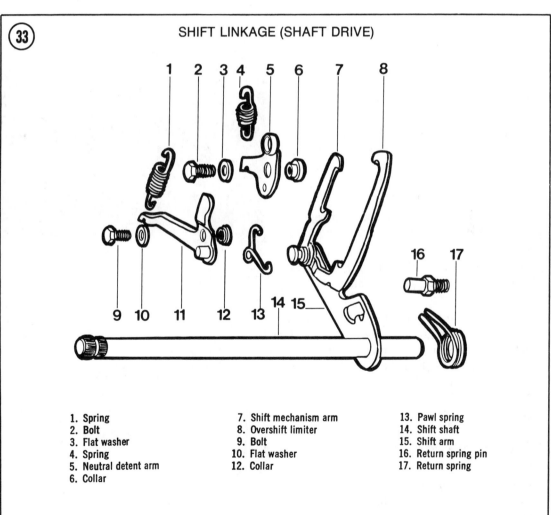

SHIFT LINKAGE (SHAFT DRIVE)

1. Spring
2. Bolt
3. Flat washer
4. Spring
5. Neutral detent arm
6. Collar
7. Shift mechanism arm
8. Overshift limiter
9. Bolt
10. Flat washer
12. Collar
13. Pawl spring
14. Shift shaft
15. Shift arm
16. Return spring pin
17. Return spring

Shift Linkage Removal (Shaft Drive)

1. Remove the front bevel drive (see *Front Bevel Removal*).

2. Remove the shift shaft; pull the pawls away from the shift drum, turn the shaft counterclockwise (to the left) and pull out the shaft assembly (B, **Figure 29**).

3. Remove the gear position detent (A) and neutral detant (B, Figure 34) springs.

4. Remove the detent arm pivot bolts and arms (**Figure 34**).

> NOTE: *Do not pull the shift rod (A, **Figure 35**) out. If it is pulled out by 1½ in. (40 mm), the internal shift forks within the crankcase will fall to the bottom of the oil pan. This would require removal and disassembly of the engine to reposition them.*

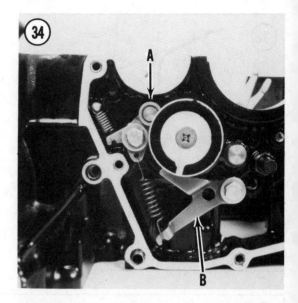

5. To expose the pegs on the shift drum, remove the screw and cover plate.

Shift Linkage Inspection (Shaft Drive)

1. If the transmission fails to shift gears, check for: a weak pawl spring; bent, worn, or binding pawls; worn shifter drum pegs; a broken return spring; or a broken return spring stop.

2. If the transmission undershifts or overshifts, check for: a binding, bent, or worn detent; a weak detent spring; bent or worn pawls; worn pegs; a loose return spring stop; or a bent or weak return spring.

3. If the transmission jumps out of gear, check for: a binding, bent, or worn detent; or a weak detent spring.

4. To check the tension of the detent springs, measure the free length with a caliper (**Figure 36**). Replace the springs if they measure more than 0.85 in. (21.6 mm) for the neutral detent or 1.47 in. (37.3 mm) for the gear position detent.

5. Replace any other broken, bent, binding, or worn parts, including shifter drum pegs.

Shift Linkage Installation (Shaft Drive)

Refer to **Figure 33**.

1. If any of the shift drum pins were removed, make certain the long peg which turns on the "neutral" light is assembled in the position shown (**Figure 37**). Use Loctite on the pin plate screw.

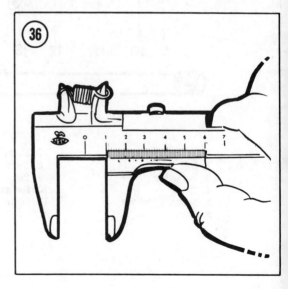

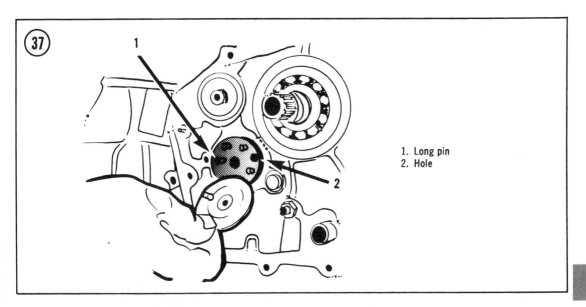

1. Long pin
2. Hole

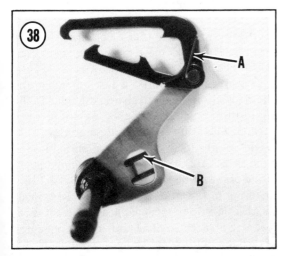

2. Check that the shift return spring pin is tight (B, **Figure 35**). If loose, apply Loctite and torque it to 14.5 ft.-lb. (2.0 mkg).

3. Put the shift drum in NEUTRAL (**Figure 35**).

4. Insert the flat washers, detent arms, and collars on the detent bolts (**Figure 33**).

5. Check that the return spring (B) and pawl spring (A) are on the shift shaft linkage (**Figure 38**).

6. Install the shift mechanism and shaft; place the shift pawls onto the pins of the shift drum (**Figure 39**).

7. Install the front bevel case (see *Front Bevel Installation*).

TRANSMISSION INTERNAL PARTS

Several transmission parts can only be repaired after splitting the engine cases. See *Engine Removal* and *Crankcase Separation* in Chapter Four. These internal parts are the:

    a. Shift drum and forks

    b. Input shaft and gears

    c. Output shaft and gears

    d. Kickstarter ratchet

These internal parts are described in the following sections.

If the transmission fails to shift properly or jumps out of gear, check the functioning of the shift linkage before splitting the engine cases (see *Shift Linkage Inspection*).

Transmission Gears

The basic transmission consists of 5 gears on the input shaft meshed with 5 gears on the output shaft (**Figure 40**). Each pair of meshed gears constitutes one speed (one gear ratio). In each pair, one of the gears is locked to its shaft and must turn with its shaft. The other gear is not attached to its shaft and can spin freely on it. Located next to the free spinning gear is a third gear which is splined to the shaft and must turn with it. This third gear can be slid from side to side along the splines of the shaft. The side of the splined gear and the side of the free-spinning gear have mating tongues and grooves ("dogs"). When the splined gear is slid up against the free-spinning gear, the 2 gears are locked together. This locks the free-spinning gear to its shaft. Since both of the meshed gears are now locked to their respective shafts, the power is transmitted from the input shaft to the output shaft through that gear ratio.

Neutral "Finder"

In 4th gear on the output shaft are 3 steel balls, spaced 120 degrees apart, which help prevent the transmission from overshooting to 2nd gear when the rider wants to shift from 1st to neutral. As long as the bike is moving and the output shaft is turning, the balls are thrown away from the shaft and will allow upshifting to 2nd. When the bike stops, a ball falls into a groove in the shaft and keeps the gear from sliding into position for higher gears.

Shift Drum and Forks

Each sliding gear has a deep groove machined in its face (**Figure 41**). In this groove rides the curved arm of a shift fork. When the shift fork is moved sideways, it moves the sliding gear sideways on its shaft.

Only 2 of the 3 shift forks—the ones working the sliding gears on the output shaft—are mounted on the shift fork shaft. The rear ends of the shift forks are pegs, which ride in camming slots in the face of the shift drum (**Figure 42**). When the gear selector mechanism rotates the shift drum, the zigzag camming slots move the

shift forks from side to side along their shaft. In turn, the shift forks move the sliding gears from side to side.

The third shift fork, which operates the sliding gear on the input shaft, is sleeved to the shift drum instead of being mounted on a separate shaft. But it works the same way.

On 1973–1978 models, a spring-loaded plunger beneath the shift drum rises into a notch in the drum at the NEUTRAL position, stabilizing the drum in NEUTRAL. For 1979 and later models, this shift drum-mounted neutral detent is replaced by an external neutral detent mounted next to the shift linkage and gear position detent.

SHIFT DRUM AND FORKS

Removal

Refer to **Figure 43**.

1. Remove the engine from the motorcycle (see *Engine Removal,* Chapter Four).

2. Split the engine cases (See *Crankcase Separation,* Chapter Four).

3. In the lower engine case, use a drift to push against the end of the shifter fork shaft nearest the clutch. Pull out the shaft from the other end of the engine case, taking off the 2 shift forks as you go (**Figure 44**).

4. On the outside of the engine case, to the left of the shift drum, remove the gear detent (A) and

6

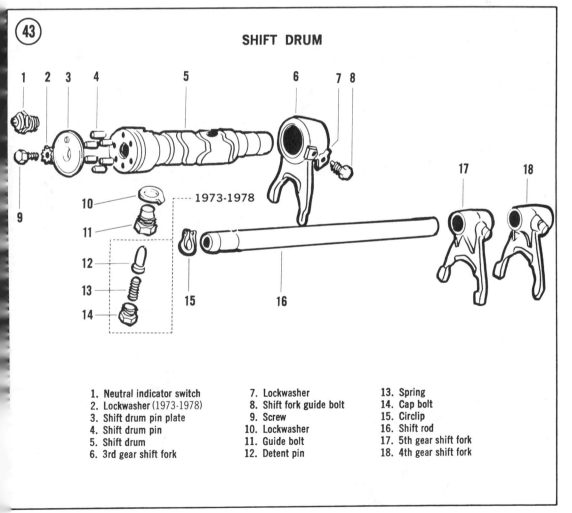

SHIFT DRUM

1973-1978

1. Neutral indicator switch
2. Lockwasher (1973-1978)
3. Shift drum pin plate
4. Shift drum pin
5. Shift drum
6. 3rd gear shift fork

7. Lockwasher
8. Shift fork guide bolt
9. Screw
10. Lockwasher
11. Guide bolt
12. Detent pin

13. Spring
14. Cap bolt
15. Circlip
16. Shift rod
17. 5th gear shift fork
18. 4th gear shift fork

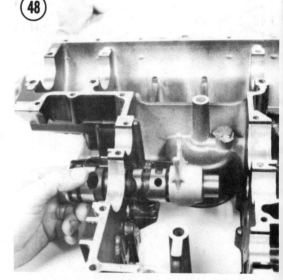

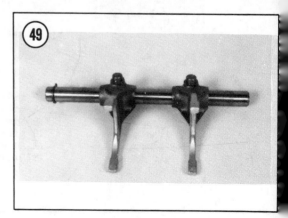

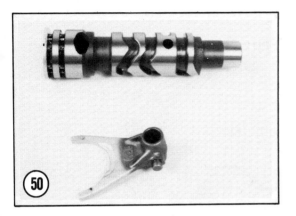

neutral detent (B) arm(s) (**Figure 45**). See *Shift Linkage Removal.*

5. On the remaining shift fork, flatten the tab washer and unscrew the peg (**Figure 46**).

6. Turn the engine case upside down. Flatten the tab washer that locks the shift drum guide bolt. Unscrew the guide bolt assembly (**Figure 47**).

7. Pull the shift drum out of the engine case, taking off the third shift fork as you go (**Figure 48**).

Shift Drum and Fork Inspection

Specifications for transmission parts not given here are listed in **Table 1** at the end of this chapter.

1. Inspect each shift fork for signs of wear or cracking. Make sure the forks slide smoothly on their respective shafts. Make sure the shafts are not bent (see **Figure 49**).

> NOTE: *Check for any arc-shaped wear or burned marks on the shift forks. If this is apparent, the fingers are worn beyond use and fork must be replaced.*

2. Measure the thickness of each shift fork arm with a caliper. Replace any fork measuring less than 0.22 in. (5.7 mm).

3. Check grooves in the shift drum (**Figure 50**) for wear or roughness.

4. Check the cam pin follower in each shift fork. It should fit snug but not too tight. Check the end that rides in the shift drum for wear or burrs. Replace as necessary.

Shift Drum and Fork Installation

Refer to **Figure 43**.

1. Apply molybdenum disulfide grease to new parts.

2. Push the shift drum into the engine case. Position the 3rd gear shift fork so that the drum will enter the short end of the fork first.

3. *1973–1978:* Rotate the shifter drum to the neutral position, so that the neutral dimple is aligned beneath the mounting hole for the neutral plunger.

4. *1973–1978:* Apply Loctite to the threads of the neutral plunger and install it.

5. To complete the reassembly of the shift mechanism, follow the remainder of the disassembly procedures in reverse order.

INPUT SHAFT

Disassembly

Refer to **Figure 51**.

Note the position of any additional shims for reassembly.

1. Remove the input shaft assembly from the engine case (**Figure 52**).

2. Take off the outer clutch hub, the clutch needle bearing, the clutch bushing, and the thrust washer.

3. From the other end of the input shaft, take off the drive shaft bushing, O-ring *(Shaft Drive only),* and the circlip.

4. Pull off the needle bearing, the 2 washers, 2nd gear, 5th gear, the 5th gear bushing, and the splined washer.

5. Take off the snap ring, and pull off 3rd gear.

6. Take off the last snap ring. Pull off the splined washer and 4th gear.

7. Remove the ball bearing assembly with a bearing puller.

Input Shaft Assembly

Refer to **Figure 51**.

1. Check each gear for excessive wear, burrs, pitting, or chipped or missing teeth. Make sure the lugs on ends of gears are in good condition.

> NOTE: *Defective gears should be replaced, and it is a good idea to replace*

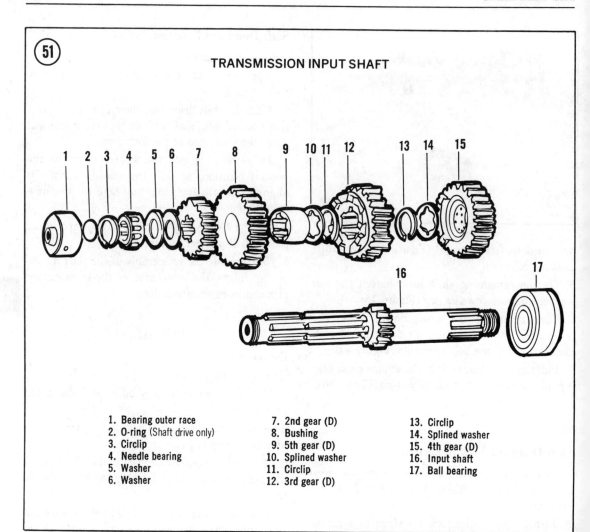

TRANSMISSION INPUT SHAFT

1. Bearing outer race
2. O-ring (Shaft drive only)
3. Circlip
4. Needle bearing
5. Washer
6. Washer
7. 2nd gear (D)
8. Bushing
9. 5th gear (D)
10. Splined washer
11. Circlip
12. 3rd gear (D)
13. Circlip
14. Splined washer
15. 4th gear (D)
16. Input shaft
17. Ball bearing

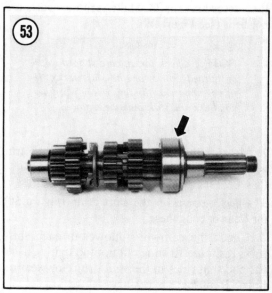

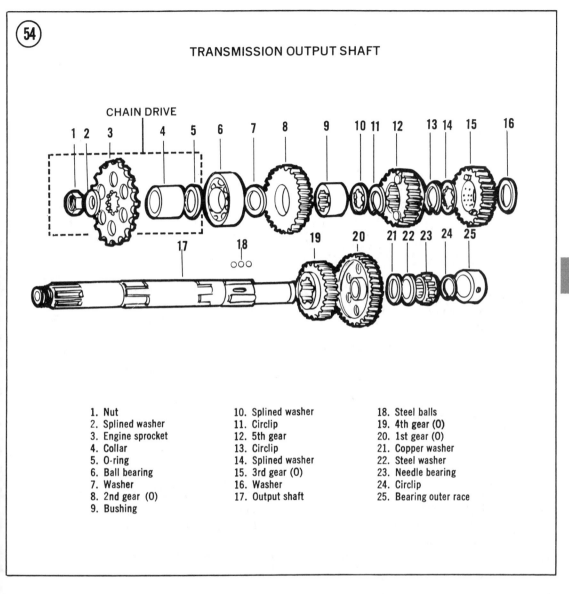

54

TRANSMISSION OUTPUT SHAFT

CHAIN DRIVE

1 2 3 4 5 6 7 8 9 10 11 12 13 14 15 16

17 18 19 20 21 22 23 24 25

1. Nut	10. Splined washer	18. Steel balls
2. Splined washer	11. Circlip	19. 4th gear (O)
3. Engine sprocket	12. 5th gear	20. 1st gear (O)
4. Collar	13. Circlip	21. Copper washer
5. O-ring	14. Splined washer	22. Steel washer
6. Ball bearing	15. 3rd gear (O)	23. Needle bearing
7. Washer	16. Washer	24. Circlip
8. 2nd gear (O)	17. Output shaft	25. Bearing outer race
9. Bushing		

6

the mating gear on the other shaft even though it may not show signs of wear or damage.

2. Make sure all gears slide smoothly on the shaft splines.

3. Check the condition of the bearing. Make sure it rotates smoothly with no signs of wear or damage. Replace it if necessary.

4. Follow the disassembly procedures in the reverse order, along with the additional procedures listed below.

5. To install the ball bearing assembly on the clutch end of the drive shaft, turn the bearing so

that its groove faces away from the drive shaft (**Figure 53**). Put the bearing on the drive shaft and press it into place.

6. When fitting 3rd gear and the 5th gear bushing to the splines of the drive shaft, turn them so that their oil holes will be aligned with the oil holes in the splines of the drive shaft.

OUTPUT SHAFT

Disassembly

Refer to **Figures 54 and 55**.

Note the position of any additional shims for reassembly.

1. Remove the output shaft assembly from the engine case (**Figure 56**).

2. Remove the output shaft bushing and circlip.

3. Pull off the needle bearing, the 2 washers, and 1st gear.

4. Pull off 4th gear. To remove the gear, spin the shaft in a vertical position, holding onto 3rd gear. Pull the 4th gear up and off the shaft.

> NOTE: *Perform this procedure over and close down to a workbench with some shop cloths spread over it. This will lessen the chance of losing the neutral locating balls when the gear comes off.*

5. *Shaft drive:* Pry out the staked part of the damper cam nut (**Figure 57**). Be careful not to damage the output shaft.

6. *Shaft drive:* Hold the damper cam in a soft-jawed vise, and remove the damper cam nut, washer, and the cam.

7. Use a bearing puller to remove the ball bearing assembly from the shaft.

8. Pull off the washer, 2nd gear, the 2nd gear bushing, and the splined washer.

9. Remove the first snap ring. Pull off 5th gear.

10. Remove the second snap ring. Pull off the splined washer, 3rd gear, and the last washer.

Output Shaft Assembly

Refer to **Figures 54 and 55**.

1. Check each gear for excessive wear, burrs, pitting, or chipped or missing teeth. Make sure the lugs on ends of gears are in good condition.

> NOTE: *Defective gears should be replaced, and it is a good idea to replace the mating gear on the other shaft even though it may not show as much wear or damage.*

2. Make sure that all gears slide smoothly on the shaft splines.

3. Check the condition of the bearing. Make sure it rotates smoothly with no signs of wear or damage. Replace if necessary.

4. Follow disassembly procedures in the reverse order along with the procedures listed below.

5. When fitting 5th gear and the 2nd gear bushing to the splines of the output shaft, turn them so that their oil holes will be aligned with the oil holes in the output shaft.

6. Put the ball bearing assembly on the threaded end of the output shaft with the groove in the bearing facing toward the shaft (**Figure 56**). Press the bearing into place.

7. When installing 4th gear and its 3 steel balls, do not grease the balls; they must be free to roll easily.

8. *Shaft drive*: Torque the damper cam nut to 90 ft.-lb. (12.0 mkg). Stake it into the shaft notch as shown in **Figure 57**.

KICKSTARTER

Refer to **Figure 58** for this procedure.

The kickstarter shaft is to the rear of the output shaft. When the kickstarter is operated

with the transmission in neutral and the clutch engaged, the kickstarter gear turns 1st gear on the input shaft, which turns the input shaft, which turns the clutch, which turns the crankshaft. Whenever the engine is running and the clutch is engaged and the input shaft is turning, the kickstarter gear is also turning.

When the kickstarter shaft is in its normal position, a camming ramp on the engine case holds the arm and keeps the ratchet gear from engaging kickstarter gear (see **Figure 59**).

When the kickstarter shaft is rotated clockwise, the arm on the ratchet gear is freed from the camming ramp. The engaging spring moves the ratchet gear against the kickstarter gear. The teeth engage, and the ratchet gear locks the kickstarter gear to the kickstarter shaft.

6

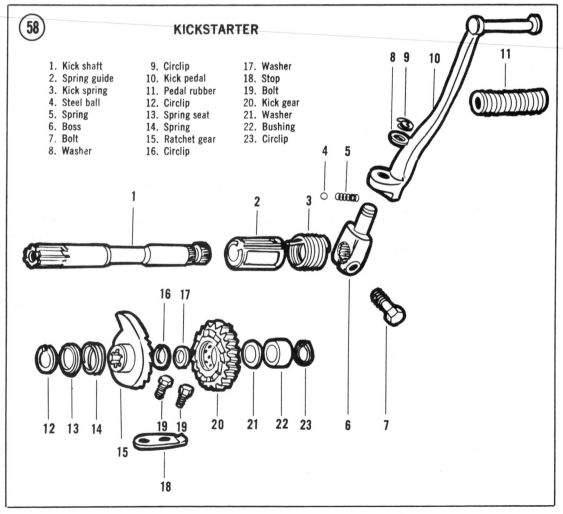

KICKSTARTER

1. Kick shaft
2. Spring guide
3. Kick spring
4. Steel ball
5. Spring
6. Boss
7. Bolt
8. Washer
9. Circlip
10. Kick pedal
11. Pedal rubber
12. Circlip
13. Spring seat
14. Spring
15. Ratchet gear
16. Circlip
17. Washer
18. Stop
19. Bolt
20. Kick gear
21. Washer
22. Bushing
23. Circlip

Kickstarter Ratchet Removal

1. Remove the engine from the frame.

2. Split the engine cases.

3. Remove the kickstarter ratchet assembly (**Figure 59**).

4. To strip the kickstarter shaft, remove the 2 circlips from the splined portion of the shaft. Then slide off the cap, the engaging spring, the ratchet gear, the washer, the kickstarter gear, the other washer, and the bushing.

Kickstarter Ratchet Inspection

1. Visually inspect the arm on the ratchet gear and the camming ramp bolted to the upper engine case. If either component shows excess wear or damage, replace it with a new one.

2. Check for broken, chipped, or missing teeth on all gears. Replace any if necessary.

3. Make sure the engagement gear operates smoothly on its shaft.

4. Check all parts for uneven wear; replace any that are questionable.

Kickstarter Ratchet Installation

1. Reassemble the components on the kickstarter shaft in the reverse order of removal.

2. When fitting the ratchet gear to the splines of the shaft, align the mark on the gear with the mark on the end of the shaft (**Figure 60**).

Table 1 TRANSMISSION SPECIFICATIONS

Item	Specification	
	Standard	Wear Limit
Clutch housing/primary gear backlash @ housing teeth	0–0.002 in. (0.01–0.06 mm)	0.004 in. (0.11 mm)
Clutch housing ID	———	1.458 in. (37.03 mm)
Clutch housing sleeve ID	———	1.258 in. (31.96 mm)
Transmission gear backlash		
900 cc first gear	0.001–0.007 in. (0.02–0.19 mm)	0.010 in. (0.25 mm)
All others	0.002–0.009 in. (0.06–0.23 mm)	0.012 in. (0.30 mm)
Shift fork finger thickness	———	0.224 in. (5.70 mm)
Gear fork groove width	———	0.246 in. (6.25 mm)
Shift drum groove width	———	0.325 in. (8.25 mm)
Shift fork guide pin width	———	
Fourth, fifth		0.309 in. (7.85 mm)
Third	———	0.312 in. (7.92 mm)
Shift drum neutral detent spring free length	———	1.26 in. (32.0 mm)
Gear/shaft or bushing clearance	———	
Output first		0.006 in. (0.16 mm)
Output second, input fifth	———	0.007 in. (0.17 mm)
Output third, input fourth	———	0.006 in. (0.16 mm)
Kickstarter gear ID	———	0.868 in. (22.05 mm)
Kickstarter shaft OD	———	0.863 in. (21.91 mm)

6

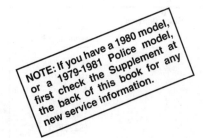

NOTE: If you have a 1980 model, or a 1979-1981 Police model, first check the Supplement at the back of this book for any new service information.

CHAPTER SEVEN

FUEL AND EXHAUST SYSTEMS

The fuel system consists of the fuel tank, shut-off valve, fuel filter, four Mikuni slide needle carburetors, and an air cleaner.

The exhaust system consists of the exhaust pipes, collectors, crossover pipe, and mufflers.

This chapter includes service procedures for all parts of the fuel and exhaust systems.

FUEL TANK

All the fuel tanks have vented gas caps that could stop fuel flow to the carburetors if plugged.

Fuel Tank Removal

1. Swing the seat open.

2. Remove the side cover.

3. *1973-1977:* Turn the fuel tap OFF (manual tap). *1978 and later*: Turn the fuel ON (vacuum tap).

4. Disconnect the fuel (and vacuum) lines at the fuel tap; raise the rear of the tank slightly, if required.

5. *Models with fuel level gauge:* Disconnect the fuel sender wires.

6. Lift the rear of the tank and pull it back and off.

Fuel Tank Installation

Reverse the removal steps, and note:

a. *Models with vacuum fuel tap:* The vacuum hose is smaller than the fuel hose (**Figure 1**).

b. Insert the front brackets carefully on the rubber grommets on the frame (**Figure 2**). Don't pinch any wires or control cables.

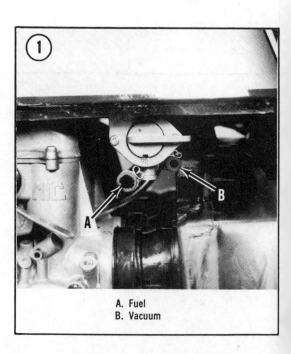

A. Fuel
B. Vacuum

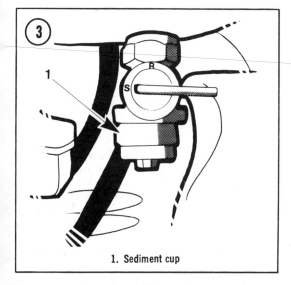

1. Sediment cup

Fuel Tank Sealing (Pin Hole)

A small pin hole size leak can be sealed with the use of a product called Thextonite Gas Tank Sealer Stick or equivalent. Follow the manufacturer's instructions.

Fuel Tank Sealing (Small Hole)

This procedure requires the use of a non-flammable non-petroleum solvent.

If you feel unqualified to accomplish it, take the tank to your dealer and let him seal the tank.

WARNING
Before attempting any service on the fuel tank be sure to have a fire extinguisher

rated for gasoline or chemical fires within reach. Do not smoke or work where there are any open flames. The work area must be well ventilated.

1. Remove the tank as described under *Fuel Tank Removal/Installation* in this chapter.

2. Mark the spot on the tank where the leak is visible with a grease pencil.

3. Turn the fuel shutoff valve to the RESERVE position and blow the interior of the tank completely dry with compressed air.

4. Turn the fuel shutoff valve to the OFF position and pour about 1 qt. (1 liter) of the non-flammable solvent into the tank, install the fuel fill cap and shake the tank vigorously one or two minutes. This is used to remove all fuel residue.

5. Drain the solvent/gasoline solution into a safe storable container. This solution may be reused.

6. Remove the fuel shutoff valve by unscrewing the fitting from the tank. If necessary, plug the tank with a cork or tape it closed with duct tape.

7. Again blow the tank interior completely dry with compressed air.

8. Position the tank so that the point of the leak is located at the lowest part of the tank. This will allow the sealant to accumulate at the point of the leak.

9. Pour the sealant into the tank (a silicone rubber base sealer like Pro-Tech Fuel Tank Sealer, or equivalent, may be used). This is available at most motorcycle supply stores.

10. Let tank set in this position for at least 48 hours.

11. After the sealant has dried, install the fuel shutoff valve, turn it to the OFF position, and refill the tank with fuel.

12. After the tank has been filled, let it sit for at least 2 hours and recheck the leak area.

13. Install the tank on the motorcycle.

FUEL TAP

Manual fuel taps have sediment bowls and screens that should be cleaned at regular intervals (**Figure 3**).

Vacuum fuel taps have no OFF position. This tap should not pass fuel in ON or RES until a running engine provides the vacuum to operate the diaphragm valve. In PRI (prime) the tap will pass fuel whether there is vacuum or not.

7

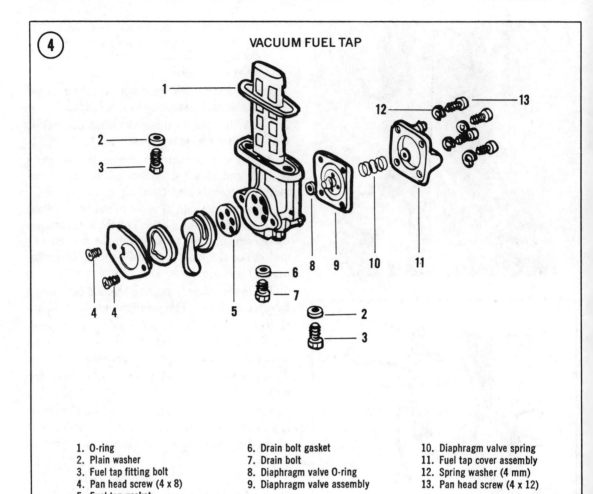

④ **VACUUM FUEL TAP**

1. O-ring
2. Plain washer
3. Fuel tap fitting bolt
4. Pan head screw (4 x 8)
5. Fuel tap gasket
6. Drain bolt gasket
7. Drain bolt
8. Diaphragm valve O-ring
9. Diaphragm valve assembly
10. Diaphragm valve spring
11. Fuel tap cover assembly
12. Spring washer (4 mm)
13. Pan head screw (4 x 12)

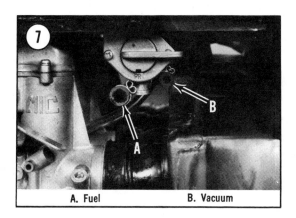

A. Fuel   B. Vacuum

Vacuum Fuel Tap Removal

1. Remove the fuel tank.

2. Turn the fuel tap to PRI and drain the gasoline into a suitable container.

> **WARNING**
> *Gasoline is extremely flammable. Do not smoke or work near flames or sparks. Keep a BC rated fire extinguisher on hand, and provide plenty of ventilation.*

3. Remove the fuel tap mounting bolts, gasket, and the tap. Take care not to damage the filter.

Vacuum Fuel Tap Inspection

Disassemble the tap (**Figure 4**) and check that the O-rings and diaphragm valve are clean and undamaged. Any bit of debris on the valve O-ring (**Figure 5**) will prevent the valve from closing.

Vacuum Fuel Tap Installation

Reverse the removal procedure, and note:

a. Assemble the tap with the diaphragm cover as shown (**Figure 6**).

b. The vacuum hose is smaller than the fuel hose (**Figure 7**).

CARBURETORS

Kawasaki uses the same basic Mikuni slide needle carburetors with minor variations on all the 900 and 1000cc engines. See **Table 1** at the end of the chapter for complete specifications. Some of the major differences are given here.

a. The 1974 and later carburetors have overflow tubes.

b. The 1977–1978 bikes and all LTD's use a pilot screw on the bottom to adjust pilot fuel, rather than pilot air flow. This is a more critical adjustment than air screw adjustment.

c. Late 1977 and later bikes have a spring-loaded floating mount jet needle.

d. The 1979 and later bikes have an accelerator pump on carburetor No. 2, with accelerator port check valves in the base of each float bowl.

e. The 1979 LTD has a vacuum sensor on the bottom of carburetor No. 2 that disables the accelerator pump when the engine is *not* running.

Basic Principles

An understanding of the function of each of the carburetor components and their relationship to one another is a valuable aid for pinpointing a source of carburetor trouble.

The carburetor's purpose is to supply and atomize fuel and mix it in correct proportions with air that is drawn in through the air intake. At the primary throttle opening—at idle—a small amount of fuel is siphoned through the pilot jet by the incoming air (**Figure 8**). As the throttle is opened further, the air stream begins to siphon fuel through the main jet and needle jet. The tapered needle increases the effective flow capacity of the needle jet, as it is lifted with the air slide, in that it occupies decreasingly less of the area of the jet. In addition, the amount of cutaway in the leading edge of the throttle slide aids in controlling the fuel/air mixture during partial throttle openings.

At full throttle, the carburetor venturi is fully open and the needle is lifted far enough to permit the main jet to flow at full capacity (**Figure 9**).

Troubleshooting

If the bike stalls or bogs down under hard acceleration, check the fuel level as described under *Fuel Level Adjustment* in this chapter.

If the mixture is too lean at any or all throttle settings, the engine may overheat. It may generate brown exhaust smoke. It may stutter at high rpm. The performance (acceleration and top speed) will fall off. You may be able to confirm this by checking the spark plugs. If the mixture is too lean across the rpm scale, the spark plugs will be white, and their electrodes

7

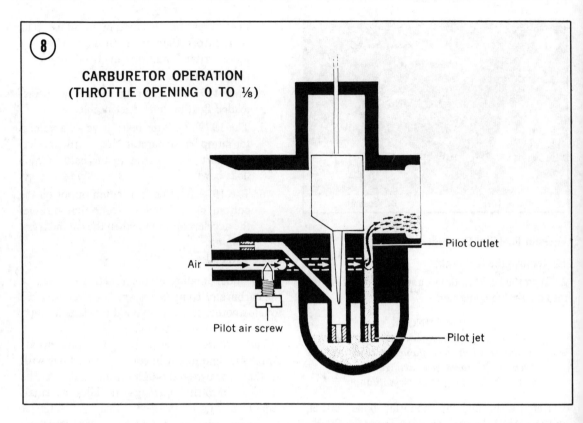

⑧ CARBURETOR OPERATION
(THROTTLE OPENING 0 TO ⅛)

Pilot outlet

Air

Pilot air screw

Pilot jet

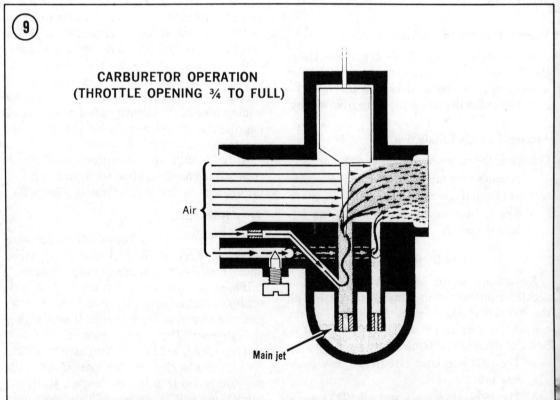

⑨ CARBURETOR OPERATION
(THROTTLE OPENING ¾ TO FULL)

Air

Main jet

may be rounded. While riding the motorcycle, turn on the carburetor starting system to see it the performance improves with what would normally be an overrich mixture.

If the mixture is too rich at any or all throttle settings, the engine may run sluggish and blubbery. It may generate black exhaust smoke. It may perform best while still cold. If the mixture is too rich across the rpm scale, the spark plugs may be black and sooty. Take out the air cleaner element and ride the motorcycle to see if the performance improves with what would normally be too lean a mixture. Don't ride without the air cleaner any longer than it takes to see if the mixture was too rich.

Diagnosing the Problem

The fact that the mixture being burned is too rich or too lean does not necessarily indicate that the carburetion is at fault. The motorcycle may as easily have an ignition or compression problem.

If the mixture is wrong all up and down the rpm range, check the obvious fuel system components. For example, if the mixture is too rich, check for a clogged air cleaner element or too high a fuel level. If the mixture is too lean, check the petcock strainer and the fuel lines for foreign material, check for too low a fuel level, and check for an air leak at the intake manifold.

Before taking apart the carburetors, you should first check out the spark plugs, the contact breaker points and ignition timing, and the cylinder compression.

Rejetting the Carburetors

Do not try to solve a carburetion problem by rejetting if all the following conditions hold true.

NOTE
This book covers U.S. models subject to governmental emissions control laws. These laws subject motorcycle dealers and their employees to heavy fines for modifying emissions related components. Although Federal law does not cover modification by the motorcycle owner, some states have laws that prohibit emission-related modifications by owners. Check the laws in your area before you change carburetor parts.

1. The engine has held a good tune in the past with the standard jetting and needle positions.

2. The engine has not been modified.

3. The motorcycle is being operated in the same geographic region under the same general climatic conditions as in the past.

4. The motorcycle was and is being ridden at average highway speeds.

If those conditions all hold true, the chances are that any problem is due to a malfunction in the carburetion or in another component that needs to be adjusted or repaired. Changing the carburetion probably won't solve the problem.

Rejetting the carburetors may be needed if any of the following conditions hold true.

1. A nonstandard type of air filter element is being used.

2. A nonstandard exhaust system is being used.

3. Any of the top end components in the engine (pistons, valves, compression ratio, etc.) have been modified.

4. The motorcycle is in use at considerably higher or lower altitudes, or in a markedly hotter or colder climate, than in the past.

5. The motorcycle is being operated at considerably higher speeds than before, and changing to colder spark plugs did not solve the problem.

6. Someone has changed the jetting or the needle positions in your motorcycle.

7. The motorcycle has never held a satisfactory engine tune.

If rejetting the carburetors is needed, check with a Kawasaki dealer for recommendations as to the sizes of jets to install.

CARBURETOR ADJUSTMENT

The carburetor service recommended at 6,000 mile intervals involves routine idle speed, synchronization, and idle mixture adjustment.

Alterations in jet size, throttle slide cutaway, changes in needle position, etc., should be attempted only if you're experienced in this type of "tuning" work; a bad guess could result in costly engine damage or, at the very least, poor performance. If after servicing the carburetors and making the adjustments described in Chapter Three, the motorcycle does not perform correctly (and assuming that other factors affecting performance are correct, such as ignition timing and condition, valve adjustment, etc.), the motorcycle should be checked by a Kawasaki dealer or a qualified performance tuning specialist.

Mechanical Synchronization

Initial rough synchronization should be performed any time the throttle linkage has been disturbed, after a carburetor has been removed, or any time the idle is so rough that vacuum synchronization won't work.

1. Remove the carburetor assembly from the engine (see *Carburetor Removal*).

2. *1976 and later:* Turn the idle adjust knob to get 1/16–1/8 in.(1.6–2.0 mm) clearance between the throttle cable bracket and the pulley stopper (**Figure 10**).

3. *1973–1975:* Check the closed throttle stop clearance.

   a. Turn the idle speed adjust knob until the bottom of the knob is ⅜ in. (10 mm) from its bracket (**Figure 11**).

   b. Loosen the locknut on the closed-throttle stop at the rear of the throttle pulley (**Figure 12**).

   c. Turn the eccentric throttle stop to set clearance between the stop and pulley. Clearance should be 1/16 in. (1.5-2.0mm) on 1973 models and 1/8 in. (2.0-3.0mm) on 1974-1975 models.

4. *1973–1975:* Loosen the synchronizing screw locknut next to the top of each carburetor (**Figure 13**). Your dealer can supply a handy special tool for doing this without removing the fuel tank. Otherwise, a wrench and screwdriver will do.

5. *1976 on:* The synchronizing screws are inside the carburetors, so you'll have to remove the fuel tank to get at them. If you can synchronize the carburetors before the float bowls run dry, fine; if not, you'll have to supply fuel from a temporary hookup.

> WARNING
> *When supplying fuel by temporary means, make sure the tank is secure and that all fuel lines are tight—no leaks.*

   a. Remove the fuel tank (see *Fuel Tank Removal*).

   b. Remove the carb top covers (**Figure 14**).

> WARNING
> *Make sure no dirt or parts fall into the carburetor, or you may wind up with a stuck throttle and no place to go.*

   c. Loosen each synchronizing screw lock. On 1976 models flatten the lockwasher and loosen the lockbolt (**Figure 15**). On *1977 and later models,* loosen the locknut (**Figure 16**).

6. Adjust each synchronizing screw to get 0.028 in. (0.7 mm) clearance from the bottom of the carburetor bore to the bottom of the throttle slide (**Figure 17**), or to the top of the notch in the carburetor slide. See **Figure 18** for 1973–1976 models.

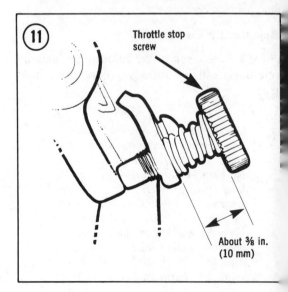

Throttle stop screw

About ⅜ in. (10 mm)

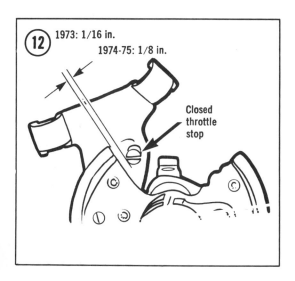

12 1973: 1/16 in.

1974-75: 1/8 in.

Closed throttle stop

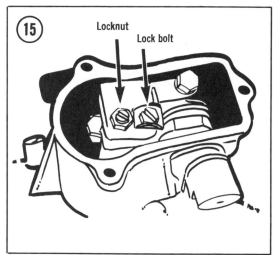

15 Locknut

Lock bolt

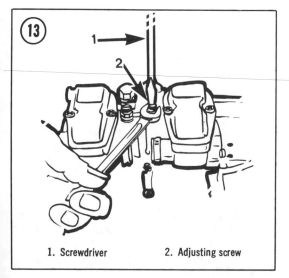

13

1

2

1. Screwdriver   2. Adjusting screw

16

7

14

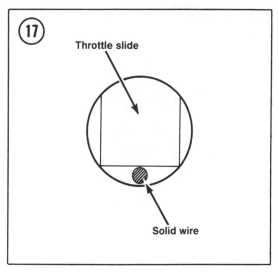

17 Throttle slide

Solid wire

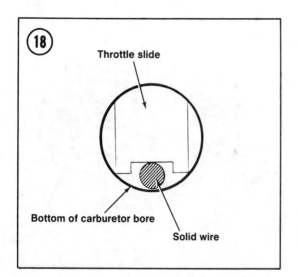

(18)

Throttle slide

Bottom of carburetor bore

Solid wire

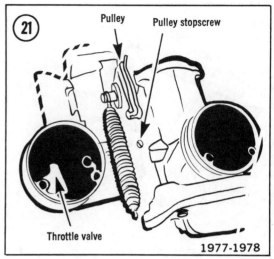

(21)

Pulley   Pulley stopscrew

Throttle valve

1977-1978

(19)

(22)

1979 and Later

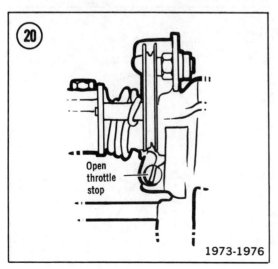

(20)

Open
throttle
stop

1973-1976

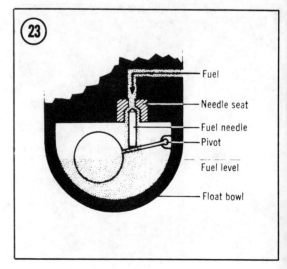

(23)

Fuel

Needle seat

Fuel needle

Pivot

Fuel level

Float bowl

NOTE: *An easy way to do this is to put a piece of 0.028 in (0.7 mm) diameter wire in the carburetor bore under the throttle slide, hold the carburetor on end, and turn the synchronizing screw until the wire just drops out of the carburetor.*

7. Repeat for the other carburetors. Each should be set *exactly* the same.

8. Tighten the locknut or bolts, fold up any locking washer tabs, and install the carburetor caps and gaskets.

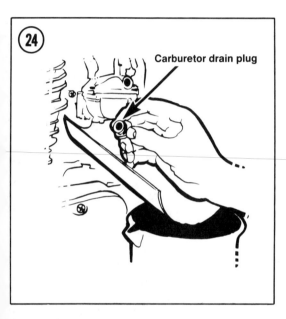

Carburetor drain plug

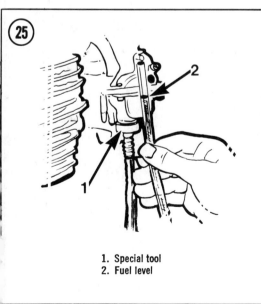

1. Special tool
2. Fuel level

9. Rotate the pulley until the bottom edge of the lowest of the 4 carburetor slides is level with the top edge of its carburetor throat (viewed from the intake manifold end). See **Figure 19**. Hold the pulley in that position. Turn the open throttle stop screw until it bottoms against the pulley at that point (**Figures 20, 21, 22**).

10. Install the carburetor assembly (see *Carburetor Installation*).

Fuel Level Adjustment

The distance from the bottom of the carburetor bore to the top of the fuel level in the float bowl is critical in a slide/needle carburetor. The flow rate of fuel from the float bowl up to the carburetor bore depends not only upon the amount of vacuum in the bore and the size of the jet(s) in the venturi tube or fuel passage, but also upon the distance the fuel has to travel to get to the bore (measured from the fuel level in the float bowl to the bore venturi). Therefore, this distance must remain constant at all times.

To maintain the fuel at a constant level, the float bowl is equipped with an intake valve through which gasoline flows by gravity from the gas tank into the bowl (**Figure 23**). Inside the bowl is a float, which floats on the surface of the gasoline. Linked to the float is a needle, which rides inside the float valve. As the float rises, the float needle rises inside the float valve and blocks it, so that when the fuel has reached its specified level in the float bowl, no more gasoline can enter.

To Check Fuel Level:

Obtain a special fuel level gauge from a Kawasaki dealer with fittings for your particular set of carburetors.

Check and adjust the float level as follows:

1. Turn fuel shutoff valve to OFF.

NOTE: *On models equipped with the vacuum controlled valve, turn it ON.*

2. Remove the drain plug from the bottom of the carburetor. Place a small container under the carburetor to catch the fuel from the float bowl (**Figure 24**).

3. Screw the fuel level gauge into the drain plug hole (**Figure 25**).

NOTE
The carburetor must be kept level to the ground during the fuel level check steps. Block up the front wheel until the carburetors are level.

4. Hold the clear tube of the tool up against the carburetor body and turn the fuel shutoff valve to ON or PRIME.

5. Check the fuel level in the clear tube. It should be *about* ⅛ in. (3.2 mm) from the top edge of the float bowl (**Figure 26**). See **Table 1** at the end of this chapter for the exact setting for your model.

To Adjust Fuel Level:

1. If the fuel level is not within specification, turn the fuel shutoff valve OFF (ON for vacuum tap). Remove the 4 screws securing the float bowl and remove it (**Figure 27**).

2. Remove the float pin and remove the float. Catch the float needle as the float is removed.

3. Bend the tang (**Figure 28**) toward the float valve to lower the fuel level; bend the tang away from the float valve to raise the fuel level.

4. If the fuel level was very far off you can set the float height (**Figure 28**) to *approximate* the desired fuel level. See **Table 1** at the end of this chapter for float height specifications.

5. Reassemble the carburetor and recheck the fuel level. Readjust if necessary.

6. Repeat for the 3 remaining carburetors.

CARBURETOR SERVICE

There is no set rule regarding frequency of carburetor overhaul. A carburetor used primarily for street riding may go 30,000 miles without overhaul. Poor engine performance, hesitation, and little response to idle mixture adjustment are all symptoms of possible carburetor malfunctions.

Carburetor Removal

Remove all 4 carburetors as a unit with their mounting bracket.

1. Place the bike on the centerstand; remove the right-hand and left-hand side covers.

2. Hinge up the seat and disconnect the battery ground lead.

3. Remove the fuel tank (see *Fuel Tank Removal*).

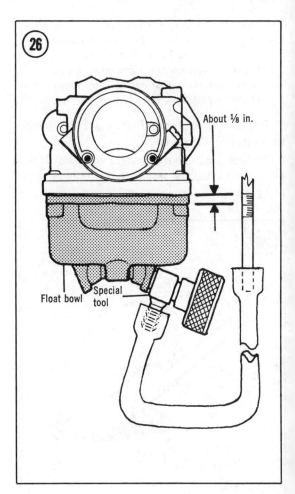

About ⅛ in.

Float bowl   Special tool

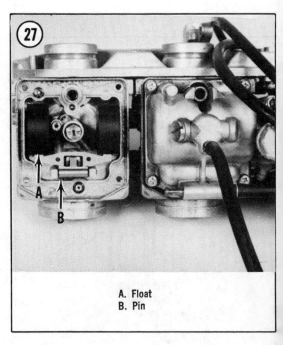

A. Float
B. Pin

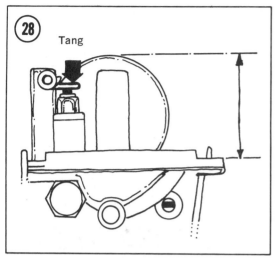

(28) Tang

(31)

(29)

4. Loosen the screws of the 4 clamps mounting the carburetors to the intake manifolds (**Figure 29**).

5. Loosen the screws of the 4 clamps mounting the air intake hoses to the carburetors.

6. Shorten the cable adjusters at the throttle grip to give plenty of cable play.

7. Atop the throttle linkage in the center of the carburetor block, loosen the throttle cable locknuts and shorten the adjusters (**Figure 30**). Remove the throttle cables from the pulley.

8. Pull the carburetor assembly back. Tilt the front up to release it from the rubber intake tubes on the cylinder head (**Figure 31**).

9. Pull the carburetor assembly to the front and release it from the rubber tubes on the air cleaner box.

10. Free the 4 overflow tubes from the rubber retainer on the frame.

11. Slide the carburetor assembly to the right and remove it.

(30)

Carburetor Installation

1. If the throttle linkage was disturbed, or a carburetor was disassembled, check the rough synchronization of the throttle valves (see *Mechanical Synchronization*).

2. Install by reversing the removal steps.

3. *1977 and later:* Check that the air cleaner ducts have the "UP" marks up, with "R" on the right (**Figure 32**).

SHAFT DRIVE

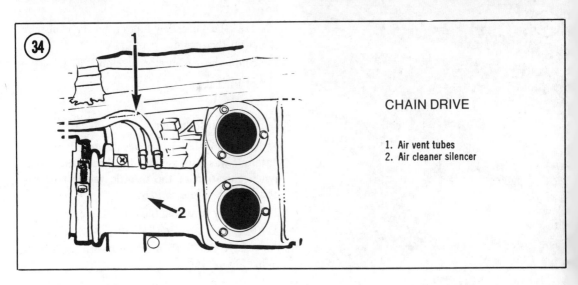

CHAIN DRIVE

1. Air vent tubes
2. Air cleaner silencer

4. Be sure the throttle cables are not twisted, kinked, or have any sharp bends.

5. Route the carburetor overflow tubes to the right-hand rear side of the engine (**Figure 33**).

6. Route the 2 carburetor air vent tubes back through the frame by the rear swing arm. On *1979 and later models,* connect the vent tubes to the air cleaner housing (**Figures 34 and 35**).

7. Make sure the carburetor bodies are fully seated forward in the rubber carburetor holders (**Figure 36**). You should feel a solid "bottoming-out" when they're correctly installed.

8. Hook the decelerator (closing) cable end onto the front of the pulley (**Figure 37**), pull the cable into position, and tighten both nuts.

9. Hook the accelerator (opening) cable end onto the pulley. Pull the cable up into position, and tighten the nuts.

10. Adjust the throttle cables (see *Throttle Cable Adjustment,* Chapter Three).

11. Adjust the carburetors (see *Carburetor Adjustment*).

Carburetor Disassembly

We recommend that only one carburetor be disassembled at a time. This will prevent the intermix of parts.

NOTE: *All 4 carburetors look the same, but slight differences exist between all of them. Prior to disassembly, note the position of the air passage plug (pilot-screw type) or air screw (air-screw type), the position of the drain plug and where the fuel line(s) joint is located.*

With the exception of the linkage mechanism and starter plunger, all parts can be removed from the carburetors without removing them from the mounting plate.

Float and Jet Removal/Installation

Refer to **Figures 38 through 40**.

1. *Pilot screw models:* Note the pilot screw limiter setting and mark it on the mounting plate (**Figures 41 and 42**).

2. Remove the 4 float bowl screws and the float bowl.

3. Remove the float pin and the float (**Figure 43**).

4. Remove the float needle valve (**Figure 44**).

5. *Pilot screw models:* Count the number of turns it takes to lightly seat the pilot screw. Then remove the pilot screw and limiter as an assembly. Inspect the pilot screw seating surface. It should be smooth and free of nicks with the O-ring in good condition (**Figure 45**).

6. Remove the main jet and the air bleed pipe it mounts in (**Figure 43**).

7. Remove the pilot jet (**Figure 43**).

8. To remove the needle jet (**Figure 46**), remove the throttle slide (see *Slide Removal/Installation*), insert a soft rod down on top of the needle jet and push it out the bottom.

NOTE: *Further disassembly is not recommended. If throttle or choke shafts or butterflies are damaged, take the body to your dealer for replacement.*

9. Assemble by reversing these disassembly steps, noting the following.

10. Replace any O-rings and gaskets that appear to be damaged or deteriorated. If they have become hardened, their ability to seal is greatly reduced.

11. On pilot screw models, turn pilot screw in carefully *until it seats lightly,* then back it out the number of turns you counted when removing it

7

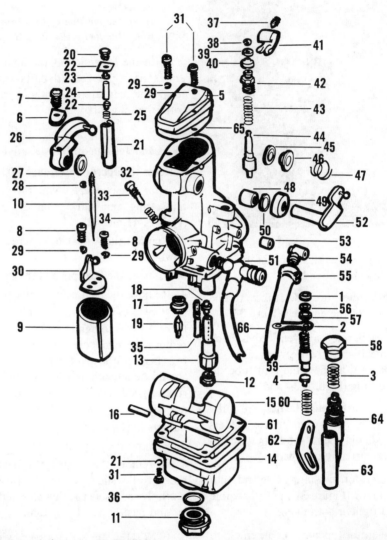

38 CARBURETOR — 1973-1975

1. Throttle stop screw locknut
2. Double washer link
3. Spring
4. Spring seat
5. Top cover
6. Lockwasher
7. Bolt
8. Screw
9. Slide
10. Jet needle
11. Drain plug
12. Main jet
13. Air bleed pipe
14. Float bowl
15. Float
16. Pin
17. Valve seat

18. Needle jet
19. Float valve needle
20. Guide screw
21. Connector
22. Lockwasher
23. Spring seat
24. Pin
25. Spring
26. Lever assembly
27. Spacer
28. Circlip
29. Lockwasher
30. Bracket assembly
31. Bolt
32. Mixing chamber
33. Air screw
34. Spring

35. Pilot jet
36. O-ring
37. Screw
38. Circlip
39. Ring
40. Cap
41. Lever
42. Guide screw
43. Spring
44. Plunger assembly
45. Oil seal
46. Collar
47. Spring
48. Hose
49. Cup
50. Washer

51. Fuel pipe fitting
52. Lever assembly
53. Hose
54. Air vent pipe fitting
55. Clamp
56. Lockwasher
57. Washer
58. Cap nut
59. Slide stop adjusting screw
60. Spring
61. Gasket
62. Rubber washer
63. Tube
64. Connector
65. Gasket
66. Air vent pipe

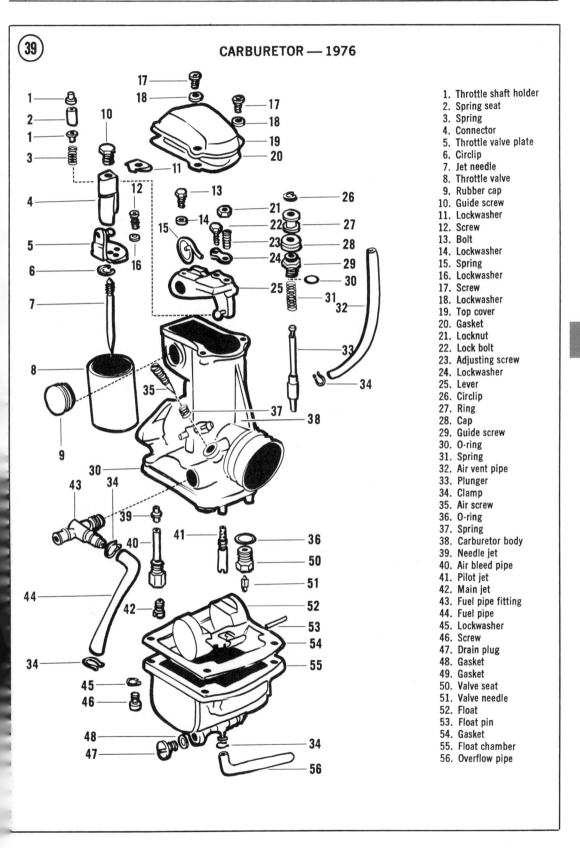

CARBURETOR — 1976

1. Throttle shaft holder
2. Spring seat
3. Spring
4. Connector
5. Throttle valve plate
6. Circlip
7. Jet needle
8. Throttle valve
9. Rubber cap
10. Guide screw
11. Lockwasher
12. Screw
13. Bolt
14. Lockwasher
15. Spring
16. Lockwasher
17. Screw
18. Lockwasher
19. Top cover
20. Gasket
21. Locknut
22. Lock bolt
23. Adjusting screw
24. Lockwasher
25. Lever
26. Circlip
27. Ring
28. Cap
29. Guide screw
30. O-ring
31. Spring
32. Air vent pipe
33. Plunger
34. Clamp
35. Air screw
36. O-ring
37. Spring
38. Carburetor body
39. Needle jet
40. Air bleed pipe
41. Pilot jet
42. Main jet
43. Fuel pipe fitting
44. Fuel pipe
45. Lockwasher
46. Screw
47. Drain plug
48. Gasket
49. Gasket
50. Valve seat
51. Valve needle
52. Float
53. Float pin
54. Gasket
55. Float chamber
56. Overflow pipe

7

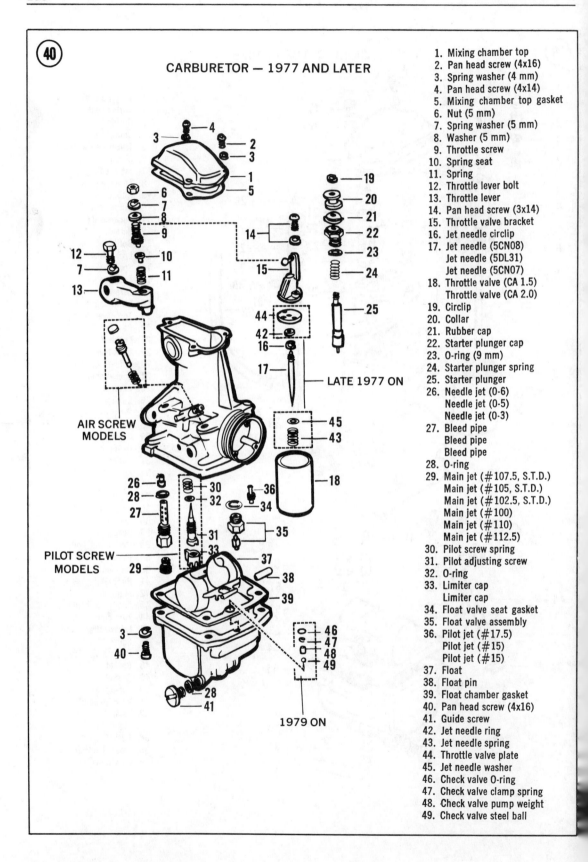

CARBURETOR — 1977 AND LATER

AIR SCREW MODELS

PILOT SCREW MODELS

LATE 1977 ON

1979 ON

1. Mixing chamber top
2. Pan head screw (4x16)
3. Spring washer (4 mm)
4. Pan head screw (4x14)
5. Mixing chamber top gasket
6. Nut (5 mm)
7. Spring washer (5 mm)
8. Washer (5 mm)
9. Throttle screw
10. Spring seat
11. Spring
12. Throttle lever bolt
13. Throttle lever
14. Pan head screw (3x14)
15. Throttle valve bracket
16. Jet needle circlip
17. Jet needle (5CN08)
    Jet needle (5DL31)
    Jet needle (5CN07)
18. Throttle valve (CA 1.5)
    Throttle valve (CA 2.0)
19. Circlip
20. Collar
21. Rubber cap
22. Starter plunger cap
23. O-ring (9 mm)
24. Starter plunger spring
25. Starter plunger
26. Needle jet (O-6)
    Needle jet (O-5)
    Needle jet (O-3)
27. Bleed pipe
    Bleed pipe
    Bleed pipe
28. O-ring
29. Main jet (#107.5, S.T.D.)
    Main jet (#105, S.T.D.)
    Main jet (#102.5, S.T.D.)
    Main jet (#100)
    Main jet (#110)
    Main jet (#112.5)
30. Pilot screw spring
31. Pilot adjusting screw
32. O-ring
33. Limiter cap
    Limiter cap
34. Float valve seat gasket
35. Float valve assembly
36. Pilot jet (#17.5)
    Pilot jet (#15)
    Pilot jet (#15)
37. Float
38. Float pin
39. Float chamber gasket
40. Pan head screw (4x16)
41. Guide screw
42. Jet needle ring
43. Jet needle spring
44. Throttle valve plate
45. Jet needle washer
46. Check valve O-ring
47. Check valve clamp spring
48. Check valve pump weight
49. Check valve steel ball

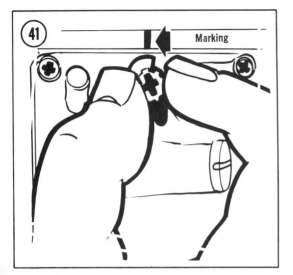

Marking

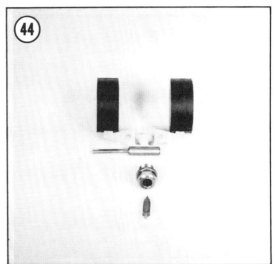

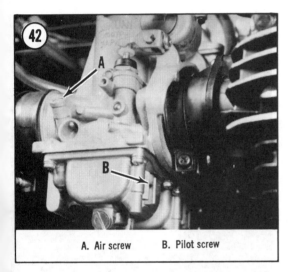

A. Air screw   B. Pilot screw

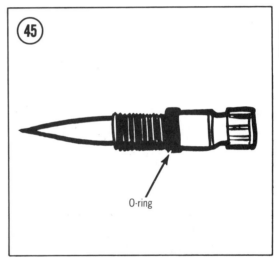

O-ring

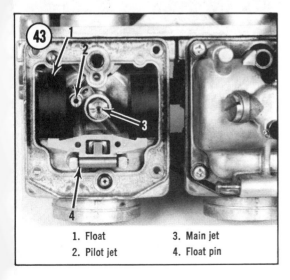

1. Float   3. Main jet
2. Pilot jet   4. Float pin

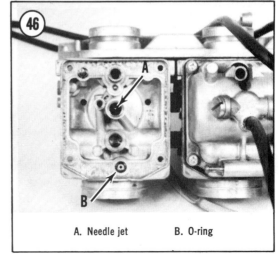

A. Needle jet   B. O-ring

7

(Step 5). Install the limiter with its tab pointing to the mark you made.

12. On accelerator pump models, make sure the O-ring is in place at the accelerator pump outlet check valve (**Figure 46**).

13. Turn the carburetors upside-down and check the float level. It should be *about* 1.0 in. (25–26 mm) above the carburetor body (**Figure 47**). See **Table 1** at the end of this chapter for your bike's specification.

> NOTE: *Float level setting is only a preliminary adjustment. Check the fuel level after the carburetors are assembled. See **Fuel Level Adjustment** earlier in this chapter.*

14. See **Table 1** at the end of this chapter for jet specifications for your bike.

Air Screw Removal/Installation

1. On air screw models, remove the plug (if installed) and count the number of turns it takes to lightly seat the air screw (**Figure 48**).

2. Remove the air screw and inspect the tapered seating surface. It should be smooth and free of nicks with the O-ring in good condition (**Figure 49**).

3. Install the air screw and turn it in *until it seats lightly,* then back it out the number of turns you counted in Step 1.

4. Install the plug (if equipped).

Slide Removal/Installation

Slides with different amounts of cutaway are available to regulate the mixture ratio differently at ⅛ to ¼ throttle openings.

1973–1975 Models:

Refer to **Figure 38**.

1. Remove the 2 screws from the top of the carburetor. Take off the top.

2. Flatten the tab washer beneath the mounting screw in the top of the slide operating lever beneath the carburetor top. Remove the mounting screw.

3. Remove the 2 screws which mount the operating linkage to the slide.

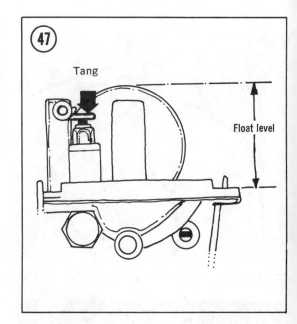

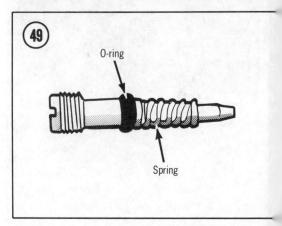

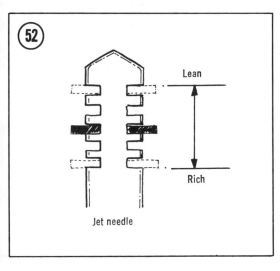

Jet needle

4. Lift up the linkage and take out the slide.

5. Install the slide in the reverse order.

1976 and Later Models:

Refer to **Figures 39 and 40**.

1. Remove the top covers (**Figure 50**).

2. Unscrew throttle arm set bolts (**Figure 51**).

3. Remove throttle return spring.

4. Remove throttle shaft set plate between carburetors No. 1 and No. 2.

5. Pull off the throttle shaft.

6. Remove screws and pull out the slide and jet needle.

7. Install the slide in reverse order.

8. Apply a light coat of grease to the throttle shaft before installing it.

Jet Needle Removal/Installation

7

The needle has a number of grooves around the top. A clip fitted to one notch suspends the needle in the slide. By fitting the clip to another notch, you can raise or lower the needle in the slide, thus raising or lowering the needle in the needle jet and changing the fuel volume and mixture ratio between ¼ throttle and ¾ throttle. The needle has 5 notches and the clip is usually fitted to the middle notch.

Different sizes of needle jets are available, as are needles with different tapers. Refer to **Figures 38 through 40**.

1. Remove the carburetor assembly from the engine (see *Carburetor Removal*).

2. Remove the throttle slide and needle assembly (see *Slide Removal*).

3. Remove the 2 screws securing the needle into the throttle valve and remove the needle.

4. Note the original position of the needle clip. Raising the needle (lowering the clip) will enrich the mixture during mid-throttle opening, and lowering it (raising the needle clip) will lean the mixture (**Figure 52**). See **Table 1** at the end of this chapter for settings for your model.

CAUTION
The needle jet settings should be the same for all 4 carburetors.

5. Reassemble the needle and throttle slide.

NOTE
On models with a floating, spring-mounted needle, install the needle plate with the projection facing down (1, Figure 53).

6. Install the throttle slide (see *Slide Installation*).

7. Install the carburetor assembly (see *Carburetor Installation*).

Single Carburetor Separation

Almost all carburetor parts can be replaced without removing the carburetors from the linkage and mounting plate. If you want to clean a carburetor internally, it's best to take it to a Kawasaki dealer for soak cleaning of air passages. There are many rubber and plastic parts that *must* be removed before using a caustic carburetor cleaner.

Disassemble only one carburetor at a time. This will prevent intermix of parts.

NOTE: *All 4 carburetors look the same, but slight differences exist between all of them. Prior to disassembly, note the position of the air passage plug (pilot-screw type) or air screw (air-screw type), the position of the drain plug and where the fuel line(s) joint is located.*

With the exception of the linkage mechanism and starter plunger, all parts can be removed from the carburetors without removing them from the mounting plate.

Carburetor Separation (1973–1975)

1. The carburetors are linked in pairs—a left pair and a right pair. In the pair from which you wish to remove a carburetor, unscrew the locknut from the slide stop adjusting screw on each carburetor. Take off the double washer link (**Figure 54**).

2. Unscrew the slide stop adjusting screw from each of the 2 carburetors. Lift off the springs and spring seats.

3. On the carburetor you wish to remove, unscrew the linkage cap nut, keeping finger pressure on it to prevent the spring beneath it from flying out. Take out the spring and the spring seat (**Figure 55**).

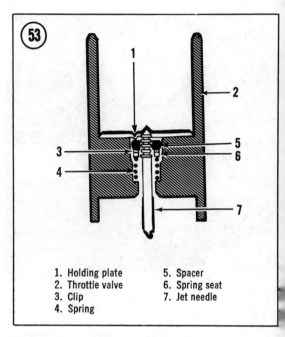

1. Holding plate   5. Spacer
2. Throttle valve   6. Spring seat
3. Clip   7. Jet needle
4. Spring

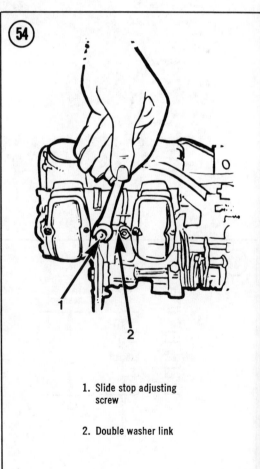

1. Slide stop adjusting
   screw

2. Double washer link

4. Remove the 4 screws that mount the 2 carburetors to the linkage mounting plate. Swing the carburetors away from the plate and remove the carburetor you want. Remove the fuel line and the vent tube (and the overflow tube on the 1974–1975 models).

5. Reassemble the carburetor in the reverse order. Apply Loctite to the carburetor mounting screws.

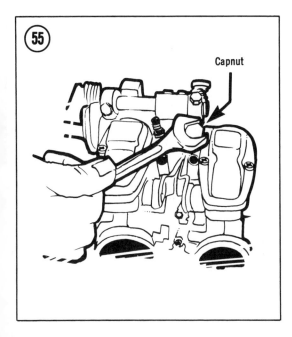

Capnut

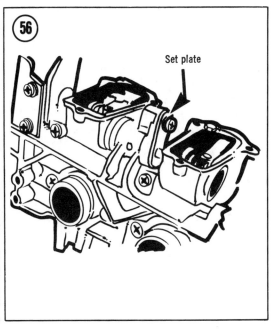

Set plate

Carburetor Separation (1976)

1. In the pair (left or right) containing the single carburetor to be removed, remove the top covers and plate.

2. Unscrew throttle arm mounting bolts (**Figure 51**).

3. Remove throttle shaft set plate (**Figure 56**).

4. Disconnect the throttle return spring.

5. Remove the rubber cap from each side of carburetor assembly.

6. Pull off the throttle shaft.

7. Remove the mounting screws and detach the 2 carburetors from the plate.

8. Pull off the wanted single carburetor from the side.

9. Reassemble carburetor in reverse order. Apply Loctite to carburetor mounting screws. Apply a light coat of grease to the throttle shaft before inserting in the carburetors.

Carburetor Separation (1977 and Later)

Refer to **Figures 57 to 59**.

1. Remove the idle adjust screw and spring.

2. Remove the screws securing the top covers and remove them.

3. Remove the throttle arm mounting bolts and washers.

4. Remove the pulley mounting bolt.

5. Remove the throttle return spring (**Figure 60**).

6. Remove the screw and lockwasher securing the throttle shaft set plate (**Figure 56**).

7. Remove the rubber caps at each end of the carburetor assembly.

8. Withdraw the throttle shaft from the left side; push it out from the right side.

9. Remove the mounting screws (**Figure 61**) securing the carburetors to the mounting plate and remove each carburetor.

10. Assemble by reversing the *Separation* steps. Apply Loctite to the carburetor mounting screws. Apply a light coat of grease to the throttle shaft before inserting in the carburetors.

ACCELERATOR PUMP

The 1979 and later models are equipped with an accelerator pump to provide an extra squirt of

7

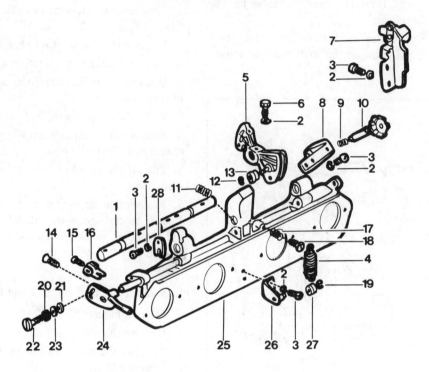

CARBURETOR MOUNT
(EARLY 1977, 1976 LTD)

1. Carburetor connection shaft
2. Spring washer (5 mm)
3. Pan head screw (5x14)
4. Throttle pulley spring
5. Throttle cable pulley
6. Throttle lever bolt
7. Throttle cable pulley bracket
8. Throttle stop screw holder
9. Throttle stop screw spring
10. Throttle stop screw
11. Throttle cable bracket spring
12. Circlip (3 mm)
13. Ring
14. Countersunk head screw
15. Pan head screw
16. Starter plunger lever
17. Adjuster screw spring
18. Adjuster screw
19. Circlip (3 mm)
20. Starter lever screw spring
21. Ring
22. Circlip (3 mm)
23. Throttle stop screw holder
24. Starter plunger shaft
25. Carburetor mounting holder
26. Throttle cable pulley bracket
27. Ring

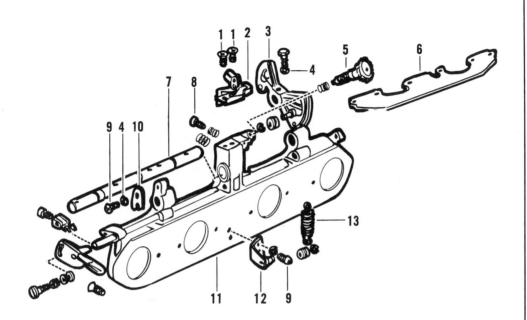

CARBURETOR MOUNT
(1977-1/2 - 1978-1/2)

1. Countersunk head screw
2. Throttle cable pulley bracket
3. Throttle cable pulley
4. Spring washer
5. Throttle stop screw
6. Carburetor connection plate
7. Carburetor connection shaft

8. Adjuster screw
9. Pan head screw
10. Shaft stopper plate
11. Carburetor mounting holder
12. Throttle cable pulley bracket
13. Throttle cable pulley spring

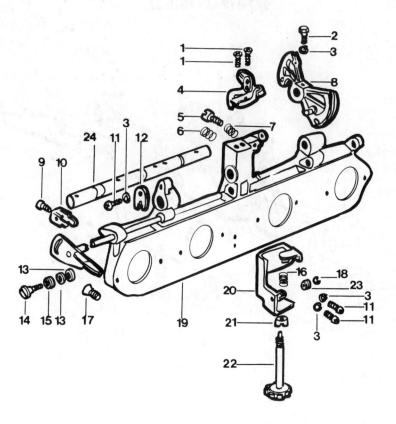

**CARBURETOR MOUNT
(1979 AND LATER)**

1. Countersunk head screw (5x10)
2. Throttle lever bolt
3. Spring washer (5 mm)
4. Throttle cable pulley bracket
5. Adjuster screw
6. Throttle cable bracket spring
7. Adjuster screw spring
8. Throttle cable pulley
9. Pan head screw
10. Starter lever
11. Pan head screw
12. Shaft stopper plate
13. Starter plunger shaft
14. Starter lever screw
15. Starter lever screw spring
16. Throttle stop screw spring
17. Countersunk head screw
18. Circlip (3 mm)
19. Carburetor mounting holder
20. Throttle pulley bracket
21. Bushing
22. Throttle stop screw
23. Ring
24. Carburetor connection shaft

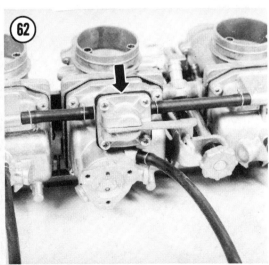

fuel as the throttle is opened. This allows leaner overall jetting for lower emissions. The pump is mounted on carburetor No. 2 and supplies all carburetors through connecting lines (**Figure 62**). The 1979 and later LTD also has an engine vacuum sensor that disables the accelerator pump when the engine is not running.

Testing (Except LTD)

1. Remove the carburetors from the engine (see *Carburetor Removal*).

2. Supply the float bowls with fuel and open the throttles quickly with the pulley.

3. The pump nozzle at the mouth of each carburetor should eject an equal amount of fuel into the center of each carburetor throat.

4. If the flow is unequal, a passage or check valve is restricted—take the carburetor to your dealer for repair.

5. If no fuel is ejected in any carburetor check the pump diaphragm.

Accelerator Pump Disassembly/Assembly

Refer to **Figure 63**.

1. Remove the 4 pump cover screws and the cover (**Figure 62**).

2. Remove the pump diaphragm and spring from the carburetor body.

3. Inspect the diaphragm. Replace it if it is torn or has a pinhole.

4. To reassemble, put the spring in the carburetor body, then the diaphragm.

5. Install the cover with 4 screws and lockwashers.

6. Check the pump rod adjustment. Clearance between the nut and the end of the rod (**Figure 64**) should be as follows:

    a. Z1R: 0.15 in. (3.8 mm)

    b. All others: 0.42-0.43 in. (10.7-10.9 mm)

7. Apply Loctite to the adjusting nut threads.

Vacuum Sensor Disassembly/Assembly

Refer to **Figure 63**.

1. Remove the 3 sensor cover screws and the cover.

2. Remove the spring and sensor diaphragm with rod from the carburetor.

3. Inspect the diaphragm. Replace it if it is torn or has a pinhole.

7

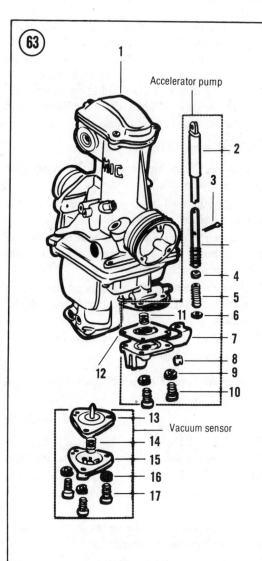

63

1

Accelerator pump

2

3

4
5
6
11
7
8
9
12
10

13
14
15
16
17

Vacuum sensor

1. Carburetor left hand, inside
2. Rod assembly pump
3. Cotter pin (1.0 x 6)
4. Pump rod washer
5. Pump rod spring
6. Pump rod washer
7. Pump cover assembly
8. Pump rod nut
9. Spring washer (4/4 mm)
10. Pan head screw (4x14)
11. Pump diaphragm spring
12. Pump diaphragm
13. Diaphragm
14. Sensor diaphragm spring
15. Sensor cover
16. Spring washer (4 mm)
17. Pan head screw (4x14)

64

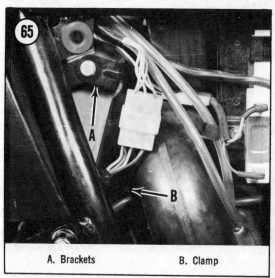

65

A

B

A. Brackets   B. Clamp

66

4. To reassemble, put the diaphragm/rod in the carburetor, then the sensor spring.

> NOTE: *The sensor spring is more closely wound than the accelerator pump spring. Don't mix them up.*

5. Align the holes at the front of the carburetor body, sensor diaphragm, and sensor cover.

6. Install the 3 cover screws and lockwashers.

CRANKCASE BREATHER

The crankcase breather separates oil mist droplets from blowby gas and routes the oil back to the crankcase via a drain hole. The vapors are routed to the air cleaner housing. No maintenance is required; but if careful attention is not paid to keeping the oil drain clear during engine assembly and to not overfilling the engine with oil, oil can be sucked up into the air cleaner housing.

For any 900cc bike with a chronic air cleaner oiling problem not caused by overfilling the crankcase, Kawasaki has a special oil return pipe kit available to reduce the problem (Service Bulletin 75 Z-39).

Breather Disassembly/Assembly

1. *Shaft drive:* Remove the fuel tank, carburetors, and air cleaner housing. The housing has 2 mounting brackets with bolts and a clamp (**Figure 65**) under the side covers.

2. Remove the breather hose and cover bolt with its O-ring (**Figure 66**).

3. Remove the cover and O-ring.

4. Remove the 2 breather plate screws and the plates, tubes, and spacers (**Figure 67**).

5. To install, reverse the procedure.

AIR SUCTION SYSTEM (1979 AND LATER)

The air suction system (**Figure 68**) consists of a vacuum switch valve, 2 air suction valves (reed valves), and air and vacuum hoses. This system does not use an air pump but does introduce fresh air into the exhaust system, in the exhaust ports, by pressure differentials generated by the exhaust gas pulses.

The vacuum switch normally allows fresh air pulses into the exhaust port but shuts off air flow during engine braking. This helps prevent backfiring in the exhaust system due to the greater amount of unburned fuel in the exhaust gas during deceleration.

The air suction valves, located within the valve cover, are basically check valves. They allow the fresh air to enter the exhaust port and prevent any air or exhaust from reversing back into the system.

Suction Valve Removal/Installation

If the engine idle is not smooth, if engine power decreases, or if there are any abnormal engine noises, remove the air suction valves and inspect them (see **Figure 69**).

1. Remove the fuel tank.

2. Slide up the lower hose clamp (**Figure 70**) and pull the hose off the air suction cover.

3. Remove the 4 bolts and flat washers (**Figure 71**) securing the cover and remove it.

4. Remove the air suction valve assembly from the valve cover (**Figure 72**).

5. Check the reed valves for cracks, folds, warpage or any other damage.

6. Check the sealing lip coating around the perimeter of the assembly. It must be free of

7

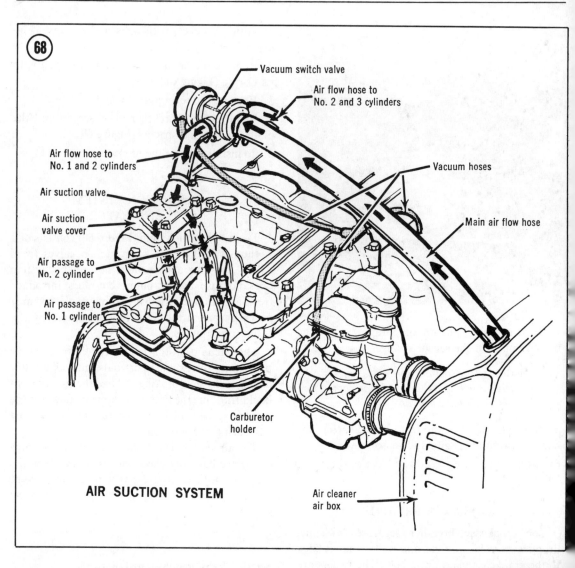

Vacuum switch valve

Air flow hose to
No. 2 and 3 cylinders

Air flow hose to
No. 1 and 2 cylinders

Air suction valve

Air suction
valve cover

Air passage to
No. 2 cylinder

Air passage to
No. 1 cylinder

Vacuum hoses

Main air flow hose

Carburetor
holder

AIR SUCTION SYSTEM

Air cleaner
air box

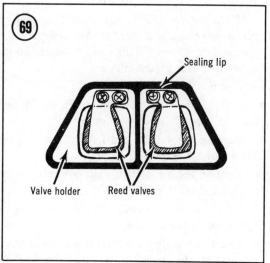

Sealing lip

Valve holder   Reed valves

grooves, scratches or signs of separation from the metal holder.

> NOTE: *The valve assembly cannot be serviced but must be replaced if defective.*

7. Wash off any carbon deposits between the reed and the reed contact area with solvent.

> CAUTION
> *Do not scrape off the deposits as the assembly will be damaged.*

8. Install the air suction valve assembly into the valve cover with the reeds facing down into the cam cover and with the projection on the holder facing up (**Figure 72**).

9. Install the cover and 4 bolts. Don't forget the flat washers under each bolt. Tighten the bolts to 11 ft.-lb. (1.5 mkg).

10. Install the air hose on the cover and slip the hose clamp into place. Ensure that all hoses are in place and the hose clamps are securely in place.

11. Repeat Steps 2–10 for the other valve assembly.

12. Install the fuel tank.

Vacuum Switch Test

Inspect the vacuum switch if there is backfiring on deceleration or other abnormal engine noise.

1. Run the engine until it is warm.

2. Rev the engine to 4,000 rpm and snap the throttle shut. Note the intensity and frequency of the backfiring for comparison later in this test.

3. Shut the engine off and, at the air cleaner housing, disconnect and plug the hose from the vacuum switch (**Figure 73**).

4. Start the engine, rev it to 4,000 rpm and compare the backfiring to what you heard before. If the backfiring is the same, there is nothing wrong with the vacuum switch.

5. If the backfiring is different, the vacuum switch is faulty. Install a new switch (**Figure 74**).

EXHAUST SYSTEM
(900CC—EXCEPT LTD)

The exhaust system consists of the 4 exhaust pipes with mufflers, and their mounting hardware. The 2 mufflers on each side are interconnected, so that exhaust gases from each cylinder are sent through 2 mufflers.

No maintenance is required except to see that the connecting clamps are tight, and that the drain holes in the outer muffler shell are kept clear (**Figure 75**).

Removal

1. Unscrew the 2 nuts and remove the 2 lock-washers mounting each finned exhaust pipe collar to the studs on the cylinder head. Pull each exhaust pipe collar off its studs.

2. Pull each slotted spacer out of the cylinder head (**Figure 76**).

3. Remove the muffler mount nut and bolt from the frame lug on each side of the motorcycle.

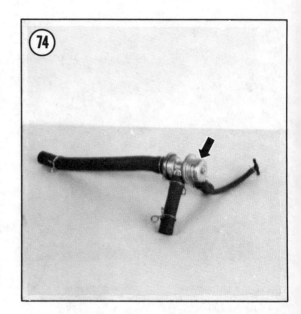

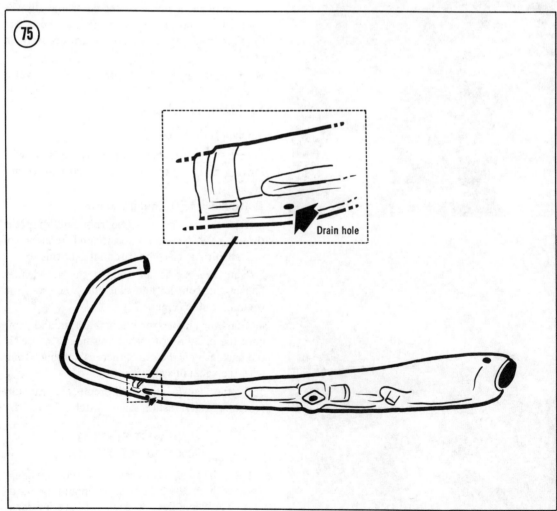

Drain hole

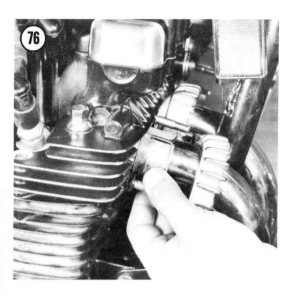

4. Push the 2 left exhaust pipes (and mufflers) forward, to free them from the cylinder head. Remove them from the motorcycle. Remove the right exhaust pipes in the same manner.

> NOTE: *The exhaust gaskets may remain in the cylinder head, or fall out when you remove the exhaust pipes.*

5. To separate a pair of pipes, loosen the screw of the hose clamp on the rubber tube connecting the mufflers (**Figure 77**). Pull one of the muffler nipples free of the rubber tube.

Installation

1. If either of the rubber tubes connecting the mufflers has been leaking gas, and the hose clamp screw is tight, replace the tube with a new one.

2. Begin with the exhaust pipe/muffler for cylinder 2 or 3. Place the exhaust gasket in the exhaust port for that cylinder.

3. On the exhaust pipe, butt the slotted spacer against the mouth of the exhaust pipe, and hold it in place with the finned exhaust collar. Push the exhaust pipe and the spacer into the exhaust port, and fit the collar to its mounting studs on the cylinder head.

4. Loosely mount the lockwashers and the nuts on the studs.

5. Install the outside exhaust pipe on the same side of the motorcycle in the same way.

6. With motorcycle completely reassembled, run the engine and check for gas blow-by at the exhaust ports and at muffler connecting tubes.

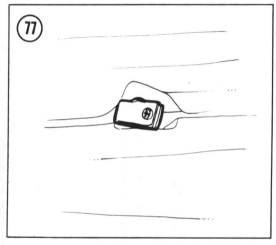

**EXHAUST SYSTEM
(1000CC—EXCEPT 1978 Z1R)**

Removal

1. Loosen the clamps holding the muffler connecting pipe, and the No. 2 and No. 3 exhaust pipe clamps (**Figures 78 and 79**).

2. Remove the No. 2 and No. 3 exhaust pipe holder self-locking nuts and slide the holders off the stud (**Figure 76**).

3. Remove the mounting bolt and washers at the rear (each side) and remove the mufflers (**Figure 80**).

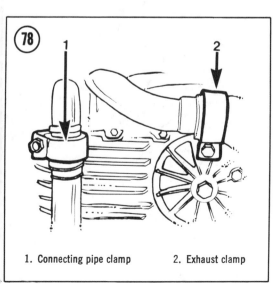

1. Connecting pipe clamp   2. Exhaust clamp

Installation

1. Separate No. 2 and 3 exhaust pipes from the left and right muffler.

2. Install a new gasket into No. 1 and 4 exhaust ports and place an exhaust pipe holder on the stud bolts.

3. Fit the end of the exhaust pipes into the exhaust ports and attach the muffler parts to the frame. Connect both mufflers with the connecting pipe. Tighten the bolts loosely.

4. Fit split keeper in position and tighten the exhaust pipe holder nuts evenly to avoid leakage. Tighten the muffler clamp bolts (**Figure 78**).

5. Install new No. 2 and 3 exhaust port gaskets and place an exhaust pipe holder on the stud bolts.

6. Fit No. 2 and 3 exhaust pipes into the exhaust ports and insert their lower ends into mufflers.

> NOTE: *Do not mix up the exhaust pipes. There is an identification mark on No. 2 and 3 exhaust pipes (Figure 81).*

7. Fit the split keeper in place and tighten the exhaust pipe holder nuts evenly. Tighten the exhaust pipe clamp bolt, and tighten the clamp bolts on the muffler connecting pipe.

8. Retighten all connecting clamps after riding 100 miles.

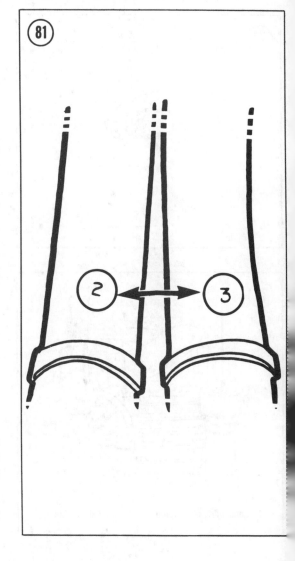

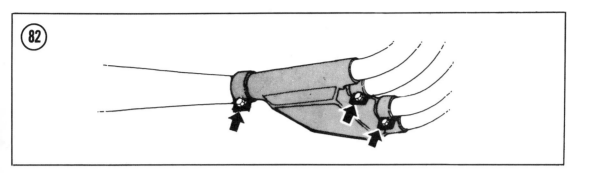

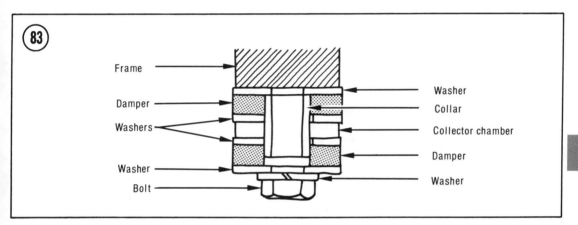

EXHAUST SYSTEM (Z1R)

Exhaust Removal/Installation

1. Put the motorcycle up on its centerstand.

2. Loosen the muffler clamp bolt at the rear of the collector chamber and the clamps holding the No. 2 and No. 3 exhaust pipes to the collector chamber (**Figure 82**).

3. Remove the rear footpeg mounting bolt and pull the muffler out of the collector chamber.

4. At the cylinder head, remove the exhaust pipe collar nuts and slide the collars down out of the way. Remove the split keepers from behind the collars.

5. Pull the No. 2 and No. 3 exhaust pipes out of the collector chamber.

6. Remove the 2 bolts that mount the collector chamber to the frame.

7. To install, reverse the removal steps. Note the following.

   a. Do not re-use exhaust pipe gaskets. Install new ones.

   b. Install the collector chamber bolts, collars, washers, and dampers as shown in **Figure 83**.

   c. Install the No. 2 and No. 3 exhaust pipes in their proper position. They have identification marks (**Figure 81**), No. 2 on the left and No. 3 on the right.

Table 1 CARBURETOR SPECIFICATIONS

| | 1979 | | | 1978½ emissions |
	Std.	LTD	Shaft	Std. LTD
Mikuni				
Carburetor model	VM28SS	VM26SS	VM28SS	VM26SS
Fuel level (±1 mm)	4 mm	4 mm	4 mm	4 mm
Float level (±1 mm)	26 mm	26 mm	26 mm	26 mm*
Main jet	102.5	102.5	110	102.5
Jet needle	5CN17-3rd	5CN18-3rd	5CN17-3rd	5CN7-4th
Needle jet	0-4	0-6	0-4	0-3
Throttle valve Cutaway	2.0	2.0	2.0	2.0
Pilot jet	15	15	15	15
Pilot screw	—	Turn screws fully clockwise when viewed from below	—	Turn screws fully clockwise when viewed from below
Air screw	1⅛	—	1⅛	—

| | 1978 non-emissions | | | 1977 |
	Z1R	Std.	LTD	Std.
Mikuni				
Carburetor model	VM28SS	VM26SS	VM26SS	VM26SS
Fuel level (±1 mm)	4 mm	4 mm	3 mm	3 mm
Float level (±1 mm)	26 mm	26 mm	25 mm	25 mm
Main jet	107.5	105	105	107.5
Jet needle	5CN15-3rd	5DL31-3rd	5DL31-3rd	5CN8-3rd
Needle jet	0-1	0-5	0-5	0-6
Throttle valve Cutaway	1.5	1.5	1.5	1.5
Pilot jet	15	15	15	17.5
Pilot screw	1⅜ ±¼	1¼ ±¼	1 ±¼	1¼ ±¼
Air screw	—	—	—	—

	1976	1975 (Z1B)	1974 (Z1A)	1973 (Z1)
Mikuni				
Carburetor model	VM26SS	VM28SC	VM28SC	VM28SC
Fuel level (±1 mm)	3 mm	3.5 mm	3.5 mm	3.5 mm
Float level (±1 mm)	22 mm	24 mm	24 mm	24 mm
Main jet	115	112.5	112.5	112.5
Jet needle	5DL31-3rd	5J9-2nd	5J9-3rd	5J9-3rd
Needle jet	0-6	0-8	P-8	P-8
Throttle valve Cutaway	1.5	1.5	2.5	2.5
Pilot jet	17.5	17.5	20	20
Pilot screw	—	—	—	—
Air screw	1⅜ ±¼	1¼	1½	1½

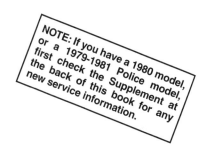
NOTE: If you have a 1980 model, or a 1979-1981 Police model, first check the Supplement at the back of this book for any new service information.

CHAPTER EIGHT

BRAKES

Brake systems on the 900/1000 Kawasakis began with a mechanical drum rear brake and single hydraulic front disc on the original Z1, an optional dual front disc kit with larger master cylinder, and progressed to standard dual front discs and single rear disc for 1979 and later models.

Repair of brake systems is extremely critical work. Don't take shortcuts and don't work with makeshift tools. If you do, you're gambling with your life. When a procedure calls for a locking agent (Loctite or equivalent), use it. If a torque specification is give, use a torque wrench. Recheck your work, and when you're finished, test the brakes in a safe area. If you have any doubts about your ability to do the job according to these procedures, take your bike to your Kawasaki dealer.

WARNING
Brake fluid is an irritant. Keep it away from your skin and eyes.

The following precautions *must* be observed when servicing the brake systems.

1. Never reuse old brake fluid.

2. Never use fluid from a container that has been left open.

3. Use only disc brake fluid clearly marked "DOT 3 for disc brake systems."

4. Don't leave the fluid reservoir cap off for too long. The fluid will absorb moisture from the air and will boil at lower temperatures.

8

5. Don't contaminate the brake discs or pads with brake fluid, gasoline, or any lubricants (including graphite or pencil lead).

6. Brake fluid ruins paint and plastic. If you spill any, wipe it up immediately.

7. If you open a bleed valve or loosen a brake line fitting, bleed air from the system.

8. When working on drum brakes, wear a protective mask to keep from inhaling any dust from the brake linings. The brake linings contain asbestos fiber; asbestos has been connected with lung scarring and cancer. Do not use compressed air to clean the brake drums or linings; dump any dust onto a newspaper and dispose of it in the trash. Wash your hands after handling the brake parts.

BRAKE FLUID BLEEDING

Bleed the hydraulic brake system whenever the brake lever or pedal action feels spongy or soft; after brake fluid has been changed; or whenever a brake line fitting has been loosened.

1. Remove the reservoir cap to observe the brake fluid. Don't let the fluid run out during this procedure.

2. Slowly pump brake lever or pedal several times (reservoir cap still off) until no air bubbles rise up through the fluid from holes at the bottom of the reservoir. (This bleeds air from the master cylinder end of the line.)

3. Install the reservoir cap. Connect a clear plastic hose to the bleed valve at the caliper (**Figure 1**). Run the other end of the hose into a clean container. Fill the container with enough fresh brake fluid to keep the end submerged. The tube should be long enough so that a loop can be made higher than the bleed valve to prevent air from being drawn into the caliper during bleeding.

4. Slowly apply the brake lever or pedal several times. Pull the lever in or push the pedal down. Hold the lever or pedal in the ON position. Open the bleed valve about one-half turn. Allow the lever or pedal to travel to its limit. When this limit is reached, tighten the bleed screw. As the fluid enters the system, the level will drop in the reservoir. Maintain the level at about ⅜ in. from the top of the reservoir to prevent air from being drawn into the system.

5. Continue to pump the lever or pedal and fill the reservoir until the fluid emerging from the hose is completely free of bubbles.

> NOTE: *Do not allow the reservoir to empty during the bleeding operation or more air will enter the system. If this occurs, the entire procedure must be repeated.*

6. Hold the lever or pedal down, tighten the bleed valve, remove the bleed tube, and install the bleed valve dust cap.

7. If necessary, add fluid to correct the level in the reservoir.

> NOTE: *On dual hydraulic disc models, always bleed the caliper furthest away from the master cylinder first. Otherwise air bubbles may remain in the brake system causing a soft lever.*

8. Install the reservoir cap tightly.

9. Test the feel of the brake lever and pedal. It should be firm and should offer the same resistance each time it's operated. If it feels spongy, it is likely that there is still air in the system and it must be bled again. When all air has been bled from the system, and the fluid level is correct in the reservoir, double check for leaks and tighten all the fittings and connections.

> WARNING
> *Before riding the motorcycle, make certain that the brakes are operating correctly by operating the lever and pedal several times.*

BRAKE FLUID CHANGE

Change the brake fluid every 6,000 miles (or yearly, or when the fluid is contaminated by dirt or water, whichever comes first). Brake fluid changing is the same as brake fluid bleeding, except that you keep the bleeder valve open and pump the lever or pedal until all fluid runs out of the system. After draining the old fluid, fill and bleed the system.

FRONT BRAKE PADS

There is no recommended mileage interval for changing the friction pads in the disc brake. Pad wear depends greatly on riding habits and conditions. See *Brake Pad Inspection* in Chapter Three.

Always replace all pads (2 per disc) at the same time.

The 1979 and later models use sintered-metal pads with insulated caliper pistons.

> WARNING
> *Do not try to use later sintered-metal pads in calipers with early non-insulated pistons. The heat produced could boil the brake fluid and cause brake failure.*

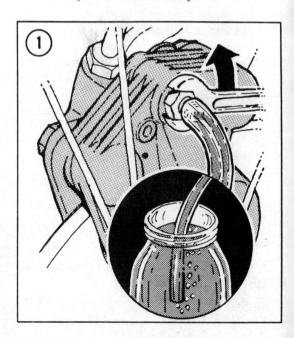

Front Brake Pad Removal

1. *1973–1977:* Remove the front wheel (see *Front Wheel Removal,* Chapter Nine).

2. *1978 and later:* Disconnect the speedometer cable at the wheel.

3. *1978 and later:* Remove the 2 caliper mounting bolts (**Figure 2**).

4. *1977 and later:* Remove the screw, lockwasher, and plate securing the inboard pad (**Figure 3**).

5. *1973–1976:* Remove the screw (**Figure 4**).

6. Take out the inboard pad.

7. Slide the caliper holder toward the bleed valve and remove the outboard pad.

> NOTE: *If the pad won't come out, squeeze the brake lever a few times until the piston pushes the caliper out.*

Front Brake Pad Installation

1. Remove the cap from the master cylinder and slowly push the piston into the caliper while checking the reservoir to make sure the brake fluid does not overflow (**Figure 5**). Remove fluid if necessary prior to overflowing. The piston should move freely. If it does not and there is any evidence of it sticking in the cylinder, the caliper should be removed and serviced by your Kawasaki dealer or a brake specialist.

2. Install the outboard pads against the caliper piston.

8

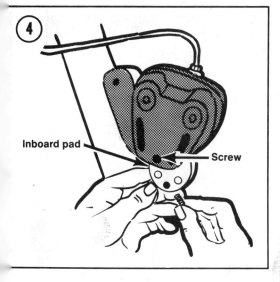

NOTE: *The inboard pad has a tapped hole in the back. The outboard has none (Figure 6).*

On *1973–1976* models, make sure the shim is toward the front (**Figure 7**) and align the groove in the pad with the ridge in the caliper.

On *1979 and later* models, align the brake pad tab with the caliper holder slot (**Figure 8**). If there is no tab, turn the flat, stepped side of the pad to the outside of the disc.

3. Install the inboard pad, using Loctite Lock 'N' Seal on the mounting screw threads.

4. *1979 and later:* Install the caliper. You may find this easier if you first insert a piece of soft tubing between the pads to keep them in place (**Figure 9**), then pull the tubing out as you slide the caliper in place (**Figure 10**).

5. *1979 and later:* Torque the caliper mounting bolts, with washers and lockwashers, to 22 ft.-lb. (3.0 mkg) on shaft drive models or to 29 ft.-lb. (4.0 mkg) on chain drive models.

6. *1979 and later:* Connect the speedometer cable.

7. *1973–1978:* Install the front wheel (see *Front Wheel Installation,* Chapter Nine).

8. Block the motorcycle up so that the front wheel is off the ground. Spin the front wheel and activate the brake lever for as many times as it takes to refill the cylinder in the caliper and correctly locate the pads.

9. Refill the fluid in the reservoir, if necessary, and replace the top cap.

> **WARNING**
> *Use brake fluid clearly marked DOT-3 only. Others may vaporize and cause brake failure.*

> **WARNING**
> *Do not ride the motorcycle until you are sure that the brake is operating correctly with full hydraulic advantage. If necessary, bleed the brakes.*

10. Bed new pads in gradually for the first 50 miles by using only light pressure as much as possible. Immediate hard applications will glaze the new friction pads and greatly reduce the effectiveness of the brakes.

FRONT BRAKE CALIPER

Caliper Rebuilding

If the caliper leaks, the caliper should be rebuilt. If the piston sticks in the cylinder, indicating severe wear or galling, the entire unit should be replaced. Rebuilding a leaky caliper requires special tools and experience.

The factory recommends that the piston fluid seal and dust seal be replaced every other time the pads are replaced.

Caliper service should be entrusted to your Kawasaki dealer or brake specialist. Considerable money can be saved by removing the caliper yourself and taking it in for repair.

Front Caliper Removal

1. *1973–1976:* Remove the front wheel (see *Front Wheel Removal,* Chapter Nine).

2. *1979 and later:* Disconnect the speedometer cable at the wheel.

3. Disconnect the brake line at the caliper (**Figure 11**) and cap it with the rubber bleed valve cap or tie it up high to prevent loss of brake fluid.

4. Remove the 2 caliper mounting bolts (**Figures 11 and 12**) and remove the caliper.

Front Caliper Installation

1. Torque the 2 caliper mounting bolts with flat washers and lockwashers to 22 ft.-lb. (3.0 mkg) on shaft drive models or to 29 ft.-lb. (4.0 mkg) chain drive models.

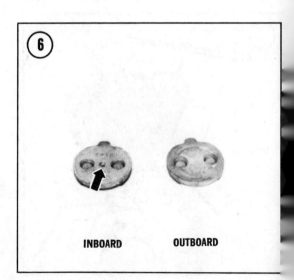

6

INBOARD   OUTBOARD

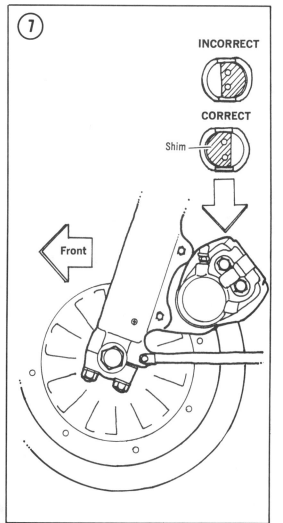

INCORRECT

CORRECT

Shim

Front

8

2. Connect the brake line. On *1978 and later* models, use new washers on either side of the banjo bolt and torque the bolt to 22 ft.-lb. (3.0 mkg).

3. Bleed the brakes (see *Brake Fluid Bleeding*).

WARNING
Do not ride the motorcycle until you are sure that the brakes are operating properly.

REAR BRAKE PADS

There is no recommended mileage interval for changing the friction pads in the disc brake. Pad wear depends greatly on riding habits and conditions. See *Brake Pad Inspection* in Chapter Three. Always replace both pads at the same time.

The 1979 and later models use sintered-metal pads with insulated caliper pistons.

WARNING
Do not try to use later sintered-metal pads in calipers with early non-insulated pistons. The heat produced could boil the brake fluid and cause brake failure.

Rear Pad Removal

Refer to **Figure 13.**

1. Remove the pad cover from the caliper.

2. Remove the clips from the pins, then hold your thumb on the anti-rattle springs to keep them from flying off. Pull the pins off the caliper.

3. Remove the pads and shims (if any) from the caliper.

Rear Pad Installation

1. Remove the cap from the master cylinder and slowly push the piston into the caliper while checking the reservoir to make sure the brake fluid does not overflow. Remove fluid if necessary prior to overflowing. The piston should move freely. If it does not and there is any evidence of it sticking in the cylinder, the caliper should be removed and serviced by your Kawasaki dealer or a brake specialist.

2. *1973–1978:* Put the shim on the back of each pad (**Figure 13**). Install the shim so the triangular hole points forward.

3. Insert the pads on either side of the caliper.

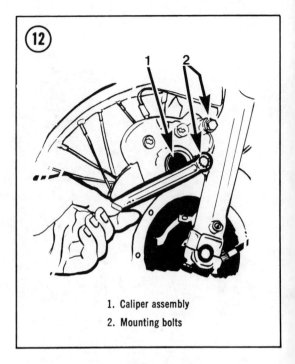

1. Caliper assembly
2. Mounting bolts

CAUTION
Don't dislocate the rubber dust seals while inserting the pads.

4. Insert 2 pins (the end with the hole is toward the outside) through the outer wall of the caliper, shim (if equipped), and outboard pad.

5. Install the anti-rattle spring with the ends under the pins and the top portion on top of the pad (**Figure 14**).

6. Install the other pad and shim (if equipped) in the same manner as the first. Press down on the anti-rattle springs so the pin goes over the ends of the springs (**Figure 15**).

7. Install the clips through the holes in the pins, between the outboard shim (or pad) and the caliper.

WARNING
Do not forget to install these clips as they keep the brake pins and pads in place. If these are lost, it could result in loss of braking at the rear wheel.

8. Install the cover.

9. Block the motorcycle up so that the rear wheel is off the ground. Spin the rear wheel and activate the brake pedal for as many times as it takes to refill the cylinder in the caliper and correctly locate the pads.

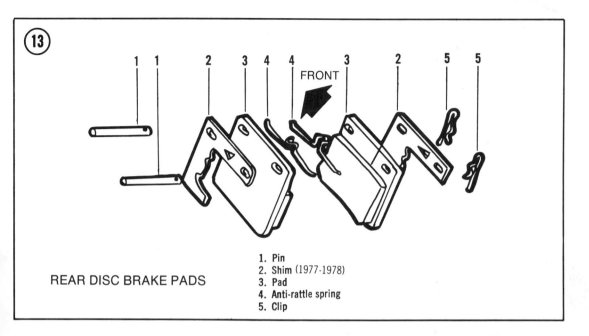

REAR DISC BRAKE PADS

1. Pin
2. Shim (1977-1978)
3. Pad
4. Anti-rattle spring
5. Clip

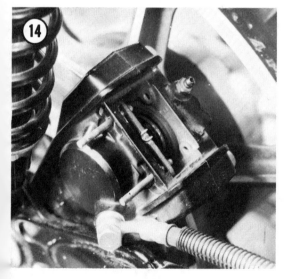

10. Refill the fluid in the reservoir, if necessary, and replace the top cap.

WARNING
Use brake fluid clearly marked DOT-3 only. Others may vaporize and cause brake failure.

WARNING
Do not ride the motorcycle until you are sure that the brake is operating correctly with full hydraulic advantage. If necessary, bleed the brakes.

11. Bed the pads in gradually for the first 50 miles by using only light pressure as much as possible. Immediate hard application will glaze the new friction pads and greatly reduce the effectiveness of the brake.

REAR BRAKE CALIPER

Caliper Rebuilding

If the caliper leaks, the caliper should be rebuilt. If the piston sticks in the cylinder, indicating severe wear or galling, the entire unit should be replaced. Rebuilding a leaky caliper requires special tools and experience.

The factory recommends that the piston fluid seal and dust seal be replaced every other time the pads are replaced.

Caliper service should be entrusted to your Kawasaki dealer or brake specialist. Considerable money can be saved by removing the caliper yourself and taking it in for repair.

Rear Caliper Removal

1. Remove the rear wheel (see *Rear Wheel Removal,* Chapter Nine).

2. Disconnect the brake line at the caliper and tie it up high to prevent loss of brake fluid.

Rear Caliper Installation

1. Install the rear wheel (see *Rear Wheel Installation*).

2. Connect the brake line. Use new washers on either side of the banjo bolt and torque it to 22 ft.-lb. (3.0 mkg).

3. Bleed the brakes (see *Brake Fluid Bleeding*).

WARNING
Do not ride the motorcycle until you are sure the brakes are operating properly.

BRAKE DISCS

Inspection

It is not necessary to remove the disc from the wheel to inspect it. Small marks on the disc are not important, but scratches deep enough to snag a fingernail reduce braking effectiveness and increase pad wear.

1. Measure the thickness at several points around the disc with vernier caliper or micrometer (**Figure 16**). The disc must be replaced if the thickness, at any point, is less than 0.24 in. (6 mm) on single disc or 0.18 in. (4.5 mm) on dual disc.

2. Check the disc runout with a dial indicator. Raise the wheel being checked and set the arm of the dial indicator against the surface of the disc (**Figure 17**) and slowly rotate the wheel while watching the indicator. If the runout is greater than 0.012 in. (0.3 mm), disc must be replaced.

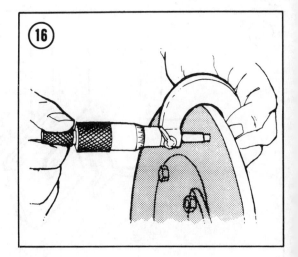

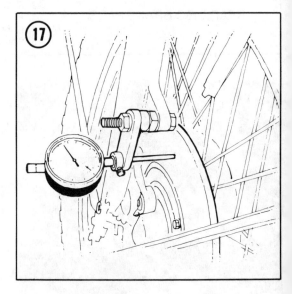

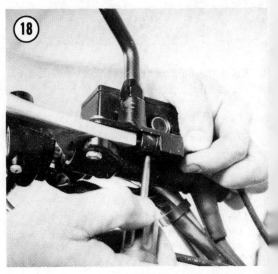

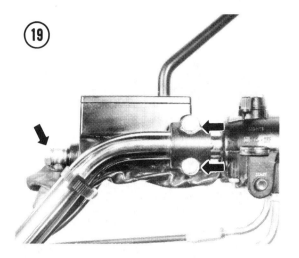

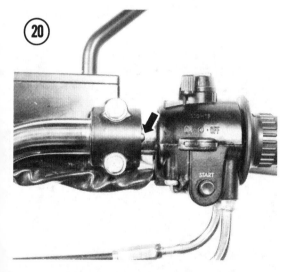

Disc Removal/Installation

See *Front Wheel Disassembly* or *Rear Wheel Disassembly* in Chapter Nine for brake disc replacement.

MASTER CYLINDERS

If the master cylinder leaks, or if it has to be pumped to brake, it should be rebuilt. If the piston sticks in the body, indicating severe wear or galling, the entire unit should be replaced. Rebuilding a leaky master cylinder requires special tools and experience.

Master cylinder repair should be entrusted to your Kawasaki dealer or a brake specialist. You can save money and possibly your life by removing the master cylinder yourself and taking it in for repair.

FRONT MASTER CYLINDER

Front Master Cylinder Removal (All except Z1R)

1. Remove the rear view mirror.

2. *Shaft drive:* Push up on the front brake switch locking tab (**Figure 18**) and pull the switch free from the master cylinder.

3. Pull back the rubber boot and remove the banjo bolt (**Figure 19**) securing the brake hose to the master cylinder and remove it.

> CAUTION
> *Brake fluid ruins paint and plastic surfaces. If you spill any, wipe it up immediately.*

4. Remove the 2 clamp bolts and the clamp (**Figure 19**). Take off the master cylinder.

Front Master Cylinder Installation (All except Z1R)

1. Install the master cylinder with the projection on the clamp toward the throttle grip (**Figure 20**).

2. Tighten the upper clamp bolt first, then the lower one.

3. Connect the brake line. Use new washers on either side of the banjo bolt, and torque it to 22 ft.-lb. (3.0 mkg).

4. Bleed the brake fluid (see *Brake Fluid Bleeding*).

Front Master Cylinder Removal (Z1R)

1. Remove the fairing and headlight to expose the front brake master cylinder.

2. Adjust for maximum free play of the brake cable. Align the slot in the knurled adjuster on the brake lever.

3. Remove the cable from the handlebar lever.

4. Loosen and remove the banjo bolts to disconnect the 2 brake hoses from the master cylinder (**Figure 21**).

> CAUTION
> *Brake fluid ruins paint and plastic surfaces. If you spill any, wipe it up immediately.*

5. Loosen and remove the 3 brake master cylinder reservoir screws.

8

6. Remove the 2 screws holding the master cylinder. Remove the master cylinder, fluid reservoir and cable as a unit.

Front Master Cylinder Installation (Z1R)

Installation is simply the reverse of removal with the following changes.

1. Replace the flat washers on each side of the banjo fitting; do not reuse the old ones.

2. Bleed the front brakes (see *Brake Fluid Bleeding*).

3. Adjust brake cable for ¼–⅜ in. (6.4–9.5 mm) of free play.

4. Check for proper brake fluid level and lever feel before riding.

REAR MASTER CYLINDER

The rear master cylinder is rigidly mounted through 1978. Beginning with the 1979 models, the master cylinder is free-floating on its mounting bolts.

A. Banjo bolt

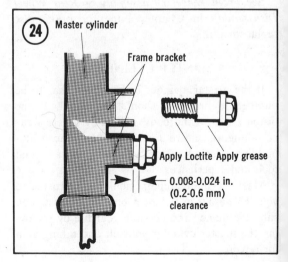

Rear Master Cylinder Removal

1. Remove the right side cover.

2. *Shaft drive:* Remove the electrical cover (**Figure 22**).

3. Remove the banjo bolt (**Figure 23**) and washers.

> CAUTION
> *Brake fluid ruins paint and plastic surfaces. If you spill any, wipe it up immediately.*

4. Remove the 2 rear master cylinder mounting bolts (**Figure 23**). Pull the master cylinder up and off the brake pushrod.

Rear Master Cylinder Installation

1. Inspect the pushrod boot on the bottom of the master cylinder. Replace it if cracked or worn out.

2. Remove any old locking compound from the mounting bolt and master cylinder threads.

3. *1979 and later:* Grease the shoulder of the mounting bolts (**Figure 24**). Apply Loctite Lock'N'Seal to the threads and install the master cylinder without any washers or shims. There should be 0.008–0.024 in. (0.2–0.6 mm) side play of the master cylinder when installed.

4. *1977–1978:* Apply Loctite Lock'N'Seal to the bolt threads and install the master cylinder with flat washers and lockwashers.

5. Torque the 2 master cylinder mounting bolts to 13 ft.-lb. (1.8 mkg).

6. Connect the brake line. Use new washers on either side of the banjo bolt, and torque it to 22 ft.-lb. (3.0 mkg).

7. Bleed the brake fluid (see *Brake Fluid Bleeding*).

8. Adjust the rear brake (see *Brake Pedal Play* in Chapter Three).

9. *Shaft drive:* Install the electrical cover.

10. Replace the side cover.

REAR DRUM BRAKE (1973–1976)

Drum Brake Disassembly.

Refer to **Figure 25**.

> WARNING
> *When working on drum brakes, wear a protective mask to keep from inhaling any dust from the brake linings. The brake linings contain asbestos fiber; asbestos has been connected with lung scarring and cancer. Do not use compressed air to clean the brake drums or linings; dump any dust onto a newspaper and dispose of it in the trash. Wash your hands after handling the brake parts.*

1. Remove the rear wheel (see *Rear Wheel Removal*, Chapter Nine).

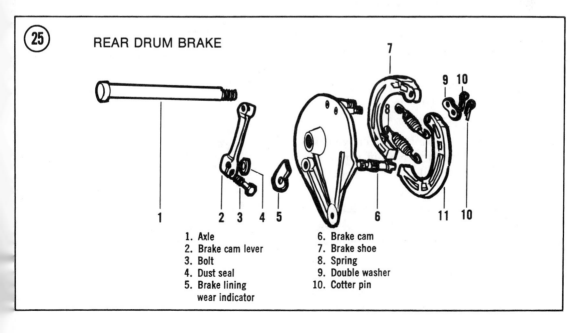

㉕ REAR DRUM BRAKE

1. Axle
2. Brake cam lever
3. Bolt
4. Dust seal
5. Brake lining wear indicator
6. Brake cam
7. Brake shoe
8. Spring
9. Double washer
10. Cotter pin

2. Pull out the axle.

3. Pull the rear brake backing plate (panel assembly) out of the rear hub.

4. Pull the 2 cotter pins out of the brake shoe pivots on the backing plate. Take off the double washer.

5. Scribe a line across the face of the brake camshaft and the brake cam lever, so that you will know how to reassemble them.

6. Remove the mounting bolt from the brake cam lever and pull the lever off the brake camshaft.

7. On 1974–1976 models, pull the brake lining wear indicator off the brake camshaft.

8. Pull the dust seal off the brake camshaft.

9. Pry the 2 brake shoes up their pivot shafts. Lift them off, together with the brake camshaft.

10. Remove the brake camshaft from the shoes. Remove brake springs and separate the shoes.

Drum Brake Inspection

1. Thoroughly clean and dry all the parts except the linings.

2. Check the contact surface of the drum for scoring. If there are deep grooves, deep enough to snag a fingernail, the drum should be reground.

3. Measure the inside diameter of the brake drum with vernier calipers (**Figure 26**). If this measurement is 7.904 in. (200.75 mm) or greater, the drum must be replaced.

4. If the brake drum is turned, the linings will have to be replaced and the new ones arced to the new drum contour.

5. Check the brake linings. They should be replaced if worn within 0.079 in. (2 mm) of the metal shoe table (**Figure 27**).

6. Inspect the linings for imbedded foreign material. Dirt can be removed with a stiff wire brush. Check for any traces of oil or grease. If they are contaminated, they must be replaced.

7. Inspect the cam lobe and the pivot pin area of the shaft for wear and corrosion. Minor roughness can be removed with fine emery cloth.

8. Inspect the brake shoe return springs for wear (**Figure 28**). The free length should not exceed 2.72 in. (69 mm). Replace both springs if either has stretched beyond this length. If they are

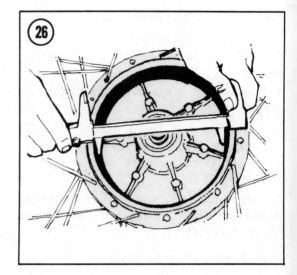

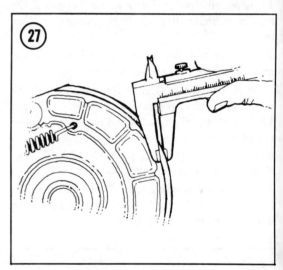

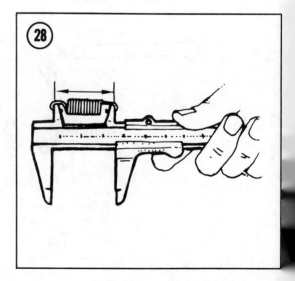

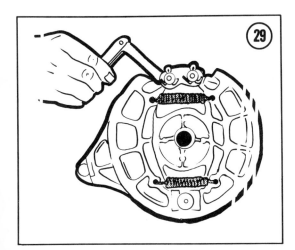

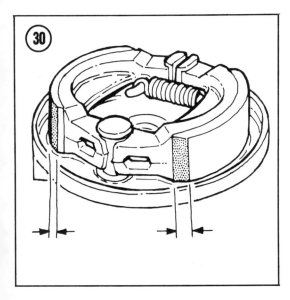

stretched, they will not fully retract the brake shoes and they will drag and wear out prematurely.

Drum Brake Assembly

Assemble the brake by reversing the disassembly steps. Note the following:

   a. Grease the shaft, cam, and pivot post with a light coat of molybdenum disulfide grease; avoid getting any grease on the brake plate where the linings may come in contact with it.

   b. If your rear drum brake squeals a lot, Kawasaki has brake shoe side clearance shims that may help. Shim the shoes to get 0.008–0.010 in. (0.20–0.25 mm) side play (**Figure 29**).

> WARNING
> *Brake shoe side clearance less than 0.008 in. (0.20 mm) may cause the brake to stick or lock.*

   c. When installing the brake lever onto the brake camshaft, be sure to align the 2 parts with the 2 marks made in *Removal,* Step 5.

   d. If new linings are being installed, file off the leading edge of each shoe a little (**Figure 30**) so that the brake will not grab when applied.

   e. Adjust the rear brake (see *Rear Brake Adjustment*).

8

CHAPTER NINE

WHEELS AND TIRES

This chapter describes disassembly and repair of the front and rear wheels, hubs and tires. For routine maintenance, see Chapter Three.

Separate procedures are given for wheel removal and disassembly for 900cc, 1000cc chain drive, and shaft drive models. Make sure you use the procedure and illustrations applicable to your bike.

FRONT WHEEL (900cc)

Removal

1. Unscrew the serrated mounting nut at the bottom of the speedometer cable with pliers. Pull out the speedometer cable.
2. Prop up the motorcycle so that the front wheel is several inches off the ground.
3. Use a grease pencil to draw a vertical line across the mating surfaces at the bottom of each front fork tube and the axle clamp, in front, for reference as to location and position when reinstalling them.
4. Unscrew the 4 axle clamp nuts. Take off the clamps, and allow the wheel to drop out of the forks.

Installation

1. Position the wheel in the forks.
2. Put on the axle clamps and the axle clamp nuts. Screw the nuts down finger-tight. There should be a

gap at the rear of the clamp (**Figure 1**). The arrow on the bottom of the clamp should point to the front.

3. Torque the front nuts and then the rear ones to 13-14 ft.-lb.

4. Install the speedometer cable; position the wheel so that the cable nut and its mount are aligned (**Figure 2**).

5. Check the wheel balance, and the axial and radial rim runout. For the checking and adjustment procedures. see *Wheel Inspection*.

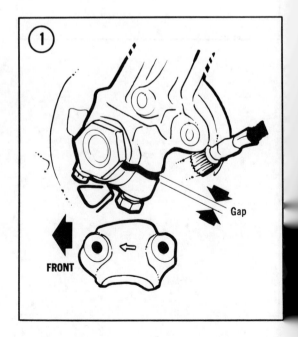

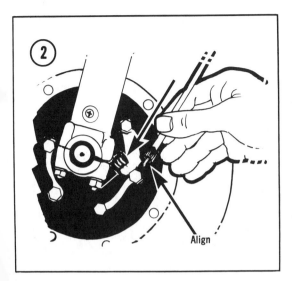

Align

Front Hub Disassembly
(1973-1975 Models)

Refer to **Figure 3**.

1. Remove the front wheel from the motorcycle.

2. Clamp the speedometer gearbox so it cannot turn (and thus damage the speedometer gear), and unscrew the front axle from it.

3. Remove the speedometer gearbox and the front axle.

4. Remove the 3 screws that mount the wheel cap to the right side of the hub. Remove cap and the collar.

5. Insert a drift from the right side of the hub and tap evenly around the inner race of the left wheel bearing to drive it out of the hub.

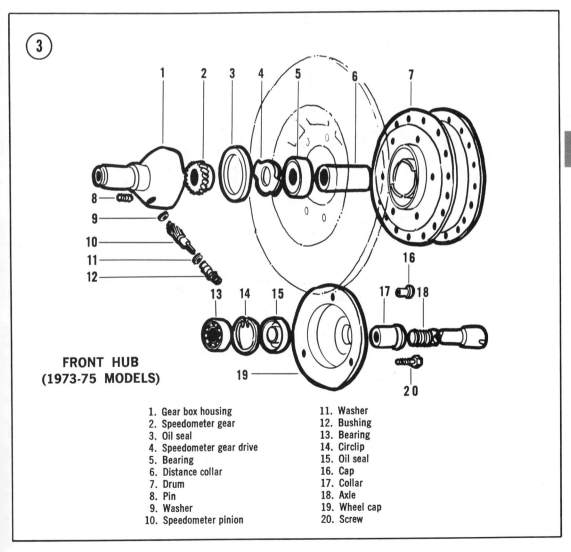

FRONT HUB
(1973-75 MODELS)

1. Gear box housing
2. Speedometer gear
3. Oil seal
4. Speedometer gear drive
5. Bearing
6. Distance collar
7. Drum
8. Pin
9. Washer
10. Speedometer pinion
11. Washer
12. Bushing
13. Bearing
14. Circlip
15. Oil seal
16. Cap
17. Collar
18. Axle
19. Wheel cap
20. Screw

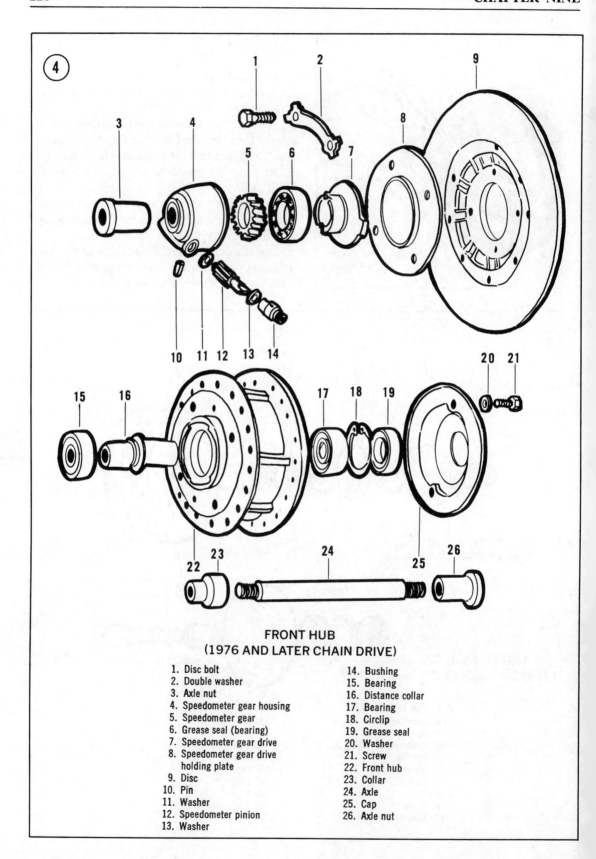

FRONT HUB
(1976 AND LATER CHAIN DRIVE)

1. Disc bolt
2. Double washer
3. Axle nut
4. Speedometer gear housing
5. Speedometer gear
6. Grease seal (bearing)
7. Speedometer gear drive
8. Speedometer gear drive holding plate
9. Disc
10. Pin
11. Washer
12. Speedometer pinion
13. Washer
14. Bushing
15. Bearing
16. Distance collar
17. Bearing
18. Circlip
19. Grease seal
20. Washer
21. Screw
22. Front hub
23. Collar
24. Axle
25. Cap
26. Axle nut

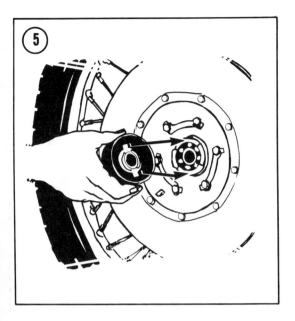

6. Take out the distance collar.

7. Pry out the oil seal from the right side of the hub.

8. Take out the snap ring from the right side of the hub.

9. Insert a drift from the left side of the hub, and drive out the right-hand wheel bearing.

10. Check the axle for runout and inspect and lubricate the wheel bearings (see *Wheel Inspection*).

Front Hub Disassembly (1976 Models)

Refer to **Figure 4**.

1. Remove the axle nut on the disc side of the front wheel.

2. Pull off the speedometer gear housing.

3. Pull out the axle (along with the right axle nut). Remove the collar.

4. Flatten the disc bolt's double washers.

5. Remove the bolts, double washers, speedometer gear drive holding plate, speedometer gear drive, and disc.

6. Remove the screws, washers, and cap from the right side of the hub.

7. Pull out the grease seal and remove the circlip.

8. Remove the right side ball bearing (along with the distance collar) by inserting a rod into the opposite side and tapping it evenly around the bearing inner race.

9. Remove the left side bearing in the same manner.

10. Check the axle for runout and inspect and lubricate the wheel bearings (see *Wheel Inspection*).

Front Hub Reassembly (All 900cc)

1. Reassemble the hub in the reverse order of disassembly, using the additional steps below.

2. When installing the wheel bearings and the right side grease seal, drive them in until they are fully seated. Use a new grease seal.

3. Grease the speedometer gearbox housing and gear.

4. When installing the gearbox hub for the speedometer drive, align it with the speedometer drive (**Figure 5**).

FRONT WHEEL (1000cc CHAIN DRIVE)

Removal

1. Loosen lower end of the speedometer cable with pliers.

2. Loosen the 4 front axle clamp nuts (but do not remove them). Loosen the front axle nuts.

3. Remove the 4 front axle clamp nuts, lock-washers, and clamps.

4. Lift the front of motorcycle with a jack under the engine (or by other suitable means) and drop the front wheel out of the forks.

> NOTE: *Dual disc models may have insufficient clearance to remove the front wheel in this manner. Removal may be made easier if one caliper is removed and eased gently out of the way. Loosen the 2 caliper mounting bolts. Remove the bolts and lift the caliper. Remove the wheel from the forks. Replace the caliper on the fork leg and replace the caliper mounting bolts, but do not tighten them.*

5. Insert a wood wedge between the disc brake pads to prevent them from moving out of position should the brake lever be accidentally squeezed.

6. Check the wheel balance, and the axial and radial rim runout (see *Wheel Inspection*).

9

Front Wheel Installation (1000cc Chain Drive)

1. Remove the wood wedge(s) from between disc brake pads and position the front wheel in place between front fork tubes. Lower the front fork tube (bottom ends) on the front axle.

2. Mount the front axle clamps and install nuts finger-tight.

> NOTE: *The arrow at the bottom clamp must point toward front. See* **Figure 6**.

3. Turn the speedometer gear housing to the left (counterclockwise) as far as it will go. It should be at about a 2 o'clock position. Make sure the stopping boss on the gear housing doesn't interfere with the fork leg.

4. Tighten the front axle nut to 60 ft.-lb. (8 mkg).

5. Torque the front axle clamp nut to 14 ft.-lb. (1.9 mkg). Tighten the rear axle clamp nut to the same torque.

> NOTE: *There should be a gap at the rear of the clamp after tightening. Refer to* **Figure 6**.

WARNING
Loss of control could result if clamps are installed wrong or improperly tightened, as clamps and/or studs could fail.

6. Guide the speedometer inner cable into the housing while turning the wheel. The slot in the end of the cable will seat in the tongue of the speedometer cable.

7. If the caliper was removed to facilitate wheel removal, replace the 2 caliper mounting bolts. Tighten to 30 ft.-lb. (4.0 mkg).

Front Hub Disassembly (1000cc Chain Drive)

Refer to **Figure 7**. The parts are the same for both wire wheels and cast wheels, except for the wheel hub itself.

1. Remove the disc side axle nut and pull off the speedometer gear housing.

2. Straighten the portion of the disc double washers that are folded over the disc bolts. Remove the bolts, double washers, speedometer gear drive holding plate, speedometer gear drive, and disc.

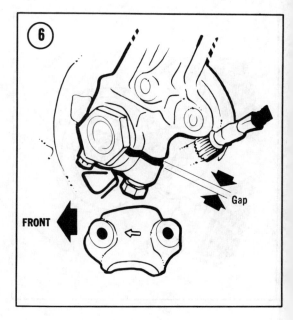

3. Remove the axle and right axle nut. Then remove the collar.

4. Remove the screws and washers, then take the cap off the right side of the hub.

5. Pull out the grease seal with a hook. Remove the circlip.

6. Remove the bearing on the right side by tapping evenly around the bearing inner face by inserting metal rod into the hub from the speedometer gear side. The distance collar will also come out with the bearing.

7. Insert a rod into the hub from the right side and remove the other bearing by tapping evenly around the bearing inner face.

8. Check the axle for runout and inspect and lubricate the wheel bearings (see *Wheel Inspection*).

Front Hub Reassembly (1000cc Chain Drive)

Refer to **Figure 7**.

1. Install the bearing. Press the bearing in until it bottoms in the hole.

2. Install a new grease seal. Press the seal in until its face is level with the surface of the front hub.

3. Grease the speedometer gearbox housing and gear.

4. Fit the speedometer gear drive into the hub notches. The speedometer gear drive holding

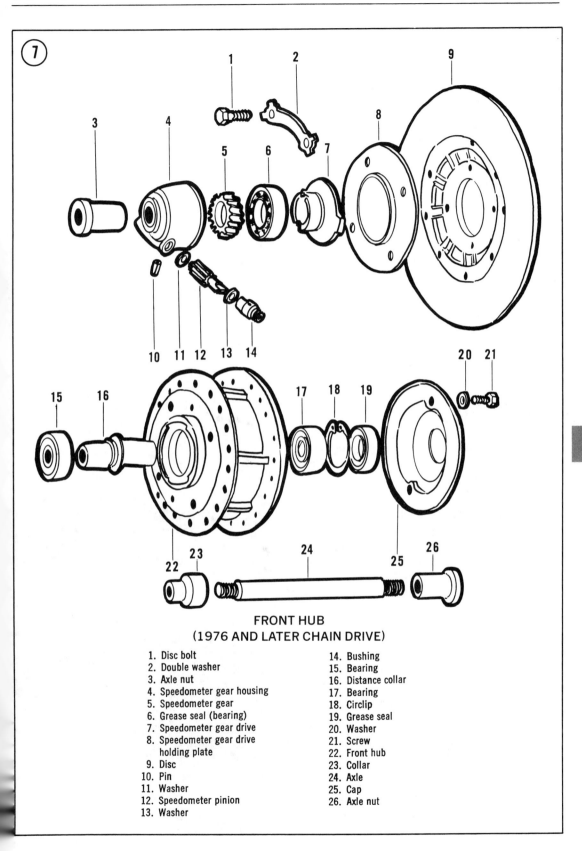

FRONT HUB
(1976 AND LATER CHAIN DRIVE)

1. Disc bolt
2. Double washer
3. Axle nut
4. Speedometer gear housing
5. Speedometer gear
6. Grease seal (bearing)
7. Speedometer gear drive
8. Speedometer gear drive
   holding plate
9. Disc
10. Pin
11. Washer
12. Speedometer pinion
13. Washer

14. Bushing
15. Bearing
16. Distance collar
17. Bearing
18. Circlip
19. Grease seal
20. Washer
21. Screw
22. Front hub
23. Collar
24. Axle
25. Cap
26. Axle nut

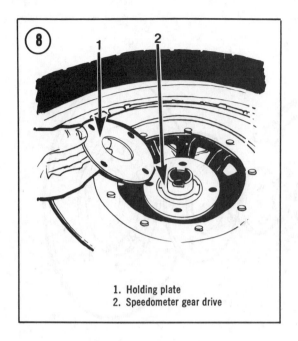

1. Holding plate
2. Speedometer gear drive

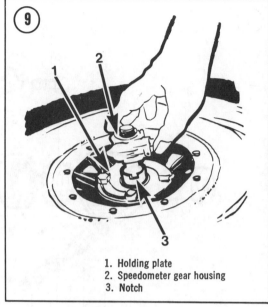

1. Holding plate
2. Speedometer gear housing
3. Notch

plate must be installed with the plain side facing in (**Figure 8**).

5. Tighten the disc mounting bolts to 30 ft.-lb. (4.0 mkg), then bend the washer tabs back over the bolts.

6. Install the speedometer gear housing so that it fits into the speedometer gear drive notches (**Figure 9**).

7. Remove any grease that may have gotten onto the disc (use a high flash-point solvent).

> WARNING
> *Never use a solvent which leaves an oily residue.*

FRONT WHEEL (SHAFT DRIVE)

Removal

1. Place a wooden block under the crankcase to lift the front wheel off the ground.

2. Disconnect the speedometer cable at the wheel.

3. Remove a brake hose clamp bolt (**Figure 10**).

4. Remove 2 brake caliper mounting bolts (A, **Figure 11**) and support the caliper to keep tension off the brake hose (**Figure 12**).

5. Remove the axle nut (B, **Figure 11**), and loosen the 4 axle clamp bolts (C).

6. Pull out the front axle and remove the wheel.

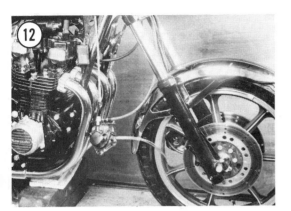

CAUTION

Do not set the wheel down on the disc surface as it may get scratched or warped.

NOTE: *Insert a piece of wood in the caliper in place of the disc. That way, if the brake lever is inadvertently squeezed, the piston will not be forced out of the cylinder. If this does happen, the caliper might have to be disassembled to reseat the piston, and the system will have to be bled.*

7. Check the wheel balance, and axial and radial rim runout (see *Wheel Inspection*).

Front Wheel Installation (Shaft Drive)

1. Remove the wood piece from the caliper.

2. Position the wheel in place, carefully inserting the disc between the pads.

3. Insert the axle through the right fork leg, collar, wheel, speedometer gear housing, and the left fork leg. Put the nut on finger-tight.

4. Turn the speedometer gear housing to about a 3 o'clock position, up against the fork leg stop (**Figure 13**).

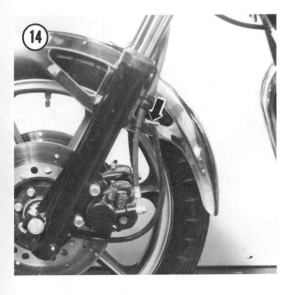

5. Stick a metal bar through the axle head and torque the axle nut to 60 ft.-lb. (8.0 mkg).

6. Torque the 4 axle clamp nuts to 15 ft.-lb. (2.0 mkg).

7. Mount the brake caliper and torque its 2 mounting bolts to 22 ft.-lb. (3.0 mkg).

8. Mount the brake hose clamp next to the fender.

9. Route the speedometer cable through its guide and connect it to the gearbox (**Figure 14**).

NOTE: *Slowly rotate the wheel while inserting the cable so it will engage properly.*

10. After the wheel is installed, rotate it and apply the brake several times to make sure it rotates freely and that the brake pads are seated against the discs.

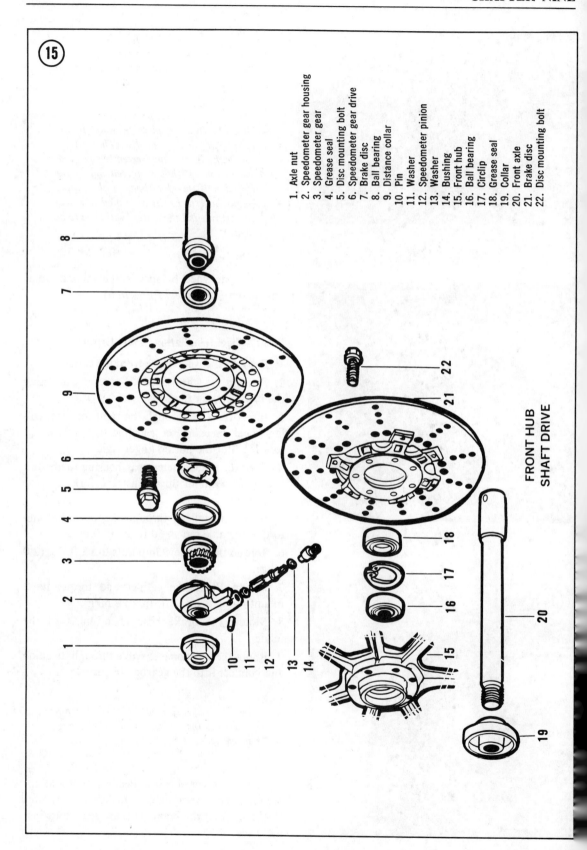

⑮

1. Axle nut
2. Speedometer gear housing
3. Speedometer gear
4. Grease seal
5. Disc mounting bolt
6. Speedometer gear drive
7. Brake disc
8. Ball bearing
9. Distance collar
10. Pin
11. Washer
12. Speedometer pinion
13. Washer
14. Bushing
15. Front hub
16. Ball bearing
17. Circlip
18. Grease seal
19. Collar
20. Front axle
21. Brake disc
22. Disc mounting bolt

FRONT HUB
SHAFT DRIVE

Front Hub Disassembly (Shaft Drive)

Refer to **Figure 15**.
1. Remove the speedometer gear housing from the left side and the collar from the right.
2. Remove the 7 brake disc bolts on each side and remove the discs (**Figure 16**).
3. On the right side, remove the grease seal and circlip.
4. Remove the left bearing and distance collar. Tap the bearing out with a soft aluminum or brass drift.
5. Remove the opposite bearing in the same manner.
6. Check the axle for runout and inspect the wheel bearing (see *Wheel Inspection*).

Front Hub Reassembly (Shaft Drive)

Refer to **Figure 15**.
1. Install the left bearing, pushing it in until it seats (sealed bearings should have the flush side out).

> *CAUTION*
> *Tap the bearings squarely into place and tap on the outer race only. Use a socket that matches the outer race diameter. Do not tap on the inner race or the bearing might be damaged. Be sure that the bearings are completely seated.*

2. Install the distance collar and the right bearing and circlip.
3. Install a new grease seal on the right side. Press it in so the face of the seal is flush with the surface of the hub.
4. Install the brake discs and torque the bolts (7 each side) to 16.5 ft.-lb. (2.3 mkg).

5. Grease the speedometer gearbox housing and gear.
6. Install the speedometer gear housing. Make sure the tangs fit in the notches in the hub (**Figure 17**).

REAR WHEEL (900cc)

Removal/Installation

> *WARNING*
> *When removing the wheels or working on the brakes, wear a protective mask to keep from inhaling any dust from the brake linings. The brake linings contain asbestos fiber; asbestos has been connected with lung scarring and cancer. Do not use compressed air to clean the brake drums or linings; dump any dust onto a newspaper and dispose of it in the trash. Wash your hands after handling the brake parts.*

1. Loosen the right side muffler mounts, to make it easier to get at the rear axle nut.
2. Remove the 2 bolts that mount chain-guard to the swing arm brackets.
3. Remove the cotter pin from the rear axle. Loosen the rear axle nut.
4. Remove the spring clip from the end of the bolt that mounts torque link to rear brake backing plate (panel). Remove the nut and bolt.
5. Remove the brake rod nut from the end of the brake rod. Remove the return spring. Remove the brake rod from the brake cam lever.
6. Loosen the locknuts on both chain adjuster bolts, and back out the bolts.
7. Unscrew both chain adjuster stop bolts, and remove the stops.

CHAPTER NINE

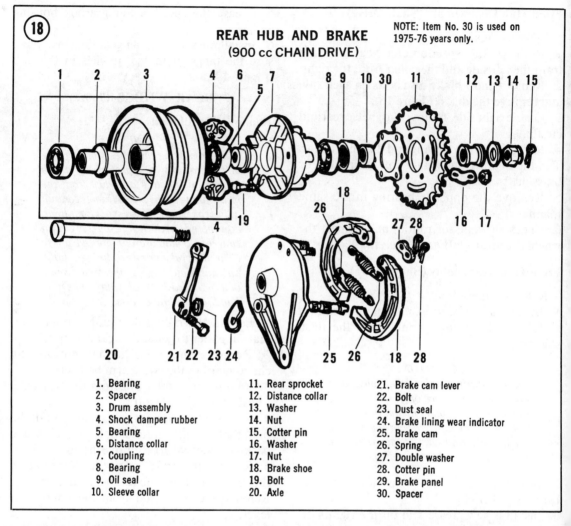

18

REAR HUB AND BRAKE
(900 cc CHAIN DRIVE)

NOTE: Item No. 30 is used on
1975-76 years only.

1. Bearing
2. Spacer
3. Drum assembly
4. Shock damper rubber
5. Bearing
6. Distance collar
7. Coupling
8. Bearing
9. Oil seal
10. Sleeve collar
11. Rear sprocket
12. Distance collar
13. Washer
14. Nut
15. Cotter pin
16. Washer
17. Nut
18. Brake shoe
19. Bolt
20. Axle
21. Brake cam lever
22. Bolt
23. Dust seal
24. Brake lining wear indicator
25. Brake cam
26. Spring
27. Double washer
28. Cotter pin
29. Brake panel
30. Spacer

8. Push the rear wheel forward in the swing arm. Remove the rear chain from the rear sprocket.

9. Pull the wheel rearward and remove it from the motorcycle. Check the wheel balance, and the axial and radial rim runout, and sprocket runout (see *Wheel Inspection*).

10. Install the wheel in the reverse order of removal, with the additional steps below.

11. Adjust the rear chain tension with the brake rod nut positioned flush with the end of the brake rod before torquing the rear axle nut or the torque link bolt. Follow the *Drive Chain Tension* checking and adjustment procedures, both in Chapter Three.

NOTE: *Before tightening the axle nut, spin the wheel and stop it forcefully with the brake pedal. Hold the pedal down*

while tightening the axle nut. This "centers" the brake shoes in the drum, and will help prevent a "spongy" feel of the drum brake.

12. Adjust the rear brake linkage, following the adjustment procedures in Chapter Three.

Rear Hub Disassembly (900cc)

Refer to **Figure 18**.

1. Remove the rear wheel from the motorcycle.

2. On the outer face of the coupling, flatten the bent-up tabs of the double washers. Remove the 6 bolts that mount the rear sprocket, and the 3 double washers. Remove the rear sprocket (and sprocket spacer on 1975 models).

3. Pull the coupling assembly from the left side of the hub.

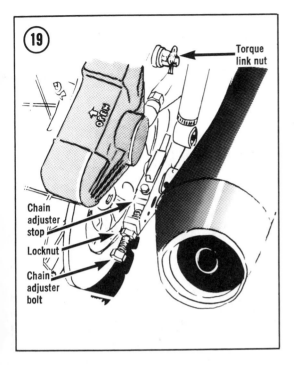

(19)

Torque
link nut

Chain
adjuster
stop

Locknut

Chain
adjuster
bolt

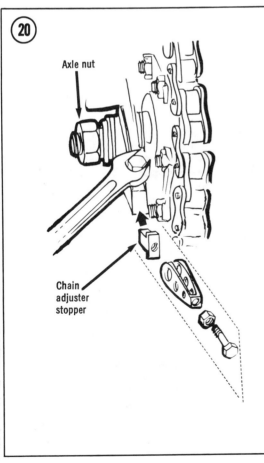

(20)

Axle nut

Chain
adjuster
stopper

4. Remove the rubber shock dampers from the hub.

5. Remove the distance collar from the inner side of the coupler.

6. Take the axle sleeve collar from the outer side of the coupler.

7. Pry out the oil seal.

8. Insert a drift into the coupler from the inner side. With it, tap evenly around the inner race of the coupler bearing, and drive it out of the coupler.

9. Remove the brake backing plate from the rear hub.

10. Insert a drift through the coupling side of the hub. With it, tap gently around the inner race of the brake side wheel bearing, and drive it out of the hub.

11. Take out the distance collar from the brake side of the hub.

12. Insert a drift from the brake side of the hub, tap gently around the inner race of the coupling side wheel bearing, and drive it out of the hub.

13. Check the axle for runout, and inspect and lubricate the wheel bearings.

Rear Hub Reassembly (900cc)

Reassemble the wheel in the reverse order of disassembly, adding the following procedures:

    a. Discard the old oil seal and install a new one.

    b. Torque the rear sprocket mounting bolts to 26.5 ft.-lb. (3.5 mkg).

REAR WHEEL (1000cc CHAIN DRIVE)

Removal/Installation

1. Set the motorcycle on its centerstand.

2. Remove the cotter pin, nut, lockwasher, and bolt from the rear end of the torque link. Refer to **Figure 19**.

3. Remove the 2 chain guard bolts and washers and take off the chain guard.

4. Remove the axle cotter pin and loosen the axle nut. Refer to **Figure 20**.

5. Loosen the left and right chain adjuster locknuts and both chain adjusting bolts. Push the wheel forward so the chain can be removed from

9

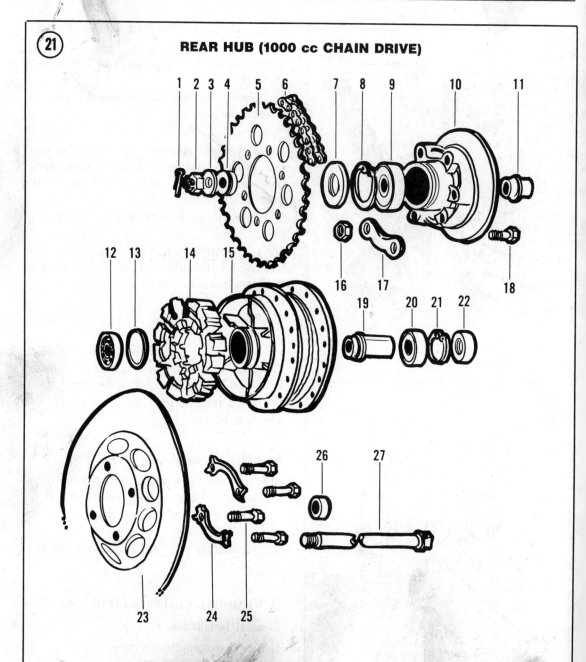

21 REAR HUB (1000 cc CHAIN DRIVE)

1. Cotter pin
2. Axle nut
3. Washer
4. Coupling collar
5. Rear sprocket
6. Drive chain
7. Grease seal
8. Circlip
9. Ball bearing
10. Coupling
11. Coupling sleeve
12. Ball bearing
13. O-ring
14. Rubber damper
15. Rear hub
16. Nut
17. Double washer
18. Bolt
19. Spacer
20. Ball bearing
21. Circlip
22. Grease seal
23. Disc
24. Double washer
25. Bolt
26. Collar
27. Axle

the sprocket. Remove the bolts and lockwashers and remove the chain adjuster stoppers.

6. Loosen the brake line from the grommets on the swing arm.

7. Slide the wheel rearward until it drops out of the swing arm.

> NOTE: *Note carefully the position of the rear wheel spacers and their location on the axle.*

8. Check the wheel balance, axial and radial rim runout, and sprocket runout (see *Wheel Inspection*).

9. Install in reverse order of removal.

Rear Hub Disassembly (1000cc Chain Drive)

Refer to **Figure 21**.

1. Straighten the bent portions of the double washer.

CAUTION
Do not lay the wheel on the ground with the disc facing down (damage to the disc could result). Lay blocks under the wheel so the disc does not touch the ground.

2. Remove the rear sprocket nuts and double washers to separate the rear sprocket and wheel coupling.

3. Remove the rear sprocket and coupling from the rear wheel. Pull the coupling collar from the left and the coupling sleeve from the right.

4. Remove the circlip and grease seal.

5. Tap lightly and evenly around the bearing inner race from the wheel side to remove the bearing.

6. Remove the rubber damper from the rear hub.

7. Pull out the collar from the disc side.

8. Straighten the bent portions of the double washers and remove the bolts, double washers, and circlip.

9. Remove the left side bearing by inserting a metal rod into the hub from the disc side, and tapping evenly around the bearing inner race. The distance collar will come out with the bearing.

10. Tap out the remaining bearing by inserting a metal rod into the hub from the other side.

11. Check the axle for runout and inspect and lubricate the wheel bearings (see *Wheel Inspection*).

Rear Hub Reassembly (1000cc Chain Drive)

Refer to **Figure 21**.

1. Press the wheel bearing in until it bottoms in the hole.

2. Install the circlip.

3. Replace the grease seal with a new one. Press the seal in until it stops at the bottom of the hole.

4. Install the rear sprocket (numbered side facing out), bolts, new double washers, and nuts. Tighten the nuts loosely.

5. Install the coupling sleeve on the right side and the coupling collar on the left side of the coupling.

6. Inspect the O-ring on the rear hub. Replace it if it has deteriorated. Apply grease sparingly to the O-ring.

7. Install the rubber damper and wheel coupling on the rear hub. Tighten the sprocket nuts to 30 ft.-lb (4.0 mkg).

8. Bend the tabs of the double washers over the nuts.

REAR WHEEL (SHAFT DRIVE)

Removal

1. Put the bike on its centerstand.

2. Remove the mufflers (see *Exhaust System Removal*, Chapter Seven).

3. Remove the rear brake caliper anchor bolt **(Figure 22)**.

4. Remove the axle nut, then pull out the axle while holding the caliper up (**Figure 23**).

> NOTE: *Prop the caliper securely on the swing arm, or tie it up to keep tension off the brake hose.*

5. Slide the wheel to the right to free it from the splined drive coupling, and remove the wheel from the motorcycle. You may find it necessary to let some air out of the tire, or to tilt the bike to get adequate clearance.

> WARNING
> *Do not tilt the motorcycle too far. It is a very heavy machine.*

> CAUTION
> *Do not set the wheel down on the disc surface as it may get damaged. Place the outer edges of the wheel on wooden blocks.*

> NOTE: *Insert a piece of wood in the caliper in place of the disc. That way, if the brake pedal is inadvertently pushed, the piston will not be forced out of the cylinder. If this does happen, the caliper might have to be disassembled to reseat the piston, and the system will have to be bled.*

6. Check the wheel balance, axial and radial rim runout (see *Wheel Inspection*).

Rear Wheel Installation (Shaft Drive)

1. Remove the wood from the brake caliper.

2. Grease the splined coupling (**Figure 24**).

3. Install the distance collar into the rear bevel case (**Figure 25**).

4. Push the wheel into place, align the coupling splines and slide the wheel to the left.

5. Slide the brake caliper over the disc, align it with the wheel, and insert the axle. Don't forget the cap outside the left swing arm.

6. Torque the rear axle nut to 100 ft.-lb. (14.0 mkg).

7. Install the caliper anchor bolt (**Figure 26**) and torque it to 22 ft.-lb. (3.0 mkg).

8. Install the mufflers (see *Exhaust System Installation*, Chapter Seven).

9. Rotate the wheel and apply the rear brake to make sure the wheel turns freely and the brake pads are seated.

Rear Hub Disassembly (Shaft Drive)

CAUTION
Do not lay the wheel on the ground or workbench with the disc facing down. Set the outer edges of the wheel on wooden blocks.

Refer to **Figure 27**.

1. Remove the circlip from the drive side (**Figure 28**).

2. Remove the wheel coupling and the rubber dampers (**Figure 29**).

3. Remove the short collar from the brake side of the wheel.

4. Remove the 7 disc bolts and the brake disc (**Figure 30**).

5. Remove the grease seal and circlip.

6. Remove the right side bearing and distance collar. Tap the bearing out with a soft aluminum or brass drift.

CAUTION
Tap only on the outer race. The bearing will be damaged if struck on the inner race.

7. Remove the left side bearing in the same manner.

8. Check the axle for runout and inspect the bearings (see *Wheel Inspection*).

Rear Hub Reassembly (Shaft Drive)

Refer to **Figure 27**.

1. Install the left bearing (sealed bearings should have the flush side out).

CAUTION
Tap the bearing squarely into place and tap only on the outer race. Use a socket that matches the outer race diameter. Do not tap on the inner race or the bearing will be damaged. Be sure to tap the bearings until they seat completely.

2. Install the right bearing and distance collar.

3. Apply a small amount of grease to the O-ring on the left side of the hub.

4. On the right side, install the circlip and a new grease seal. Press it in so the face of the seal is even with the face of the seal hole.

5. Install the brake disc and torque its 7 mounting bolts to 16.5 ft.-lb. (2.3 mkg).

6. Insert the short collar on the right side.

WHEEL INSPECTION

Alignment (Chain Drive Only)

1. Measure the width of the 2 tires at their widest points.

2. Subtract the smaller dimension from the larger.

3. Make an alignment tool out of wood, approximately 7 feet long, with an offset equal to one half of the dimension obtained in Step 2. See (D) in **Figure 31**.

4. If the wheels are not aligned as in (A) and (C), **Figure 31**, the rear wheel must be shifted to correct the situation.

5. Adjust the rear wheel with the chain adjuster bolts until the wheels align.

NOTE: *After this procedure is completed, refer to **Drive Chain Adjustment** in Chapter Three to make sure drive chain slack is within tolerance.*

Rim Runout

Measure the lateral and vertical runout of the wheel rim with a dial indicator as shown in **Figure 32**. The maximum lateral runout for a wire spoke type wheel is 0.12 in. (3.0 mm) and is 0.02 in. (0.5 mm) for the cast aluminum wheel. The

9

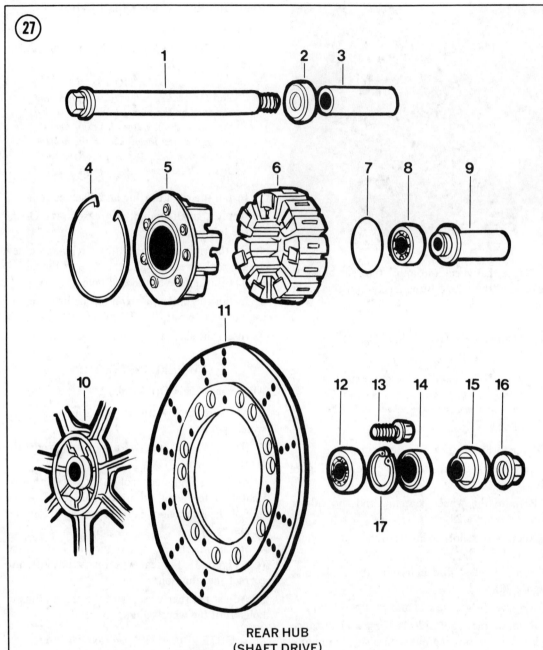

**REAR HUB
(SHAFT DRIVE)**

1. Rear axle
2. Cap
3. Distance collar
4. Retainer
5. Wheel coupling
6. Rubber damper
7. O-ring
8. Ball bearing
9. Distance collar
10. Rear hub
11. Brake disc
12. Bearing
13. Disc mounting bolt
14. Grease seal
15. Collar
16. Axle nut
17. Circlip

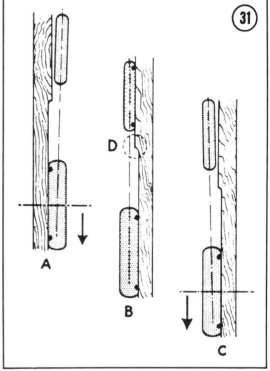

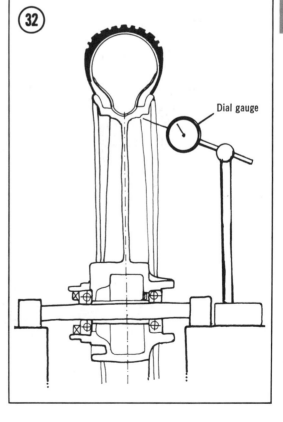

Dial gauge

9

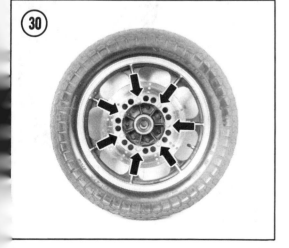

maximum vertical runout for the wire spoke type wheel is 0.08 in. (2.0 mm) and is 0.03 in. (0.8 mm) for the cast aluminum wheel. If the runout exceeds these dimensions, check the wheel bearing condition.

On models with wire spoke wheels, some of this condition can be corrected as described under *Spoke Adjustment*.

The stock Kawasaki cast aluminum wheel cannot be serviced, but must be replaced.

Inspect the cast aluminum wheels for any signs of cracks, fractures, dents, or bends. If it is damaged in any way, it must be replaced.

WARNING
Do not try to repair any damage to this type wheel as it will result in an unsafe riding condition.

Spoke Adjustment

Spokes loosen with use and should be checked periodically. If all appear loose, tighten all spokes on one side of the hub, then tighten all the spokes on the other side. One-half to one turn should be sufficient; do not overtighten.

After tightening the spokes, check the rim runout to be sure you haven't pulled the rim out of shape.

To pull the rim out, tighten the spokes which terminate on the same side of the hub and loosen the spokes which terminate on the opposite side of the hub. See **Figure 33**. In most cases, only a slight amount of adjustment is necessary to true a rim. After adjustment, rotate the rim and make sure another area has not been pulled out of true. Continue adjustment and checking until runout is within tolerance.

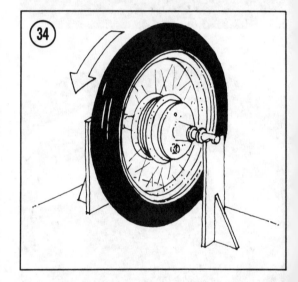

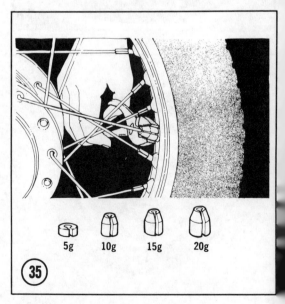

Figure 33

Hub
Loosen
Tighten
Rim

Wheel Balance

An unbalanced wheel is unsafe. Depending on the degree of unbalance and the speed of the motorcycle, the rider may experience anything from a mild vibration to a violent shimmy which may even result in loss of control.

On spoke type wheels, the balance weights are applied to the spokes on the light side of the wheel to correct this condition.

On models equipped with the cast aluminum wheels, weights are attached to the rim. A kit of Tape-A-Weight, or equivalent, may be purchased from most motorcycle supply stores. This kit contains test weights and strips of adhesive backed weights that can be cut to the desired weight and attached directly to the rim.

NOTE: *Be sure to balance the wheel with the brake disc(s) in place as they affect the balance.*

Before you attempt to balance the wheel, check to be sure that the wheel bearings are in good condition and properly lubricated and that the brakes do not drag. The wheel must rotate freely.

1. Remove the wheel as described under *Front Wheel Removal*.

2. Mount the wheel on a fixture such as the one in **Figure 34** so it can rotate freely.

3. Give the wheel a spin and let it coast to a stop. Mark the tire at the lowest point.

4. Spin the wheel several more times. If the wheel keeps coming to a rest at the same point, it is out of balance.

5. On spoke type wheels, attach a weight to the upper (or light) side of the wheel at the spoke (**Figure 35**). Weights come in 4 sizes: 5, 10, 15, and 20 grams. They are crimped onto the spoke with ordinary pliers.

NOTE: *Kawasaki offers weights that are crimped on the rim of both tubed and tubeless tires (Figure 36).*

6. On cast wheels, tape a test weight to the upper (or light) side of the wheel.

7. Experiment with different weights until the wheel, when spun, comes to rest at a different position each time.

8. On cast wheels, remove the test weight and install the correct size adhesive backed weight.

Sprocket Inspection

1. Inspect the teeth of the sprocket. If the teeth are visibly worn (**Figure 37**), replace with a new one.

2. If the sprocket requires replacement, the drive chain is probably worn also. Refer to *Drive Chain Inspection*.

3. Measure sprocket runout with a dial indicator. Runout should not exceed 0.020 in. (0.5 mm).

Axle Runout

A bent axle can cause vibration, poor handling, and instability. To check the runout of the axle:

1. Place the axle in V-blocks spaced 4 in. apart. Position a dial gauge halfway between the V-

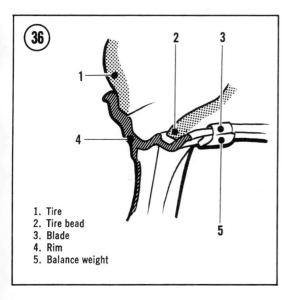

36

1. Tire
2. Tire bead
3. Blade
4. Rim
5. Balance weight

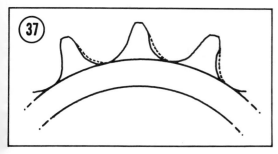

37

blocks so that its probe bears perpendicularly against the axle (**Figure 38**).

2. Rotate the axle and write down the highest and lowest dial gauge readings. The difference between them is the runout.

3. If the axle has more than 0.008 in. (0.2 mm) of runout, replace it with a new one.

Bearing Inspection/Lubrication

> NOTE: *Some of the later models come with sealed ball bearings which should last the life of the motorcycle. They are not designed to be lubricated.*

1. Clean bearings thoroughly in solvent and dry. Do not spin the bearing while drying.

2. Oil the bearing, then spin with your fingers to check its condition (**Figure 39**). It should not make noise, and it should spin smoothly. If not, replace it with a new one.

3. If the old bearing is to be reused, wash it in solvent again and pack it with a good quality wheel bearing grease. Be sure the grease is worked thoroughly into the bearing.

TIRE CHANGING

The Kawasaki cast wheel is aluminum and the exterior appearance can easily be damaged. Special care must be taken with tire irons when changing a tire to avoid scratches and gouges to the outer rim surface.

New tubeless tires, designated by TUBELESS cast into the sidewall (**Figure 40**), are designed to be used only with special TUBELESS rims that are dimensionally different from tube-type rims. The word TUBELESS is stamped into these rims (**Figure 41**).

> WARNING
> *Do not install a tubeless tire on rims not originally equipped with tubeless tires. The tire bead may not seal properly. Unexpected deflation can result.*
>
> *Do not install tube-type tires on rims originally intended for tubeless tires. The tire bead will be hard to seat, and the tire could slip on the rim.*

> CAUTION
> *Do not lay the wheel on its disc or the disc may get warped. Support the tire edges to hold the disc off the ground.*

Tube Tire Removal

1. Remove the valve core to deflate the tire. If the tire has rim locks (**Figure 42**), loosen the rim locknuts fully, but don't remove them.

2. Press the entire bead on both sides of the tire into the center of the rim.

3. Lubricate the beads with soapy water.

4. Insert the tire iron under the bead next to the valve (**Figure 43**). Force the bead on the opposite side of the tire into the center of the rim and pry the bead over the rim with the tire iron.

> NOTE: *Use rim protectors (**Figure 44**) or insert scraps of leather between the tire irons and the rim to protect the rim from damage.*

5. Insert a second tire iron next to the first to hold the bead over the rim. Then work around the tire with the first tire iron, prying the bead over the rim (**Figure 45**). Be careful not to pinch the inner tube with the tire irons.

6. Remove the valve from the hole in the rim and remove the tube from the tire.

> NOTE: *Step 7 is required only if it is necessary to completely remove the tire from the rim, such as for tire replacement.*

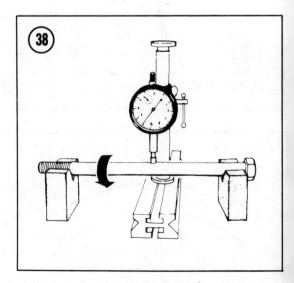

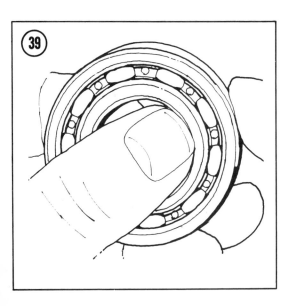

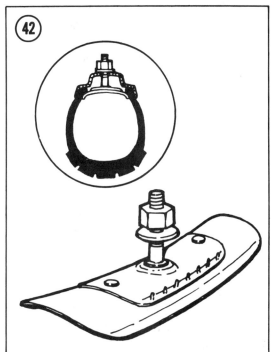

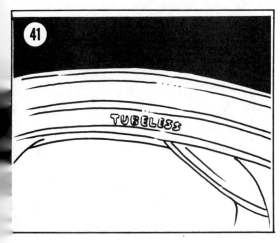

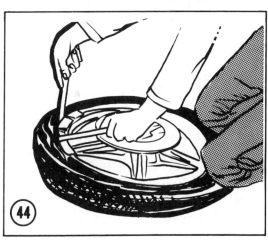

7. Stand the tire upright. Insert the tire iron between the second bead and the side of the rim that the first bead was pried over (**Figure 46**). Force the bead on the opposite side from the tire iron into the center of the rim. Pry the second bead off the rim, working around as with the first.

Tube Tire Installation

1. Carefully inspect the tire for any damage, especially inside.

2. A new tire may have balancing rubbers inside. These are not patches and should not be disturbed. A colored spot near the bead indicates a lighter point on the tire. This spot should be placed next to the valve stem.

3. If the rear tire has a rotational direction arrow molded in the sidewall (**Figure 47**), make sure it points the way the wheel turns.

4. Inflate the tube just enough to round it out. Too much air will make installation difficult.

5. Place the tube inside the tire.

6. Lubricate both beads of the tire with soapy water.

7. Place the backside of the tire into the center of the rim and insert the valve stem through the stem hole in the wheel. The lower bead should go into the center of the rim and the upper bead outside. Work around the tire in both directions (**Figure 48**). Use a tire iron for the last few inches of bead (**Figure 49**).

8. Press the upper bead into the center of the rim opposite the valve (**Figure 50**). Pry the bead into the rim on both sides of the initial point with a tire iron, working around the rim to the valve (**Figure 51**).

9. Wiggle the valve to be sure the tube is not under the bead. Set the valve squarely in its hole before screwing in the valve nut to hold it against the rim.

10. Check the bead on both sides of the tire for an even fit around the rim. Inflate the tire slowly to seat the beads in the rim. It may be necessary to bounce the tire to complete the seating. Inflate to the required pressure. Balance the wheel (see *Wheel Balance*). Tighten the rim locks, if equipped.

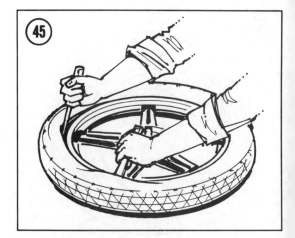

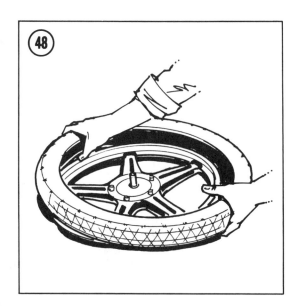

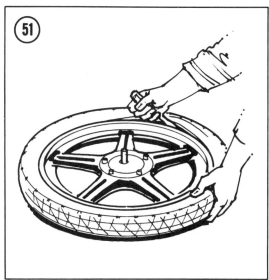

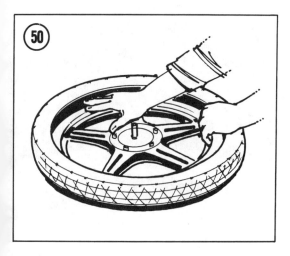

9

INNER TUBE REPAIR

Every rider eventually experiences trouble with a tire or tube. Repairs and replacement are fairly simple, and every rider should know the techniques.

Patching a motorcycle tube is only a temporary fix. A motorcycle tire flexes too much and could rub a patch right off. However, a patched tire will get you far enough to buy a new tube if you ride at moderate speeds.

Tube Repair Kits

Tube repair kits can be purchased from motorcycle dealers and some auto supply stores. When buying, specify that the kit you want is for motorcycles.

There are 2 types of tube repair kits:

a. Hot patch

b. Cold patch

Hot patches are stronger because they actually vulcanize to the tube, becoming part of it. However, they are far too bulky to carry for roadside repairs, and the strength is unnecessary for a temporary repair.

Cold patches are not vulcanized to the tube; they are simply glued to it. Though not as strong as hot patches, cold patches are still very durable. Cold patch kits are less bulky than hot and more easily applied under adverse conditions. A cold patch kit containing everything necessary tucks in easily with your emergency tool kit.

Tube Repair

1. Install the valve core into the valve stem (**Figure 52**) and inflate the tube slightly. Do not overinflate.

2. Immerse the tube in water a section at a time (see **Figure 53**). Look carefully for bubbles indicating a hole. Mark each hole and continue checking until you are certain that all holes are discovered and marked. Also make sure that the valve core is not leaking; tighten it if necessary.

> NOTE: *If you do not have enough water to immerse sections of the tube, try running your hand over the tube slowly and very close to the surface. If your hand is damp, it works even better. If you suspect a hole anywhere, apply some saliva to the area to verify it.*

3. Roughen the area around the hole slightly larger than the patch; use a cap from the tire repair kit or a pocket knife. Do not scrape too vigorously or you may cause additional damage.

4. Apply a small quantity of special cement to the puncture and spread it evenly with a finger.

5. Allow the cement to dry until it's tacky—usually 30 seconds or so is sufficient.

6. Remove the backing from the patch.

> CAUTION
> *Do not touch the newly exposed rubber with your fingers or the patch will not stick firmly.*

7. Center the patch over the hole. Hold the patch firmly in place for about 30 seconds to allow the cement to set.

8. Dust the patched area with talcum powder to prevent sticking.

9. Carefully check inside the tire casing for glass particles, nails, or other objects which may have damaged the tube. If the inside of the tire is split, apply a patch to the area to prevent it from pinching and damaging the tube again.

10. Check the inside of the rim. Make sure the rim band is in place, with no spoke ends protruding, which could puncture the tube.

11. Deflate the tube prior to installation in the tire.

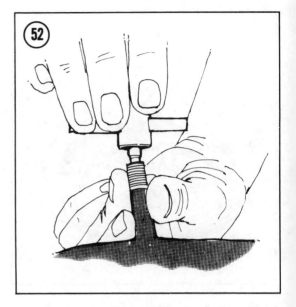

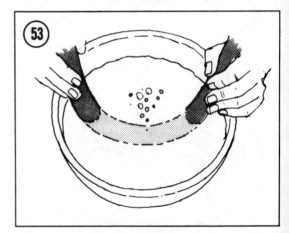

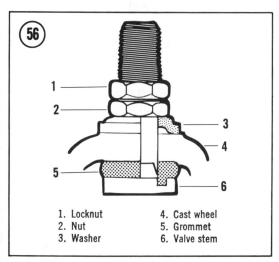

1. Locknut
2. Nut
3. Washer
4. Cast wheel
5. Grommet
6. Valve stem

TUBELESS TIRES

Tubeless tires have TUBELESS molded into the sidewall (**Figure 54**). Tire failure should be less frequent because the tires run cooler without a tube, and they have some self-sealing capability around small nails, etc.

When a tubeless tire is flat, your best recourse is to take it to a motorcycle dealer for repair. Flat tubeless tires should always be removed from the rim to inspect the inside of the tire and to apply a combination plug/patch from the inside. Don't rely on a plug or cord repair applied from outside the tire. It might be OK on a car, but it's too dangerous on a motorcycle.

After repairing a tubeless tire, Kawasaki recommends not exceeding 50 mph (80 kph) for 24 hours, and then *never* exceeding 110 mph (180 kph). So if you are a racer, don't rely on tubeless tire repair. Replace the tire.

Installing a new tubeless tire can be difficult because an initial air seal is hard to get. Your dealer has a bead seater to make the job easy.

Tubeless Tire Removal/Installation

CAUTION
The inner rim and tire bead area are the air sealing surfaces on a tubeless tire. Do not scratch the inside of the rim or damage the tire bead.

9

Tubeless tire removal and installation is similar to that of tube-type tires, with these additional requirements:

a. Always use rim protectors (**Figure 55**), and be careful not to scratch or gouge the rim or the inside of the tire.

b. Install a new valve stem whenever you have the tire off the wheel (**Figure 56**). Rubber deteriorates with age, and valve stem replacement will never be as convenient as now.

c. After the tire is on the rim, bounce it several times while rotating the wheel. This helps seal the bead.

d. After inflating the tire, check to see that the beads are fully seated, and that the rim lines molded into the sidewall are parallel to the rim (**Figure 57**). If necessary, inflate the tire to not more than 60 psi (4.0 kg/cm²) to seat the beads.

e. If the beads won't seat, deflate the tire, re-lubricate the rim and bead with soapy water, and re-inflate the tire.

WARNING
Do not ride the motorcycle if the beads are not seated. The tire could slip on the rim, or it could deflate unexpectedly.

Tubeless Tire Repair

Do not rely on a plug or cord type patch applied from outside the tire. Use a combination plug/patch applied from inside the tire (**Figure 58**).

1. Remove the tire from the rim.

2. Inspect the rim inner flange. Smooth any scratches on the sealing surface with emery cloth. If a scratch is deeper than 0.020 in. (0.5 mm) replace the wheel.

3. Inspect the tire inside and out. Replace a tire if any of the following is found:

   a. A puncture larger than ⅛ in. (3 mm)

   b. A punctured or damaged sidewall

   c. More than 2 punctures in the tire

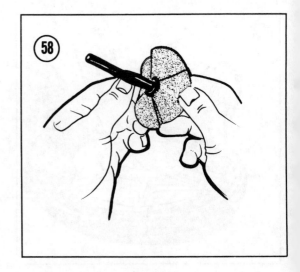

   d. Two punctures within 15 in. (40 cm) of each other

4. Apply the plug/patch, following the instructions supplied with the patch.

5. After repairing a tubeless tire, don't exceed 50 mph for the first 24 hours, and don't exceed 110 mph thereafter. The patch could work loose from the tire flexing and heat.

NOTE: If you have a 1980 model, or a 1979-1981 Police model, first check the Supplement at the back of this book for any new service information.

CHAPTER TEN

CHASSIS

This chapter covers the front forks, steering head, rear shock absorbers, swing arm, drive chain, drive shaft, and rear bevel drive unit. Chassis torque specifications (**Table 1**) are at the end of the chapter.

The 900/1000cc chain drive chassis is similar for all models, but the shaft drive chassis is unique. When different procedures are given, make sure you follow the procedures and illustrations applicable to your motorcycle.

FRONT FORKS

The Kawasaki front suspension consists of a spring-controlled, hydraulically damped telescopic fork. Before suspecting major trouble, drain the fork oil and refill it with the proper type and quality; refer to Chapter Three. If you still have trouble, such as poor damping, tendency to bottom out or top out, or leakage around the rubber seals, then follow the service procedures in this section.

To simplify fork service and to prevent the mixing of parts, the legs should be removed, serviced, and reinstalled individually.

Each front fork leg consists of the fork tube (inner tube), slider (outer tube), fork spring and damper rod with its damper components.

Front Leg Removal/Installation

1. Raise the front wheel off the ground, support the motorcycle securely under the engine.

2. Detach the brake calipers (see *Front Brake Removal*, Chapter Eight).

> NOTE: *The hydraulic brake lines do not have to be disconnected if the calipers are supported to prevent stress and bending of metal brake lines.*

> NOTE: *Insert a piece of wood in the calipers in place of the disc. That way, if the brake lever is inadvertently squeezed, the piston will not be forced out of the cylinder. If it does happen, the caliper might have to be disassembled to reseat the piston, and the system will have to be bled.*

3. Remove the front wheel (see *Front Wheel Removal*, Chapter Nine).

4. Remove the front fender bolts and the lockwashers and the fender (**Figure 1**). Note the location of any speedometer cable or brake line guides.

5. Loosen the upper triple clamp fork bolt (**Figure 2**).

6. If you are going to disassemble the fork after removal, loosen the top fork plug bolt (**Figure 2**).

10

NOTE: *On some models, the han-dlebars must be detached for access to the fork plug bolts.*

7. Loosen the lower triple clamp bolts (**Figure 3**).

8. Work the fork leg down and out with a twisting motion.

9. Install by reversing these removal steps. Note the following.

10. *1973–1977:* The top surface of each fork tube must be flush with the top of the upper fork bridge.

11. *1978 and later:* The top surface of each fork tube must be below the top surface of the upper triple clamp by 0.08 in. (2 mm). See **Figure 2**.

12. Torque the fork mounting bolts. See **Table 1** for torque specifications.

Fork Leg Disassembly

Refer to **Figures 4 through 8** for this procedure.

1. Hold the upper fork tube in a vise with a rubber sheet to grip the tube. Remove the top bolt and spring seat.

WARNING
Some forks are assembled with spring pre-load. Keep your face away from the fork end. The top bolt may spring out.

2. Remove the fork spring(s).

3. Remove the fork from the vise and pour the oil out and discard it. Pump the fork several times by hand to expel most of the remaining oil.

4. Remove the rubber boot out of the notch in the slider and slide it off of the fork tube.

5. Clamp the slider in a vise with a rubber sheet to grip the slider (**Figure 9**).

6. Remove the Allen bolt and gasket from the bottom of the slider (**Figure 10**). Hold the damper rod from turning with a Kawasaki special tool. Your dealer can tell you which tool to use. If a special tool is not available, you can often hold the damper rod with a square hardwood stick jammed into the top of the damper. The Allen bolt may come out without holding the damper rod if an impact driver is used.

7. Pull the fork tube out of the slider.

8. Remove the oil lockpiece, the damper rod, and rebound spring.

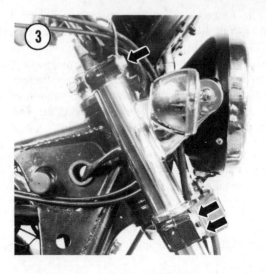

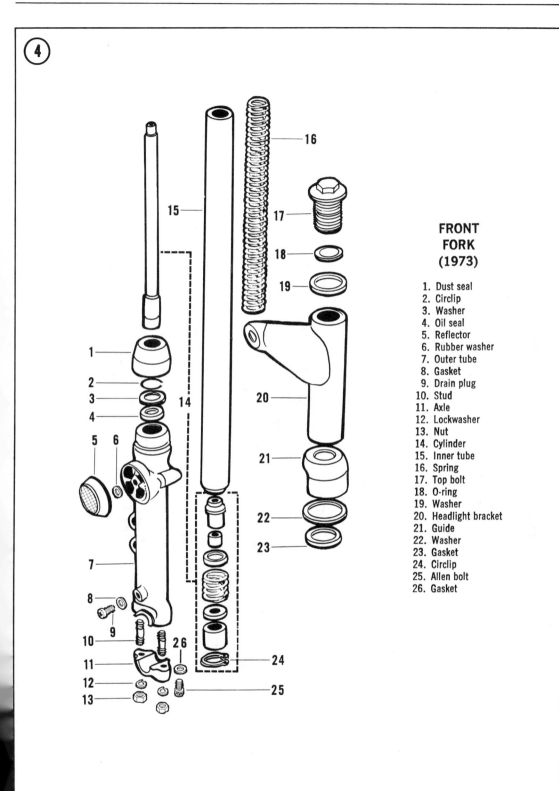

FRONT FORK (1973)

1. Dust seal
2. Circlip
3. Washer
4. Oil seal
5. Reflector
6. Rubber washer
7. Outer tube
8. Gasket
9. Drain plug
10. Stud
11. Axle
12. Lockwasher
13. Nut
14. Cylinder
15. Inner tube
16. Spring
17. Top bolt
18. O-ring
19. Washer
20. Headlight bracket
21. Guide
22. Washer
23. Gasket
24. Circlip
25. Allen bolt
26. Gasket

10

FRONT FORK
(1974-1976
MODELS)

1. Damper assembly
2. Dust seal
3. Circlip
4. Circlip
5. Washer
6. Oil seal
7. Rubber washer
8. Reflector
9. Fork slider
10. Gasket
11. Drain plug
12. Stud
13. Axle
14. Lockwasher
15. Nut
16. Fork tube
17. Gasket
18. Allen bolt
19. Spring
20. Top bolt
21. O-ring
22. Headlight stay
23. Base cover
24. Washer
25. Gasket

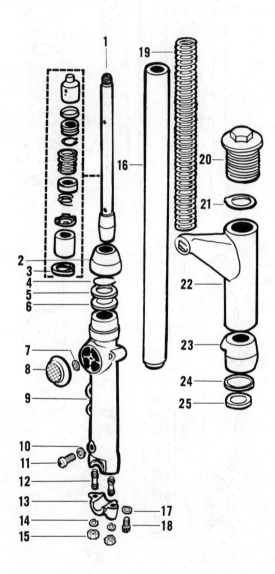

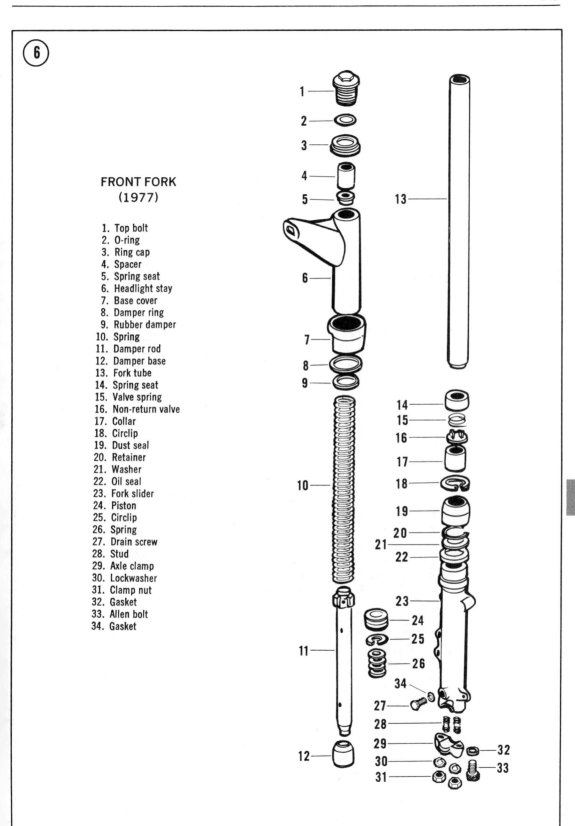

⑥

FRONT FORK
(1977)

1. Top bolt
2. O-ring
3. Ring cap
4. Spacer
5. Spring seat
6. Headlight stay
7. Base cover
8. Damper ring
9. Rubber damper
10. Spring
11. Damper rod
12. Damper base
13. Fork tube
14. Spring seat
15. Valve spring
16. Non-return valve
17. Collar
18. Circlip
19. Dust seal
20. Retainer
21. Washer
22. Oil seal
23. Fork slider
24. Piston
25. Circlip
26. Spring
27. Drain screw
28. Stud
29. Axle clamp
30. Lockwasher
31. Clamp nut
32. Gasket
33. Allen bolt
34. Gasket

10

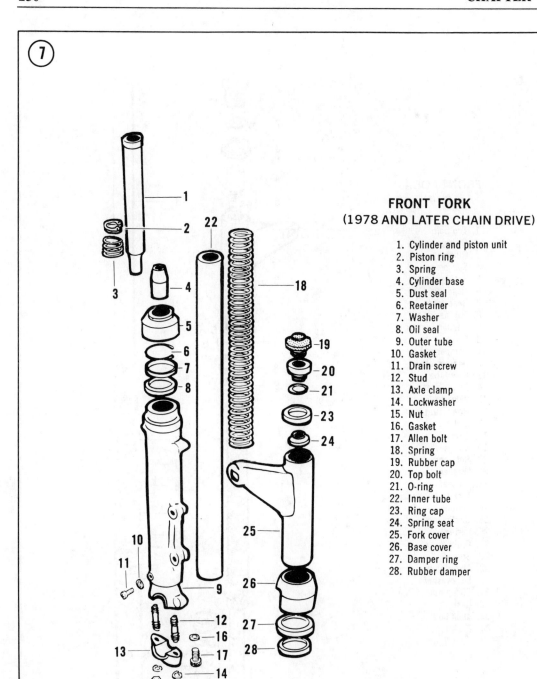

FRONT FORK
(1978 AND LATER CHAIN DRIVE)

1. Cylinder and piston unit
2. Piston ring
3. Spring
4. Cylinder base
5. Dust seal
6. Reetainer
7. Washer
8. Oil seal
9. Outer tube
10. Gasket
11. Drain screw
12. Stud
13. Axle clamp
14. Lockwasher
15. Nut
16. Gasket
17. Allen bolt
18. Spring
19. Rubber cap
20. Top bolt
21. O-ring
22. Inner tube
23. Ring cap
24. Spring seat
25. Fork cover
26. Base cover
27. Damper ring
28. Rubber damper

FRONT FORK
(SHAFT DRIVE)

1. Piston and cylinder unit
2. Piston ring
3. Spring
4. Dust seal
5. Cylinder base
6. Retainer
7. Washer
8. Oil seal
9. Left outer tube
10. Clamp bolt
11. Gasket
12. Screw
13. Locknut
14. Gasket
15. Allen bolt
16. Inner tube
17. Spring
18. Spring seat
19. Spring

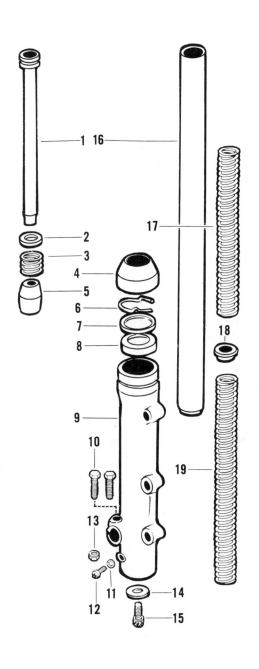

10

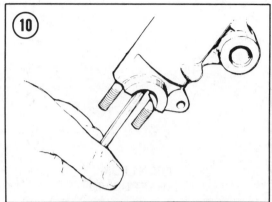

9. *1977:* Remove the circlip from inside the lower end of the fork tube. Remove the collar, valve, spring, and valve seat.

10. *1977:* Remove the spring and circlip and remove the piston from the damper rod.

11. If oil has been leaking from the top of the slider, remove the retainer from the top of the slider. Remove the washer and pull out the oil seal.

> NOTE: *It may be necessary to slightly heat the area on the slider around the oil seal prior to removal. Be careful not to damage the top of the slider.*

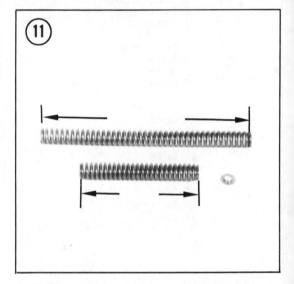

Fork Leg Inspection

Refer to **Figures 4 through 8**.

1. Thoroughly clean all parts in solvent and dry. Check the fork tube for signs of wear or scratches.

2. Check the damper rod for straightness. If bent, install a new rod.

3. Carefully check the damper valve and piston ring for wear or damage.

4. Inspect the oil seals for scoring and nicks and loss of resiliency. Replace if the condition is questionable.

5. Check the upper fork tube for straightness. If bent or severely scratched, it should be replaced.

6. Check the lower slider for dents or exterior damage that may cause the upper fork tube to hang up during riding conditions. Replace if necessary.

7. Measure uncompressed length of the spring(s) (**Figure 11**). Replace the spring(s) if shorter than

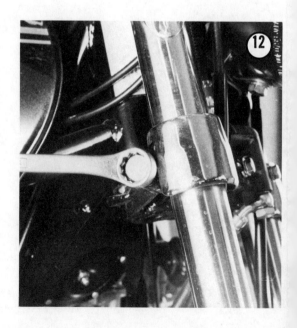

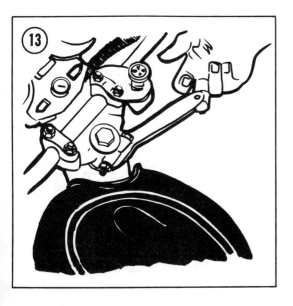

the following dimensions given in **Table 2** at the end of the chapter.

Fork Leg Assembly

To assemble, reverse the removal procedure. Note the following:

1. Install the oil seal, washer, and retainer into the top of the slider if removed.

2. When inserting the damper rod into the fork tube (inner tube) of the 1974–1976 models, use a cylinder guide tool to compress the piston ring inside the fork tube. (A Kawasaki dealer has a special tool available.)

3. *1978 and later chain drive:* Install the fork spring with the tapered end down.

4. Apply liquid gasket sealer to the Allen bolt gasket and apply Loctite Lock N' Seal to the threads of the bottom Allen bolt (**Figure 10**) before installation.

Torque the Allen bolt to 14.5 ft.-lb. (2.0 mkg) on 1977 models; to 16.5 ft.-lb. (2.3 mkg) on 1978 and later chain drive models; and to 30 ft.-lb. (4.0 mkg) on shaft drive models.

5. Add fresh fork oil to each tube (see *Fork Oil Change*).

STEERING PLAY

Steering play adjustment is critical to your motorcycle's safe handling. Make sure you follow the directions given here. If you aren't sure that you've got it right, have your dealer check it.

Steering Play Adjustment (Chain Drive)

1. Remove the fuel tank to protect its finish (see *Fuel Tank Removal*).

2. Loosen the big steering stem cap nut on top of the upper triple clamp.

3. Loosen the steering stem clamp bolt at the rear of the upper triple clamp.

4. Loosen the 2 fork tube clamp bolts on the lower triple clamp (**Figure 12**).

5. Raise the front wheel off the ground; support the motorcycle securely under the engine.

6. Fit a spanner wrench to the notched steering stem adjuster between the upper triple clamp and the steering head (**Figure 13**).

7. Back the adjuster out 2 turns, so the forks turn freely.

8. Tighten the adjuster lightly, until you just feel the steering become hard to turn.

9. Tighten the adjuster another 1/16 turn past that point.

> CAUTION
> *Don't tighten the adjuster so tight that you indent the steering ball bearings into their races. If you do, the steering will be "notchy" and you'll have to replace the bearings.*

10. Tighten the steering stem cap nut on top of the upper triple clamp.

11. Torque the steering stem clamp bolt at the rear of the upper triple clamp to 14 ft.-lb. (1.9 mkg).

12. Hit each side of the lower triple clamp from the top and bottom with a rubber mallet to reposition it on fork tubes and relieve strain.

13. Torque the 2 fork tube clamp bolts on the lower triple clamp to 40 ft.-lb. (5.7 mkg) on 900cc models or to 30 ft.-lb. (4.0 mkg) on 1000cc models.

14. Recheck steering play (see *Steering Play Inspection*).

15. Install the fuel tank.

Steering Play Adjustment (Shaft Drive)

1. Remove the fuel tank to protect its finish (see *Fuel Tank Removal,* Chapter Seven).

2. Loosen the 2 upper triple clamp fork bolts (**Figure 14**).

3. Remove the 4 handlebar clamp bolts and the clamp (**Figure 15**).

4. Loosen the upper triple clamp rear bolt and the big top cap bolt (**Figure 15**).

5. Support the motorcycle securely with the front wheel off the ground.

6. Loosen the top adjuster locknut with a spanner wrench. There is a spanner in the motorcycle's tool kit.

7. Tighten the bottom adjuster nut (**Figure 16**) to about 30 ft.-lb. (4.0 mkg).

> NOTE: *Practice getting the "feel" of 30 ft.-lb. by tightening another bolt with a torque wrench. Put an extension pipe on your spanner wrench to make it as long as your torque wrench.*

8. Back out the adjuster nut until the steering turns easily.

9. Tighten the adjuster nut again until the steering just starts to become hard to turn. Do not overtighten.

10. Hold the adjuster nut in position, and tighten the upper locknut with your fingers.

11. Torque the big cap bolt to 30 ft.-lb. (4.0 mkg).

12. Torque the rear upper triple clamp bolt to 14.5 ft.-lb. (2.0 mkg).

13. Torque the 2 upper triple clamp fork bolts to 20 ft.-lb. (2.8 mkg).

14. Install the handlebars, clamp, lockwashers and bolts. Torque the bolts to 14.5 ft.-lb. (2.0 mkg).

15. Recheck steering play (see *Steering Play Inspection* in Chapter Three).

16. Install the fuel tank (see *Fuel Tank Installation* in Chapter Seven).

STEERING HEAD

Removal and disassembly of the steering head is easiest if all the other parts are removed from the front of the motorcycle. In most cases, it is not necessary or desirable to disconnect any hydraulic brake lines. If you do, be sure to bleed the system when you're done (see *Brake Fluid Bleeding* in Chapter Eight).

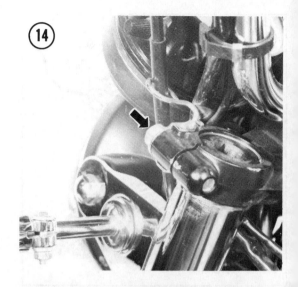

A. Rear bolt   B. Cap bolt

Front End Disassembly/Assembly

The following procedure covers all models. As you remove parts, note the location of all cable and hose guides and wiring straps for proper installation. Watch what you're doing carefully, and make a note of anything you might not remember a week from now. Pay particular attention to control, wiring and instrument cable routing.

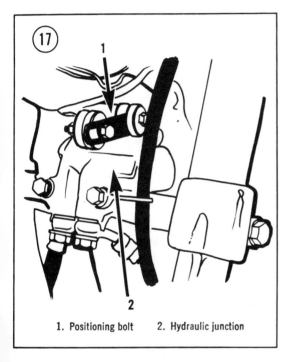

1. Positioning bolt 2. Hydraulic junction

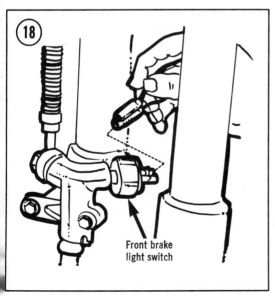

Front brake light switch

1. Support the motorcycle securely with the front wheel off the ground.

2. Remove the fuel tank to protect its finish (see *Fuel Tank Removal* in Chapter Seven).

3. Remove the bottom headlight positioning bolt (**Figure 17**—not equipped on LTD).

4. *Chain drive:* Disconnect the hydraulic brake-light switch leads (**Figure 18**).

5. Remove the hydraulic junction mounting bolts and any spacers behind the junction (**Figure 17**).

6. Remove the headlight from its shell (see *Headlight Removal* in Chapter Eleven), and disconnect the wiring connectors. Push the wiring out the back of the shell.

7. Disconnect the speedometer and tachometer cables at the wheel and engine. Tape the inner cable ends to the outer housings so they don't slip out.

8. Detach the front brake calipers (see *Front Caliper Removal,* Chapter Eight). Do not disconnect the brake lines.

> **CAUTION**
> *On models with metal brake tubing at the calipers, be careful not to bend the tubing. Support the calipers to keep stress off the tubing.*

9. Remove the front wheel (see *Front Wheel Removal,* Chapter Nine).

10. Remove the front forks (see *Fork Removal*).

11. Remove the headlight shell, mounting brackets, and turn signals. Note the bottom cover, ring, and washer at the bottom of the brackets (**Figure 19**).

12. Free all cables and hoses from guides and clamps at the steering head (**Figure 20**).

13. Remove the instrument mounting nuts, washers, and rubber dampers (**Figure 21**). Remove the instrument assembly with cables, noting the routing of the cables.

> **CAUTION**
> *Store the meters right side up. If they are upside down or sideways, the instrument fluids inside will leak and the meters won't work.*

14. Remove the front master cylinder from the handlebars (see *Front Master Cylinder Removal,*

10

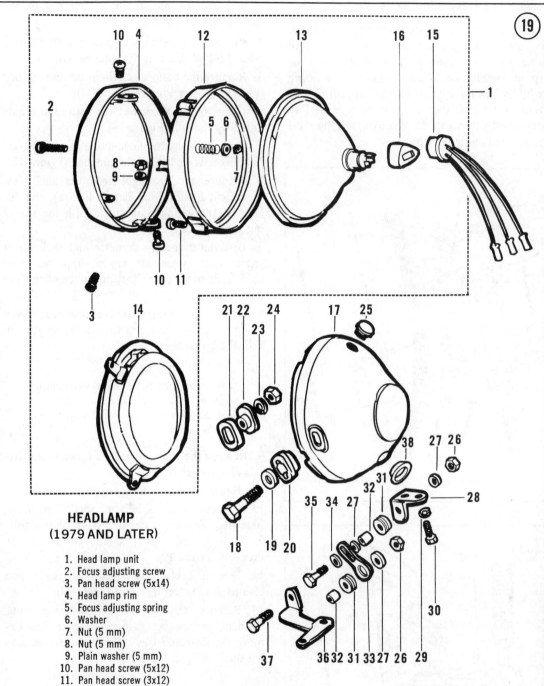

HEADLAMP
(1979 AND LATER)

1. Head lamp unit
2. Focus adjusting screw
3. Pan head screw (5x14)
4. Head lamp rim
5. Focus adjusting spring
6. Washer
7. Nut (5 mm)
8. Nut (5 mm)
9. Plain washer (5 mm)
10. Pan head screw (5x12)
11. Pan head screw (3x12)
12. Retainer
13. Sealed beam unit
14. Head lamp mounting ring
15. Head lamp socket
16. Head lamp socket cover
17. Head lamp body
18. Hex head bolt (10 mm)
19. Plain washer (10 mm)
20. Damper rubber A

21. Damper rubber B
22. Collar
23. Spring washer (10 mm)
24. Nut (10 mm)
25. Rubber plug
26. Lock nut (6 mm)
27. Plain washer
28. Head lamp body bracket
29. Spring washer (8 mm)

30. Hex head bolt (8x16)
31. Damper rubber
32. Collar
33. Bracket
34. Plain washer (6 mm)
35. Hex head bolt (6x28)
36. Head lamp bracket
37. Hex head bolt (6x25)
38. Grommet

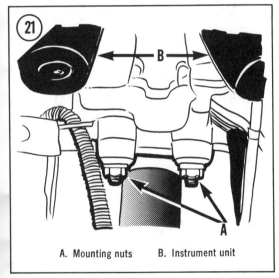

A. Mounting nuts   B. Instrument unit

Chapter Eight), and remove the whole front brake assembly (master cylinder-to-caliper) from the bike.

CAUTION
Don't bend any metal brake lines.

15. Remove the handlebar clamp bolts and clamps. Let the handlebar assembly hang down in front of the motorcycle, being careful not to damage any cables or wires.

16. If there are any other parts attached to the triple clamps, remove them now.

17. To assemble the front end, reverse the disassembly procedure.

WARNING
Control and instrument cables must:
a. Be routed through existing guides
b. Be free of sharp bends
c. Not get pinched by or interfere with the steering
d. Not rub on the tire

NOTE: *Be sure to install a rubber damper above and below the fork bridge on the instrument cluster mounting bolts, followed by the flat washer, lockwasher, and nut. This is to minimize instrument cluster vibration.*

Steering Head Disassembly/Assembly

Refer to **Figures 22 through 24**.

1. Loosen the upper triple clamp rear bolt; then remove the big top cap bolt, flatwasher, and wave washer.

2. Remove the upper triple clamp. If necessary, tap it up from the bottom with a soft mallet.

3. *Shaft drive:* Remove the upper notched adjuster locknut.

4. Hold up the lower triple clamp to keep it from falling out, and remove the notched steering adjuster nut, using a spanner wrench (**Figure 25**).

5. Remove the lower triple clamp and steering stem assembly from the bottom of the steering head (**Figure 26**).

10

NOTE: *On chain drive models, catch the lower bearing balls as they fall out. There should be 20 of them. Remove any stuck in the bottom of the steering head.*

6. Remove the steering stem cap from the top of the steering head. On *chain drive* models, remove the upper inner race and 19 balls and on *shaft drive* models remove the upper roller bearing.

7. To assemble, reverse the removal procedure. Note the following:

   a. Lubricate the steering head bearings. On *chain drive* models stick the 19 upper and 20 lower ball bearings in place with grease while you install the lower triple clamp/ steering stem (**Figure 27**).

   b. Adjust the steering play (see *Steering Play Adjustment*) after installing the lower triple clamp/steering stem.

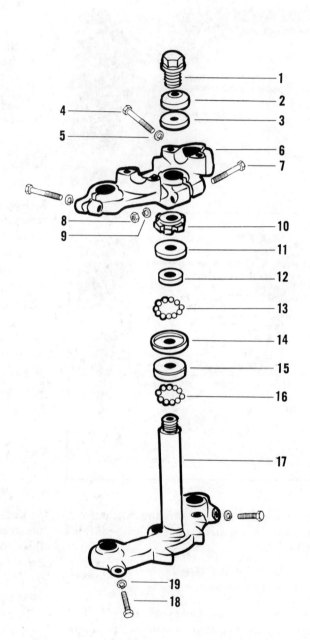

㉒

**STEERING HEAD
(1973-1975)**

1. Steering head stem bolt
2. Steering stem head washer
3. Wave washer
4. Clamp bolt
5. Lockwasher
6. Stem head
7. Clamp bolt
8. Nut
9. Lockwasher
10. Steering stem head nut
11. Steering stem head cap
12. Steering stem head upper cone
13. Balls
14. Race
15. Race
16. Balls
17. Steering stem
18. Bolt
19. Lockwasher

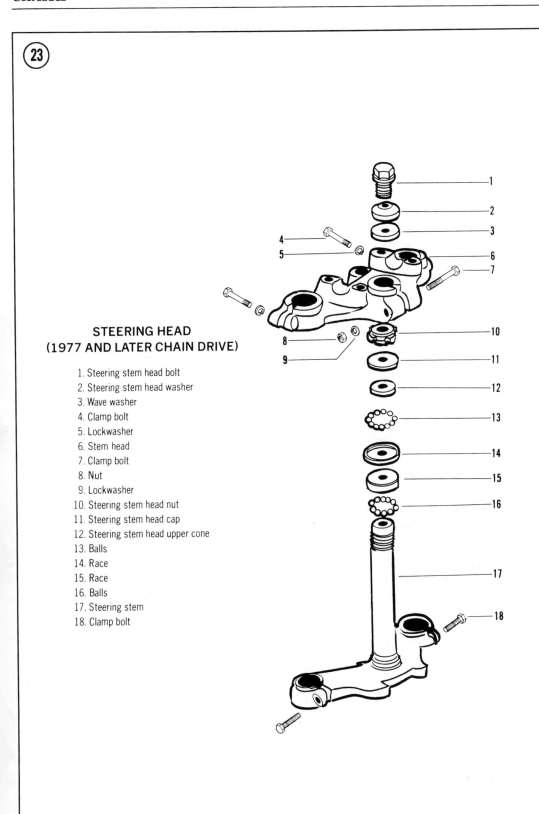

**STEERING HEAD
(1977 AND LATER CHAIN DRIVE)**

1. Steering stem head bolt
2. Steering stem head washer
3. Wave washer
4. Clamp bolt
5. Lockwasher
6. Stem head
7. Clamp bolt
8. Nut
9. Lockwasher
10. Steering stem head nut
11. Steering stem head cap
12. Steering stem head upper cone
13. Balls
14. Race
15. Race
16. Balls
17. Steering stem
18. Clamp bolt

10

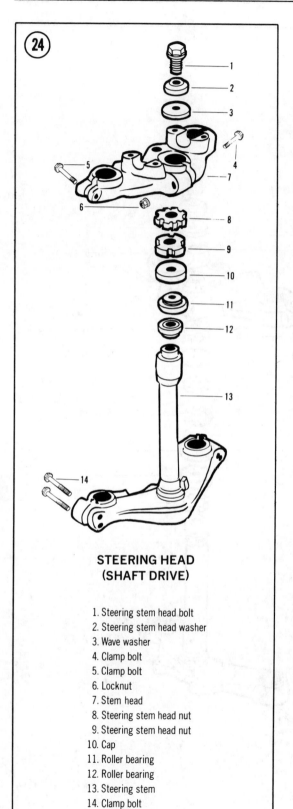

**STEERING HEAD
(SHAFT DRIVE)**

1. Steering stem head bolt
2. Steering stem head washer
3. Wave washer
4. Clamp bolt
5. Clamp bolt
6. Locknut
7. Stem head
8. Steering stem head nut
9. Steering stem head nut
10. Cap
11. Roller bearing
12. Roller bearing
13. Steering stem
14. Clamp bolt

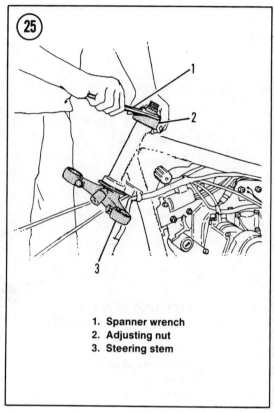

1. Spanner wrench
2. Adjusting nut
3. Steering stem

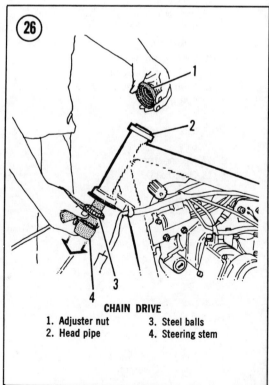

CHAIN DRIVE

1. Adjuster nut
2. Head pipe
3. Steel balls
4. Steering stem

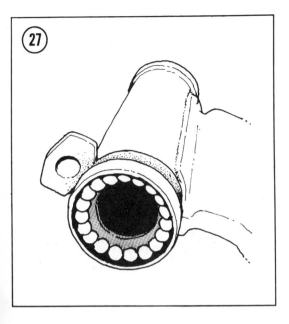

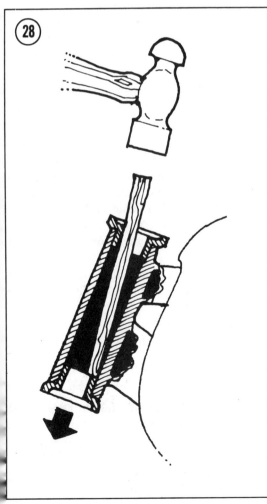

c. Leave the upper triple clamp top cap bolt and clamp bolt loose until after you insert and align the fork legs.

d. Torque the top cap bolt to 30 ft.-lb. (4.0 mkg) and the rear upper clamp bolt to 14 ft.-lb. (1.9 mkg).

Steering Head Inspection & Lubrication

1. Clean the bearing races in the steering head, the steering stem races, and all the bearings with solvent.

2. Check for broken welds on the frame around the steering head.

3. Check each of the balls or rollers for pitting, scratches, or discoloration indicating wear or corrosion. Replace them in sets if any are bad.

4. Check the upper and lower races in the steering head. See *Bearing Race Replacement* if races are pitted, scratched, or worn.

5. Check the steering stem for cracks. Check the bearing race on the stem for pitting, scratches, or excessive wear.

6. Check the inside of the top ball race for pitting, scratches, or wear.

7. Grease the bearings and races.

Bearing Race Replacement

The head and steering stem bearing races are pressed into place. Because they are easily bent, do not remove them unless they are worn and require replacement. Take old races to your dealer to ensure exact replacement.

Steering Head

To remove a steering head race, insert a hardwood stick into the head tube and carefully tap the race out from the inside (**Figure 28**). Tap all around the race so that neither the race nor the head tube are bent. To install a race, grease it and fit it into the end of the head tube. Tap it slowly and squarely with a block of wood (**Figure 29**). Make sure it is fully seated. You will notice a distinct change in the hammering sound as the race "bottoms-out."

> NOTE: *The upper and lower races are different. Be sure that you install them at the proper ends of the head tube.*

10

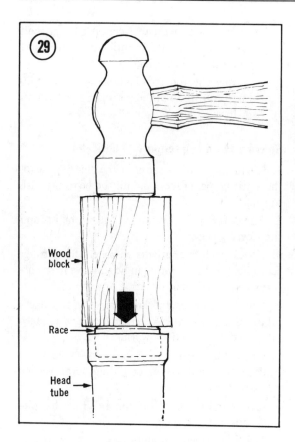

Wood
block

Race

Head
tube

Steering Stem

To remove the steering stem race, try twisting
and pulling it up by hand. If it will not come off,
carefully pry it up with a screwdriver, while
working around in a circle, prying a little at a
time. Remove the race and the grease seal.

> NOTE: *A bearing puller may be re-*
> *quired to remove the stem race.*

Install a new grease seal on the steering stem.
Slide the race over the steering stem with the
bearing surface pointing up. Tap the race down
with a piece of hardwood; work around in a circle
so that the race will not be bent. Make sure it is
seated squarely and all the way down.

REAR SHOCK ABSORBERS

The shock absorbers are not considered main-
tainable. Check them by removing them from
the motorcycle, compressing them by hand and
observing the extension stroke, and comparing
their "feel." If one has a different feel from the
other, replace them both with a new pair.

Shock Absorber Removal/Installation

Removal and installation of the rear shocks are
easier if they are done separately. The remaining
shock will support the rear of the bike and maintain the correct distance between the top and bottom shock mounts.

1. Place the bike on the centerstand.
2. Remove the nuts from the upper shock absorber mounts (**Figure 30**).
3. Remove the grab bar mounting bolt(s) inside
the fender (**Figure 31**), and remove the grab bar.
4. Remove the lower shock absorber mounting
bolt or nut (**Figure 30**). If the bolt is difficult to
loosen and the mufflers get in the way, loosen the
exhaust pipe mounts, or take off the exhaust
pipes (see *Exhaust System Removal,* Chapter
Seven).
5. Pull the top end of the shock absorber free of
its mounting stud and remove the shock absorber
from the motorcycle.
6. Install the shock absorber in the reverse order
of removal, adding the following procedures.

> NOTE: *Install the grab bar outside the*
> *shock.*

7. For bikes with grab rails, install the large flat
washer, grab rail, small flat washer, then cap nut.
8. Torque the upper shock absorber mounting
nuts and lower mounting bolts or nuts to 22 ft.-lb.
(3.0 mkg) on chain drive models or to 18 ft.-lb.
(2.5 mkg) on shaft drive models.

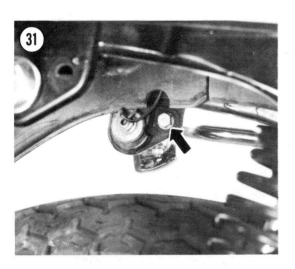

9. Check to see that the cam adjuster on each shock absorber is turned to the same notch before riding the motorcycle (**Figure 32**).

SWING ARM (CHAIN DRIVE)

The original Z1 and all the 900cc machines have plain sleeves on the swing arm pivot, riding inside bushings pressed into the swing arm.

The 1977 and later 1000cc chain drive machines have needle roller bearings; one on each side for 1977, 2 on each side for 1978 and later.

In time, the bushings (or bearings) will wear and the swing arm will become loose on the pivot shaft. If not replaced, this will cause loss of high speed stability.

Kawasaki uses an endless drive chain with no master link. The swing arm must be removed to replace the drive chain. Do not attempt to install a master link or chain failure will occur.

SWING ARM (900cc)

Swing Arm Removal

Refer to **Figure 33**.

1. Remove the rear wheel from the motorcycle.

2. Take out the lower shock absorber mounting bolt on each side.

3. Unscrew the swing arm pivot shaft nut, and remove the washer and cap.

4. Pull out the pivot shaft, and remove the swing arm.

5. Pull the sleeve out of each end of the pivot tube.

6. Insert a thin drift into the pivot tube. Hammer it gently against the near end of the distance collar to drive out the bushing at the other end of the tube.

7. Insert the drift into the other end of the pivot tube and drive out the remaining bushing.

Swing Arm Inspection (900cc)

Check the sleeves for wear. Install new bushings when the swing arm is reassembled. Check the pivot shaft for runout.

1. Measure the outside diameter of the sleeve with a micrometer.

2. If either sleeve has an outside diameter of less than 0.864 in. (21.95 mm), replace both sleeves as a set.

3. If either sleeve is visibly damaged, replace both sleeves as a set.

4. Measure the inside diameter of the bushings at both ends. If the dimension is 0.881 in. (22.37 mm) or greater, both bushings must be replaced.

> NOTE: *Always replace both bushings even though only one may be worn.*

5. Measure the runout of the pivot shaft. If the runout exceeds 0.008 in. (0.2 mm), the shaft must be replaced.

Swing Arm Installation (900cc)

Reassemble the swing arm in the reverse order of disassembly, adding the following procedures:

10

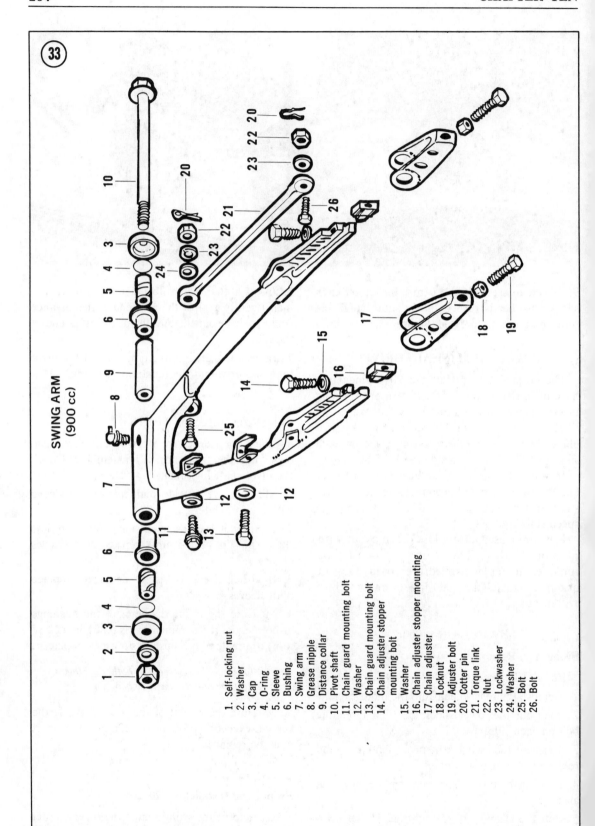

SWING ARM
(900 cc)

1. Self-locking nut
2. Washer
3. Cap
4. O-ring
5. Sleeve
6. Bushing
7. Swing arm
8. Grease nipple
9. Distance collar
10. Pivot shaft
11. Chain guard mounting bolt
12. Washer
13. Chain guard mounting bolt
14. Chain adjuster stopper
    mounting bolt
15. Washer
16. Chain adjuster stopper mounting
17. Chain adjuster
18. Locknut
19. Adjuster bolt
20. Cotter pin
21. Torque link
22. Nut
23. Lockwasher
24. Washer
25. Bolt
26. Bolt

1. Grease the swing arm pivot, sleeves, and bushings thoroughly.

2. Torque the pivot shaft nut to 100 ft.-lb. (13.5 mkg).

SWING ARM (1000cc CHAIN DRIVE)

Swing Arm Removal

Refer to **Figure 34**.

1. Place the motorcycle on its centerstand.

2. Remove the mufflers (see *Exhaust System Removal*, Chapter Seven).

3. Remove the rear wheel (see *Rear Wheel Removal*, Chapter Nine).

4. Disconnect the rear brake hose from its guides on the swing arm and fasten the brake hose so its end is higher than the rear brake reservoir to prevent fluid loss.

5. Remove the mounting bolt from the bottom of each shock absorber. A lockwasher comes off with each bolt.

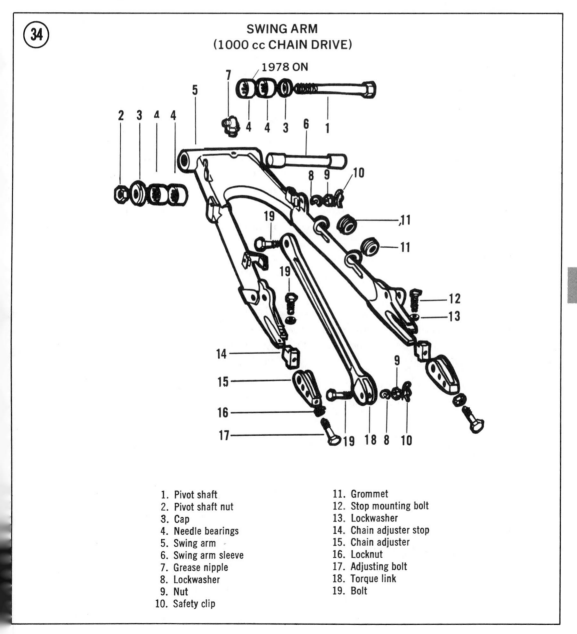

34

**SWING ARM
(1000 cc CHAIN DRIVE)**

1978 ON

10

1. Pivot shaft
2. Pivot shaft nut
3. Cap
4. Needle bearings
5. Swing arm
6. Swing arm sleeve
7. Grease nipple
8. Lockwasher
9. Nut
10. Safety clip
11. Grommet
12. Stop mounting bolt
13. Lockwasher
14. Chain adjuster stop
15. Chain adjuster
16. Locknut
17. Adjusting bolt
18. Torque link
19. Bolt

6. Move the swing arm up and down to check for abnormal friction.

7. Remove the pivot shaft nut and pull out the pivot shaft.

8. Pull back the swing arm (a cap on each side of the pivot will also come off).

> NOTE: *The swing arm is equipped with needle bearings at each end. The bearings will be damaged when removed, so don't remove them unless absolutely necessary.*

9. Remove the clip from the torque link bolt. Take out the nut and bolt, then remove the torque link from the swing arm.

10. Pull out the swing arm sleeve.

11. Insert a bar into one side and hammer on it gently to remove the needle bearing on the opposite side.

12. Remove the needle bearing on the opposite side in the same manner as Step 3, preceding.

> NOTE: *The 1978 and later models use 2 needle bearings on each side of the swing arm, and they should be replaced as a unit with the swing arm sleeve.*

Swing Arm Inspection (1000cc Chain Drive)

1. Withdraw the sleeve and remove the grease fitting. Wash all parts in solvent.

2. Measure the outside diameter of the sleeve with a micrometer at both ends. If the diameter is 0.864 in. (21.95 mm) or less at either end, the sleeve must be replaced.

> NOTE: *If the sleeve is replaced, all needle bearings must be replaced at the same time.*

3. Measure the runout of the pivot shaft. If the runout exceeds 0.006 in. (0.14 mm), install a new shaft.

Swing Arm Installation (1000cc Chain Drive)

Refer to **Figure 34**.

> CAUTION
> *Never reinstall a needle bearing that has been removed. During removal it becomes slightly damaged and is no longer true to alignment.*

1. Oil the outside surface of the new bearings and install them with a press.

2. Install the torque link and tighten the torque link nut to 22 ft.-lb. (3.0 mkg). Install a cotter pin or safety clip.

3. Lubricate the swing arm pivot.

4. Apply grease to the cap inner surfaces.

5. Install a cap on each end of the swing arm pivot. Insert the left side of the swing arm through the drive chain loop.

> NOTE: *Be sure to slip the swing arm through the drive chain—the chain must be on the inside of the swing arm.*

6. Position the swing arm pivot in the frame, then slide in the pivot shaft from right to left. Insert a screwdriver into the left side of the pivot to keep the left cap in place (**Figure 35**).

7. Install the pivot shaft nut and torque it to 70 ft.-lb. (10.0 mkg).

8. Install the rear shock absorber bolts and lockwashers, and torque each bolt to 22 ft.-lb. (3.0 mkg).

9. Fasten the brake hose in its guides with rubber grommets, then install the brake hose fitting in the caliper and torque the banjo bolt to 22 ft.-lb. (3.0 mkg). Use a new flat washer on each side of the fitting.

10. Install the right side cover.

11. Install the rear wheel (see *Rear Wheel Installation* in Chapter Nine).

12. Install the mufflers (see *Exhaust System Installation* in Chapter Seven).

13. Bleed the brake system if the brake line was disconnected (see *Brake Fluid Bleeding* in Chapter Eight).

14. Adjust the drive chain (see *Drive Chain Adjustment*).

DRIVE CHAIN

Removal/Installation

The swing arm must be removed to remove the drive chain.

> CAUTION
> *The drive chain is manufactured as a continuous closed loop with no master link. Do not cut it with a chain cutter as this may result in future chain failure.*

1. Remove the swing arm (see *Swing Arm Removal*).

2. Remove the drive sprocket cover (see *Sprocket Cover Removal* in Chapter Six).

3. Remove the drive chain.

4. Clean the drive chain with kerosene and check it for wear (see *Drive Chain Inspection* in Chapter Three).

5. Install by reversing these steps.

REAR BEVEL DRIVE

The rear bevel drive unit is mounted on the end of the left swing arm. It connects to the drive shaft with a sliding spring-loaded coupling; and to the rear wheel through a splined coupling gear (see **Figure 36**). Trouble should be very infrequent, as long as the recommended lubrication is adhered to (see Chapter Three). The rear bevel drive uses hypoid gear oil as a lubricant.

Bevel gear backlash, tooth contact patterns, and tapered roller bearing preload are all critical to bevel drive strength, quietness and longevity. Assembly to the proper tolerances requires several special tools and a high degree of skill. In the event of bevel drive trouble, we recommend you remove the unit from the motorcycle and take it to your Kawasaki dealer for repair.

The rear bevel drive unit must be removed to lubricate the rear drive shaft sliding joint, and to replace the drive shaft.

Rear Bevel Removal

1. Remove the rear wheel (see *Rear Wheel Removal* in Chapter Nine).

2. Loosen the left shock absorber top and bottom nuts (**Figure 37**).

3. Remove the 4 rear bevel/swing arm nuts (**Figure 38**).

4. Separate the rear bevel unit from the swing arm. A spring should come off with the rear bevel unit (**Figure 39**).

5. Remove the bottom shock mounting nut and remove the rear bevel unit.

NOTE: *Prop the rear bevel drive in a vertical position to prevent lubricant seepage out of the breather hole (Figure 40).*

Disassembly and Inspe

Although it may assemble the beve₁ cannot replace the bear₁₁₉ quire bearing removal) withou₁ there is trouble in the drive unit, it ma₁ remove the unit, take it to your Kawasaki ₁ and let him overhaul it.

Check rear bevel gear backlash at the ring gear splines. Standard backlash is 0.003–0.004 in. (0.08–0.11 mm).

Rear Bevel Installation

Reverse the removal procedure, and note the following:

1. Lubricate the drive shaft/rear bevel sliding joint. Coat the splines, and pack the coupling pocket forward of the splines with 25 cc (a little more than half a shot glass) of high temperature grease.

2. Make sure the spring is in place on the rear bevel input shaft (**Figure 41**).

3. Torque the rear bevel/swing arm nuts to 22 ft.-lb. (3.0 mkg).

SWING ARM (SHAFT DRIVE)

The shaft drive model's swing arm rides on tapered roller bearings at the pivots. It houses the drive shaft and it must be removed to replace the drive shaft.

There is no grease fitting on the shaft drive model's swing arm, so the swing arm must be removed to lubricate the bearings.

CAUTION
If you install a grease fitting on the swing arm, be careful not to contaminate the swing arm grease and bearings with metal filings.

The swing arm bearings have grease seals which could be damaged by pressure lubrication. If you install a grease fitting in the swing arm, be sure to loosen or remove the pivot shafts to allow the grease some place to escape (see Swing Arm Installation).

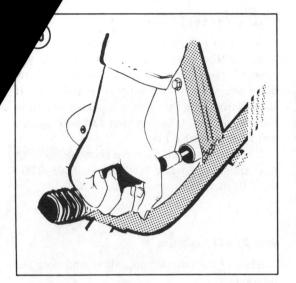

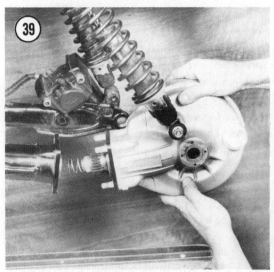

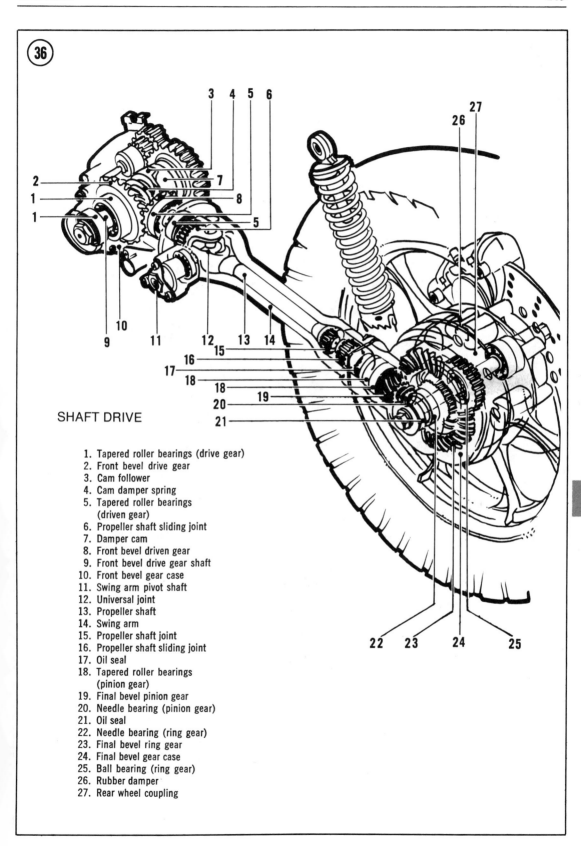

36

SHAFT DRIVE

1. Tapered roller bearings (drive gear)
2. Front bevel drive gear
3. Cam follower
4. Cam damper spring
5. Tapered roller bearings
   (driven gear)
6. Propeller shaft sliding joint
7. Damper cam
8. Front bevel driven gear
9. Front bevel drive gear shaft
10. Front bevel gear case
11. Swing arm pivot shaft
12. Universal joint
13. Propeller shaft
14. Swing arm
15. Propeller shaft joint
16. Propeller shaft sliding joint
17. Oil seal
18. Tapered roller bearings
    (pinion gear)
19. Final bevel pinion gear
20. Needle bearing (pinion gear)
21. Oil seal
22. Needle bearing (ring gear)
23. Final bevel ring gear
24. Final bevel gear case
25. Ball bearing (ring gear)
26. Rubber damper
27. Rear wheel coupling

10

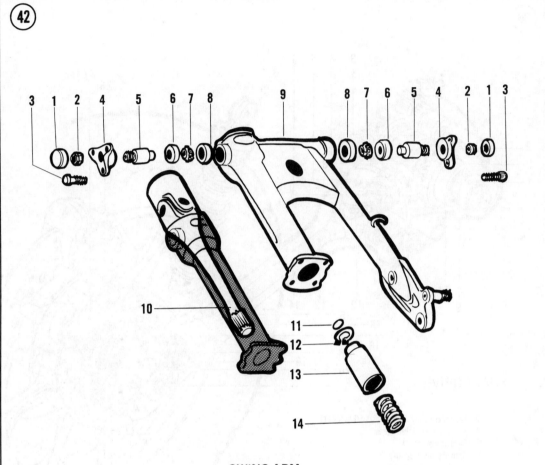

SWING ARM
(SHAFT DRIVE)

1. Rubber cap
2. Locknut
3. Allen bolt
4. Pivot shaft stop
5. Pivot shaft
6. Grease seal cap
7. Tapered roller bearing inner race
8. Tapered roller bearing outer race
9. Swing arm
10. Propeller shaft
11. O-ring
12. Circlip
13. Propeller shaft joint
14. Spring

Swing Arm Removal (Shaft Drive)

Refer to **Figure 42**.

1. Remove the exhaust system (see *Exhaust System Removal* in Chapter Seven).

2. Remove the rear wheel (see *Rear Wheel Removal* in Chapter Nine).

3. Pull the rear brake line and grommet out of the guide clip on the swing arm, and support the caliper to keep tension off the brake line.

4. Remove the rear bevel drive unit (see *Rear Bevel Removal*).

5. Loosen the right shock absorber top nut, remove the bottom nut, and pull the bottom of the shock off the swing arm stud.

6. Remove the circlip from inside the rear drive shaft joint, and pull out the splined joint (**Figure 43**).

7. At the front bevel case, pull the dust cover forward from the swing arm flange and remove the rubber caps from the left and right swing arm pivots (**Figure 44**).

8. Loosen the locknuts on the pivot shafts, then remove the 3 Allen bolts from the pivot shaft stops (**Figure 45**).

9. Remove the pivot shafts and shaft stops (**Figure 46**).

10. Pull the swing arm back and out, leaving the drive shaft attached to the front bevel drive.

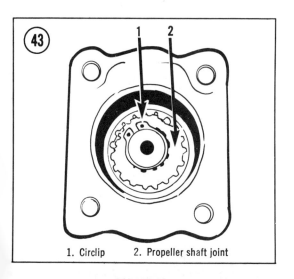

1. Circlip   2. Propeller shaft joint

10

Swing Arm Disassembly/Assembly (Shaft Drive)

Refer to **Figure 42**.

> NOTE: *Do not remove the grease seals and bearings unless you plan to install new ones. The old ones will probably be damaged during removal.*

1. Pry out the grease seals, and remove the inner bearing cone and rollers from both sides.

2. Insert a rod into one side, and hammer on it gently to push out the opposite side's bearing outer race.

3. To install new outer races, oil them and tap them slowly and squarely into place with a wood block (**Figure 47**). Be sure the races are *fully seated*.

4. Grease the new bearing rollers thoroughly before installing them.

5. Install new grease seals.

Swing Arm Installation (Shaft Drive)

Refer to **Figure 42**.

1. Pull back on the drive shaft to check that the front coupling is secure.

2. Install the swing arm over the drive shaft.

3. Install the pivot shaft stops and pivot shafts. Make sure the shaft screws are backed out to provide plenty of clearance. Tighten the 3 Allen bolts on each side.

4. Position the swing arm in the frame by inserting a 0.060 in. (1.5 mm) feeler gauge or a piece of shim stock between the inside of the frame boss and the left end of the swing arm (**Figure 48**).

5. Turn in the right pivot shaft until it meets resistance. Tighten the locknut.

6. Remove the gauge or shim stock, and torque the left pivot shaft to 11 ft.-lb. (1.5 mkg). Tighten the left locknut.

7. Swing the swing arm up and down and try to move it side-to-side. There should be no play, and the swing should be smooth. Readjust the pivots, if necessary.

8. Replace the rubber caps and the front coupling dust cover.

9. Install the right shock absorber, and torque its mounting nuts to 18 ft.-lb. (1.5 mkg).

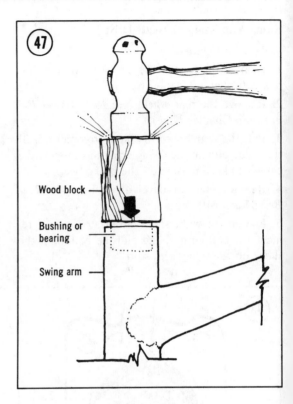

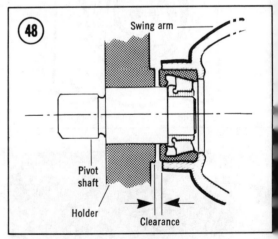

10. Lubricate the rear drive shaft joint, install the joint, and secure it with the circlip.

11. Install the rear bevel drive unit (see *Rear Bevel Installation*).

12. Install the rear wheel and caliper (see *Rear Wheel Installation* in Chapter Nine).

13. Secure the rear caliper hose in its swing arm guide clip grommet (**Figure 49**).

14. Install the exhaust system (see *Exhaust System Installation* in Chapter Seven).

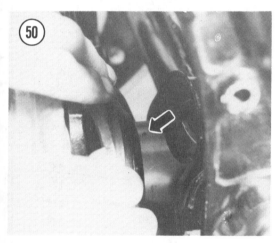

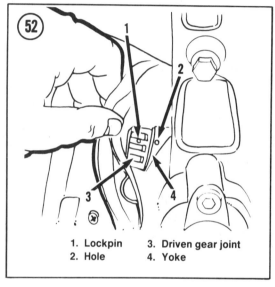

1. Lockpin   3. Driven gear joint
2. Hole   4. Yoke

10

DRIVE SHAFT

The drive shaft connects the front and rear bevel drive units. It has a pin-locked coupling at the front, a U-joint at the swing arm pivot center line, and a sliding splined coupling at the rear. The entire assembly is spring-loaded to the front. No maintenance is required. If the U-joint wears out, the drive shaft must be replaced.

Drive Shaft Removal

1. Remove the swing arm (see *Swing Arm Removal*).

2. At the front drive shaft coupling, pull the dust cover forward and turn the drive shaft until you can see a hole in the smooth rim of the coupling (**Figure 50**). In the hole is a pin that locks the coupling in the forward position.

3. Push the coupling lockpin in about 3/16 in., and pull the drive shaft assembly back and out.

Drive Shaft Installation

1. Check that the coupling lockpin and spring are in place in the front bevel drive gear (**Figure 51**).

2. Lubricate the front coupling splines with high temperature grease.

3. Position the drive shaft and align the coupling hole and lockpin (**Figure 52**).

4. Push the lockpin in just far enough to let the coupling slide forward over the gear.

> NOTE: *Don't push the lockpin in too far. It can fall inside the bevel drive gear.*

5. Maneuver the coupling as required to allow the lockpin to spring out and seat in the coupling.

6. Pull back on the drive shaft to check that the front coupling is secure.

7. Install the swing arm (see *Swing Arm Installation*).

Table 1 CHASSIS TORQUE AND LOCKING AGENT

Fastener	Chain Drive		Shaft Drive	
	Foot-pounds	Meter/Kilograms	Foot-pounds	Meter/Kilograms
Brake pedal pivot cap nut	14	1.9	14	1.9
Front axle clamp nuts	14	1.9	14	1.9
Front axle nuts	60	8.0	60	8.0
Front brake light switch PT ⅛	20	2.8	N/A	N/A
Front fork bottom Allen bolts	14.5	2.0	30	4.0
Front fork clamp bolts				
Upper	14	1.9	20	2.8
Lower	30 (1000 cc)	4.0	14.5	2.0
	40 (900 cc)	5.7	N/A	N/A
Front fork top bolts	20	2.8	20	2.8
Handlebar clamp bolts	14	1.9	14	1.9
Pad mounting screw	Use locking agent		Use locking agent	
Rear axle nut	90	12	100	14.0
Rear shock absorber mounting	22	3.0	18	2.5
	30 (900 cc upper)	4.0	N/A	N/A
Rear sprocket nuts	30	4.0	N/A	N/A
Spokes	26 in.-lb.	0.3	N/A	N/A
Steering stem head bolt	33	4.5	30	4.0
Steering stem head rear clamp bolt	14	1.9	14	1.9
Swing arm pivot shaft nut: chain drive	70	10.0	N/A	N/A
Torque link nuts	22	3.0	22	3.0
Disc brake (front and rear)				
Brake lever	50 in.-lb.	0.6	26 in.-lb.	0.3
Brake lever adjuster locknut	14.5	2.0	14.5	2.0
Master cylinder clamp	65 in.-lb.	0.8	80 in.-lb.	0.9
Banjo bolts	22	3.0	22	3.0
Brake pipe nipple	13	1.8	13	1.8
3-way joint	70 in.-lb.	0.8	70 in.-lb.	0.8
Front brake light switch	20	2.8	20	2.8
Caliper holder shafts	19	2.6	19	2.6
Caliper mounting bolts	30	4.0	30	4.0
Bleed valve	70 in.-lb.	0.8	70 in.-lb.	0.8
Disc mounting bolts	30	4.0	16.5	2.3
Rear caliper Allen bolts	22	3.0	22	3.0
Master cylinder plug (rear)	33	4.5	33	4.5
Rear bevel mounting bolts	N/A	N/A	22	3.0
Rear bevel drain plug	N/A	N/A	14.5	2.0
Rear bevel pinion nut	N/A	N/A	90	12.0
Swing arm pivot shaft: shaft drive	N/A	N/A	11	1.5

NOTE: "N/A" means "Not Applicable"

Table 2 FORK SPRING LENGTHS

1973	19 in. (485 mm)
1974–75	19.5 in. (495 mm)
1976–77	17.9 in. (455 mm)
1978 and later chain drive	20.1 in. (511 mm)
1978 and later shaft drive	7.6 in. (153 mm) *and* 14.4 in. (366 mm)

10

NOTE: If you have a 1980 model, or a 1979-1981 Police model, first check the Supplement at the back of this book for any new service information.

ELECTRICAL SYSTEM

The electrical system includes the battery, ignition system, charging system, starter system, lighting, gauges, and horn. All tables are at the end of this chapter.

Wiring diagrams are located at the end of this book.

FUSES

There are 3 fuses used on the 900/1000. All are located in the fuse panel. On standard models, the fuse panel is under the side cover (**Figure 1**). Remove the electrical cover on 1979 and later bikes (**Figure 2**). On shaft drive models, the panel is under the seat (**Figure 3**) and on Z1R models it is found in both places.

The main fuse is 20A, and the headlight and taillight are 10A.

Inside the cover are spare fuses; always carry spares.

Whenever a fuse blows, find out the reason for the failure before replacing the fuse. Usually, the trouble is a short circuit in the wiring. This may be cause by worn-through insulation or a disconnected wire shorting to ground.

CAUTION
Never substitute tinfoil or wire for a fuse. Never use a higher amperage fuse than specified. An overload could result in fire and complete loss of the bike.

BATTERY

The bike is equipped with a 12 volt, 14 ampere-hour battery (16 amp-hr for shaft) with a specific gravity of 1.280 at 68° F when fully charged.

Battery electrolyte testing and battery charging may be required after long periods (more than a month) of inactivity or when electrical trouble arises.

The battery is the heart of the electrical system. The majority of electrical system troubles can be attributed to neglect of this vital component.

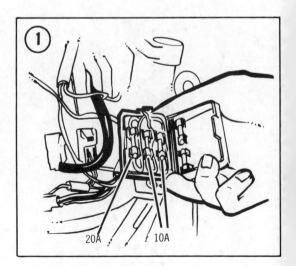

20A   10A

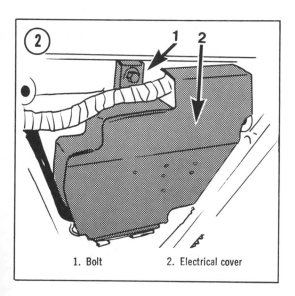

1. Bolt   2. Electrical cover

Batteries evaporate more water in warmer climates, but excessive use of water may be an indication that the battery is being overcharged. The 2 most common causes of overcharging are high battery temperature and high voltage regulator setting. It is advisable to check the voltage regulator if this situation exists.

> **WARNING**
> *Read and thoroughly understand the section of safety precautions before doing any battery service.*

Safety Precautions

While working with batteries, use care to avoid spilling or splashing the electrolyte. Electrolyte contains sulfuric acid, which can destroy clothing and cause serious chemical burns. If any electrolyte is spilled or splashed on clothing, body, or other surface, neutralize it *immediately* with a solution of baking soda and water, then flush with plenty of clean water.

> **WARNING**
> *Electrolyte splashed into the eyes is extremely dangerous. Safety glasses should always be worn while working with batteries. If electrolyte is splashed into the eye, call a physician immediately, force the eye open, and flood with cool, clean water for about 5 minutes.*

If electrolyte is splashed onto painted or unpainted surfaces, it should be neutralized immediately with baking soda solution and then rinsed with clean water.

When batteries are being charged, highly explosive hydrogen gas forms in each cell. Some of this gas escapes through the filler openings and may form an explosive atmosphere around the battery. *This explosive atmosphere may exist for several hours.* Sparks, flames, or a lighted cigarette can ignite the gas, causing an internal explosion and possible serious personal injury. The following precautions should be taken to prevent an explosion.

1. Do not smoke or permit any flame near any battery being charged or which has been recently charged.

2. Do not disconnect live circuits at battery terminals, because a spark usually occurs where a live circuit is broken. Care must always be taken when connecting or disconnecting any battery charger; be sure its power switch is off before making or breaking connections. Poor connections are a common cause of electrical arcs which cause explosions.

Specific Gravity Testing

Hydrometer testing is the best way to check battery condition. Use a hydrometer with numbered graduations from 1.100 to 1.300 rather

11

than one with color-coded bands (**Figure 4A**). To use the hydrometer, squeeze the rubber ball, insert the tip into the cell and release the ball.

Draw enough electrolyte to float the weighted float inside the hydrometer. Note the number in line with surface of the electrolyte; this is the specific gravity for this cell. Return the electrolyte to the cell from which it came.

The specific gravity of the electrolyte in each battery cell is an excellent indication of that cell's condition. A fully charged cell will read 1.260-1.280, while a cell in good condition reads from 1.230-1.250 and anything below 1.140 is discharged.

Specific gravity varies with temperature. For each 10° that electrolyte temperature exceeds 80° F, add 0.004 to the reading indicated on the hydrometer. Subtract 0.004 for each 10° below 80° F.

Repeat this measurement for each battery cell. If there is more than 0.050 difference (50 points) between cells, battery condition is questionable.

If the cells test in the poor range, the battery requires recharging. The hydrometer is useful for checking the progress of the charging operation. **Figure 4B** shows approximate state of charge.

It is most important to maintain batteries fully charged during cold weather. A fully charged battery freezes at a much lower temperature than does one which is partially discharged. Freezing temperature depends on specific gravity, as shown on **Table 1**.

Battery Removal

Disconnect the ground, or negative (–) cable first, then the positive (+) cable.

If the motorcycle is not to be used for an extended period, charge the battery fully, remove it from the machine, and store it in a cool, dry place. Recharge the battery every 2 months while it is in storage, and again before it is put back into service.

Be very careful when installing the battery to connect it properly. If the battery is installed backward, the rectifier and alternator will be damaged.

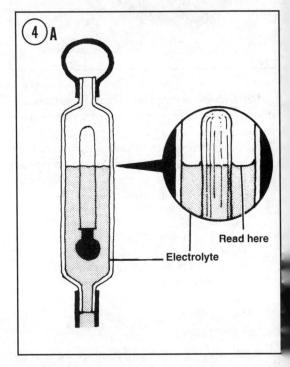

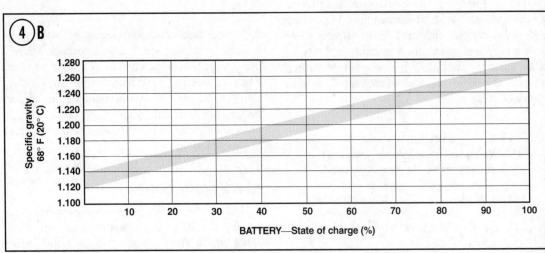

Battery Installation

1. When installing the battery, connect the positive terminal first, then the negative one. Don't overtighten the clamps.

2. Check to make sure the cable terminals won't rub against any metal parts (like the seat). Slide the rubber boot(s) over the terminals.

3. Connect the battery vent tube and make sure it isn't pinched anywhere. Keep the end away from the mufflers and drive chain. The corrosive gases could cause damage.

Battery Charging

WARNING
*Do not smoke or permit any open flame in any area where batteries are being charged, or immediately after charging. Highly explosive hydrogen gas is formed during the charging process. Be sure to reread **Safety Precautions** in the beginning of this section.*

CAUTION
Always remove the battery from the motorcycle before connecting charging equipment, or you may damage part of the bike's charging system.

Motorcycle batteries are not designed for high charge or discharge rates. It is recommended that a motorcycle battery be charged at a rate not exceeding 10 percent of its ampere-hour capacity. That is, do not exceed 0.5 ampere charging rate for a 5 ampere-hour battery or 1.5 amperes for a 15 ampere-hour battery. This charge rate should continue for 10 hours if the battery is completely discharged, or until specific gravity of each cell is up to 1.260–1.280, corrected for temperature.

Some temperature rise is normal as a battery is being charged. Do not allow the electrolyte temperature to exceed 110 degrees F. Should the temperature reach that figure, discontinue charging until the battery cools, then resume charging at a lower rate.

1. Connect the positive (+) charger lead to the positive battery terminal and the negative (−) charger lead to the negative battery terminal.

2. Remove all vent caps from the battery, set the charger at 12 volts, and switch it on. If the output of the charger is variable, it is best to select a low setting—1½ to 2 amps.

3. After the battery has been charged for about 8 hours, turn the charger off, disconnect the leads and check the specific gravity. It should be within the limits specified in **Figure 4B**. If it is, and remains stable for one hour, the battery is charged.

4. Clean the battery terminals, case, and tray and reinstall them in the bike, reversing the removal steps. Coat the terminals with Vaseline or silicone spray to retard decomposition of the terminals.

CHARGING SYSTEM

The charging system consists of the battery, alternator, voltage regulator, and rectifier. **Figure 5**

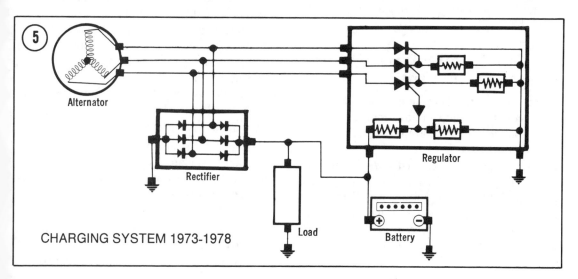

CHARGING SYSTEM 1973-1978

Alternator

Rectifier

Regulator

Load

Battery

11

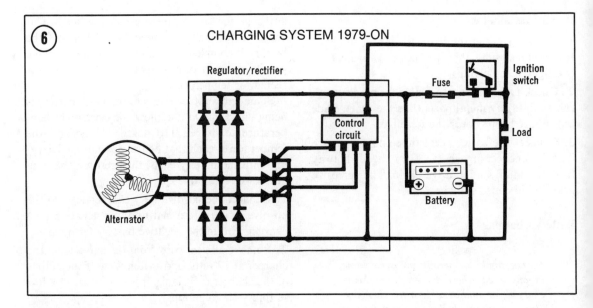

⑥ CHARGING SYSTEM 1979-ON

Regulator/rectifier

Control circuit

Fuse

Ignition switch

Load

Battery

Alternator

is for 1973–1978, as it uses a mechanical contact point type voltage regulator. **Figure 6** (1979 and later) shows the solid state type non-adjustable voltage regulator/rectifier.

The alternator generates an alternating current (AC) which the rectifier converts to direct current (DC). The regulator maintains the voltage to the battery and load (lights, ignition, etc.) at a constant voltage, regardless of variations in engine speed and load.

Whenever a charging system trouble is suspected, make sure the battery is good before going any further. Clean and test the battery (see *Specific Gravity Test*).

Prior to starting the test, start the bike and let it reach normal operating temperature; and then shut it off.

CHARGING SYSTEM TEST (1973–1978)

Voltage Regulator (1973–1978)

The voltage regulator limits the amount of charging current that can flow from the rectifier to the battery, so as to avoid overcharging the battery. See **Figure 7**.

If the battery is continually discharging or overcharging, the voltage regulator may have gone bad. If the battery is being overcharged, the electrolyte level will drop, necessitating frequent addition of water to the cells. Also, the lights will burn out frequently when the engine is running at high rpm.

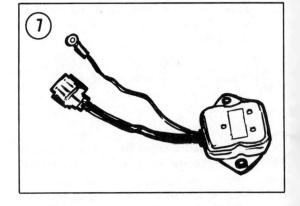

Check the voltage regulator as follows:

1. Check that the battery is fully charged and in good condition (12–15 volts).

2. Connect a voltmeter across the battery with the positive (+) lead on the positive (+) terminal and negative (-) lead on the negative (-) terminal (**Figure 8**).

3. Start the engine and turn off all the lights. Run the engine at 4,000 rpm.

4. Voltmeter should read 14–15 volts.

5. If the meter reads more than 15 volts, either the voltage regulator is bad, or it is hooked up with a loose connection or to a bad wire. Check those possibilities before replacing the regulator with a new one.

6. If the meter reads less than 14 volts, either the regulator or the rectifier or the alternator is bad. Shut off the engine and unplug the green voltage

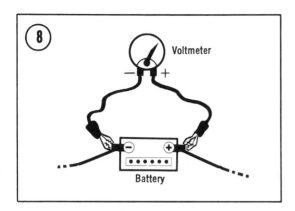

regulator plug from its socket behind the side cover.

7. Restart the engine and run it at 4,000 rpm.

8. Check the voltmeter. If the meter reads 14–20 volts, the alternator and the rectifier are good, and the voltage regulator is defective. If the meter reads less than 14 volts, the voltage regulator is probably good, and either the rectifier or the alternator is defective.

Rectifier Resistances (1973–1978)

1. With the engine turned off, unplug the white rectifier plug from its socket behind the side cover, and unplug the white wire going to the battery.

2. Set up the ohmmeter to read RX1 or RX10.

3. Make a series of resistance measurements between the rectifier wires, as described below. Take a measurement across 2 wires, and then take the same measurement with the ohmmeter test leads reversed. In one of the 2 readings, the resistance should be very low. In the other reading, the resistance should be at least 10 times greater.

4. Check the resistance between the white wire and each of the 2 yellow wires, and the black wire and each of the 2 yellow wires. This gives 6 combinations of wires to measure, and a total of 12 measurements.

5. In taking the 2 readings across a pair of wires, if you find that the resistance is either low or high in both directions, replace the rectifier with a new one.

Alternator Stator Resistance (1973–1978)

If no charging current is going to the battery, check the alternator coils as follows:

1. Behind the side cover, unplug the blue plug from its socket.

2. Set up the ohmmeter to read RX1.

3. Read the resistance between each 2 of the 3 alternator wires going into the plug: between the blue wire and the pink wire; between the blue wire and the yellow wire; and between the pink wire and the yellow wire.

4. In each measurement, the meter should read 0.45-0.70 ohms. If it reads much less, the coils are short-circuited and the stator must be replaced. If the resistance is much higher, the coils have an open circuit and the stator must be replaced.

5. Set up the ohmmeter for its highest resistance readings.

6. Ground one of the meter leads to the engine case. With the other lead, take resistance readings across each of the 3 alternator wires you just finished checking.

7. In each case, the meter should read infinity. If there is any other reading, the stator is short-circuited and must be replaced.

Alternator Output (1973–1978)

If the battery is receiving an insufficient amount of charging current, check the alternator as follows:

1. Check the rectifier to verify that it is working properly.

2. Check the battery to verify that it is in good condition; if necessary, charge it to 12 volts.

3. Take off the right side cover and remove the green regulator plug from its socket.

4. Set up the voltmeter to read 30 VDC.

5. Start the engine, turn off the lights, and run the engine at 4,000 rpm.

6. Connect the voltmeter across the battery with the (+) lead to the (+) terminal and the (−) lead to the (−) terminal.

7. Read the meter. If the voltage is less than 15, the alternator is defective.

8. To determine whether the stator or the rotor is at fault, make the ohmmeter measurements listed above. If the voltage is down, but the resistance readings are within tolerance, the problem is probably weakened magnets in the rotor.

CHARGING SYSTEM TEST
(1979 AND LATER)

See **Figure 6**.

Whenever charging system trouble is suspected, make sure the battery is good before going any further. Check the specific gravity (see *Specific Gravity Testing*). Battery voltage should be above 12 volts. If not, charge the battery.

Initial Inspection (1979 and Later)

1. Start the engine and let it reach normal operating temperature.

2. Connect a 0–15 DC voltmeter to the battery as shown in **Figure 8**.

3. Bring the engine speed from idle to 4,000 rpm, observing the voltage as you go.

4. The voltage should be at or near battery voltage at idle, and it should increase with engine speed, up to about 14.5 volts. If the reading is higher (more than about 16 volts), the regulator/rectifier is defective and should be replaced. If the reading is less than specified, or does not increase with rpm's, check the alternator output and resistance and regulator/rectifier resistance.

Alternator Output (1979 and Later)

1. *Shaft drive:* Remove the left side cover and disconnect the 6-pin connector from the alternator (**Figure 9**).

2. *Chain drive:* Remove the sprocket cover and disconnect the 3 yellow leads from the alternator.

3. Start the engine and connect a voltmeter (set on 250 volt AC scale) to every pair of yellow leads (pins) in turn. The voltage should read about 50 volts AC. If it is much lower, the alternator is defective. Check stator coil resistance.

Alternator Stator Resistance (1979 and Later)

1. With the engine OFF and an ohmmeter set on the 1 ohm scale, check resistance between each pair of yellow leads as described in *Alternator Output*.

2. Resistance should be about 0.5–0.7 ohms.

3. Set the ohmmeter on the highest scale and check resistance between each yellow lead and ground. Resistance should be infinite (∞).

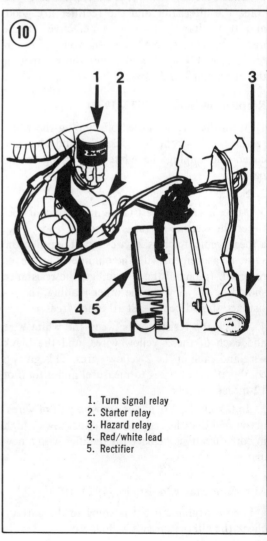

1. Turn signal relay
2. Starter relay
3. Hazard relay
4. Red/white lead
5. Rectifier

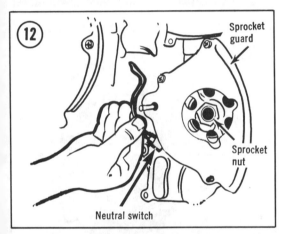

Sprocket
guard

Sprocket
nut

Neutral switch

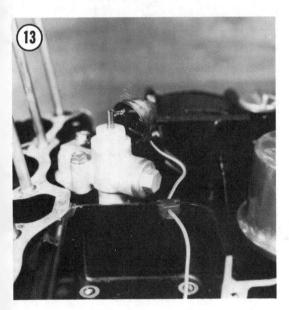

4. If the stator coil resistance is OK, but alternator output is low, the rotor has probably been demagnetized. Replace the rotor.

Regulator/Rectifier Resistance (1979 and Later)

1. Remove the side cover and open the electrical panel (**Figure 10**).

2. Disconnect the 6-pin connector and the regulator red/white lead (**Figure 11**).

CAUTION
The red/white lead is "hot." Do not short circuit the voltage regulator when connecting the test leads.

4. Use an ohmmeter, set at RX10 or RX100, and measure the resistance between each yellow lead and the red/white lead, and between each yellow lead and the black lead. Keep the same meter lead on the red/white and the black leads, in turn. Note the readings.

5. Reverse the meter polarity (use the opposite probes to make the connections) and repeat the tests.

6. There should be more than 10 times as much resistance in one direction as in the other. If any 2 leads show the same resistance in both directions, the regulator/rectifier is faulty.

ALTERNATOR REMOVAL

The alternator rotor is mounted to the left end of the crankshaft. The stator is mounted inside the left engine cover.

Removal/Installation (1973–1978)

1. Pull off the side cover. Behind it, on the bottom row of electrical components, unplug the blue alternator connector.

2. Remove the chain cover (see *Sprocket Cover Removal* in Chapter Six).

3. Below the lower left side of the sprocket guard, disconnect the wire to the neutral switch (**Figure 12**).

4. Atop the engine cases to the rear of the cylinder block, pull the rubber cap off the oil pressure switch. Disconnect the wire to the switch (**Figure 13**).

11

5. Remove the 8 Phillips screws from the alternator cover. Lightly tap the cover with a soft mallet to loosen it (**Figure 14**).

> NOTE: *The alternator stator is mounted to the inside of the cover with Allen screws (**Figure 15**).*

6. Remove the bolt holding the rotor to the shaft (**Figure 16**).

> NOTE: *To lock the engine without a special tool, shift the transmission into 5th gear, and have a friend step on the brake pedal.*

7. Remove the starter idler gear and shaft (**Figure 17**).

8. Fabricate a rotor removing tool by using a large ball bearing and one of the top fork cap bolts. Slip the bearing in first, then thread in the cap bolt (see **Figure 18**).

9. Tighten the bolt against the ball bearing (which is riding against the crankshaft).

10. After tightening the bolt down it might be necessary to tap the bolt with a hammer to jar the rotor loose (see **Figure 19**). Remove the rotor. Be sure to put the fork cap bolt back where it belongs.

11. Remove the Woodruff key that held the armature in place (**Figure 20**).

12. Remove the shim and starter clutch gear (**Figure 21**).

13. Remove the collar and needle bearing. Do not forget the thrust washer (still shown on the end of the shaft in **Figure 22**). The chamfered edge goes toward the engine.

14. To install, reverse the preceding.

> NOTE: *Apply Loctite to the rotor mounting bolt before screwing it into the crankshaft. Torque to 18 ft.-lb.*

> NOTE: *Inspect the starter clutch gear needle bearing. If it is damaged or if a new rotor, clutch gear, thrust washer, or crankshaft is being installed, check crankshaft bearing/clutch gear clearance (see **Damper Selection**).*

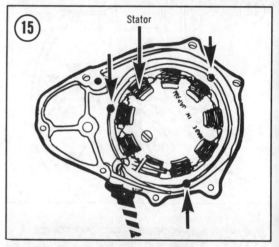

Stator

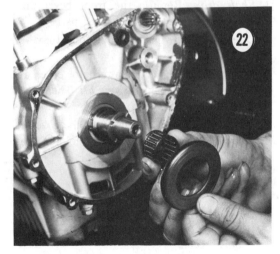

Damper Selection

The starter clutch gear damper is available in 3 different thicknesses, designated by the star mark molded into the damper (**Figure 23**). Select the proper damper to provide proper clutch gear/crank bearing clearance (**Figure 24**).

> CAUTION
> *If the damper is too thin, the starter clutch gear will wobble and damage the gear's needle bearing. Too thick a damper will accelerate shim and thrust washer wear.*

1. Put a ball of clay on the crankshaft bearing outer race (thrust washer removed).

2. Install the starter clutch gear and thrust washer, and push the alternator rotor onto the crankshaft by hand.

3. Remove the starter clutch gear and measure the thickness of the clay (**Figure 25**). Select the proper rubber damper according to specifications in **Table 2**.

4. After installing the alternator rotor, turn the starter clutch gear to the right (clockwise) with the starter idler gear removed. The gear should not be hard to turn, but there should be a slight drag.

Alternator Removal/Installation (1979 and Later)

1. *Chain drive:* Remove the engine sprocket cover (see *Sprocket Cover Removal,* Chapter Six).

2. *Shaft drive:* Remove the front bevel drive cover (see *Front Bevel Removal,* Steps 1–6).

3. Disconnect the 3 yellow leads from the alternator (**Figure 26**).

4. Put an oil pan under the alternator cover, and remove the 8 cover bolts (**Figure 27**). There are 2 locating dowel pins.

5. To remove the stator coils from the cover, remove the 3 coil bolts and the 2 holding plate screws (**Figure 28**).

6. Remove the rotor bolt (**Figure 29**).

> NOTE: *To lock the engine without a special tool, shift the transmission into 5th gear and have a friend step on the brake pedal.*

7. Screw in a flywheel puller (**Figure 30**) until it stops. Use a wrench on the puller and tap on the end of it with a hammer until the rotor disengages (**Figure 31**). Remove the puller and the rotor with the starter clutch assembly.

> CAUTION
> *Do not hit the rotor with a hammer. You could destroy its magnetism.*

8. Remove the thin washer (B) and starter clutch gear (A, **Figure 32**).

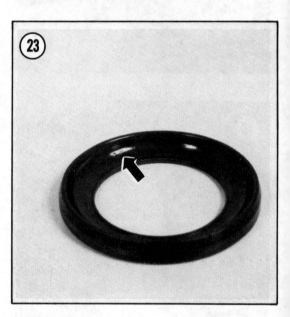

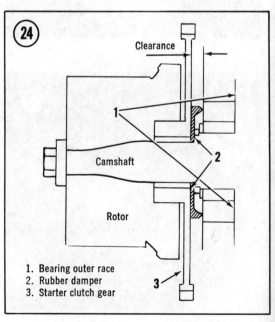

1. Bearing outer race
2. Rubber damper
3. Starter clutch gear

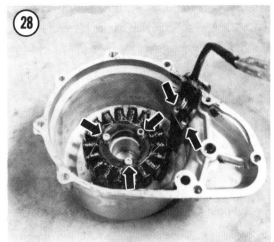

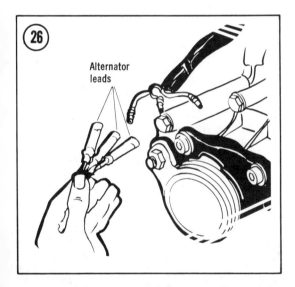

Alternator
leads

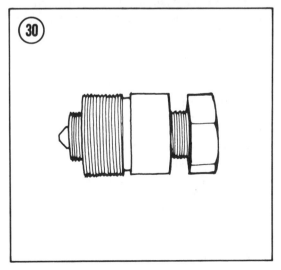

11

9. Remove the rubber damper (**Figure 33**), if it did not come out with the starter clutch gear.

10. Remove the needle bearing (B) and thick thrust washer (A, **Figure 34**).

11. Remove the starter idler shaft (A) and gear (B, **Figure 35**).

12. To install the alternator, reverse the removal procedure. Note the following:

   a. Inspect the starter clutch gear needle bearing. If it is damaged, *or* if a new rotor, clutch gear, thrust washer, or crankshaft is being installed, check crankshaft bearing/clutch gear clearance (see *Damper Selection*).

   b. Install the chamfered face of the thrust washer toward the engine.

   c. Apply molybdenum disulfide grease to the starter idler shaft, and to the starter clutch gear needle bearing and damper.

   d. Use a solvent to clean any oil from the tapered crankshaft end.

   e. Clean off any metal bits that may cling to the rotor magnets.

   f. Rotor bolt torque is 95 ft.-lb.

   g. Use Loctite on the stator coil bolts and the cover bolt that goes through the upper dowel pin.

   h. Check the engine oil and top it up if necessary.

IGNITION SYSTEM

Operation (Breaker Point Ignition)

Figure 36 is a diagram of the ignition circuit used on all models with contact breaker point ignition.

The ignition system is equipped with 2 coils and 2 sets of points, each of which fires 2 spark plugs wired in series, simultaneously. One of the spark plugs in the pair is fired on the compression stroke; the other is fired (harmlessly) on the exhaust stroke.

Ignition takes place every 180 degrees of crankshaft rotation; each set of points opens every 360 degrees of crankshaft rotation. The firing order is 1–2–4–3. The left set of points fires cylinders 1 and 4; the right set of points fires cylinders 2 and 3.

Because the ignition coil fires through 2 spark plugs wired in series, if one of the plugs fails to

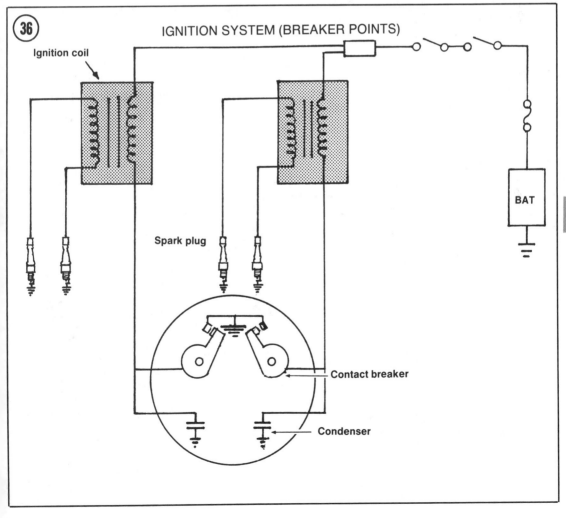

IGNITION SYSTEM (BREAKER POINTS)

Ignition coil

Spark plug

BAT

Contact breaker

Condenser

11

fire, so will the other. If one plug develops a weak spark, so will the other.

When the breaker points are closed, current flows from the battery through the primary winding of the ignition coil, thereby building a magnetic field around the coil. The breaker cam rotates and is so adjusted that the breaker points open as the piston reaches the firing position (F-mark on the advancer rotor).

As the points open, the magnetic field collapses. When this occurs, a very high voltage is induced (up to approximately 15,000 volts) in the secondary winding of the ignition coil. This high voltage is sufficient to jump the gap at the spark plug causing the plug to fire.

The condenser assists the coil in developing high voltage, and also serves to protect the points. Inductance of the ignition coil primary winding tends to keep a surge of current flowing through the circuit even after the points have started to open. The condenser stores this surge and thus prevents arcing at the points.

Operation (Transistorized Ignition)

Figure 37 is a diagram of the ignition circuit used on all models with transistorized ignition.

The Kawasaki transistorized ignition system is similar to the conventional point/coil system used in 1973–1978 models. It works much the same, with these differences:

a. Mechanical contact points are replaced by magnetic triggering pickup coils.

b. An intermediate electronic switch, the battery-powered IC igniter, receives the weak signals from the pick-up coils and uses them to turn the ignition coil primary current ON and OFF.

c. The ignition coil has a special low resistance primary winding that helps it produce a powerful spark at high rpm.

d. An ignition coil primary resistor is added to limit current and keep the coil from burning out at low rpm.

e. The transistorized ignition system's dwell angle *increases* slightly as rpm's increase. This is a characteristic of the magnetic pickup coils.

f. Ignition timing is *not* adjustable.

The ignition coil primary current is normally OFF until the ignition timing rotor approaches the pickup coil.

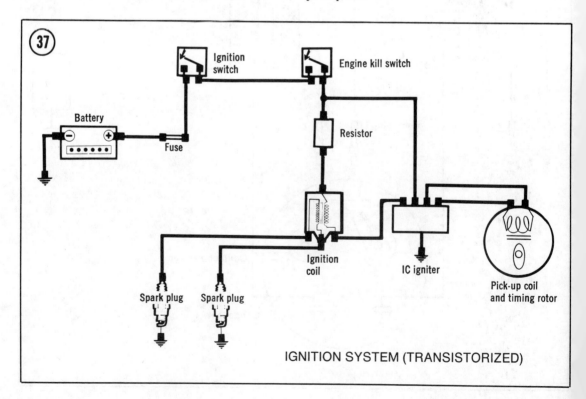

IGNITION SYSTEM (TRANSISTORIZED)

The pickup coil signal builds to a level that turns the IC igniter ON, allowing primary current to flow through the ignition coil. As the timing rotor passes the pickup coil, the trigger signal reverses polarity and turns the IC igniter OFF. The sudden stoppage of current through the ignition coil primary winding then produces a spark, as in a conventional point/coil system.

The elimination of contact breaker points means that periodic adjustment of point gap and ignition timing are no longer required. Once set properly, initial timing should not require adjustment for the life of the motorcycle.

SPARK PLUGS

See *Engine Tune-Up and Troubleshooting* (Chapter One) for regular inspection and adjustment of spark plugs.

On 1977 and later models, a resistor-type spark plug cap is used to reduce radio interference (**Figure 38**). If you have a high speed misfire, check the resistance between the plug terminal and the plug wire spike. Normal is 10,000 (ohms). If resistance is more than 20,000 (ohms), the cap is faulty and should be replaced.

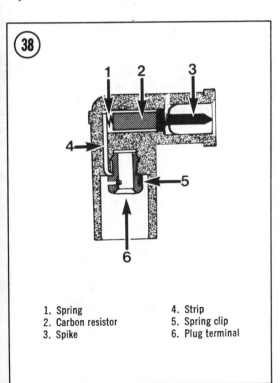

1. Spring
2. Carbon resistor
3. Spike
4. Strip
5. Spring clip
6. Plug terminal

Troubleshooting Spark Plugs

If you suspect that 2 of the spark plugs are failing to fire, or are delivering weak sparks, check them as follows:

1. Remove the spark plugs from the engine and compare them to the spark plug chart in Chapter One.

2. If visual inspection shows that one or both of the spark plugs are defective, discard them and install new ones.

3. Check both spark plugs (whether new or used) by putting on their spark plug wires and taping them to the cylinder head fins, so that metal touches metal.

4. Wheel the motorcycle over to a dark corner. Turn on the ignition, operate the starter, and observe the sparks. If the plugs throw sparks that are intermittent, feeble, or orange-yellow in color, and that do not make snapping sounds when they jump, the sparks are weak.

5. If one or both of the spark plugs throwing weak sparks are old, fit new plugs to the spark plug wires and observe the sparks again. Watch also for arcing inside the spark plug cap.

6. If the used spark plugs fail to fire or generate weak sparks, and if the new spark plugs throw strong sparks (bluish in color, accompanied by a snapping sound), then one or both of the old spark plugs are defective.

IGNITION ADVANCE

The ignition advance mechanism advances to the ignition (fires the spark plugs sooner) as engine speed increases. If it does not advance smoothly, the ignition will be incorrect at high engine rpm. It must be lubricated periodically to make certain it operates freely.

The ignition advance mechanism is bolted to the right end of the crankshaft, inside the right engine cover.

Advancer Removal/Installation

1. Remove the 2 ignition cover screws and the cover and gasket (**Figure 39**).

2. Remove the 3 point plate/pickup coil plate screws and the plate (**Figures 40 and 41**).

11

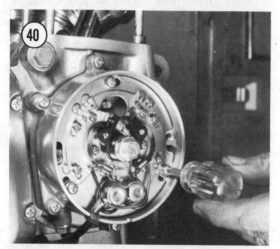

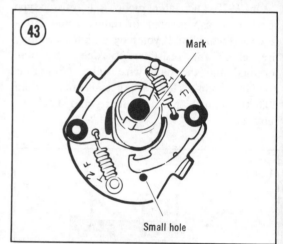

Mark

Small hole

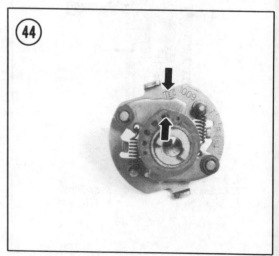

3. Hold the larger nut, and remove the advancer mounting bolt and the advancer (**Figure 42**).

4. Remove the cam from the advancer body. Grease groove around the body, the weight pivots, and the arms that fit into the advancer.

5. Install by reversing these removal steps. Note the following:

  a. Check for free movement and full return by the advancer springs.

  b. When assembling the advancer unit itself, align the cam mark and hole on advancer (**Figure 43**), on contact point models; and the rotor peak and TEC mark (**Figure 44**) on transistorized models.

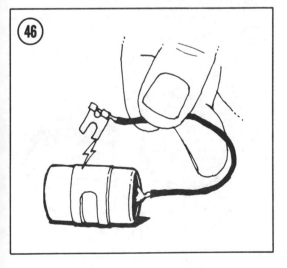

  c. When installing the advancer assembly, align the notch in the back of the advancer with the pin in the crank (**Figure 45**).

  d. Advancer bolt torque is 18 ft.-lb. (2.5 mkg).

  e. *Contact point models:* Adjust ignition timing (see *Ignition Timing* in Chapter Three).

CONDENSER (CONTACT POINT MODELS)

The condenser normally requires no service. If the condenser has deteriorated internally, it will no longer store current temporarily. It will allow a spark to jump across the points after they have opened, causing the electromagnetic field in the ignition coil to collapse more slowly. This will lower the voltage generated in the secondary windings of the coil, and weaken the ignition sparks.

Troubleshooting

If the condenser has gone bad, the points will be pitted or dirty because they have been sparking, in which case replace the condensers. Also, replace both condensers whenever you replace a set of points.

The condenser specifications are: 0.25 ± 0.03 microfarads. In the event that no test equipment is available, a quick test of the condenser may be made by connecting the condenser case to the negative terminal of a 12-volt battery, and the positive lead to the positive battery terminal. Allow the condenser to charge for a few seconds, then quickly disconnect the battery and touch the condenser pigtail to the condenser case (**Figure 46**). If you observe a spark as the pigtail touches the case, you may assume that the condenser is good.

IGNITION COIL

An ignition coil can fail in any of 3 ways. It can develop an open circuit (broken wire) in the primary windings or the secondary windings, in which case the coil won't function at all, or it can develop a partial short circuit, arcing to bridge some of the secondary windings. If that happens, the coil will generate weak sparks at the electrodes of the spark plugs.

11

Removal/Installation

1. Disconnect the battery ground lead.

2. Remove the fuel tank (see *Fuel Tank Removal,* Chapter Seven).

3. Disconnect the leads to the coil.

4. Detach the coil and remove it.

5. Install by reversing these removal steps. Make sure to connect the primary electrical wires to the correct coils (resistor on the 1979 and later chain drive) and the spark plug leads to the correct spark plug.

Testing

1. If coil condition is doubtful, there are several checks which may be made. Disconnect the coil wires before testing. Measure coil primary resistance, using an ohmmeter set at RX1. The resistance should be *about* 4.0 ohms on contact point models and *about* 1.5 ohms on transistorized models.

2. Measure coil secondary resistance (remove resistor-type plug caps from the wires and measure between the wires). The resistance should be *about* 13,500 ohms.

3. Measure the resistance between the coil primary lead and ground (coil core) and between the coil secondary lead and ground (coil core). The resistance should be ∞ (infinte). A low reading indicates a short circuit.

4. If the coil resistance values do not meet these specifications, the coil(s) must be replaced. If the coil exhibits visible damage, it should be replaced.

5. If a coil is generating weak sparks, substitute the other coil in the circuit and check the sparks again. If the other coil generates stronger sparks at the electrodes of the spark plugs, there is a short circuit in the secondary windings of the original coil; replace it with a new one.

Ignition Coil Resistor (Transistorized Models)

The ignition coil resistor is mounted in front of the coil on chain drive models and under the left side cover (**Figure 47**) on shaft drive models; disconnect the resistor leads and measure the resistance with an ohmmeter set at RX1. It should be 1.7 ohms.

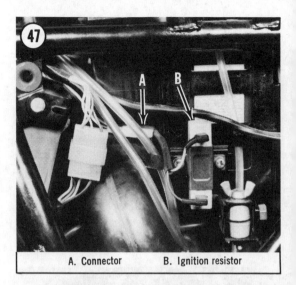

A. Connector   B. Ignition resistor

SHAFT DRIVE

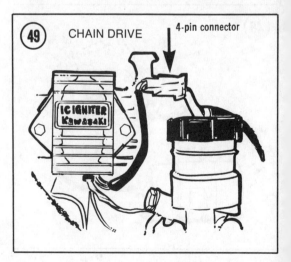

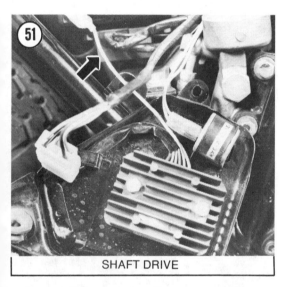

SHAFT DRIVE

PICK-UP COILS
(TRANSISTORIZED MODELS)

Testing

1. Remove the side cover and disconnect the 4-pole pick-up coil connector (**Figure 48** and **Figure 49**).

2. With an ohmmeter set at RX100, measure the resistance between the 2 pairs of leads: black and blue (No. 1, 4) and yellow and red (No. 2, 3). The resistance should be 400-500 ohms.

3. Set the ohmmeter at its highest scale and check the resistance between either lead for each pair of cylinders and chassis ground. The reading should be ∞ (infinite).

4. If the pickup coils fail either of these tests, check the wiring to the coils, and replace the coil(s) if the wiring is OK (**Figure 50**).

IC IGNITER (TRANSISTORIZED MODELS)

The operation of the IC igniter (**Figures 49 and 51**) can be checked simply by removing one of each pair of spark plugs, grounding it against the cylinder head while the plug lead is connected, turning the ignition ON, and touching a screwdriver or a magnet to the pickup coil core (**Figure 52**). If the IC igniter is good, the plug will spark.

Remember that the IC igniter is battery powered and will not function if the battery is dead. The following IC igniter test can be made on the motorcycle.

1. Remove one of each pair of spark plugs and ground it against the cylinder head while its plug wire is connected.

2. Disconnect the 4-pole connector from the pickup coils (**Figure 53**).

11

3. Turn the ignition ON, and connect positive (+) 12 volts to the black lead, and negative (-) to the blue lead. As the voltage is connected, the plug should spark.

4. Repeat the test for the other pair of plugs, positive (+) to the yellow lead from the IC igniter and negative (−) to the red lead.

5. If the IC igniter fails these tests, install a new one. If the IC igniter passes these tests but you still have an ignition problem that can't be traced to any other part of the ignition system, substitute an IC igniter that you know is good, and see if that solves the problem. Some transistorized ignition troubles just don't show up on your workbench.

STARTING SYSTEM

The starting system consists of the starter motor, starter solenoid, and the starter button.

The layout of the starting system is shown in **Figure 54**. When the starter button is pressed, it engages the solenoid switch that closes the circuit. The electricity flows from the battery to the starter motor.

The starter motor is a 12-volt DC motor geared to the left side of the crankshaft through idler gears behind the alternator rotor. The starter motor is connected mechanically to the crankshaft, and can rotate it, when the engine is not running. The starter clutch (between the rotor and the idler gear) uncouples the idler gear from the crankshaft when the engine is running.

Table 3 lists possible starter problems, probable causes and the most common remedies.

Starter Removal/Installation

1. Place the bike on the centerstand.

2. Disconnect the battery ground (−) lead.

3. Remove the fuel tank (see *Fuel Tank Removal,* Chapter Seven).

4. Remove the carburetor assembly (see *Carburetor Removal,* Chapter Seven).

5. Remove the 2 starter cover bolts and the cover **(Figure 55)**.

6. Remove the 2 long starter motor mounting bolts and lockwashers **(Figure 56)**.

7. Pry the starter to the right, away from the alternator housing, and disconnect the starter cable at the motor **(Figure 57)**.

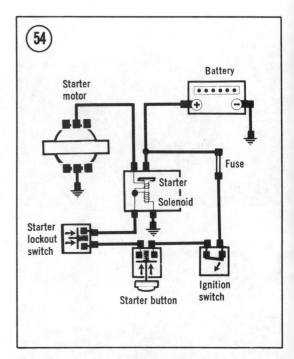

8. To install the starter, reverse the removal steps. Note the following:

a. Make sure the starter case terminal and mounting bosses are clean.

b. Oil the O-ring on the left end cap of the motor assembly.

c. Apply Loctite to the 2 long starter motor mounting bolts.

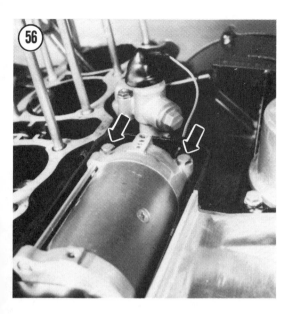

Starter Disassembly/Assembly

The overhaul of a starter motor is best left to an expert. This section shows how to determine if the unit is defective.

Refer to **Figure 58**.

1. Remove the starter motor case screws and separate the case.

NOTE: *Write down how many thrust washers are used and install the same number when reassembling the starter.*

2. Clean all grease, dirt, and carbon dust from the armature, case, and end covers.

CAUTION
Do not immerse brushes or the wire windings in solvent or the insulation might be damaged. Wipe the windings with a cloth lightly moistened with solvent and dry thoroughly.

3. Remove the brushes and use a vernier caliper (**Figure 59**) to measure the length of the brush. If it is worn shorter than ¼ in. (6 mm), it should be replaced.

4. Inspect the condition of the commutator (**Figure 60**). The mica in the normal commutator is cut below the copper. A worn commutator is also shown; the copper is worn to the level of the mica. A worn commutator can be undercut, but it requires a specialist. Take the job to your Kawasaki dealer or motorcycle repair shop.

5. Inspect the commutator bars for discoloration. If a pair of bars are discolored, that indicates grounded armature coils.

6. Check the electrical continuity between pairs of armature bars and between the commutator bars and the shaft. If there is a short, armature should be replaced.

7. Inspect the field coil by checking continuity from the cable terminal to the motor case. Also check from the cable terminal to the brush wire. If there is a short or open, the case should be replaced.

8. Assemble the case; make sure that the punch marks on the case and covers align (**Figure 61**).

9. Inspect the front and rear cover bearings for damage. Replace the starter if they are worn or damaged.

STARTER CLUTCH

The starter clutch is mounted on the left end of the crankshaft, behind the alternator rotor. The starter motor is meshed with an idle gear, which in turn is meshed with the starter clutch on the crankshaft. The starter clutch gear spins freely (on a needle bearing) on the crankshaft.

The starter clutch locks the starter clutch gear to the rotor when the starter motor is turning the engine (**Figure 62**). In this case, the clutch rollers

11

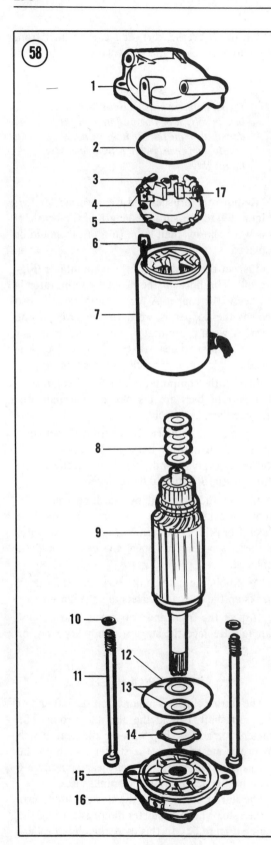

(58)

1
2
3
4 — 17
5
6
7
8
9
10
12
11
13
14
15
16

**STARTER
MOTOR**

1. End cover
2. O-ring
3. Brush lead
4. Screw
5. Brush plate
6. Field coil lead
7. Yoke assembly
8. Shim
9. Armature
10. Lockwasher
11. Screw
12. O-ring
13. Shim
14. Toothed washer
15. Grease seal
16. End cover
17. Brush

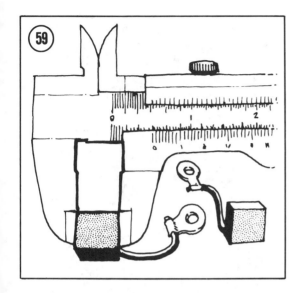

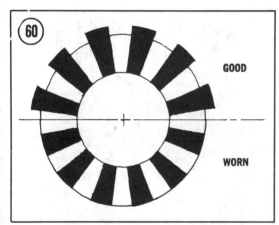

GOOD

WORN

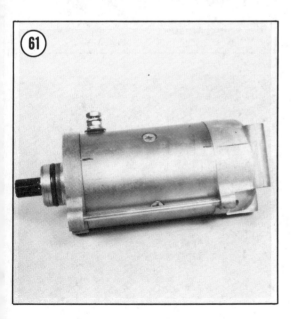

are pushed out by the springs and jammed between the crankshaft and clutch. After the engine starts, the stationary clutch gear hub rolls the rollers back against their springs and frees the crank from the clutch (**Figure 62**).

Starter Clutch Inspection

To check the operation of the starter motor clutch, remove the left engine cover and the idle gear. Try turning the starter clutch gear in both directions by hand. The gear should not turn at all to the left (counterclockwise). It should turn freely and quietly to the right (clockwise). If the gear fails to operate in that manner, the clutch assembly is malfunctioning.

Starter Clutch Disassembly/Assembly

1. Remove the alternator rotor (see *Alternator Removal*).

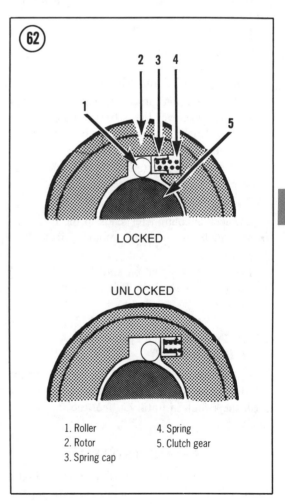

LOCKED

UNLOCKED

1. Roller   4. Spring
2. Rotor   5. Clutch gear
3. Spring cap

11

2. Remove the 3 rollers, spring caps, and springs from the clutch (**Figure 63**).

3. Wrap the rotor with cloth and mount it in a lead jaw vise. Remove the 3 Allen screws that mount the clutch body to the rotor.

4. To assemble, reverse the *Disassembly* steps. Use Loctite on the 3 starter clutch Allen bolts.

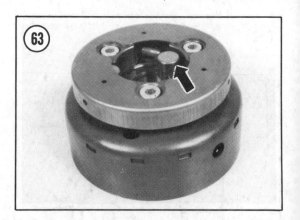

STARTER SOLENOID

Test

1. Remove the side cover (and electrical panel, if required). See **Figure 64**. On *shaft drive* models the solenoid is under the seat (**Figure 65**).

2. Turn on the ignition, check that the kill switch is ON (and pull in the clutch lever if your model has a starter lockout), and operate the starter pushbutton. Listen for the clicking noise that tells you the solenoid is working.

3. If the solenoid does not click, set up a voltmeter to read 30 VDC.

4. Remove the starter button yellow/black and black wires from the solenoid. Connect the (+) lead from the meter to the black wire, and connect the (−) lead to the yellow/black wire.

5. With the ignition turned on, read the meter. It should read whatever the battery voltage is. If it does, the solenoid is no good. If it does not, there is an open somewhere in the circuit.

6. Push the starter button. If the solenoid clicks, remove the starter motor wires from the solenoid.

7. Set up an ohmmeter to read RX1.

8. Connect the ohmmeter leads to the terminals from which the starter motor wires were removed.

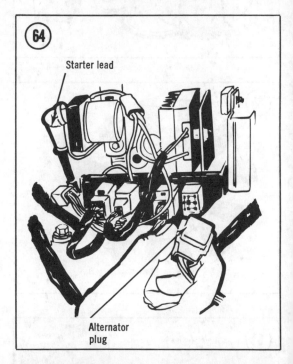

Starter lead

Alternator plug

9. Push the starter button and check the meter. It should read zero ohms. If it does not, the solenoid is bad.

Starter Lockout Switch Replacement (Shaft Drive and Z1R)

Push up on the bottom of the switch locking tab (**Figure 66**) and pull out the switch. To install, push the switch in until you feel the tab lock in place.

LIGHTING SYSTEM

The lighting system consists of the headlight, taillight/brakelight combination, directional sig-

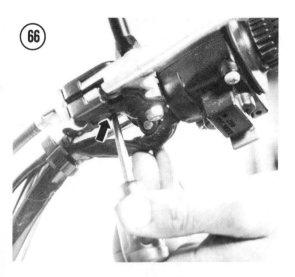

nals, warning lights and speedometer and ta-chometer illumination lights. **Table 4** lists replacement bulbs for these components.

If a light stops burning, check first for a burned-out or broken bulb. If bulbs burn out frequently, check for a low level of electrolyte in the battery, or for a defective voltage regulator overcharging the battery.

If the problem is not in the bulb, check the wiring from the socket back to the battery. Measure voltages with the ignition turned on, or resistances with the ignition switch turned on and the fuse removed from its holder.

Headlight Replacement

1. Remove the 2 mounting screws (**Figure 67**) on each side of the headlight housing.

2. Pull the trim bezel and headlight unit out and disconnect the electrical connector from the backside (**Figure 68**).

3. *Quartz-Halogen headlight models:* Remove the dust cover from the back of the light housing, open the spring clip, and remove the lighting element. Install a new 55/60 watt element.

> CAUTION
> *Don't handle the quartz bulb with your bare fingers. They'll leave oil on the bulb and will cause it to burn out early.*

4. Remove the 2 top and bottom pivot screws and the horizontal adjusting screw (**Figure 69**). Take off the outer rim.

11

5. Remove the 2 screws from the inner rim (**Figure 70**) and remove the sealed beam unit.

6. Install by reversing these removal steps. Be sure to install the sealed beam unit with the TOP mark facing up.

7. Adjust the headlight as described under *Headlight Adjustment,* following.

Headlight Adjustment

Adjust the headlight horizontally and vertically according to Department of Motor Vehicle regulations in your area.

To adjust headlight horizontally, turn the screw (**Figure 71**). For vertical adjustment, loosen the bottom positioning bolt (**Figure 71**) and tilt the headlight as required. Tighten the positioning bolt.

> *NOTE*
> *The Z1R has a lockbolt to the rear of, and above the pivot bolt.*

> NOTE: *If the headlight is too tight to move, remove the headlamp assembly and loosen the headlight mounting nuts (Figure 72).*

Front Brakelight Switch
Hydraulic Switch Replacement

Remove the electrical wires from the switch (**Figure 73**). Unscrew the switch from the brake line coupling.

> CAUTION
> *If any brake fluid spills out of the coupling when the switch is removed, wipe it up. Wash any brake fluid off of painted or plastic surfaces immediately, as it will destroy the finish.*

Apply a small amount of Loctite Lock 'N' Seal to the threads of the switch prior to installation. To avoid getting any of it in the brake fluid, do not apply any to the lower ¼ of the threads. Tighten the switch to 20 ft.-lb. (2.8 mkg). Attach the electrical leads and bleed the front brake as described under *Bleeding the System* in Chapter Eight.

Lever Switch Replacement

Push up on the bottom of the switch locking tab (**Figure 74**). Remove the headlight unit and disconnect the wires inside the headlight shell.

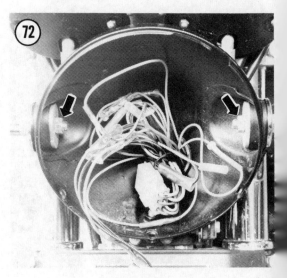

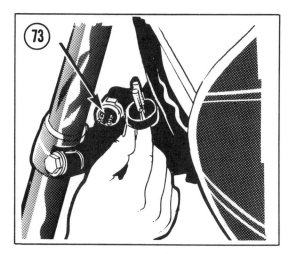

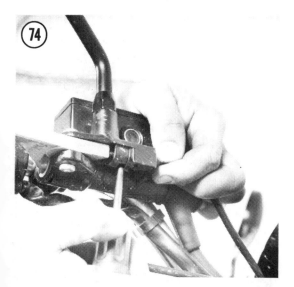

Turn Signal Flasher (900cc)

The turn signal flasher is under the right side cover.

Turn Signal Flasher (1000cc Chain Drive)

The turn signal flasher is under the left side cover.

Turn Signal Flasher (1000cc Shaft Drive)

The turn signal flasher is under the right side cover (**Figure 75**).

Hazard Flasher (1000cc only)

On *chain drive* models the hazard flasher is under the right side cover. On *shaft drive* models the hazard flasher is under the seat (**Figure 76**).

FUEL GAUGE

The fuel gauge has a built-in 7-volt voltage regulator, with an electrical sending unit inside the fuel tank.

Gauge Inspection

1. Remove the fuel tank and disconnect the 2-pole sending unit coupler.

2. Turn the ignition switch ON. The gauge should read E.

3. Short the black/yellow and white/yellow leads from the gauge. The gauge should read F.

11

4. If these readings are correct, but the gauge indicates erroneous fuel level, the sending unit is probably bad.

Sending Unit Inspection

1. Remove the fuel tank (see *Fuel Tank Removal,* Chapter Seven).

2. Drain all fuel into a safe container.

3. Remove the 6 sending unit mounting bolts and the sending unit.

4. Check that the float arm moves up and down smoothly throughout its range.

5. Measure the resistance of the sending unit with an ohmmeter. At the full position, resistance should be 1–5 (ohms). At the empty position, resistance should be 103–117 (ohms). If resistance does not vary smoothly as the arm is moved, the sending unit is faulty.

HORN

As the horn wears, it may be adjusted with the locknut and adjusting screw on the back of the horn (**Figure 77**).

Z1R CIRCUITS

The Z1R has extra circuits for its automatic turn signal cancelling system (**Figure 78**), and its reserve lighting system (**Figure 79**). Also, refer to the color wiring diagram at the back of this book.

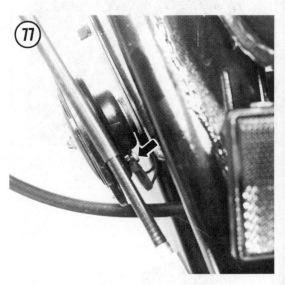

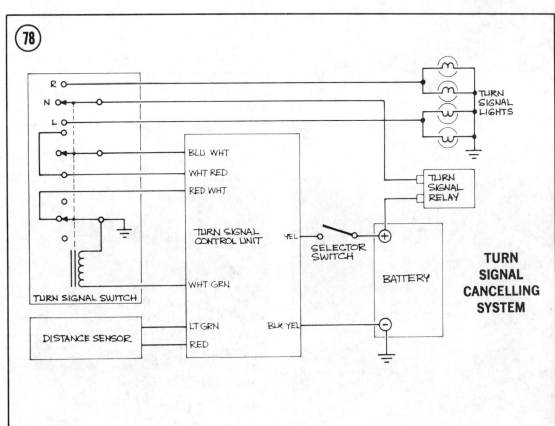

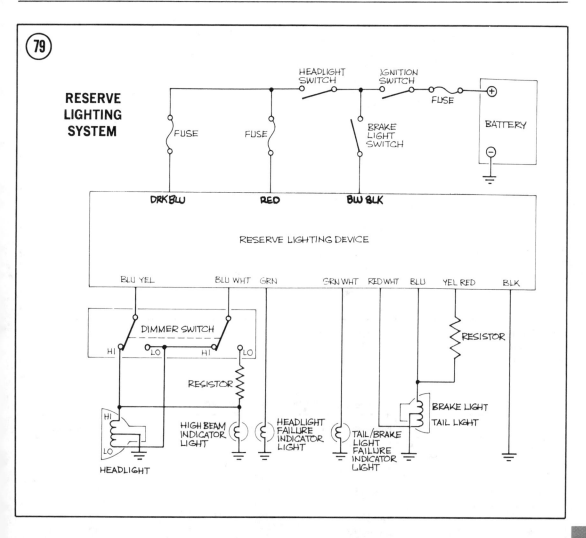

Table 1   BATTERY FREEZING TEMPERATURES

Specific Gravity	Freezing Temperature Degrees F.	Specific Gravity	Freezing Temperature Degrees F.
1.100	18	1.200	—17
1.120	13	1.220	—31
1.140	8	1.240	—50
1.160	1	1.260	—75
1.180	—6	1.280	—92

Table 2 DAMPER SPECIFICATIONS

Clearance	I.D. Mark	Thickness
0.20–0.23 in. (5–6 mm)	*	6.3 mm
0.24–0.27 in. (6–7 mm)	**	7.3 mm
0.28–0.32 in. (7–8 mm)	***	8.3 mm

11

Table 3   STARTER TROUBLESHOOTING

Symptom	Probable Cause	Remedy
Starter does not work	Low battery	Recharge battery
	Worn brushes	Replace brushes
	Defective relay	Repair or replace
	Defective switch	Repair or replace
	Defective wiring or connection	Repair wire or clean connection
	Internal short circuit	Repair or replace defective component
Starter action is weak	Low battery	Recharge battery
	Pitted relay contacts	Clean or replace
	Worn brushes	Replace brushes
	Defective connection	Clean and tighten
	Short circuit in commutator	Replace armature
Starter runs continuously	Stuck relay	Replace relay
Starter turns; does not turn engine	Defective starter clutch	Replace starter clutch

Table 4 LIGHT BULB REPLACEMENT

Item	Number	Wattage	Candle Power
Headlight		Z1R 60/55	
		1978 & later: 60/50	
		1973–77: 50/35	
Tail/brakelight	SAE 1157	8/27	3/32
Directional signals			
Front	SAE 1034	23	32
Rear	SAE 1073	23	32
Instrument lights	SAE 57	3.4	2
Running light	SAE 1034	8	3

SUPPLEMENT

1980-1981 SERVICE INFORMATION

This supplement contains all procedures and specifications unique to the models listed below. If a specific procedure is not includes, refer to the procedure in the prior chapters in the main body of this book.

1980 KZ1000, Standard, LTD, Classic, Z1R and Shaft Drive

For 1979-1981 Police models, refer to the procedures for the 1979 KZ1000.

The 1980 Classic is essentially the same as the 1980 LTD with the addition of fuel injection. Use the procedures and specifications listed for the 1979 LTD unless otherwise noted in this supplement.

This supplement is divided into sections that correspond to those in the other chapters of this book.

CHAPTER ONE

GENERAL INFORMATION

Troubleshooting and Tune-up Equipment
(Fuel Injected Models Only)

All fuel injection service procedures described in this supplement can be performed with the tools described in Chapter One in the main body of this book, plus the following special tools for troubleshooting:

a. Fuel/oil pressure gauge, T-adapter and extension hose.

b. Ohmmeter with 1 ohm scale.

c. Test light (3.4 watt).

CHAPTER THREE

LUBRICATION, MAINTENANCE AND TUNE-UP

SCHEDULED MAINTENANCE

The maintenance for 1980 models is the same as for 1979 models, with the following exception for the fuel injected KZ1000 Classic:

a. Fuel injected models require fuel filter replacement at each yearly or 6000 mile (10000 km) maintenance interval. See chapter Seven in this supplement. Periodic cleaning of the fuel injection system is not necessary unless indicated by a troubleshooting procedure.

b. Fuel injected models require high-pressure fuel hose replacement every two years. See Chapter Seven in this supplement.

WEEKLY MAINTENANCE

Tire and Tire Pressure

1980 Standard, LTD, Classic

There is an alternate tire size designation for these models. Inflation pressures are unchanged:

MN90-19 is an alternate to 3.25V-19

MP90-18 is an alternate to 4.00V-18

Police models: front wheel MN90-18, rear wheel MR90-18

1980 Z1R

The 1980 Z1R tire specification is upgraded to a V-rating, with a higher load inflation specification of 40 psi at the rear for loads over 215 lb.

Rear Brake Pedal
(Police Model)

Adjustment

The rear brake pedal adjustment should not be required once it is set correctly. The rear brake must have 0.08-0.12 in. (2-3 mm) from the at-rest position prior to contacting the master cylinder. Also the brake pedal and linkage must not contact the engine case or any other adjacent parts.

The brake pedal adjustment consists of two separate adjustments; pedal position and pushrod length. Each adjustment is separate, are inter-related and must be performed in the following order.

1. Place the motorcycle on the sidestand.
2. Check to be sure that the brake pedal is in the at-rest position.
3. Loosen the locknut and turn the adjusting bolt so there is clearance between the brake pedal and the engine case.

Idle speed adjust

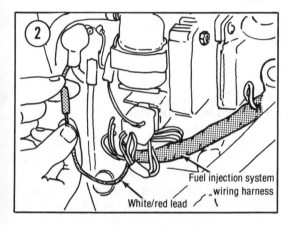

Fuel injection system wiring harness

White/red lead

4. Remove the clevis pin from the master cylinder pushrod clevis.

5. Rotate the clevis in either direction until the push rod has 0.080in. (2 mm) of free travel prior to contacting the master cylinder piston. Insert the clevis pin and recheck the clearance and readjust if necessary.

6. Adjust the rear brake light switch, see *Rear Brake Light Switch Adjustment* in Chapter Three in the main body of this book.

TUNE-UP

Tune-up procedures for the 1980-1981 models are the same as for earlier comparable models with the following exceptions.

Spark Plug Inspection
(1980 Z1R)

The standard spark plug gap is 0.039-0.043 in. (1.0-1.1 mm). All other models retain the 1979 specifications.

Suction Valve Inspection
(Fuel Injected Models Only)

See *Fuel Tank Removal* in Chapter Seven in this supplement before removing the fuel tank for this procedure on fuel injected models.

Valve Clearance Inspection
(Fuel Injected Models Only)

See *Fuel Tank Removal* in Chapter Seven in this supplement before removing the fuel tank for this procedure on fuel injected models.

Throttle Cable Adjustment
(Fuel Injected Models Only)

A single throttle is used on these models. The specified cable play remains at about 1/8 in. (2-3 mm).

Idle Speed
(Fuel Injected Models)

The idle speed adjuster is below the throttle valve (**Figure 1**). If idle speed on fuel injected models is unstable, see Chapter Seven in this supplement for troubleshooting.

Idle Mixture
(All Carburetted Models)

On 1980 and 1981 models, the idle mixture screw is set and sealed at the factory and requires no adjustment.

Throttle Valve Synchronization
(Fuel Injected Models)

Synchronization of the throttle valves is not required on a regular basis. If you suspect that a problem may be caused by poor synchronization, see Chapter Seven in this supplement for fuel injection troubleshooting.

Cylinder Compression
(Fuel Injected Models)

Check cylinder compression for fuel injected models the same way as for carbureted models, but disconnect the white/red lead from the starter solenoid to the fuel injection harness to temporarily disable the fuel injectors (**Figure 2**).

YEARLY MAINTENANCE

Fork Oil Change
(Except Police Model)

The fork oil weight for chain drive models is changed from SAE 15W to SAE 10W.

12

Fork Oil Change
(Police Models)

Fork oil change is the same as on previous KZ1000 chain drive models with the following exceptions:
1. Fill the fork tubes with approximately 5.75 oz. (170 cc) 15W non-detergent fork oil.
2. After filling both fork tubes, pump the forks several times to expel air from the upper and lower fork chambers.

3. Stick a long wire (at least 24 in.) down into the fork tube. Measure the distance from the top of the fork oil to the top of the fork tube. The distance should be 18.23 in. (463 mm).

STORAGE
(FUEL INJECTED MODELS ONLY)

Do not add any preservative to the fuel tank when storing the fuel injected motorcycle. The fuel injectors and filter may be damaged.

CHAPTER FOUR

ENGINE

The following specifications are changed for all models:
  a. Combustion chamber volume (measured from the bottom surface of the cylinder head) is increased to 39 cc.
  b. The minimum inner valve spring tension limit is decreased to 54 lb. at 0.93 in. compression (24.5 kg at 23.6 mm).
  c. The minimum outer valve spring tension limit is decreased to 99 lb. at 1.01 in. compression (44.7 kg at 25.6 mm).

Follow the engine repair procedures described in Chapter Four of the basic book, except as noted here for the KZ1000 Classic.

Camshaft Removal
(Fuel Injected Models Only)

Before starting to remove the camshaft on fuel injected models, turn the ignition switch to OFF and disconnect the white/red lead from the starter solenoid to the fuel injection wiring harness (**Figure 2**).

Cylinder Head Removal
(Fuel Injected Models Only)

On fuel injected models, the fuel injection intake system must be removed before removing the cylinder head. See *Fuel Injection Disassembly* in Chapter Seven of this supplement.

Engine Removal
(Fuel Injected Models Only)

Before starting to remove the engine on fuel injected models, turn the ignition switch to OFF and disconnect the white/red lead from the starter solenoid to the fuel injection wiring harness (**Figure 2**).

On fuel injected models, the complete intake system must be removed before removing the engine. See *Fuel Injection Disassembly* in Chapter Seven of this supplement.

Engine Removal/Installation
(Police Models)

Engine removal and installation is the same as on previous models with the exception of removal of the floorboards.
1. Move the floorboard to the raised position.
2. On the left side, mark the position of the shift linkage clamp on the shift linkage.
Remove the pivot bolt and clamp bolt and remove the shift linkage. Remove the floorboard mounting bolts and remove the floorboard assembly.
3. On the right side, disconnect the rear brake light switch from the brake pedal. Remove the rear mounting bolt on the brake pedal and the floorboard, then remove the remaining floorboard mounting bolts. Remove the floorboard assembly.
4. Reverse the removal procedure. Tighten the mounting bolts securely.

CHAPTER FIVE

CLUTCH

CLUTCH PLATES AND HUB

Clutch Removal (Chain Drive)

Clutch removal and installation is the same as on previous models with the exception of removal of the floorboard.

1. Move the floorboard to the raised position.

2. Remove the two floorboard pivot bolts and remove the floorboard.

3. Reverse the removal procedure. Tighten the pivot bolts securely.

CHAPTER SIX

TRANSMISSION

DRIVE SPROCKET COVER

Removal/Installation
(Police Models)

Sprocket removal and installation is the same as on previous models with the exception of removal of the floorboards.

1. Move the floorboard to the raised position.

2. Mark the position of the shift linkage clamp on the shift linkage.

3. Remove the pivot bolt and clamp bolt and remove the shift linkage. Remove the floorboard mounting bolts and remove the floorboard.

4. Reverse the removal procedure. Tighten the bolts securely, then adjust the linkage as described in the following procedure.

SHIFT LINKAGE (CHAIN DRIVE)

Adjustment
(Police Models)

The gearshift pedals must be positioned so that each can easily be pressed down all the way to ensure full gear engagement. Also, the pedal linkage must not contact the engine case or any other adjacent parts.

1. Loosen both locknuts and turn the center adjuster in either direction to correctly position both shift pedals. The rear threaded portion of the adjuster has left-hand threads.

2. Tighten the locknuts securely.

12

CHAPTER SEVEN

FUEL SYSTEM

Fuel Tank Removal
(Fuel Injected Models Only)

See *Fuel Injection Disassembly* in this chapter of the supplement for fuel tank removal.

Idle Mixture Screw
(Carburetted Models)

Removal/installation

The idle mixture screw is covered by a plug bonded in place at the factory. When disassembling

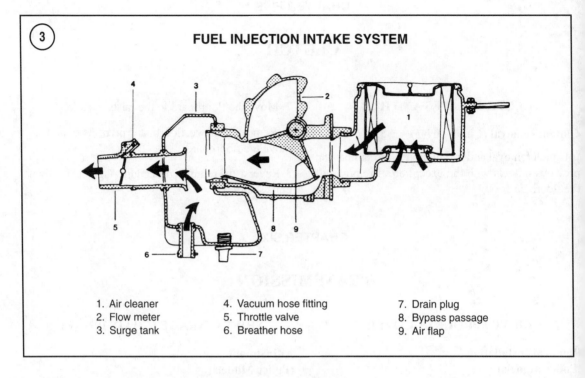

③ **FUEL INJECTION INTAKE SYSTEM**

1. Air cleaner
2. Flow meter
3. Surge tank
4. Vacuum hose fitting
5. Throttle valve
6. Breather hose
7. Drain plug
8. Bypass passage
9. Air flap

the carburetor for overhaul, the plug should be removed in order to clean the passage with compressed air.

1. Carefully scrape the bonding agent from the recess in the carburetor body.
2. Punch and pry out the plug with a small screwdriver or awl.
3. Carefully turn the mixture screw in until it seats lightly. Count and record the number of turns so it can be installed in the same position on reassembly.
4. Remove the mixture screw and spring from the carburetor body.
5. Inspect the end of the mixture screw; replace if damaged or worn.
6. Install the mixture screw, turn it in until it seats lightly, then back it out the same number of turns noted during removal.
7. Install a new plug and seal the edges of the plug with silicone sealant.

Jet Needle Removal/Installation (All Chain Drive Models)

The jet needle used on all 1980 chain drive models is 5CN29. All other carburetor specifications are unchanged.

Accelerator Pump Disassembly/Assembly (Z1R Only)

The 1980 Z1R accelerator pump should be assembled with 0.15 in. (3.8 mm) clearance between

the nut and the end of the pump rod. See **Figure 64** in Chapter Seven of the basic book.

FUEL INJECTION

The 1980 Classic is equipped with an electronic fuel injection system instead of carburetors. The fuel injection system is highly reliable, having been derived from time tested systems used in the automotive field.

Typical of complex electronic systems, most parts cannot be repaired, only replaced. This chapter describes how the fuel injection system works, how to maintain it, how to determine when a part is faulty and how to replace such parts.

CAUTION
*Servicing a motorcycle with electronic fuel injection requires special precautions to prevent damage to the expensive electronic control unit. Common electrical system service procedures acceptable on other motorcycles may cause damage to several parts of the fuel injection system. Be sure to read the **Fuel Injection Precautions** in this chapter.*

FUEL INJECTION OPERATION

The fuel injection system consists of the intake system, the fuel system and the control system. Together they measure air flow to the throttle valves, air temperature, engine temperature and engine speed. The electronic control unit (computer) then computes the best fuel mixture for smooth performance, maximum fuel economy and lowest exhaust emissions; the computer signals the injector valves to open for a specific amount of time, injecting precisely the right amount of fuel into the cylinder head intake ports.

Intake System

See **Figure 3**. The intake system routes air through the air cleaner, flow meter, surge tank, past the throttle valves and into the cylinder head intake ports.

The flow meter has an air flap that deflects in proportion to the rate of air flow past the flap. Connected to the flap is a variable resistor that tells the computer how much air is flowing into the engine. Inside the flow meter there is also an air temperature sensor that signals the computer to deliver more fuel when cold, dense air is entering the system.

At idle, the flow meter flap is fully closed and a small amount of air goes to the engine through a bypass passage around the flap.

From the flow meter, the air enters a surge tank that smooths the air pressure pulses caused by normal engine operation. This keeps the pressure pulses from affecting operation of the air flow meter. The surge tank is also the point at which combustion blow-by gases from the crankcase breather enter the intake system.

From the surge tank, the air passes through 4 individual butterfly type throttle valves into the intake ports. A rubber-capped fitting on 2 throttle valves provides intake vacuum sensing points for the fuel pressure regulator.

There is a throttle position switch on the left throttle valve that tells the computer when the throttle is fully closed or open.

Fuel System

See **Figure 4**. The fuel system routes fuel from the fuel tank through a filter, to an electric fuel pump, to the individual fuel injectors and into the cylinder head intake ports. The fuel system does not provide feedback to the electronic control system, but the control system turns the fuel pump and the injectors on and off.

The fuel pump is a constant flow pump; whatever fuel the injectors are not using is routed through a fuel pressure regulator, through a return line and a one-way check valve back into the fuel tank. The fuel pump is cooled and its bearings are lubricated by the fuel it is pumping.

CAUTION
If the pump is operated without fuel, its bearings will be damaged. The fuel pump cannot be disassembled or repaired.

The fuel pressure regulator is basically an on/off valve that dumps excess fuel back into the fuel tank when fuel pressure exceeds the regulator's limit. The regulator has a vacuum line leading to 2 of the intake ports. This line senses intake vacuum and allows the regulator to adjust fuel pressure so that it is at a constant level above intake vacuum.

The fuel injectors are simply solenoid valves that open on signal from the computer. All the injectors open at the same time: once every 360° of crankshaft rotation, regardless of whether the engine intake valves are open or closed. This means that every time an intake valve opens, its injector will have opened twice. If the intake valve is not open when the injector operates, the finely atomized fuel/air mixture stays in the intake port until the intake valve opens.

Control System

See **Figure 5**. The electronic control system consists of a relay that controls power to the fuel pump, air flow meter and central computer; the computer that senses input signals; and the various sensors described here.

a. Signals from the ignition coil primary ground leads provide engine speed information that determines how often the injectors operate.

b. The air flow meter variable resistor provides information about how much air is entering the engine, which is the most important factor in determining how long the injectors are open.

c. The computer receives signals from the engine temperature sensor and the air temperature sensor and adjusts fuel mixture to compensate for a cold engine and cold air; this is similar to the operation of a carburetor choke.

d. The throttle position switch on the left throttle valve tells the computer when the throttle valves are at idle and when they are more than about ½ open. In either position the computer slightly enriches the fuel/air mixture.

12

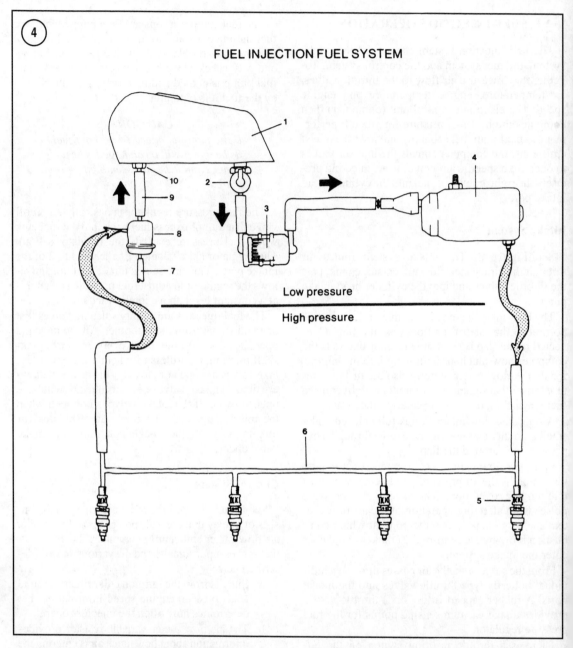

④ FUEL INJECTION FUEL SYSTEM

Low pressure

High pressure

FUEL INJECTION PRECAUTIONS

CAUTION
Servicing a motorcycle with electronic fuel injection requires special precautions to prevent damage to the expensive electronic control unit (computer). Common electrical system service procedures acceptable on other motorcycles may cause damage to several parts of the fuel injection system.

Solid state electronic parts are usually very reliable, but they are sensitive to electrical overloads or polarity reversals and to physical shock. The following precautions must always be observed when servicing a fuel injected motorcycle.

Control System Precautions

1. Unless specifically directed by a troubleshooting procedure, do not start the motorcycle while any electrical connectors are disconnected and do not disconnect the battery cables or any electrical con-

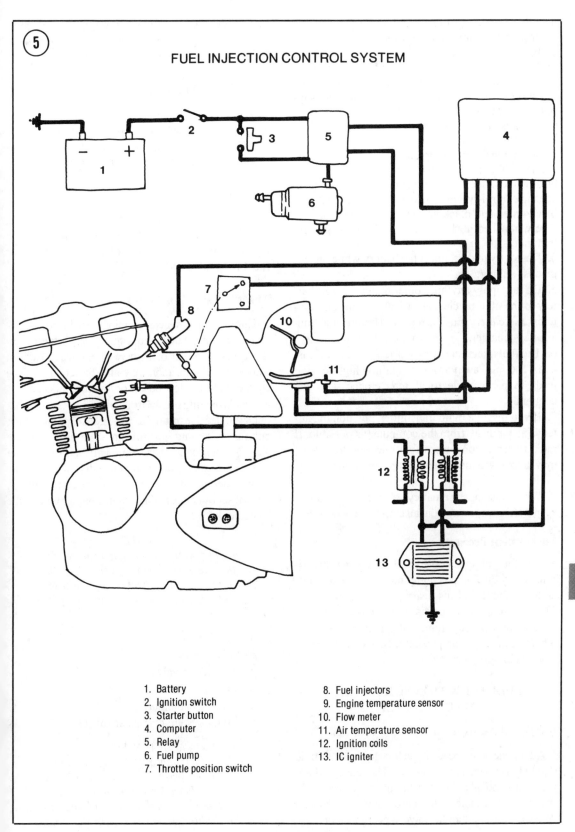

FUEL INJECTION CONTROL SYSTEM

1. Battery
2. Ignition switch
3. Starter button
4. Computer
5. Relay
6. Fuel pump
7. Throttle position switch
8. Fuel injectors
9. Engine temperature sensor
10. Flow meter
11. Air temperature sensor
12. Ignition coils
13. IC igniter

12

nectors while the ignition switch is ON. Irreparable control system damage may result.

2. Before disconnecting any electrical connectors, turn the ignition switch to OFF and disconnect the white/red lead from the starter solenoid to the fuel injection wiring harness (**Figure 2**). This lead supplies power to the computer, relay and fuel injectors at all times; it is not switched or protected by a fuse and so it is always "hot."

3. When repairs are complete, do not try to start the engine without double checking all fuel injection electrical connectors; faulty connections may damage the control system. Make sure the fuel injection black/green and black/yellow ground leads are securely attached at the battery negative (-) ground terminal.

4. Do not try to disconnect the battery while the engine is running.

5. Do not apply anything other than a 12-volt battery to the motorcycle's electrical system. The motorcycle's battery must be removed before attaching a battery charger.

6. The fuel injection wiring harness must be at least 4 in. (100 mm) away from the ignition high-tension leads to prevent electrical interference with the computer.

7. If you install a radio transmitter, position the antenna as far away from the computer as possible. If radio transmission causes fuel injection trouble, it may help to ground the computer case to the motorcycle.

8. When washing the motorcycle, take special care to keep water spray away from all electrical connectors.

Fuel System Precautions

1. The fuel pump is cooled and its bearings are lubricated by the fuel it is pumping. If the pump is operated without fuel, its bearings will be damaged. The fuel pump cannot be disassembled or repaired.

2. Do not add any lubricants, preservatives, or other additives to the gasoline; fuel system corrosion or clogging may result.

FUEL INJECTION SCHEDULED MAINTENANCE

Idle Speed Adjustment

Adjust the idle speed at each regular 3,000 mile (5,000 km) maintenance interval. The idle speed adjustment knob is below the throttle valve assembly (**Figure 1**). If the idle is unstable or rough, check throttle cable play and throttle valve synchronization.

If idling is still unstable or rough after synchronizing the throttle valves, see *Fuel Injection Troubleshooting* in this chapter of the supplement.

Fuel Filter Replacement

Fuel injected models require fuel filter replacement at each regular 6,000 mile (10,000 km) maintenance interval. See *Fuel Injection Disassembly* in this chapter of the supplement for fuel filter replacement.

Fuel Hose Replacement

Fuel injected models require high pressure fuel hose replacement every 2 years. See *Fuel Injection Disassembly* in this chapter of the supplement for fuel hose replacement.

Throttle Valve Synchronization

Throttle valve synchronization should not be required regularly, but this adjustment may be necessary if the idle is rough or if there is excessive exhaust smoke. Synchronization may also be required if the engine stalls, has low power or low fuel mileage.

Synchronizing the throttle valves makes sure that one cylinder doesn't try to run faster than the other, cutting power and gas mileage. The only accurate way to synchronize the throttle valves is to use a set of vacuum gauges (a manometer) that measures the intake vacuum of all cylinders at the same time. A typical set of gauges is shown in Chapter One in the basic book.

NOTE
Before you try to synchronize the throttle valves, make sure all of the following are checked or adjusted first. If not, you won't get a good synch.

a. Air cleaner
b. Spark plugs
c. Air suction valves
d. Valve clearance
e. Throttle cable play
f. All air system clamps are airtight

WARNING
Some fuel may spill during these procedures. Work in a well-ventilated area at least 50 feet from any sparks or flames, including gas appliance pilot lights. Do not smoke in the area.

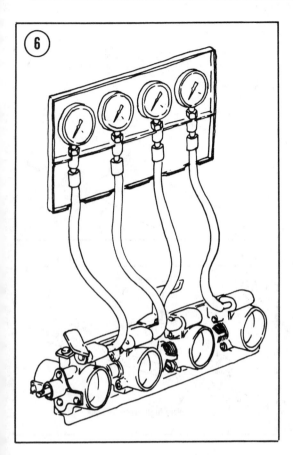

Keep a BC rated fire extinguisher handy.

1. Start the engine, warm it up fully, set the idle speed, then stop the engine.

2. Remove the fuel tank and set it on a bench so it is the same height as it was on the motorcycle; see *Fuel Tank Removal* in this chapter of the supplement. Get some long fuel tubing and connect the fuel filter to the fuel tap and the pressure regulator to the return check valve.

3. Remove the rubber cap or vacuum line from each throttle valve vacuum tap (**Figure 6**) and attach a set of vacuum gauges following the manufacturer's instructions.

4. Turn the fuel tap to ON, start the engine and adjust the idle speed.

5. Check that the vacuum difference between the cylinders is less than 1.18 in. Hg (30 mm Hg). The readings should be as close as possible.

6. If the difference is greater than specified, loosen the locknut and turn the appropriate synchronizing screw (located between the throttle valves) as required to equalize the vacuum in all cylinders (**Figure 7**).

First match No. 1 and No. 2, then match No. 3 and No. 4, and finally match the left pair of cylinder to the right pair. The left and right screws control the no. 1 and No. 4 throttle valves individually. The

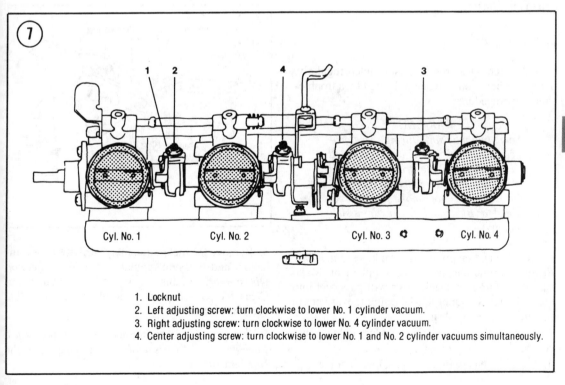

1. Locknut
2. Left adjusting screw: turn clockwise to lower No. 1 cylinder vacuum.
3. Right adjusting screw: turn clockwise to lower No. 4 cylinder vacuum.
4. Center adjusting screw: turn clockwise to lower No. 1 and No. 2 cylinder vacuums simultaneously.

center screw controls both No. 1 and No. 2 throttle valves in relation to No. 3.

7. Rev the engine once and check that all cylinders return to equal readings. Readjust if necessary and tighten the adjuster locknuts while holding the adjusters steady.

8. Reset the idle speed, stop the engine and install the fuel tank.

NOTE
Poor synchronization of fuel injection throttle valves causes more problems than poor synchronization of carburetors on a carburetted motorcycle. If one throttle valve is open more than the others, more air will flow through the air flow meter and the computer will inject more fuel into all cylinders, causing a too-rich mixture in the remaining 3 cylinders.

Surge Tank Drain Plug

The surge tank between the flow meter and the throttle valves is equipped with a drain plug in case water, oil or gas collect in the tank (**Figure 8**).

To drain the tank, simply pull the plug down and out. When installing the plug, make sure it is airtight; any air leaks will cause the fuel injection system to malfunction.

Fuel System Cleaning

Fuel system cleaning is not scheduled regularly, but it may be required when indicated by a troubleshooting procedure.

WARNING
Some fuel may spill during these procedures. Work in a well-ventilated area at least 50 feet from any sparks or flames, including gas appliance pilot lights. Do not smoke in the area. Keep a BC rated fire extinguisher handy.

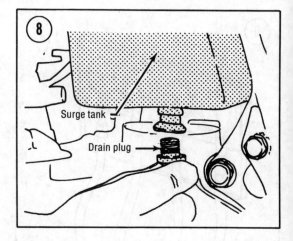

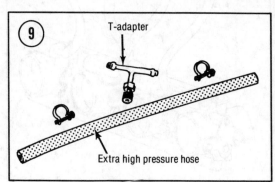

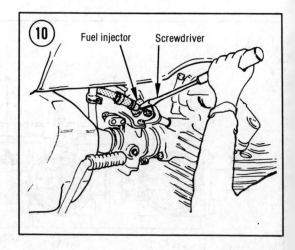

1. Remove and empty the fuel tank; see *Fuel Tank Removal* in the chapter of the supplement. Make sure the return line check valve will pass fuel into the tank, but not out of it. Make sure the air vent in the fuel tank cap is clear.

2. Remove the fuel tap and clean the fuel tap filter screen.

3. Flush the tank with clean gasoline or solvent.

4. Remove the fuel pump, fuel distribution tube, injectors and pressure regulator; see *Fuel Injection Disassembly* in this chapter of the supplement. Clean the parts in solvent. Replace any parts that can't be cleaned.

5. Install a new fuel filter and new fuel hoses; see *Fuel Injection Disassembly* in this chapter of the supplement.

FUEL INJECTION
TROUBLESHOOTING

This troubleshooting section will help you solve most fuel injection system problems quickly, minimizing unnecessary parts replacement.

Re-read the *Fuel Injection Precautions* in this chapter of the supplement before trying to troubleshoot the system. Solid state electronic parts are usually very reliable, but they are sensitive to electrical overloads or polarity reversals and to physical shock. Be very careful not to create accidental short circuits when using a test meter.

Tools

The troubleshooting procedures described here require the following special tools, in addition to the tools described in Chapter One of the basic book.

a. For fuel pressure measurement: a fuel pressure gauge, T-shaped junction tube and an extra length of high-pressure hose are required to inspect fuel pressure (**Figure 9**). Kawasaki furnishes a combination oil/fuel pressure gauge (part No. 57001-125 or 57001-164) and a T-adapter and hose kit (part No. 57001-1089). You can use any fuel or oil pressure gauge in the 50 to 100 psi range and a high-pressure hose with screw type clamps.

b. For relay and other parts inspection: An ohmmeter with a 1 ohm scale. This means the ohmmeter must be very sensitive–approximate 50,000 to 100,000 ohms/volt. You must "zero" the ohmmeter before each test: for each scale (like RX1) touch the meter probes together and adjust the meter reading to zero, using the ohmmeter adjustment knob.

c. For relay inspection: a 3.4 watt test light is required. See Test No. 8, under *Fuel Injection Test Sequence*, following, for a description of the light.

Most Common Troubles

Before you suspect the expensive parts, check the "obvious" problems that are sometimes overlooked:

a. Is there fuel in the tank?

b. Is the fuel tap turned to ON or RES?

c. Check for debris or water in the fuel filter. If there is dirt or water in the filter, clean the fuel system; see *Fuel System Cleaning* in this chapter of this supplement.

d. Is the air filter clean and in place?

e. Is the ignition fuse okay?

f. Are the throttle valves synchronized?

g. More fuel injection troubles are caused by loose or corroded connectors than by any other factor. Recheck the wiring connections, especially if the motorcycle has just been assembled. Make sure the ground wires are clean and firmly attached at the battery, the color coded wires are correctly matched, and all connectors are securely coupled.

h. Are the motorcycle's starting and ignition system operating? If not, repair them before blaming a problem on the fuel injection system; refer to Chapter Eleven in the basic book.

Troubles Unique to Fuel Injection

Now check the "not so obvious" fuel injection-related operating requirements that would not cause fuel problems in a motorcycle with carburetors. Because the fuel pressure regulator uses engine intake vacuum to control fuel pressure and because the crankcase ventilation system affects the vacuum measurement, the following items must be in order for proper fuel injection operation:

a. Is the oil level correct?

b. Are the oil filler cap, surge tank drain plug and breather hose installed and air tight?

c. Is the valve clearance correct?

d. Is the cranking compression acceptable? Refer to *Compression Test* in Chapter Three in this supplement.

BEFORE YOU START THE TEST
SEQUENCE

If all the items above are in order, perform Steps 1 and 2 following this paragraph before you proceed to the comprehensive test sequence given later. You may be able to save considerable troubleshooting time by using these preliminary checks.

1. While cranking the engine with the electric starter, feel the high-pressure hose to the fuel distribution tube. Can you feel the fuel pressure pulses that show the fuel pump is working?

a. If you can feel the fuel pressure pulses, the fuel system is probably okay; go on to Step 2.

b. If you cannot feel the fuel pressure pulses, troubleshoot the fuel system, starting the test sequence at Test No. 1.

2. Put the tip of a screwdriver on each injector body in turn and the screwdriver grip against your ear (**Figure 10**). While cranking the engine with the

12

b. If all injectors are ticking, the control system is probably okay. If both the fuel pump and injectors appear to be working but you still have a fuel injection problem, start the test sequence at *Test No. 10.*

FUEL INJECTION TEST SEQUENCE

Fuel System Tests

Test No. 1: Fuel Pump

1. Remove the left side cover and disconnect the 2-pin fuel pump connector (**Figure 11**).
2. Connect a 12 volt battery to the fuel pump socket from the fuel pump: positive (+) terminal to the orange/black lead, and negative (-) terminal to the black/yellow lead. Listen for the sound of the fuel pump operating.
   a. If the fuel pump does not operate, the pump or its wiring is bad. Replace as required.
   b. If the fuel pump operates, it is okay. Go to *Test No. 2.*

Test No. 2: Fuel pump start and run signals

1. Remove the left side cover and disconnect the 2-pin fuel pump connector (**Figure 11**).
2. Connect a voltmeter to the fuel pump plug from the wiring harness: positive (+) terminal to the orange/black lead, and negative (-) terminal to the black/yellow lead.
3. While cranking the engine with the electric starter, observe the meter reading.
   a. If the meter reads battery voltage, the relay is receiving its "start signal" from the starter solenoid and the relay is supplying power to the fuel pump. Go on to Step 4.
   b. If the meter does not read battery voltage, check the wiring from the starter solenoid to the relay. If the wiring and connectors are good, inspect the relay; go to *Test No. 8.*
4. Remove the air filter.
5. With the ignition switch ON, but without pushing the starter button, push the flow meter flap open (**Figure 12**) and observe the meter reading as the flap is pushed and released.

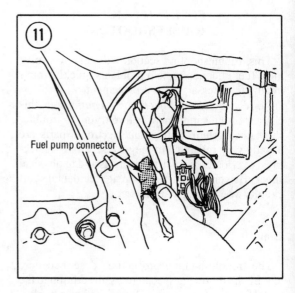

Fuel pump connector

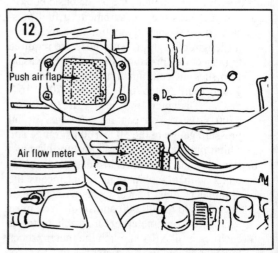

Push air flap

Air flow meter

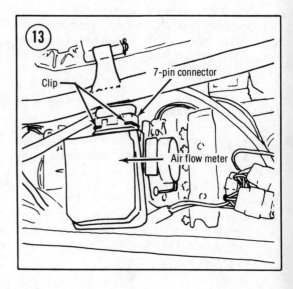

Clip

7-pin connector

Air flow meter

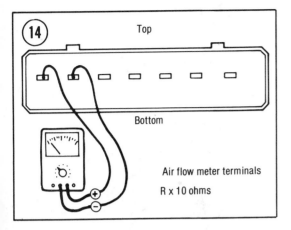

Top

Bottom

Air flow meter terminals

R x 10 ohms

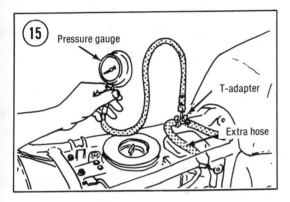

Pressure gauge

T-adapter

Extra hose

5. Connect an ohmmeter, set at a 10 ohm scale, to the 2 terminals furthest to the left on the flow meter body plug (**Figure 14**). Measure the resistance with the air flap valve closed and open. The resistance should be infinite (open circuit) at rest and 0 ohms (closed circuit) when the flap is pushed.

   a. If the switch doesn't function as described, the entire air flow meter must be replaced. The switch is not available separately.

   b. If the switch functions correctly, but the "run signal" was not present at the fuel pump connector plug in *Test No. 2*, inspect the relay; go on to *Test No. 8*.

Test No. 4: Fuel pressure inspection

WARNING
Residual fuel pressure may exist in the fuel lines. Be careful to avoid accidental spillage.

WARNING
Some fuel may spill during these procedures. Work in a well-ventilated area at least 50 feet from any sparks or flames, including gas appliance pilot lights. Do not smoke in the area. Keep a BC rated fire extinguisher handy.

NOTE
*A fuel pressure gauge, T-shaped junction tube and an extra length of high-pressure hose are required to inspect fuel pressure (**Figure 9**). Kawasaki furnishes a combination oil/fuel pressure gauge (part No. 57001-125 or 57001-164) and a T-adapter and hose kit (part No. 57001-1089). You can use any fuel or oil pressure gauge in the 50 to 100 psi range and a high-pressure hose with screw type clamps.*

a. If the meter reads battery voltage when the flap is pushed and zero voltage when the flap is released, the fuel pump is receiving its "run signal" from the flow meter's fuel pump switch and the relay. Skip to *Test No. 4*.

b. If the meter does not read battery voltage, inspect the flow meter's fuel pump switch; go on to *Test No. 3*.

Test No. 3: Flow meter fuel pump switch

1. Turn the ignition switch to OFF.
2. Disconnect the white/red lead from the starter solenoid to the fuel injection wiring harness (**Figure 2**).
3. Remove the air filter and the right side cover.
4. Remove the clip and disconnect the flow meter 7-pin connector (**Figure 13**).

CAUTION
Do not try to start the engine while the flow meter is disconnected. You may cause irrepairable electrical system damage.

1. Remove the right side cover and disconnect the fuel pump outlet hose.
2. Connect the T-adapter to the disconnected hose, attach the pressure gauge to the T and connect the T-adapter to the fuel pump outlet with the extra hose (**Figure 15**). Tighten the hose clamps.

12

3a. If the engine will start, start it and let it idle. Note the average gauge reading; at idle, the fuel pressure should be 31-34 psi (2.2-2.4 kg/cm^2). Open the throttle fully for an instant and note the gauge reading; when the throttle is first opened, the pressure should be 34-37 psi (2.4-2.6 kg/cm^2).

3b. If the engine will not start, remove the air filter, turn the ignition switch to ON and push the flow meter flap open to start the fuel pump. Note the average gauge reading; the fuel pressure should be 34-37 psi (2.4-2.6 kg/cm^2).

   a. If the fuel pressure is normal, the fuel system is okay. Skip to *Test No. 7.*

   b. If the fuel pressure was higher than specified, go on to *Test No. 5.*

   c. If the fuel pressure was lower than specified, skip to *Test No. 6.*

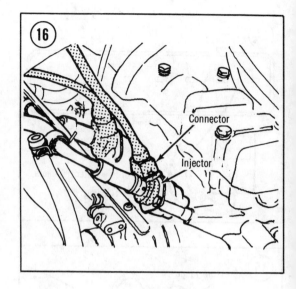

Test No. 5: High fuel pressure

If the fuel pressure was too high in *Test No. 4,* check the regulator vacuum hose for leaks and check the fuel return line and fuel tank check valve for blockage.

   a. If there is no leakage or blockage, the fuel pressure regulator is faulty and should be replaced.

   b. If there was leakage or blockage, clean or replace the parts and repeat *Test No. 4.*

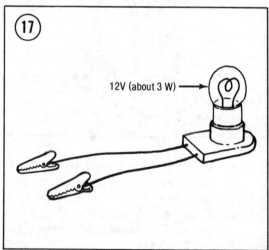

Test No. 6: Low fuel pressure

1. If the fuel pressure was too low in *Test No. 4,* check the fuel lines from the fuel tap to the fuel pump and the fuel filter for blockage. Check the fuel high-pressure hoses for leaks.

   a. If there was leakage or blockage, clean or replace the parts and repeat *Test No. 4.* See *Fuel System Cleaning* in this chapter of the supplement.

   b. If there is no leakage or blockage, go on to Step 2.

2. If there is no leakage or blockage in Step 1, clamp shut or plug the fuel return line and repeat *Test No. 4.*

   a. If the pressure is okay or too high, the fuel pressure regulator is faulty and should be replaced.

   b. If the pressure is too low, the fuel pump is faulty and should be replaced.

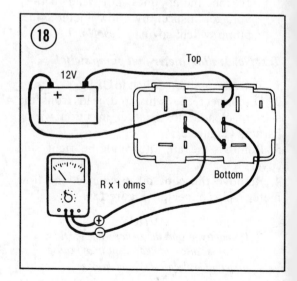

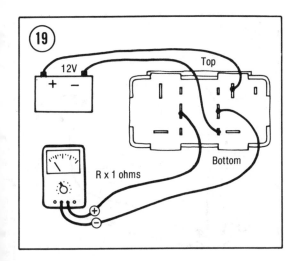

Control System Tests

Tests No. 7 through No. 9 are key tests of the electronic control system. A failure of these parts will most likely result in a bike that won't start or which dies soon after starting.

Test No. 7: Injector signal

1. Remove the fuel tank; see *Fuel Tank Removal* in Chapter Seven of this supplement.

> *CAUTION*
> *Before disconnecting any electrical connectors, turn the ignition switch to OFF and disconnect the white/red lead from the starter solenoid to the fuel injection wiring harness (Figure 2). This lead supplies power to the computer, relay and fuel injectors at all times; it is not switched or protected by a fuse and so it is always "hot."*

2. Disconnect all 4 of the fuel injector connectors (**Figure 16**), then reinstall the fuel tank.
3. Attach a voltmeter set at 10 volts to one injector socket's 2 pins (from the wiring harness).
4. Crank the engine with the electric starter and observe the voltmeter. Repeat for all the injector sockets. If the meter needle flickers at regular intervals, the electronic control system is operating.
   a. If the meter needle does not flicker on any connectors, the control system is not operating; go to *Test No. 8*.

b. If the needle flickers on *some* of the connectors but not all, check the connections and wiring back to the wiring harness.
c. If the meter needle flickers, but you could *not* hear the injectors "ticking" in Step 2 of *Before You Start The Test Sequence*, the injector is faulty. Replace the injector.

> *CAUTION*
> *If you want to test an individual injector, do not connect a 12 volt power source directly to an injector or the injector's solenoid coil will be damaged. Connect a 5-7 ohm resistor in series with a 12 volt battery or use a 3 volt power source to protect the injector.*

d. If the meter needle flickers, the control system is operating. Skip to *Test No. 10*.

Test No. 8: Relay

A faulty relay may stop the fuel pump, the control system or both from operating. Testing the relay requires a 12 volt power source (the motorcycle's battery can be used), an ohmmeter with a 1 ohm scale and a 12 volt, 3.4 watt test light (SAE No. 57); see **Figure 17**. One of the motorcycle's instrument or indicator lights will do.

The relay cannot be repaired. If faulty, it must be replaced. If another relay is available, you can bypass this procedure by simply substituting a known good relay to see if the problem is cured.

1. Remove the relay from the motorcycle; see *Relay Removal* later in this chapter of the supplement. Using an ohmmeter set on a 1 ohm scale and a 12 volt power source, make the following relay tests.
2. Connect the ohmmeter and power source as shown in **Figure 18**. The side of the relay that mates with the left black connector is marked with a black label on the top.
   a. If the meter shows infinite resistance (no continuity), the relay is faulty. Replace the relay.
   b. If the meter shows zero resistance (continuity), go on to Step 3.
3. Connect the ohmmeter and power source as shown in **Figure 19**.

12

a. If the meter shows zero resistance (continuity), the relay is faulty. Replace the relay.

b. If the meter shows infinite resistance (no continuity), go on to Step 4.

4. Connect the ohmmeter and power source as shown in **Figure 20**.

    a. If the meter shows infinite resistance (no continuity), the relay is faulty. Replace the relay.

    b. If the meter shows zero resistance (continuity), go on to Step 5.

5. Connect the ohmmeter and power source as shown in **Figure 21**.

    a. If the meter shows zero resistance (continuity), the relay is faulty. Replace the relay.

    b. If the meter shows infinite resistance (no continuity), go on to Step 6.

6. Connect the ohmmeter and power source as shown in **Figure 22**.

    a. If the meter shows infinite resistance (no continuity), the relay is faulty. Replace the relay.

    b. If the meter shows zero resistance (continuity), go on to Step 7.

7. Connect the ohmmeter and power source as shown in **Figure 23**.

    a. If the meter shows zero resistance (continuity), the relay is faulty. Replace the relay.

    b. If the meter shows infinite resistance (no continuity), go on to Step 8.

8. Connect the ohmmeter and power source as shown in **Figure 24**.

    a. If the meter shows infinite resistance (no continuity), the relay is faulty. Replace the relay.

    b. If the meter shows zero resistance (continuity), go on to Step 9.

9. Connect the test light, ohmmeter and power source as shown in **Figure 25**.

CAUTION
The test light serves as a current limiter.
Do not perform this test without the light in
series with the power source or the internal
fuel pump relay resistor will burn out.

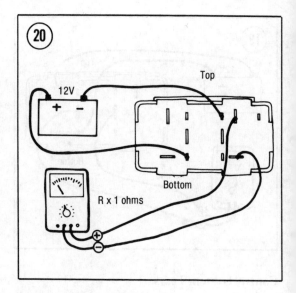

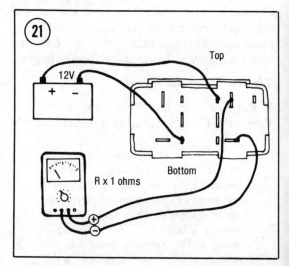

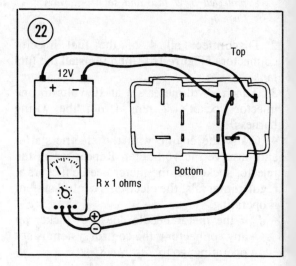

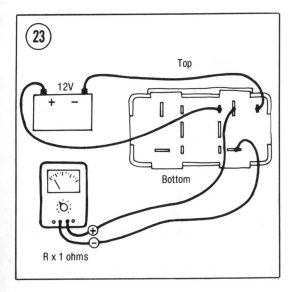

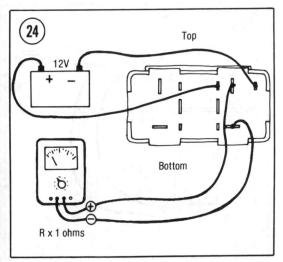

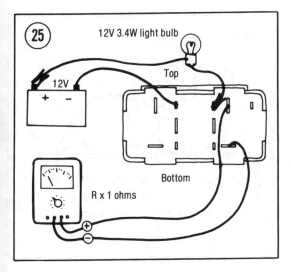

a. If the meter shows zero resistance (continuity), the relay is faulty. Replace the relay.

b. If the meter shows infinite resistance (no continuity), the relay is in good condition. Go on to *Test No. 9.*

Test No. 9: Computer

This test checks the functioning of the computer when it receives the ignition timing signal from the ignition system. If the bike fails this test it will not start or run.

If you have not already inspected the ignition system, refer to *IC Igniter* in Chapter Eleven of the basic book. The computer cannot function if the ignition system is faulty or if the relay is faulty (see *Test No. 8*).

The computer can not be repaired. If faulty, it must be replaced.

1. Disconnect one of the injector connectors (**Figure 16**).

> *CAUTION*
> *Before disconnecting any electrical connectors, turn the ignition switch to OFF and disconnect the white/red lead from the starter solenoid to the fuel injection wiring harness (**Figure 2**). This lead supplies power to the computer, relay and fuel injectors at all times; it is not switched or protected by a fuse so it it is always "hot."*

2. Attach a voltmeter set at 10 volts DC to the injector socket's pins (from the wiring harness).

3. Crank the engine with the electric starter and observe the voltmeter.

a. If the meter needle flickers at regular intervals, the computer is operating. Check the various sensors (*Test No. 10 through No. 12*).

b. If the meter needle does not flicker, and *Test No. 8* revealed no problem with the relay, the computer is faulty and must be replaced.

> *NOTE*
> *Before replacing an expensive part, be sure the problem is not caused by bad electrical connections. More fuel injection troubles are caused by loose or corroded connectors than by any other factor. Make sure the*

12

ground wires are clean and firmly attached at the battery, the color coded wires correctly matched and all connectors securely coupled.

Sensor Tests

If the previous tests did not indicate a faulty part or if the bike will run but is hard to start, runs poorly, hesitates, backfires or burns excessive fuel, the remaining tests should detect the faulty part.

Test No. 10: Flow meter

This test checks the flow meter flap, the variable resistor and the air temperature sensor. If the flow meter fails on any step, it must be replaced. Repair parts are not available from Kawasaki.

1. Remove the air flow meter; see *Flow Meter Removal* later in this chapter of the supplement.
2. Push the air flap in and let it return by itself. The flap must open and close fully and smoothly.
3. Connect an ohmmeter set at RX100 as shown in **Figure 26**.
  a. If the meter reads 350-400 ohms, go on to Step 4.
  b. If the meter reads more or less than 350-400 ohms, inspect the wiring to the meter. If the wiring is good, replace the flow meter.
4. Connect an ohmmeter set at RX100 as shown in **Figure 27**. Move the flap slowly, observing the meter reading as it changes.
  a. If the meter indicates a specific resistance other than zero or infinite at any flap position, the variable resistor is okay. Go on to Step 5.
  b. If the meter shows zero resistance (continuity) or infinite resistance (no continuity) at any flap position, the variable resistor is faulty; replace the flow meter.
5. Connect an ohmmeter set at RX1000 as shown in **Figure 28**.
  a. If the meter shows 2,100-2,900 ohms at 72° F (20° C), the air temperature sensor is okay. Go on to *Test No. 11.*

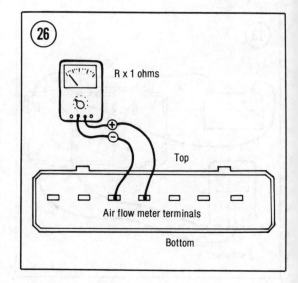

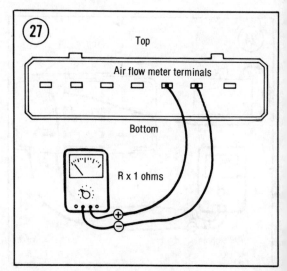

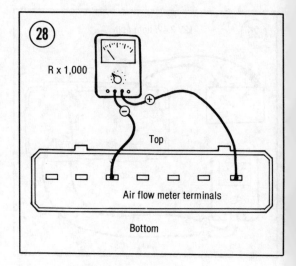

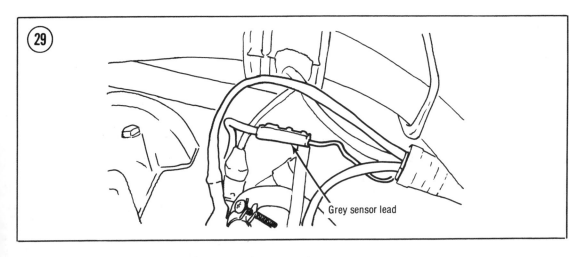

Grey sensor lead

Throttle position switch

3-pin connector

b. If the meter shows more or less than 2,100-2,900 ohms, the sensor is faulty. Replace the flow meter.

Test No. 11: Engine temperature sensor

If the engine runs rich when warm and will not rev past 5,000 or 6,000 rpm, the engine temperature sensor may be faulty.

You can check the sensor quickly by warming the engine up fully, turning the ignition switch to OFF, disconnecting the grey lead from the sensor to the computer (**Figure 29**), then grounding the grey lead from the computer to the engine. Restart and test ride the bike. If the problem goes away, the sensor is loose or faulty. Check that the sensor is tight or replace it if necessary.

The sensor resistance can be checked *when the engine is at room temperature.*

1. Turn the ignition switch to OFF.

2. Disconnect the grey lead from the engine temperature sensor (**Figure 29**).

3. Connect an ohmmeter set at RX1000: one test lead to the sensor's grey lead and the other test lead to the sensor hex head body (or engine ground).

   a. If the meter shows 2,100-2,900 ohms at 72° F (20° C), the engine temperature sensor is okay. Go on to *Test No. 12.*

   b. If the meter shows more or less than 2,100-2,900 ohms, the sensor is faulty. Replace the sensor.

Test No. 12: Throttle position switch

The throttle position switch may be faulty if the motorcycle reacts sluggishly when the throttle is opened fully.

1. With the ignition switch OFF, disconnect the 3-pin connector from the throttle position switch (**Figure 30**).

12

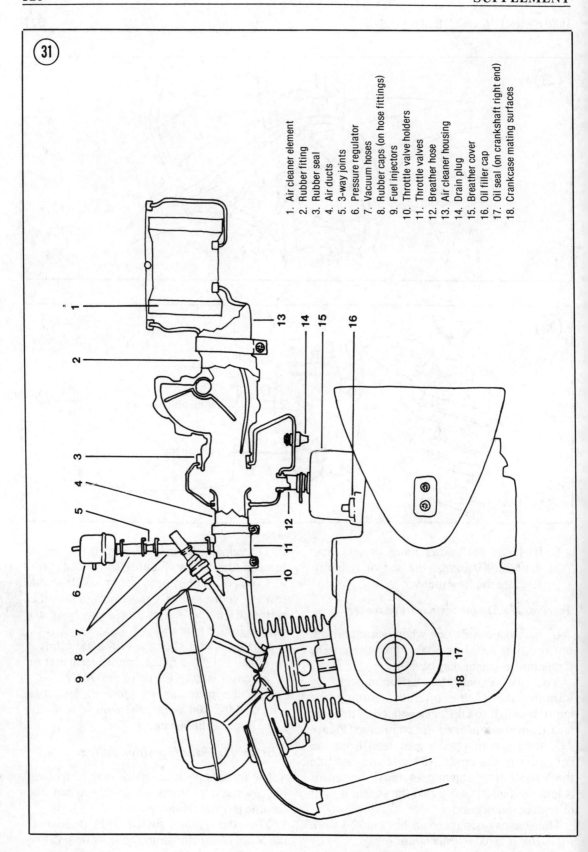

1. Air cleaner element
2. Rubber fiting
3. Rubber seal
4. Air ducts
5. 3-way joints
6. Pressure regulator
7. Vacuum hoses
8. Rubber caps (on hose fittings)
9. Fuel injectors
10. Throttle valve holders
11. Throttle valves
12. Breather hose
13. Air cleaner housing
14. Drain plug
15. Breather cover
16. Oil filler cap
17. Oil seal (on crankshaft right end)
18. Crankcase mating surfaces

2. Connect an ohmmeter set at RX100 to the *left* 2 terminals of the switch. Note the meter readings at full open and full closed throttle.

 a. If the meter shows infinite resistance (no continuity) when the throttle is open and zero resistance (continuity) when the throttle is closed, go on to Step 3.

 b. If the switch gives any other indication, the switch may be faulty; go on to Step 3.

3. Connect an ohmmeter set at RX100 to the *right* 2 terminals of the switch. Note the meter readings at full open and full closed throttle.

 a. If the meter shows infinite resistance (no continuity) when the throttle is closed and zero resistance (continuity) when the throttle is open, the switch is okay. Go on to *Test No. 13*.

 b. If the switch gives any other indication, the switch may be faulty. Loosen the switch mounting screws and turn the switch body as required to adjust it. If the switch still doesn't function properly, install a new one.

Test No. 13: Last chance

1. If you entered the test sequence at *Test No. 10*, yet all tests indicated nothing wrong, re-enter the test sequence at *Test No. 1* to troubleshoot the fuel system and control system. If there is still no sign of a faulty part, go on to Step 2, following.

2. Air leaks at any of the points shown in **Figure 31** can be the cause if the bike is hard to start, runs poorly, hesitates, backfires or burns excessive fuel. Make sure all junctions are airtight.

3. If the bike has passed all tests to this point, but it still runs poorly, remove the fuel injection wiring harness; see *Wiring Harness Removal* later in this chapter of the supplement.

 a. Check the harness for burnt, frayed or broken wires.

 b. Check all the connector pins and wires for separation. If there is an O-ring in a multiple pin connector, make sure it is in good condition.

 c. Check for continuity of all wires in the harness. All wires must conduct electricity from one color-coded end of

the wire to the other end. Wiggle the wires and connectors to see if there is an intermittent open or short circuit. Repair or replace the harness if faulty.

4. If the bike has passed all tests to this point, but it still runs poorly, grit your teeth and beg your Kawasaki dealer to substitute a known good computer for yours. If the problem clears up you'll need to buy a new computer.

FUEL INJECTION DISASSEMBLY

CAUTION
Servicing a motorcycle with electronic fuel injection requires special precautions to prevent damage to the very expensive electronic control unit. Common electrical system service procedures acceptable on other motorcycles may cause damage to several parts of the fuel injection system. Be sure to read the **Fuel Injection Precautions** *in this chapter of the supplement.*

CAUTION
*Before disconnecting any electrical connectors, turn the ignition switch to OFF and disconnect the white/red lead from the starter solenoid to the fuel injection wiring harness (**Figure 2**). This lead supplies power to the computer, relay and fuel injectors at all times; it is not switched or protected by a fuse and so it is always "hot."*

GASOLINE PRECAUTIONS

Observe the following precautions whenever removing any part of the fuel system.

WARNING
Residual fuel pressure may exist in the fuel lines. Be careful to avoid accidental spillage.

WARNING
Do not try to start the engine with the fuel return line disconnected. Gasoline will be pumped out of the return line.

12

WARNING
Some fuel may spill during these procedures. Work in a well-ventilated area at least 50 feet from any sparks or flames, including gas appliance pilot lights. Do not smoke in the area. Keep a BC rated fire extinguisher handy.

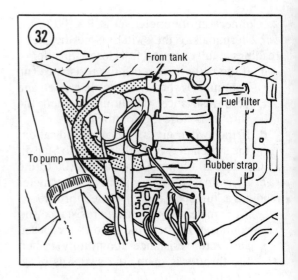

FUEL FILTER

The fuel filter is under the left side cover.

Removal/Installation

1. Turn the ignition switch to OFF and the fuel tap to OFF.
2. Unhook the rubber fuel filter strap (**Figure 32**).
3. Loosen the hose clamps, slide them back and remove the filter.
4. To install, reverse the removal steps.

NOTE
*Install the fuel filter with the IN mark on top (**Figure 33**). The line from the fuel tank goes to the top IN fitting, and the line to the fuel tank goes to the bottom OUT fitting.*

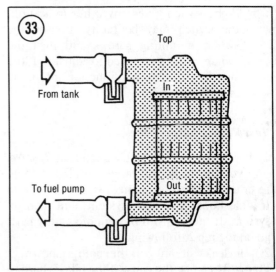

HIGH-PRESSURE FUEL HOSES

The high-pressure hoses run from the fuel pump to the fuel distribution tube and from the distribution tube to the fuel pressure regulator.

Removal/Installation

1. Loosen the hose clamps and remove the hoses.
2. Be careful not to kink or bend the hoses too sharply. If the inner plastic coating is damaged, the hoses must be replaced.
3. Kawasaki recommends using new hose clamps when the hoses are replaced. Make sure the hose extends well past the raised portion of the fitting and that there is a little extra hose space on either side of the clamp (**Figure 34**).

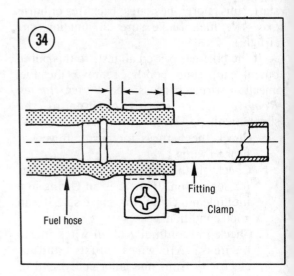

FUEL TANK

On fuel injected models there is a fuel supply line from the fuel tap on the left side of the tank to the fuel filter and a return line from the fuel pressure regulator to a one-way check valve back into the right side of the tank.

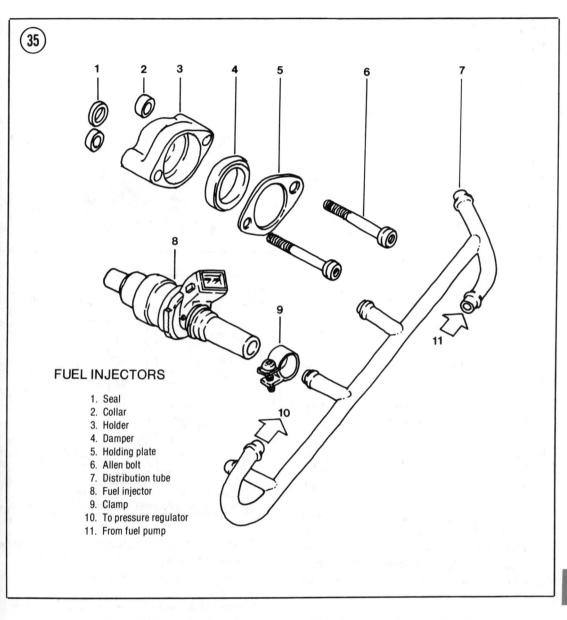

FUEL INJECTORS

1. Seal
2. Collar
3. Holder
4. Damper
5. Holding plate
6. Allen bolt
7. Distribution tube
8. Fuel injector
9. Clamp
10. To pressure regulator
11. From fuel pump

12

WARNING
Do not try to start the engine with the fuel return line disconnected. Gasoline will be pumped out of the return line.

Removal/Installation

1. Turn the ignition switch to OFF and the fuel tap to OFF.
2. Raise the seat and release the rubber strap holding the rear of the tank.
3. Slide the hose clamps down and disconnect the supply line from the fuel tap, and the return line from the check valve.

4. Pull the fuel tank up and to the rear.
5. To install, reverse the removal steps.

FUEL INJECTORS

See **Figure 35**.

CAUTION
If you want to test an individual injector, do not connect a 12 volt power source directly to an injector or the injector's solenoid coil will be damaged. Connect a 5-7 ohm resistor in series with a 12 volt battery or use a 3 volt power source to protect the injector.

Removal/Installation

1. Turn the ignition switch to OFF and the fuel tap to OFF.
2. Remove the fuel tank.
3. Disconnect the white/red lead from the starter solenoid to the fuel injection wiring harness (**Figure 2**).
4. Disconnect the injector's 2-pin electrical connector (**Figure 36**).
5. If you only need to remove one injector, loosen the injector hose clamps, and pull the distribution tube free.
6. Remove the injector holder Allen bolts and remove the injector assembly from the cylinder head.

CAUTION
Be very careful not to damage the injector nozzle.

7. The injectors cannot be disassembled. To install, reverse the removal steps. Note the following.

   a. Make sure the seal and damper (**Figure 35**) are in good condition. Install new ones if necessary.
   b. Be careful not to kink or bend the high-pressure hoses too sharply. If the inner plastic coating is damaged, the hoses must be replaced.
   c. Kawasaki recommends using new hose clamps when the hoses are disconnected. Make sure the hose extends well past the raised portion of the fitting and that there is a little extra hose space on either side of the clamp (**Figure 34**).

FUEL PUMP

The fuel pump is under the air flow meter.

Removal/Installation

1. Turn the ignition switch to OFF and the fuel tap to OFF.
2. Disconnect the white/red lead from the starter solenoid to the fuel injection wiring harness (**Figure 2**).
3. Remove the air cleaner housing; see *Air Cleaner Housing Removal* in this chapter of the supplement.

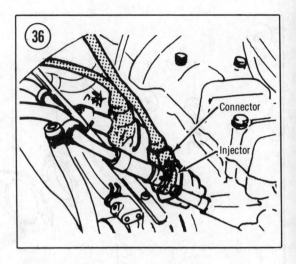

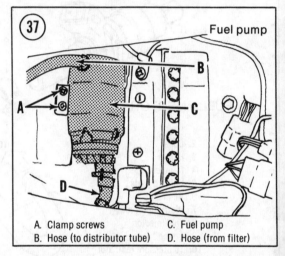

A. Clamp screws   C. Fuel pump
B. Hose (to distributor tube)   D. Hose (from filter)

4. Remove the flow meter; see *Flow Meter Removal* in this chapter of the supplement.
5. Remove the 2 fuel pump clamping screws (**Figure 37**).
6. Loosen the hose clamps and pull the fuel hoses free from the pump. Wipe up any spilled fuel.
7. Disconnect the fuel pump's 2-pin connector. Remove the pump.
8. The fuel pump cannot be disassembled. To install, reverse the removal steps. Note the following.

CAUTION
If the pump is operated without fuel, its bearings will be damaged.

   a. The orange/black lead goes to the positive (+) pump terminal, and the

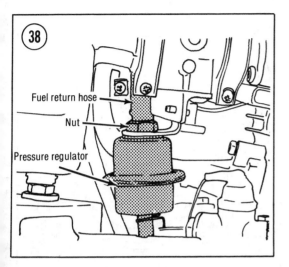

Fuel return hose

Nut

Pressure regulator

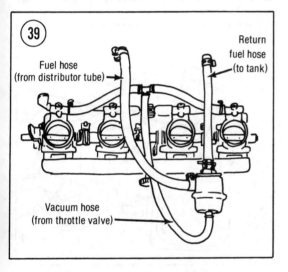

Return fuel hose (to tank)

Fuel hose (from distributor tube)

Vacuum hose (from throttle valve)

e. If a new dry fuel pump has been installed, bleed the air from the pump before trying to start the engine: before installing the air cleaner housing, turn the ignition switch and fuel tap to ON and reach through the flow meter inlet to push the meter flap open so that the fuel pump runs for about 30 seconds.

PRESSURE REGULATOR

The fuel pressure regulator is attached to the bottom of the throttle valve bracket.

Removal/Installation

1. Turn the ignition switch to OFF and the fuel tap to OFF.
2. Loosen the fuel return hose clamp on top of the regulator and slide it up away from the regulator (**Figure 38**).
3. Remove the regulator mounting nut, pushing the hose off the regulator fitting as you go.
4. Disconnect the vacuum and distribution pipe hoses and remove the regulator.
5. To install, reverse the removal steps. Note the following.
   a. Connect the regulator and hoses as shown in **Figure 39**.
   b. Be careful not to kink or bend the high-pressure hoses too sharply. If the inner plastic coating is damaged, the hoses must be replaced.
   c. Kawasaki recommends using new hose clamps when the hoses are disconnected. Make sure the hose extends well past the raised portion of the fitting and that there is a little extra hose space on either side of the clamp (**Figure 34**).

black/yellow lead goes to the negative (-) pump terminal.

b. The hose from the filter connects to the inlet fitting on the left end of the pump and the hose to the distribution tube connects to the fitting on the top of the pump (**Figure 37**).

c. Be careful not to kink or bend the high-pressure hoses too sharply. If the inner plastic coating is damaged, the hoses must be replaced.

d. Kawasaki recommends using new hose clamps when the hoses are disconnected. Make sure the hose extends well past the raised portion of the fitting and that there is a little extra hose space on either side of the clamp (**Figure 34**).

AIR CLEANER HOUSING

Removal/Installation

Raise the seat and remove the bolt at the rear of the housing (**Figure 40**), then loosen the clamp at the front of the housing and pull the housing off the flow meter.

When installing the housing, tighten the rear mounting bolt first, then the clamp.

12

FLOW METER

The air flow meter is between the air cleaner housing and the surge tank.

Removal/Installation

1. Turn the ignition switch to OFF.
2. Disconnect the white/red lead from the starter solenoid to the fuel injection wiring harness (**Figure 2**).
3. Remove the air cleaner housing.
4. Pry off the retaining clip and disconnect the meter's 7-pin electrical connector (**Figure 41**).

> *CAUTION*
> *Do not try to start the engine while the flow meter is disconnected. You may cause irrepairable damage to the computer.*

5. Pull the flow meter to the rear, out of the surge tank.

> *NOTE*
> *You may find it easier to remove the meter if you lubricate the flow meter/surge tank junction with soapy water.*

6. To install, reverse the removal steps. Make sure the meter flap and air passage are clean.

SURGE TANK

The surge tank is between the flow meter and the throttle valve assembly.

Removal/Installation

1. Remove the air cleaner housing and flow meter.
2. Loosen the clamps that connect the tank to the throttle valve assembly (**Figure 42**).

> *NOTE*
> *You may have to loosen the 2 fuel pressure regulator mounting bolts and remove the regulator to get at the No. 3 surge tank clamp.*

3. Slide the surge tank out to the right.
4. To install, reverse the removal steps. Make sure the breather hose is fastened to the breather fitting and slide the clip in place (**Figure 43**).

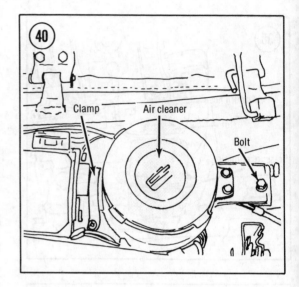

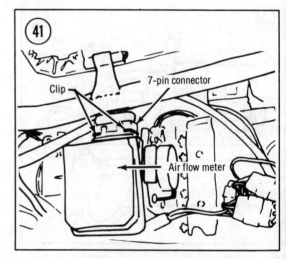

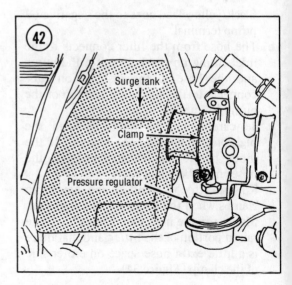

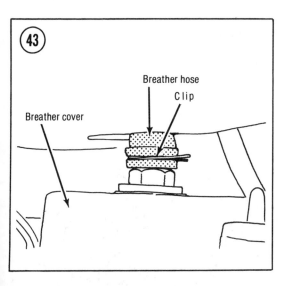

Breather hose

Clip

Breather cover

THROTTLE VALVES

See **Figure 44**.

1. Remove the air cleaner housing, flow meter and surge tank.
2. Remove the throttle position switch's 3-pin connector.
3. To remove the throttle position switch from the valve assembly, remove the 2 mounting screws and pull the switch straight off the left throttle valve shaft (**Figure 45**).
4. Pry off the retainer clip and remove the 3-pin connector from the switch.
5. Loosen the 4 clamps at the front of the throttle valves and pull the valve assembly free from the cylinder head.
6. Disconnect the throttle cable and 2 vacuum hoses. Remove the throttle valve assembly.
7. To install, reverse the removal steps. Note the following.

  a. If the throttle valves were disassembled, synchronize the throttle valve plates visually so that they each have an equal gap at the throttle bore at idle; loosen the adjuster locknuts, turn the adjusters as required and tighten the locknuts (**Figure 7**).

  b. Be careful not to kink or bend the high-pressure hoses too sharply. If the inner plastic coating is damaged, the hoses must be replaced.

  c. Kawasaki recommends using new hose clamps when the hoses are disconnected. Make sure the hose extends well past the

raised portion of the fitting and that there is a little extra hose space on either side of the clamp (**Figure 34**).

  d. The marks on the throttle position switch base should align with the center of the mounting screws (**Figure 46**). Inspect the throttle switch operation after installation is complete; see *Troubleshooting Test No. 12*.

  e. Adjust the throttle cable play and idle speed; see *Fuel Injection Maintenance* in this chapter of the supplement.

  f. If a throttle valve was replaced or disassembled, synchronize the throttle valves; see *Throttle Valve Synchronization* in this chapter of the supplement.

RELAY

The relay is under the left side cover, below the fuel filter.

Removal/Installation

1. Turn the ignition switch to OFF.
2. Disconnect the white/red lead from the starter solenoid to the fuel injection wiring harness (**Figure 2**).
3. Disconnect the black lead from the white connector to the starter solenoid (**Figure 47**). Pull the white and black 9-pin connectors off of the relay.
4. Remove the relay mounting screws and the relay.
5. To install, reverse the removal steps. Install the relay with the black label on the left and connect the black 9-pin connector to the left side of the relay.

COMPUTER

The computer is mounted inside the rear tail piece.

Removal/Installation

1. Turn the ignition switch to OFF.
2. Disconnect the white/red lead from the starter solenoid to the fuel injection wiring harness (**Figure 2**).
3. Raise the seat and remove the 2 bolts with flat washers that hold the rear fender cover in place (**Figure 48**).

12

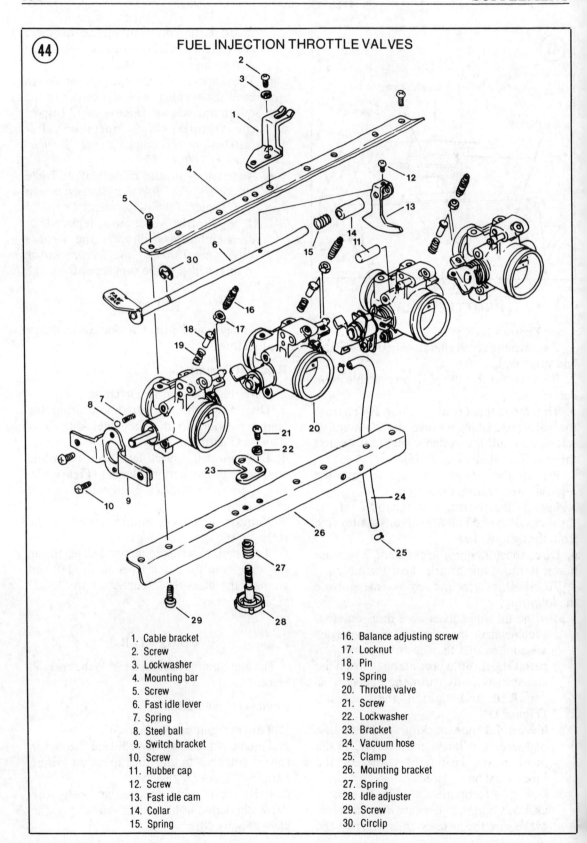

FUEL INJECTION THROTTLE VALVES

44

1. Cable bracket
2. Screw
3. Lockwasher
4. Mounting bar
5. Screw
6. Fast idle lever
7. Spring
8. Steel ball
9. Switch bracket
10. Screw
11. Rubber cap
12. Screw
13. Fast idle cam
14. Collar
15. Spring
16. Balance adjusting screw
17. Locknut
18. Pin
19. Spring
20. Throttle valve
21. Screw
22. Lockwasher
23. Bracket
24. Vacuum hose
25. Clamp
26. Mounting bracket
27. Spring
28. Idle adjuster
29. Screw
30. Circlip

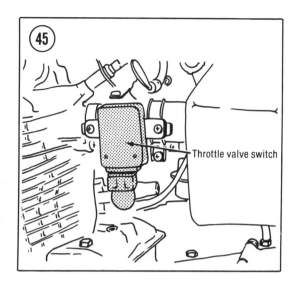

(45)

Throttle valve switch

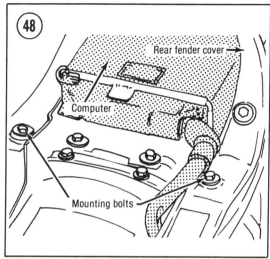

(48)

Rear fender cover

Computer

Mounting bolts

(46)

Align mark with screw

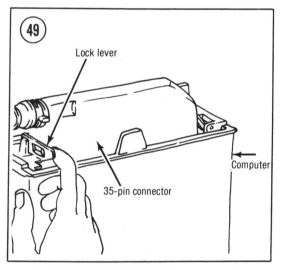

(49)

Lock lever

Computer

35-pin connector

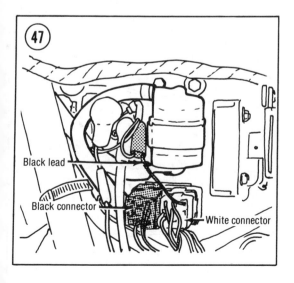

(47)

Black lead

Black connector

White connector

12

4. Slide the rear fender cover forward. To remove the computer 35-pin connector, release the connector lock by pulling it away from the connector (**Figure 49**) and pull the connector straight off the computer plug pins.

5. Remove the 4 nuts, bolts, and 8 flat washers and remove the computer from the fender cover (**Figure 50**).

6. To install, reverse the removal steps. Note the following.

   a. Flat washers must be installed between the fender cover and the rubber dampers.

   b. When attaching the 35-pin computer connector, slide the hook on the end of the connector around the pin on the computer (**Figure 51**).

ENGINE TEMPERATURE SENSOR

Removal

1. Turn the ignition switch to OFF and the fuel tap to OFF.

2. Disconnect the white/red lead from the starter solenoid to the fuel injection wiring harness (**Figure 2**).

3. Remove the fuel tank.

4. Disconnect the engine temperature sensor wire from the wiring harness and remove the sensor from the cylinder head (**Figure 52**).

5. To install, reverse the removal steps. Torque the sensor nut to 11 ft.-lb. (1.5 mkg).

WIRING HARNESS

Removal/Installation

1. Turn the ignition switch to OFF and the fuel tap to OFF.

2. Disconnect the white/red lead from the starter solenoid to the fuel injection wiring harness (**Figure 2**).

3. Remove the fuel tank.

4. Remove the computer, air cleaner housing and flow meter.

5. Disconnect the black lead from the white relay connector to the starter solenoid (**Figure 47**). Pull the white and black 9-pin connectors off of the relay.

6. Disconnect the fuel pump's 2-pin connector.

7. Disconnect the IC igniter's 4-pin connector to the wiring harness.

8. Disconnect the engine temperature sensor's grey wire.

9. Remove the throttle position switch's 3-pin connector.

10. Disconnect the ignition coil's 3 leads (green, red, black) at the frame top backbone.

11. Detach the tie straps and remove the wiring harness from the motorcycle (**Figure 53**).

12. To install, reverse the removal steps. Make sure the fuel injection ground wires (black/green and black/yellow) are securely connected to the battery's negative (-) ground terminal.

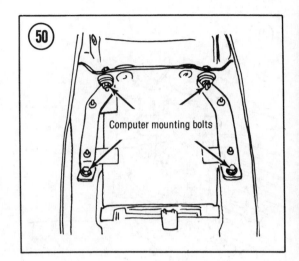

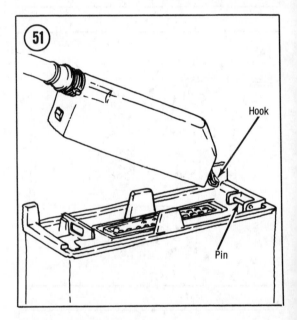

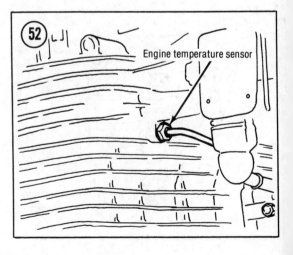

FUEL INJECTION WIRING HARNESS

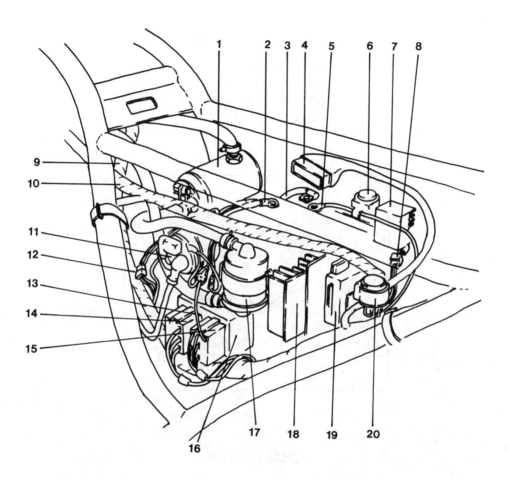

1. Fuel pump
2. Battery positive lead
3. Battery negative ground lead
4. 7-pin connector
5. Black/yellow and black green leads
6. Hazard relay
7. I.C. igniter
8. 4-pin connector
9. Injection system
10. Main wiring harness

11. Starter motor solenoid
12. 2-pin connector
13. Black lead
14. Black 9-pin connector
15. White 9-pin connector
16. Relay
17. Fuel filter
18. Regulator/rectifier
19. Fuse box
20. Turn signal relay

12

CHAPTER EIGHT

BRAKES

REAR MASTER CYLINDER

The rear master cylinder on 1980 and later models is rigidly mounted with a remote fluid reservoir (**Figure 54**). There should be no clearance between the master cylinder and frame bracket. Do not use grease or a locking agent on the master cylinder mounting bolts.

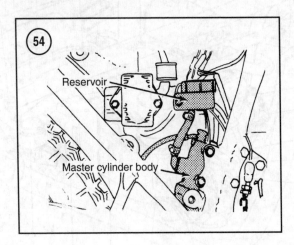

CHAPTER TEN

CHASSIS

The front fork spring minimum free length on 1980 chain drive motorcycles is increased to 21.0 in. (533 mm).

The master cylinder clamp bolt torque for 8 mm bolts is 14 ft.-lb. (1.9 mkg).

All other specifications remain as described in the basic book.

FRONT FORKS (POLICE MODELS)

Fork Leg Removal/Installation

Removal and installation is the same as on 1978 and later chain drive models. The top surface of

each fork tube must be below the top surface of the upper triple clamp by 0.08 in. (2 mm).

Fork Leg Disassembly/Assembly

Refer to Figure 55 for this procedure.

Fork leg disassembly and assembly is the same as on 1979 chain drive models except that the police model is equipped with the rubber boot and two clamps that secure the boot to the inner and outer fork tubes.

This rubber boot takes the place of two parts on the fork assembly used on the 1979 chain drive

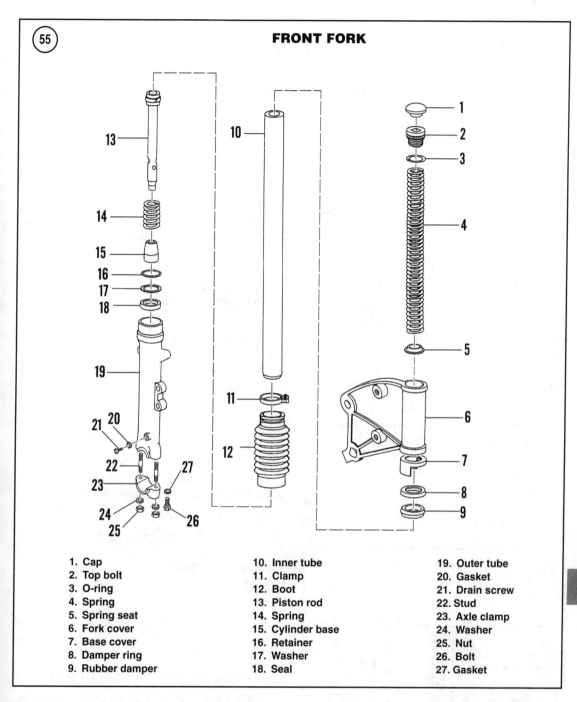

FRONT FORK

1. Cap
2. Top bolt
3. O-ring
4. Spring
5. Spring seat
6. Fork cover
7. Base cover
8. Damper ring
9. Rubber damper
10. Inner tube
11. Clamp
12. Boot
13. Piston rod
14. Spring
15. Cylinder base
16. Retainer
17. Washer
18. Seal
19. Outer tube
20. Gasket
21. Drain screw
22. Stud
23. Axle clamp
24. Washer
25. Nut
26. Bolt
27. Gasket

models described in Chapter Ten in the main body of this book. Refer to **Figure 7** in Chapter Ten and note that Item No. 5 (dust seal) and Item No. 23 (ring cap) are eliminated and replaced with a rubber boot.

When disassembling the fork leg, loosen both clamps securing the rubber boot and slide the rubber boot off the inner tube.

After the fork has been completely assembled, secure the rubber boot to the outer tube and tighten only the lower clamp screw. Install the fork assembly onto the triple clamps and tighten the bolts to 29 ft.-lb. (40 mkg). Make sure the rubber boot is not twisted, then tighten the upper clamp screw. Compress the forks several times and make sure the boot is not interfering with fork travel. Reposition if necessary.

CHAPTER ELEVEN

ELECTRICAL SYSTEM

The electrical systems are changed little for most 1980 models. The 1980 KZ1000 LTD gets the automatic turn signal cancelling and reserve lighting devices used on the Z1R. The KZ1000 Classic fuel injection wiring harness is totally new. See the wiring diagrams at the end of the book.

BATTERY
(FUEL INJECTED MODELS)

The battery is below the air flow meter on fuel injected models (**Figure 56**). Special precautions are necessary to protect the fuel injection system when servicing the battery.

Battery Removal

1. Turn the ignition switch to OFF.
2. Disconnect the white/red lead from the starter solenoid to the fuel injection wiring harness (**Figure 2**).
3. Remove the air cleaner housing and flow meter; see Chapter Seven in this supplement.
4. Remove the negative (-) ground cable first, then the positive (+) cable.

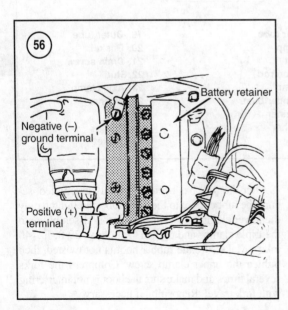

5. Remove the battery retainer bolts and the retainer. Remove the battery.

6. To install, reverse the removal steps. Make sure the fuel injection ground wires (black/green and black/yellow) are securely connected to the battery's negative (-) ground terminal.

Battery Charging
(Fuel Injected Models Only)

When charging the battery on fuel injected models, you must remove the battery from the motorcycle to prevent irreparable damage to the fuel injection system.

LIGHTING SYSTEM

A 60/55 watt quartz halogen headlight is used on the 1980 Z1R, LTD and Classic models.

ALTERNATOR

Removal/Installation
(Police Models)

Alternator removal and installation is the same as on previous models with the exception of removal of the floorboards.

1. Move the floorboard to the raised position.

2. Mark the position of the shift linkage clamp on the shift linkage.

Remove the pivot bolt and clamp bolt and remove the shift linkage. Remove the floorboard mounting bolts and remove the floorboard.

3. Reverse the removal procedure. Tighten the bolts securely, then adjust the linkage as described in the following procedure.

LIGHTING SYSTEM

Headlight Replacement
(Police Models)

1. Remove the single mounting screw at the base of the trim ring.

2. Pull straight out on the bottom of the trim ring and remove the trim ring.

3. Remove the three small mounting screws on the holding ring.

4. Pull the sealed beam and holding ring straight out of the front fairing and disconnect the electrical connector from the backside of the sealed beam.

5. Remove the holding ring from the sealed beam.

6. Install by reversing these removal steps. Be sure to install the sealed beam unit with the TOP mark facing up.

7. Adjust the headlight as described under *Headlight Adjustment* in the following procedure.

Headlight Adjustment
(Police Models)

Adjust the headlight horizontally and vertically according to Department of Motor Vehicle regulations in your area.

To adjust the headlight horizontally, turn the adjust screw on the right side of the trim ring. For vertical adjustment, turn the adjust screw at the top of the trim ring.

12

INDEX

13

13

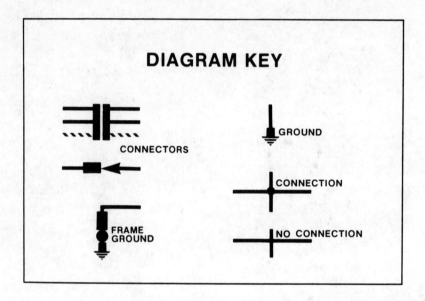

DIAGRAM KEY

CONNECTORS

GROUND

FRAME GROUND

CONNECTION

NO CONNECTION

1973-1974 Z1

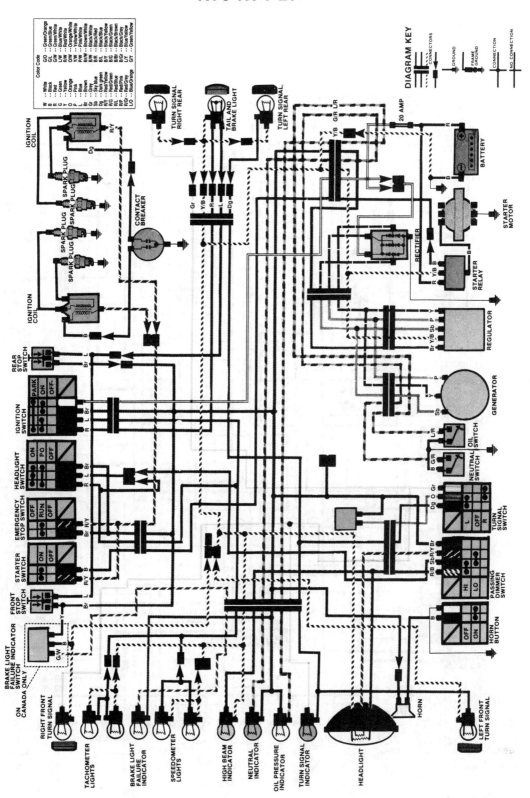

1975-1976 KZ900

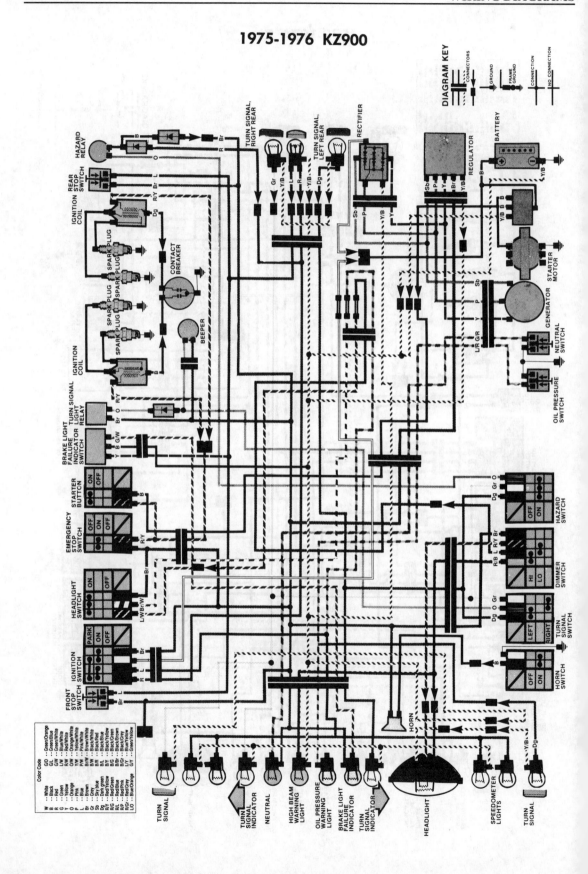

1977-1978 KZ1000 & KZ1000 LTD

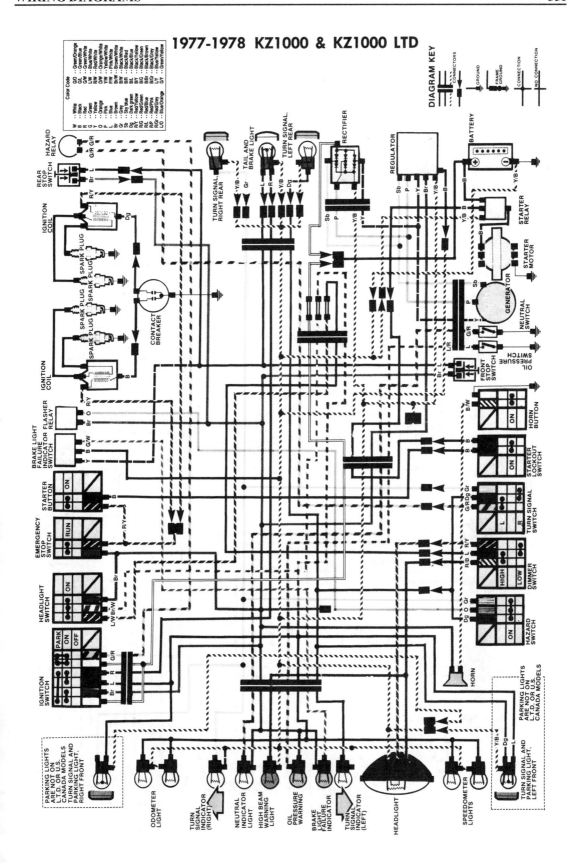

1978 KZ1000 Z1R

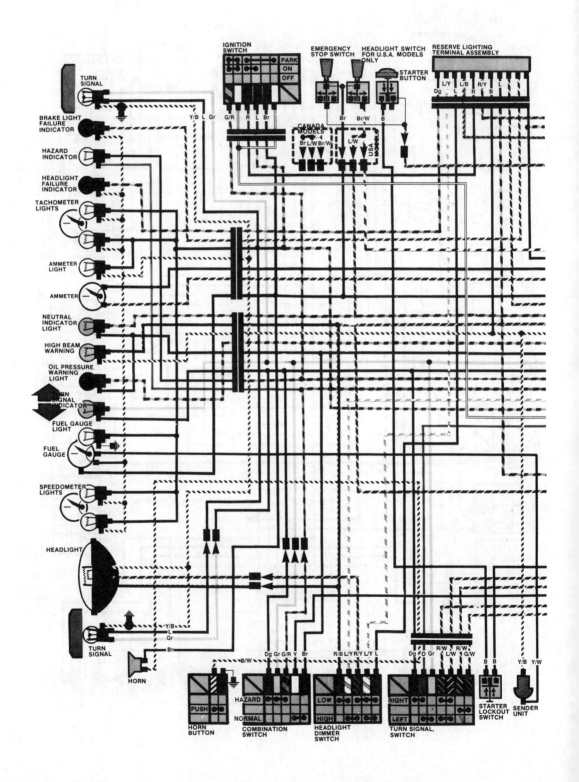

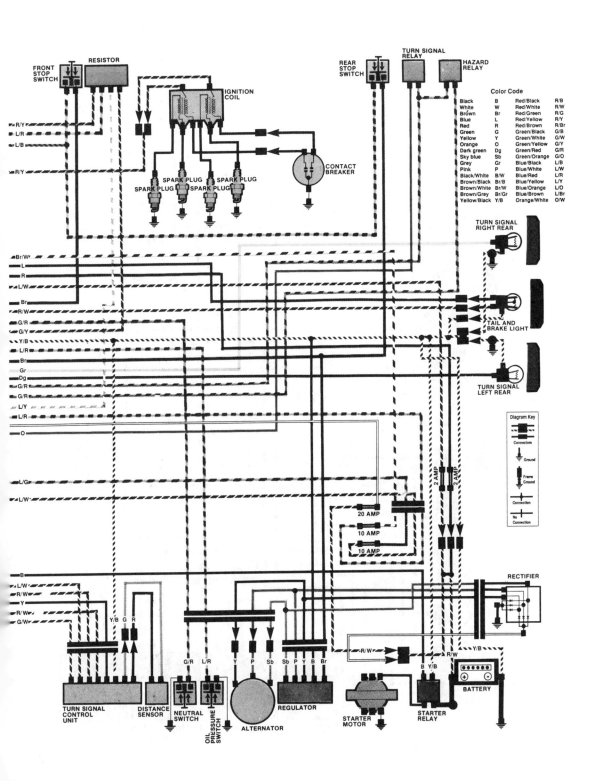

1979 KZ1000 LTD

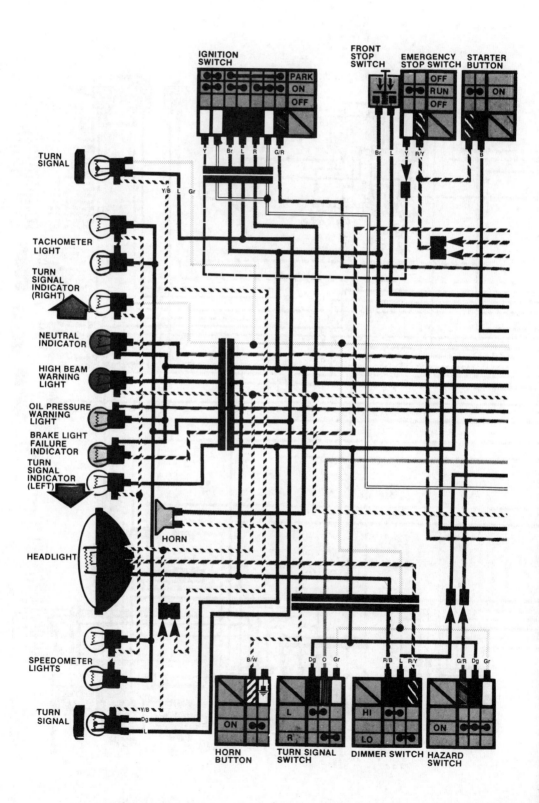

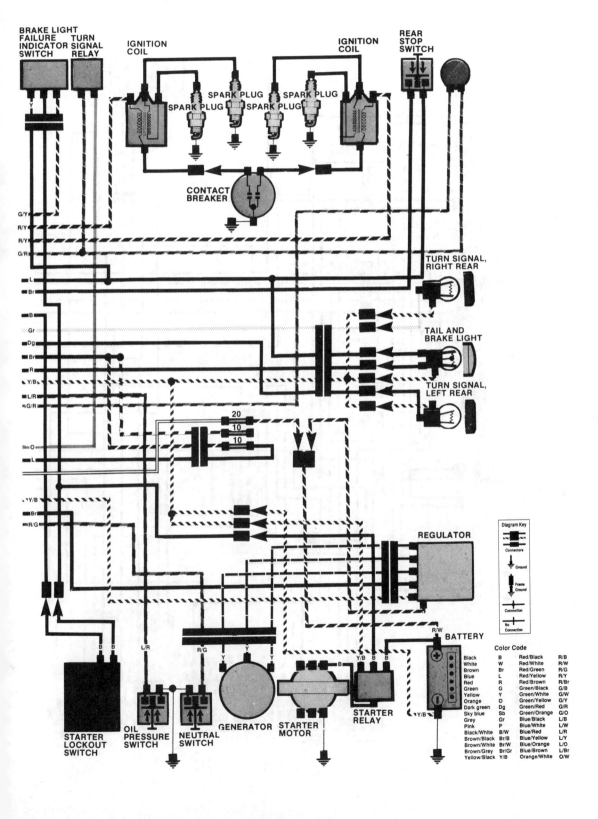

BRAKE LIGHT
FAILURE
INDICATOR
SWITCH

TURN
SIGNAL
RELAY

IGNITION
COIL

IGNITION
COIL

REAR
STOP
SWITCH

SPARK PLUG
SPARK PLUG

SPARK PLUG
SPARK PLUG

CONTACT
BREAKER

TURN SIGNAL,
RIGHT REAR

G/Y
R/Y
R/Y
G/R

L
Br

B
Gr
Dg
Br
R
Y/B
L/R
G/R

O
L

Y/B
Br
R/G

TAIL AND
BRAKE LIGHT

TURN SIGNAL,
LEFT REAR

20
10
10

REGULATOR

Diagram Key

Connectors

Ground

Frame
Ground

Connection

No
Connection

B B

L/R

R/G

Y Y Y

Y/B B B

R/W

BATTERY

Y/B

STARTER
LOCKOUT
SWITCH

OIL
PRESSURE
SWITCH

NEUTRAL
SWITCH

GENERATOR

STARTER
MOTOR

STARTER
RELAY

Color Code

Black	B	Red/Black	R/B
White	W	Red/White	R/W
Brown	Br	Red/Green	R/G
Blue	L	Red/Yellow	R/Y
Red	R	Red/Brown	R/Br
Green	G	Green/Black	G/B
Yellow	Y	Green/White	G/W
Orange	O	Green/Yellow	G/Y
Dark green	Dg	Green/Red	G/R
Sky blue	Sb	Green/Orange	G/O
Grey	Gr	Blue/Black	L/B
Pink	P	Blue/White	L/W
Black/White	B/W	Blue/Red	L/R
Brown/Black	Br/B	Blue/Yellow	L/Y
Brown/White	Br/W	Blue/Orange	L/O
Brown/Grey	Br/Gr	Blue/Brown	L/Br
Yellow/Black	Y/B	Orange/White	O/W

1979-1980 KZ1000 Standard & KZ1000 Shaft Drive

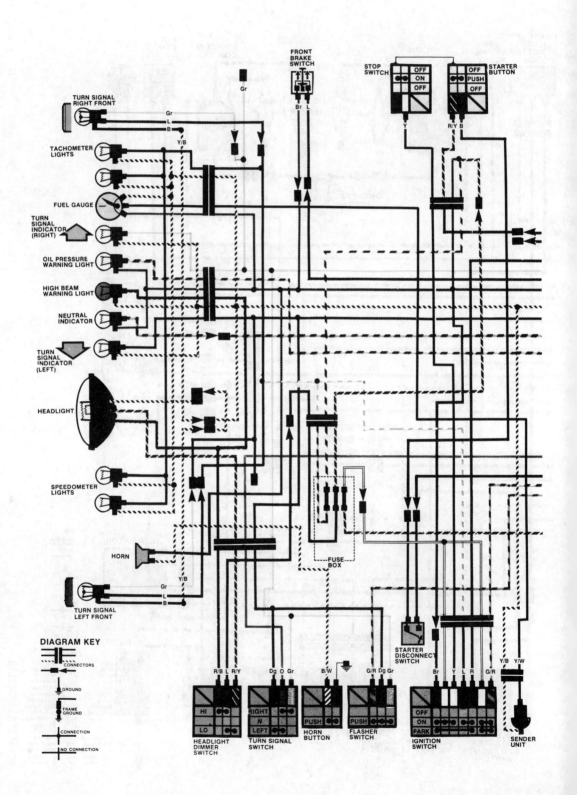

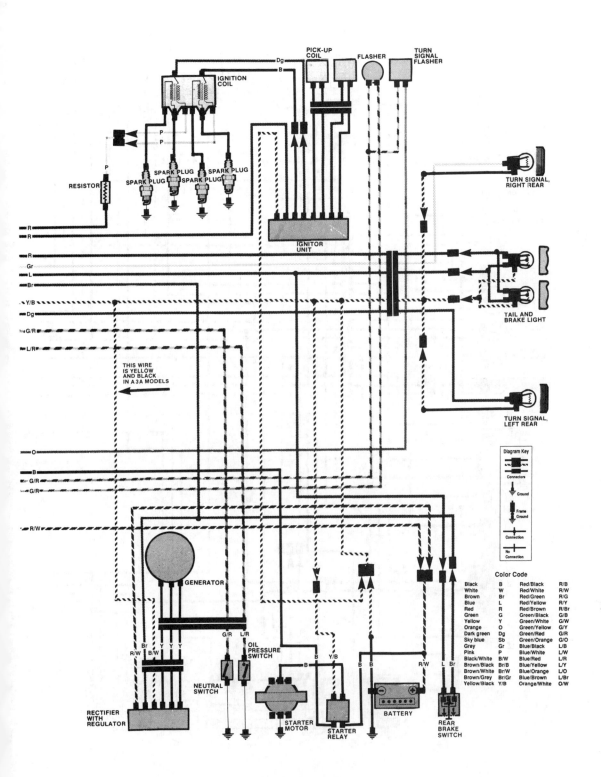

1980 KZ1000 Z1R

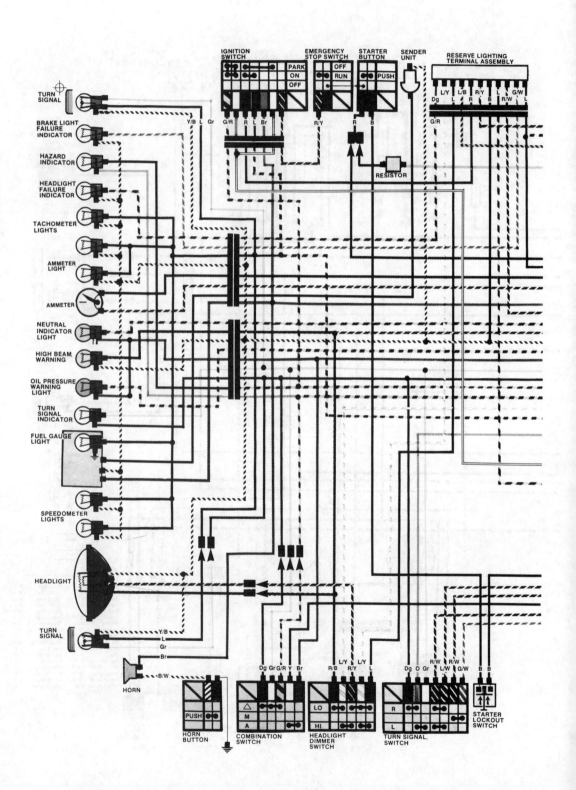

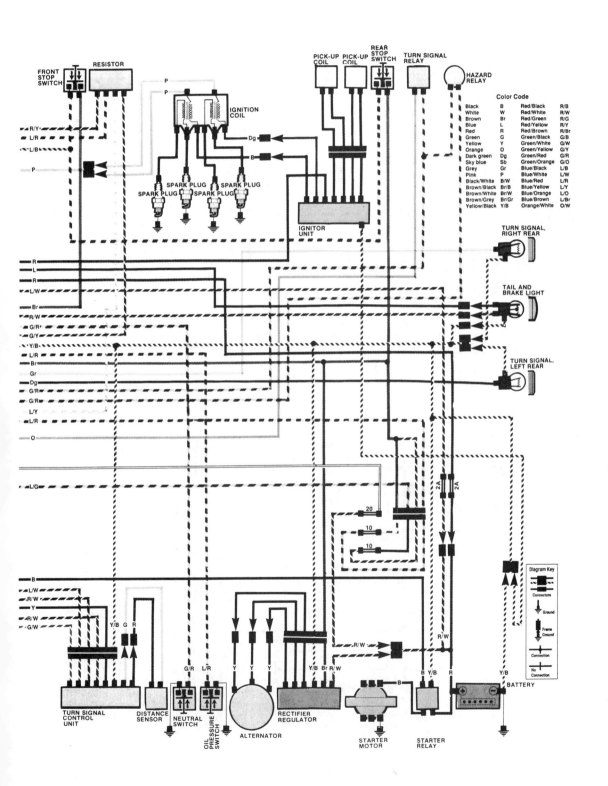

1980 KZ1000 LTD

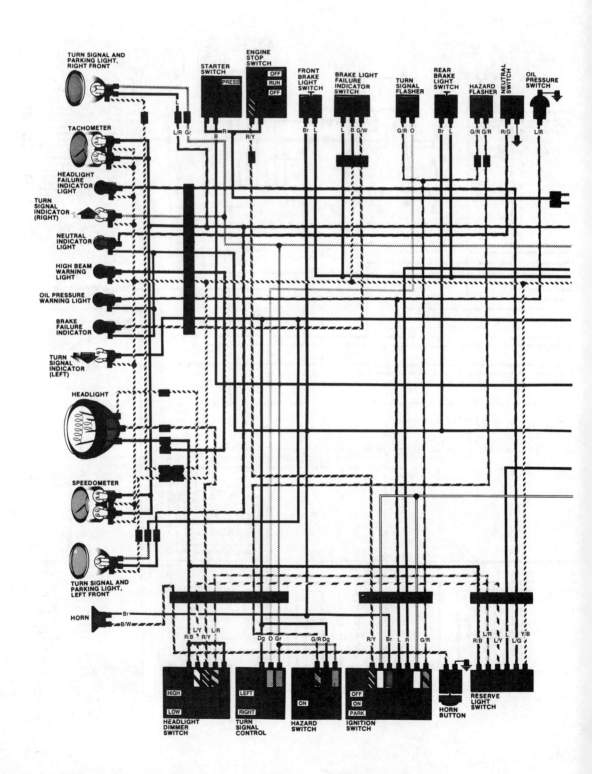

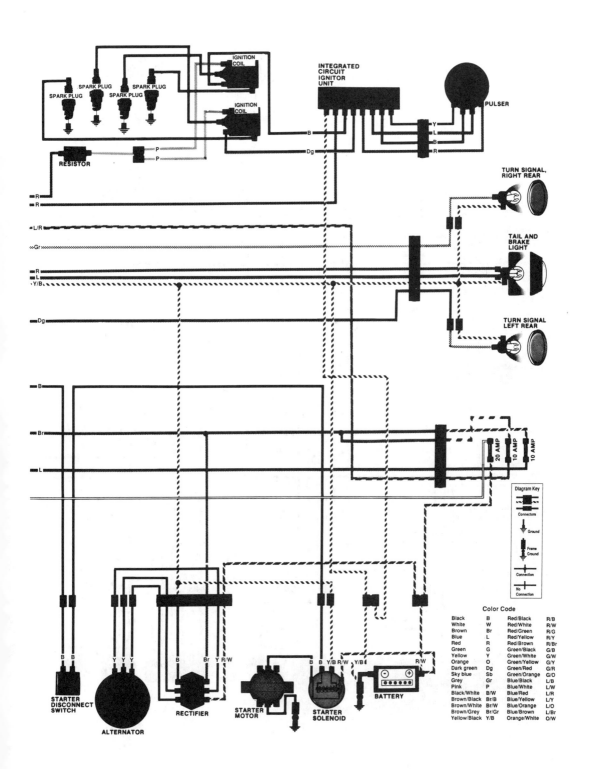

IGNITION COIL

SPARK PLUG
SPARK PLUG
SPARK PLUG
SPARK PLUG

IGNITION COIL

INTEGRATED CIRCUIT IGNITOR UNIT

PULSER

RESISTOR

P
P

B

Dg

Y
L
B
R

TURN SIGNAL, RIGHT REAR

R
R

L/R

Gr

R
L
Y/B

TAIL AND BRAKE LIGHT

Dg

TURN SIGNAL LEFT REAR

B

Br

L

20 AMP
10 AMP
10 AMP

Diagram Key

Connectors

Ground

Frame Ground

Connection

No Connection

STARTER DISCONNECT SWITCH

B B

ALTERNATOR

Y Y Y

RECTIFIER

B   Br Y R/W

STARTER MOTOR

STARTER SOLENOID

B B Y/B R/W

Y/B

BATTERY

R/W

Color Code

Black	B	Red/Black	R/B
White	W	Red/White	R/W
Brown	Br	Red/Green	R/G
Blue	L	Red/Yellow	R/Y
Red	R	Red/Brown	R/Br
Green	G	Green/Black	G/B
Yellow	Y	Green/White	G/W
Orange	O	Green/Yellow	G/Y
Dark green	Dg	Green/Red	G/R
Sky blue	Sb	Green/Orange	G/O
Grey	Gr	Blue/Black	L/B
Pink	P	Blue/White	L/W
Black/White	B/W	Blue/Red	L/R
Brown/Black	Br/B	Blue/Yellow	L/Y
Brown/White	Br/W	Blue/Orange	L/O
Brown/Grey	Br/Gr	Blue/Brown	L/Br
Yellow/Black	Y/B	Orange/White	O/W

1980 KZ1000 Classic

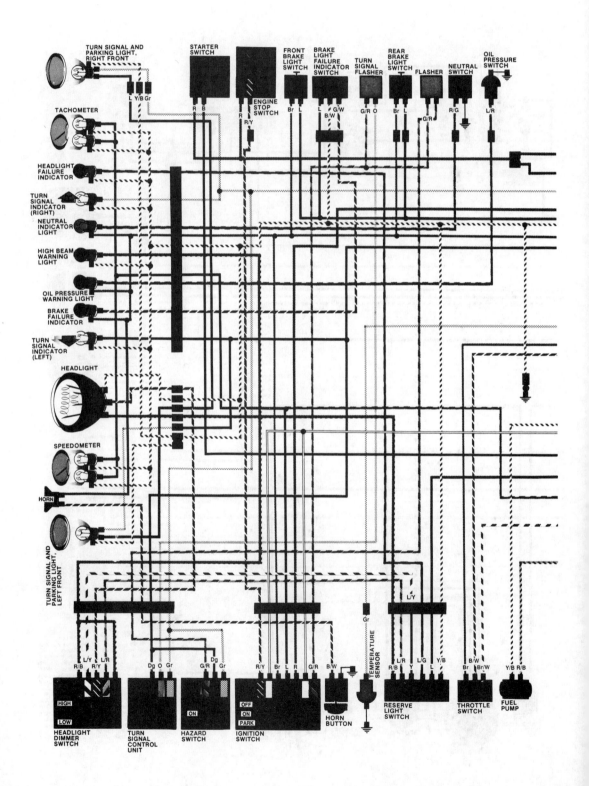

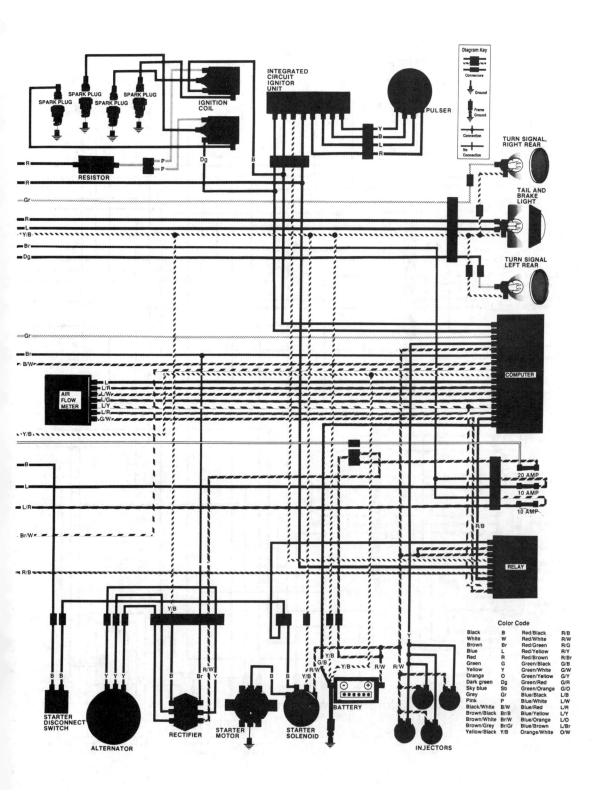

1978-1981 C SERIES POLICE

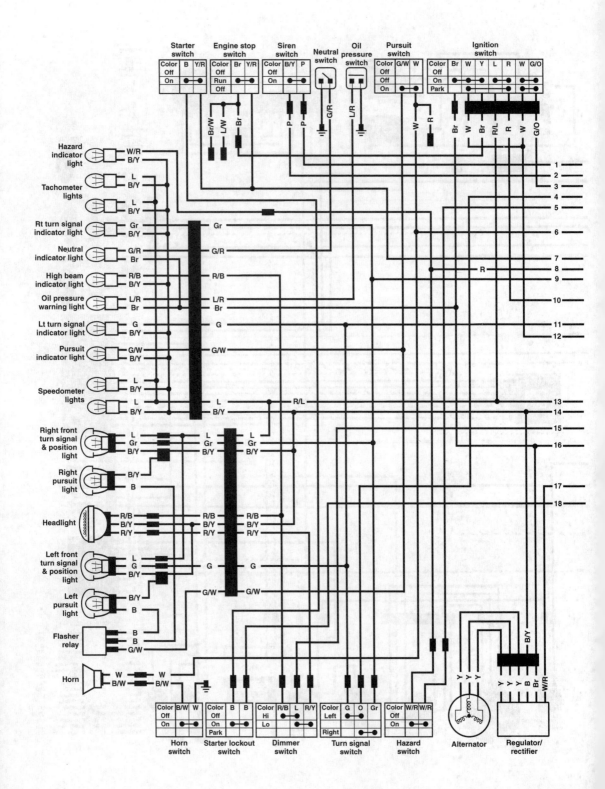

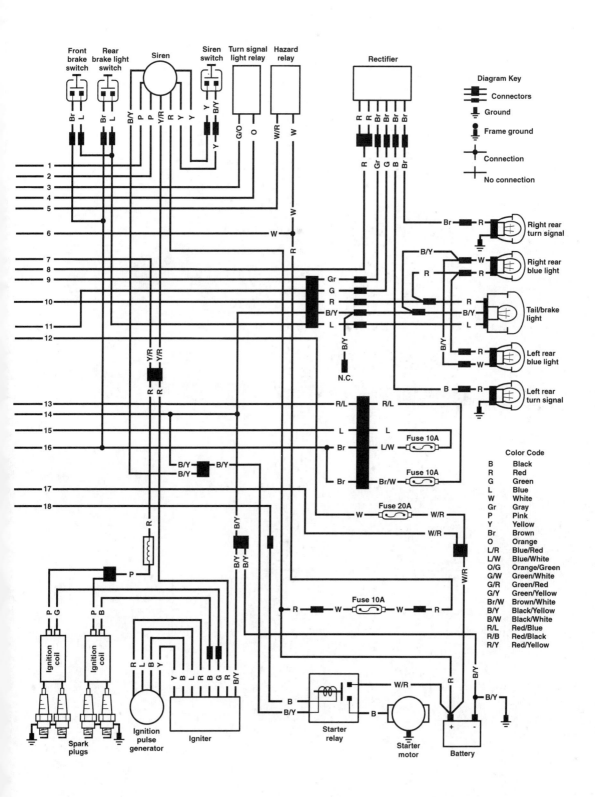

MAINTENANCE LOG

Date	Miles	Type of Service